an ASSOCIATION PRESS book $8   W9-ARI-811

12 modern religious plays fe⸱

- more theological substance—without
  - higher artistic quality
    - moderate or low-cost production (royalt⸱ props and costumes)
      - suitability for amateur performance

This new anthology of successful church drama is i⸱ tended to "meet the reasonable conditions for pla⸱ to be produced in most congregational situation⸱ Because of today's deepened Scriptural concern, Bib⸱ lical pageants and medieval mysteries have been omitted; instead the larger purpose of *contemporary* religious drama is reflected here.

The *Introduction* states: "In many churches, large and small, drama is no longer a 'frill' or a 'stunt'. It is a way in which 'the nature and destiny of man' can be explored through dramatic experiences shared by actors and audiences. It is a means by which prophetic artists evoke responses to their perspectives of life and relationships, including the divine-human encounter This ⸱⸱ction of plays has been prepared to ⸱⸱t th⸱ ⸱⸱ful leaders in locating plays suitable and so demanding a venture."

The e⸱itors are as cognizan⸱ ⸱ th⸱ ⸱ations ⸱mposed by local pr⸱ ⸱i⸱ ⸱olo⸱ ⸱ implications. Pla⸱ ⸱na⸱ ⸱ting abil⸱⸱ h⸱ ⸱ ⸱emand ⸱ ⸱ne⸱ ⸱

torily with amateur casts. . . . The [royalty] fees are modest and should not be an obstacle for any church which has serious intentions in dramatic production."

Organization of this group of plays around four major themes demonstrates the variety of subject and the appropriateness to different seasons of the church year. Contrast in historical setting is immediately evident: "Almost all of the plays involve an intimate relationship between Biblical theme and modern situation. . . . While exploring the roots of the faith, the plays not only take into account current emphases but evoke response to today's world."

Religious thinking ranges "from the Anglicanism of Philip Lamb. . . . to the humanism of Laurence Housman with his Quaker sympathies." Topics cover such diverse problems as those of an ordinary housewife, of the underprivileged in the inner city, of racial minorities in a riven world. Mood runs the gamut from humor to tragedy, while style of writing varies from direct to satirical to highly imaginative. Some of the plays require as few as three actors; others employ a more extensive cast, sometimes a speaking chorus.

The fact that almost all of the plays were written since 1959 lends unusual relevancy. Unique collaboration in this development of religious drama on both sides of the Atlantic is acknowledged: "Since the break between the theater and Protestantism was bridged earlier in England than in the United States, it is not surprising that almost half the plays are the creations of British writers, but all have been received favorably in American productions."

"Christmas in the Market Place," "The Curate's Play" and "Emmanuel" have been produced in New York City churches and were enthusiastically praised by Broadway reviewers such as Howard Taubman, Lewis Funke and Arthur Gelb. "Abraham and Isaac" received a similar response after performance on television and on tour. "A Very Cold Night" was outstanding at the Second International Conference on Religious Drama at Royaumont, France, in 1960. Most frequently performed of these 12 plays is "Christ in the Concrete City."

These popular plays will of course prove exciting and rewarding to the individual reader. This excellent collection should stimulate more church performances as shared experiences, which in turn provoke discussion of profound issues.

THE EDITORS: Dr. JOHN W. BACHMAN is Professor of Practical Theology at Union Theological Seminary in New York and Director of its Center for Communication and the Arts. He is author of *How to Use Audio-Visual Materials* (1956) and *The Church in the World of Radio-Television* (1960), both published by Association Press. E. MARTIN BROWNE was Visiting Professor of Drama at Union from 1956 to 1962, and has since served as Hon. Drama Adviser to Coventry Cathedral.

Jacket design by NORMAN POMERANTZ

BETTER PLAYS
FOR
TODAY'S CHURCHES

BETTER PLAYS

SELECTED BY

John W. Bachman

AND

E. Martin Browne

for

TODAY'S
CHURCHES

ASSOCIATION PRESS

BETTER PLAYS FOR TODAY'S CHURCHES

religious drama

Publisher's Stock Number: 1537
Library of Congress catalog card number: 64–11417

Printed in the United States of America

I

PREFACE

In city, town, and country, persons have heard and read about the twentieth century revival of religious drama. With hopes aroused they ask, "What can we produce in our congregation?" Research and correspondence with "experts" is often disappointing, always sobering. It is soon realized that many of the better plays are difficult to stage with amateur casts and limited facilities. This is a significant discovery because a poor production of a great play is unfair to both the playwright and audience. But less demanding plays often express little more than pedantic platitudes.

In most churches today a renewed theological interest has shifted emphasis from the "social gospel" of a generation ago to a deepened Scriptural concern, providing another cause for dissatisfaction with most available "religious dramas." The hosts of Biblical pageants with their bathrobe bathos are generally rejected and the medieval mysteries, available in other collections, serve only in a partial way to fill the recognized need. Hundreds of letters ask variations of the same question: where can I find a play which is theologically substantial and artistically sound, yet within the production capabilities of our cast and not utterly beyond the appreciation of our parish?

No collection of plays, certainly not this one, can satisfy all such requests. The directorial novice who searches for a "good" Lenten play which will require no scenery and no royalty, will employ a cast of one man and ten women and will be twenty minutes in length, can expect only disappointment.

In greater or lesser degrees, however, the contents of this volume meet the reasonable conditions for plays to be produced in most congregational situations. Almost all of the plays involve an intimate relationship between Biblical theme and modern situation. Historical events are portrayed in contemporary idiom, including twentieth century allusions. Current scenes, on the other hand, prepare the way for the cutting edge of prophecy. For this reason the division of the volume into four categories is admittedly arbitrary. In one play listed under "Modern Society" the lead is Eve, in another the lead is Cain. Within the Biblical categories titles such as *Christ in the Concrete City* and *Christmas in the Market Place* suggest the eternal contemporaneity of "the Word become flesh." While exploring the roots of the faith, the plays not only take into account current emphases but evoke response to today's world.

Production limitations have been taken into account in the selection of plays. At least three of them, *Christ in the Concrete City, Eyes Upon the Cross,* and *The Curate's Play,* were written specifically for production in a particular church. All have been staged satisfactorily with amateur casts. Since the break between the theater and Protestantism was bridged earlier in England than in the United States, it is not surprising that almost half the plays are the creations of British writers, but all have been received favorably in American productions. Few full-length dramas were included, allowing space for more plays running an hour or less, a length especially suitable to prevailing rehearsal limitations.

Not all of the plays will be appropriate for every congregation. They are varied in literary style and reflect a diversity of theological orientation, from the anglicanism of Philip Lamb, in the Catholic tradition, to the humanism of Laurence Housman with his Quaker sympathies. There is sufficient variation in theme to allow production groups to select dramas for different occasions during the year.

Of the three plays listed as dealing with "Modern Society," *The Case Against Eve* and *Verdict of One* have been warmly received when presented to large national assemblies. *The Case Against Eve* gives the collection a welcome note of humor—which is something much needed in Christian drama. Though in a sense a fantasy, the play is also very much on earth, for its principal character is the young housewife of today, the Eve we know.

Verdict of One deals with an incident in the lives of the "underprivileged" and "disadvantaged" in the inner-city but in the process reveals that our place of residence does not remove us from involvement in and responsibility for what happens elsewhere. Viewers of this play are also confronted by the claims of the full-time Christian ministry upon a young person at the time of occupational decision.

The Circle Beyond Fear was first written for choral speaking but with imaginative direction this drama of the love that casts out fear can go beyond that static form. Cain typifies all the pride and fear which lead men to defy God and to destroy their brothers. His trial, his flight, and his final discovery of the supporting strength of the circle surrounding him can be portrayed in movement as well as in words. As an American Negro working in the Church in India, the playwright has more than an academic knowledge of the tensions in human relationships which he portrays. *The Circle Beyond Fear* was first presented by office workers at the Inter-Church Center in New York, was later produced with a student cast in an outdoor setting at Union Seminary, and has been played under Mr. Swann's direction in India.

Among the dramas featuring "The Passion Events," *Christ in the Concrete City* is probably the one most frequently presented on both sides of the Atlantic. It has been done in seminaries, on television, by touring groups, and by hundreds of local casts. Viewers are reminded that the society of today is not in human essentials different from the first century, that we "were there" at the crucifixion. The players act as a choral ensemble, and individual actors come out from this to portray parts both in the historical scenes and in the satirical scenes from modern life. Thus this Passion Play has three dimensions: the choral-reflective, the historical, and the modern-satirical.

A Very Cold Night deviates even further from the purely historical treatment of Biblical events. It uses the style of Samuel Beckett to make a confrontation with Christ both immediate and timeless, demanding a response. The two crucified thieves are at the same time two men whose instinct for survival is struggling with an impulse toward charity. Extremely brief, *A Very Cold Night* won the first prize in a playwriting competition sponsored by Union Theological Seminary in cooperation with the National Broadcasting Company in 1960. When it was later performed at the Second International Conference on Religious Drama at Royaumont, France, in July 1960, Mrs. K. M. Baxter, then Chairman of the

Council of the Religious Drama Society of Great Britain, said, "The play, *A Very Cold Night,* performed with great effect, was a salutary corrective to the more conventional dramas presented by several European groups."

Eyes Upon the Cross is a more traditional presentation of Passion events, revealing the variety of ways in which people around the cross regarded the Crucified, and how among them we may find ourselves. The play includes nine scenes which may also be presented individually or in various combinations. When *Eyes Upon the Cross* was produced at Union Theological Seminary in 1962, President Van Dusen commented, "I have found this play not only one of the most interesting but one of the most moving instances of religious drama which I have seen. . . . In format, it is original and distinctly contemporary; but it has a strange power to bring the death of Jesus home to us all."

This Rock is a simple, straightforward dramatization of the agony of Peter after his denial of Christ; it is not difficult to perform and has a moving quality.

Among the three Christmas plays, one has an international flavor especially appropriate for the Nativity. *Christmas in the Market Place* was written by a famous French dramatist for his own group of amateur actors. For the first English performance, by the Pilgrim Players of Canterbury, Eric Crozier provided a translation which he hoped would "do what the original certainly does—bring the story of the Nativity alive in all its majesty, and contrast the simple humor of the gypsy family with their devout interpretation of the greatest of subjects." One of the more recent of many American presentations, offered in New York churches by the Lutheran Foundation for Religious Drama, was described by the New York Times reviewer as "an enchanting production" and a "rewarding experience." Lewis Funke wrote concerning the play, "The tone is a superb mixture of the secular and the reverential. There is about it, too, a buoyant air of improvisation that somehow, though it be a story two thousand years old, nevertheless, has a contemporary flavor that can only be applauded."

The Curate's Play was commissioned for the 150th Anniversary of St. George's Episcopal Church, New York City, and was described by Arthur Gelb of the New York Times as "a thoroughly felicitous Nativity play—a delight to the eye and ear," and a "perfect blending of religion and art." It begins with typical children's tableaux and interrupts them to introduce a situation of urgent human need, so that the familiar pictures and music are applied to it.

Emmanuel was written for his own English village by an author well known in London's West End and off-Broadway. It tells the story of Christmas in the traditional way, but with many a lively and colorful moment. The play has been warmly received both on stage and on television in the United States. Howard Taubman of the New York Times called it "a fresh and elevating experience . . . written with reverence and a personal poetic style." He also said, "Mr. Forsyth captures the wonder and glory of the Nativity, while setting it in a humble frame."

Old Testament themes predominate in two plays. In *Abraham and Isaac* Laurence Housman "demythologizes" the story of the sacrifice of Isaac. He shows Abraham learning, by facing the challenge of his inner voice which tells him to offer his son, to discover for himself, through the suffering involved, a new understanding of God's will for him and for his people. This play has found an enthusiastic response when presented by touring groups and on television.

Go Down Moses, like *Christ in the Concrete City,* uses choral effects and modern idiom in the telling of a Biblical story. Building toward the climax in which Moses beholds not only the Promised Land but the purpose for which God has chosen it and His people, the play explores the meaning of history from a Biblical perspective.

All of the plays are presented here in a reading version, from which production details are often omitted. In most cases acting versions are available from the publishers indicated and royalty fees are payable, of course, to them. In view of the quality of the plays the fees are modest and should not be an obstacle for any church which has serious intentions in dramatic production.

In many churches, large and small, drama is no longer a "frill" nor a "stunt." It is a way in which "the nature and destiny of man" can be explored through dramatic experiences shared by actors and audiences. It is a means by which prophetic artists evoke responses to their perceptions of life and relationships, including the divine-human encounter. This collection of plays has been prepared to assist thoughtful leaders in locating plays suitable for so significant and so demanding a venture.

In preparing it, the editors have not been oblivious to the wider range of dramatic literature—the works of Eliot, Greene, Tennessee Williams, O'Neill, Beckett, Inge and Arthur Miller, among others. We share the conviction that church groups should engage in the viewing of professional productions and the study of such plays. It is our hope that the local production of plays in this volume will help to prepare the less sophisticated for broader theatrical experiences and serve a limited, specialized purpose with the more sophisticated.

Among the playwrights and publishers' representatives who have cooperated in the editing of this volume, Miss Edna Cahill has been especially helpful. At various points in the selection process we have benefited from the judgment of Mr. Robert Seaver, whose directorial skill first brought to life several of the manuscripts. As in so many of the activities of the Center for Communication and the Arts at Union Theological Seminary, Miss Connie Clark has given valuable assistance throughout the entire project.

Each play is presented here in the printing style in which it originally appeared. This system makes possible the closest rendering of each author's intent.

JOHN W. BACHMAN
E. MARTIN BROWNE

CONTENTS

CHARACTERS AND TIME

A guide to the number of characters and the running time of each play.

THE CASE AGAINST EVE
> Cast: 4 men, 4 women, 2 boys
> Running Time: 45 minutes

VERDICT OF ONE
> Cast: 15 men, 5 women
> Running Time: 1½ hour

THE CIRCLE BEYOND FEAR
> Cast: 6 men, 6 women
> Running Time: 25 minutes

CHRIST IN THE CONCRETE CITY
> Cast: 4 men, 2 women
> Running Time: 1 hour

A VERY COLD NIGHT
> Cast: 2 men and a Voice
> Running Time: 10 minutes

EYES UPON THE CROSS
> Cast: 11 men, 11 women, 2 boys
> Running Time: 1½ hour

THIS ROCK
> Cast: 4 men, 2 women
> Running Time: 20 minutes

CHRISTMAS IN THE MARKET PLACE
> Cast: 2 men, 2 women, 1 boy
> Running Time: 1¼ hour

THE CURATE'S PLAY

> Cast: 4 men, 2 women, 11 boys, 1 girl
> Running Time: 40 minutes

EMMANUEL

> Cast: 11 men, 4 women
> Running Time: 1½ hour

ABRAHAM AND ISAAC

> Cast: 1 man, 1 woman, 1 boy
> Running Time: 40 minutes

GO DOWN MOSES

> Cast: 3 men, a chorus of 4 women, two choruses of mixed
> voices
> Running Time: 1¼ hour

BETTER PLAYS
FOR
TODAY'S CHURCHES

by
Eve McFall

THE CASE AGAINST EVE

CHARACTERS
IN ORDER OF APPEARANCE:

EVE	a suburban housewife
KEN	} her two sons
BILLY	
THE JURORS	three men and three women
1	plays ADAM
2	plays FATHER and DOCTOR
3	plays PSYCHIATRIST and MINISTER
4	plays MOTHER
5	plays MISS MUCH and DORCAS
6	plays MRS. MORE and MARTHA
THE RECORDER	who also plays a BOY and a REPAIRMAN

The scene is a courtroom. There is a Judge's chair and bench raised upstage center, with three places for Jurors on each side. Downstage is a low stool for Eve. Houselights are on dimly and stagelights are going up gradually from dark to dim as Eve enters with Ken and Billy. They walk in slowly, looking around.

KEN : Where are we, Mom?

EVE : This is a courtroom, dear.

BILLY : But there's nobody here.

EVE : No, not yet. Perhaps it's not too late . . . perhaps I needn't go through with it.

KEN : Through with what?

EVE : My trial.

BILLY : Trial? But where's the policeman?

EVE : Policeman, darling?

BILLY : I thought there would be a policeman.

EVE : Not this time. I came of my own accord. Perhaps it will count in my favor. Will you boys go and call the court for me.

(Boys go out together. Their voices fade as they move off.)

BOYS : Calling the Court . . . the court . . . the court . . . the court . . .

EVE : It's growing dark . . . *(She gropes for stool, and sits. House-lights dim.)* I wish I could hide in the dark. *(She hides her head in her arms. Stage lights up full as Jurors come in and take their places. They sit, until the Recorder enters. He is preceded by Ken, who carries a large copy of the Bible, and followed by Billy, who acts as page, carrying the gavel. Ken walks up the steps to the Judge's bench, puts the Bible down, walks down the other side. As the Recorder takes the Judge's seat, the boys leave. The Jurors sit once more and start chatting to each other.*

Eve sees none of this. She sits facing the audience, tense, listening but not looking. However, she turns around as the Recorder hammers with his gavel.)

RECORDER : Order! Order! (*He looks around him*) So this is the court room—rather a makeshift court, but one mustn't complain. After all, I'm a makeshift judge, a surrogate merely. The Courts are overcrowded and the regular judges busy. However, with this book—a record of precedents in recorded cases of contract and criminal law, lately revised, indexed, and cross-referred; with the help of this book in which no sentence is incompetent, irrelevant or immaterial. . . . Where was I? Oh, yes. With the help of this book, I say, I hope to further justice. We are met today to try this woman, Eve. The charge is . . . (*shuffles papers*) the charge is . . . What *is* the charge, my dear?

EVE : I don't remember, I'm all in the dark.

JUROR 1 : (*standing*) The charge is failure to love.

RECORDER : Failure to live, did you say? I'm a little hard of hearing.

JUROR 1 : No, I think it's an O. I'm a little blind myself. Yes, it's failure to love.

RECORDER : Not that it really matters. The human race dies of heart failure in either case. (*sycophantic laughter in court*) Young man! Will you read the charge.

JUROR 1 : The charge is that the defendant, Eve, born in the twentieth century,

CHORUS : —equal rights for women—

JUROR 2 : living in the wealthiest nation of the world,

CHORUS : —last year's income fifteen thousand dollars—

JUROR 5 : educated to her utmost capacity,

CHORUS : —IQ high in the ninety-ninth percentile—

JUROR 4 : happily married, the mother of two children,

JUROR 6 : home-owner,

CHORUS : —rumpus room, panelled den and patio—

JUROR 6 : home-maker,

CHORUS : —Duomatic washer and dryer—

JUROR 2 : vital statistics

CHORUS : —a respectable average—

JUROR 3 : The charge is that the defendant, Eve, with every advantage that the world can offer is out of love with life.

CHORUS : Out of love with life!

RECORDER : We shall try the case as stated. However, because the defendant herself brought this case to the Court's attention, I should like your indulgence to read the following: (*He finds the place in his book.*) "And this is the judgment, that the light has come into the world and men loved darkness rather than light. But he who does what is true comes to the light, that it may be clearly seen that his deeds have been wrought in God." It is possible that, although she sits in darkness, the defendant is trying to come to the light. (*To Eve*) Now, what have you to say in your defense?

(*Jurors 2 and 3 walk forward. 2 wears a physician's head reflector; 3 wears heavy hornrims, carries notebook and pencil.*)

EVE : I thought I must be sick, so I went to the doctor . . .

DOCTOR : An interesting case. She complains that she doesn't feel like herself at all. I've tested her tonsils, counted her corpuscles, checked that her vertebrae are all in alignment, reflexes responsive, blood pressure normal. There's nothing wrong with the woman at all. That's where you come in, old fellow. *You* can find something.

PSYCHIATRIST : Yes, I can find something. A little maladjustment in the infant psyche, the Electra complex not entirely resolved; trauma in the nursery, trouble in the teens; but my dear, you needn't worry with this technical jargon. Just put yourself in my hands; relax completely. . . . relax. . . . re-lax. . . . we're doing very nicely. Now, tell me all about it. Begin at the beginning.

EVE : (*drowsy*) In the beginning was the Word . . . (*She starts upright*) Now, why did I say that, I wonder?

PSYCH. : No matter. No matter. It's of no significance. Now. Start again. Relax . . . re-lax . . . Tell me all about it.

EVE : In the beginning was a garden . . . (*lights begin to dim, leaving soft spot on Eve*) Adam and I used to walk in the evening under the trees, in the cool of evening.

(*Eve rises, walks toward L. Juror 1 (Adam) walks toward her. Psychiatrist sits on Eve's stool, notebook on his knee*)

EVE : Adam, where are you?

ADAM : Here I am, waiting under the trees. (*Lights up on Adam*)

EVE : I'm sorry . . .

ADAM : Don't apologize. I think it's worth it. When we are married I shall spend a happy lifetime waiting for you. I'll stand at the foot of the stairs when I come home all for the pleasure of having you run down into my arms. (*They embrace*) You should never be punctual but never too late, for I love you so much my heart aches as I wait.

EVE : Dearest Adam. When we are married, will we come here to walk in the garden . . . and bring our children?

ADAM : I don't see why not.

EVE : It's a beautiful orchard—peach, pear, and cherry, and that old crabapple. It reminds me of our garden when I was seven years old.

PSYCH. : Seven years old. Ah, yes. A significant phase in psychic maturation. Tell me of your childhood.

(*As Eve walks back to Psychiatrist, Adam returns to his Juror's seat. Recorder takes off wig and gown, drapes them over his chair so that he still appears to be presiding there. Under gown he wears bluejeans and a checked shirt.*)

EVE : I was the only daughter. Mother and father . . . we weren't very wealthy then. The house was falling down but I loved the garden. It seemed enormous in those days, with a path to the tracks under an apple tree with friendly branches. There was a boy. . . . (*Pause*)

PSYCH. : Go on.

EVE : He lived across the tracks. He used to go fishing.

(*Recorder as Boy walks down from bench, carrying tin can and fishing pole*)

Did you catch any fish?

BOY : I haven't gone yet. I came to dig worms down by the bank there.

EVE : I know where there are worms, big ones, and wiggly. Behind the apple tree. Look, here. (*Boy starts to dig with one end of his fishing pole.*) You can't dig with that stick. I'll fetch my trowel. (*She fetches trowel from under her chair.*)

BOY : Tisn't a stick. It's a fishing pole.

EVE : Do you like fishing?

BOY : Sure, lots. Do you like gardening?

EVE : Yes. I like to plant things and watch them grow. I planted a cherry pit and when it grows up I shall give you some cherries.

BOY : When I grow up I'm going to be a fisherman . . . or perhaps a doctor.

EVE : When I grow up I'm going to be a Mummy just like my Mummy.

BOY : My dad's a carpenter. He likes to fix things.

MOTHER : (*Mother calls off:*) Eve, where are you? (*The children go on digging*)

EVE : That's my Mummy.

(*Enter Mother. She drags Eve to her feet*)

MOTHER : Eve, come here at once. Little boy, go away. Off! Off! (*She shoos him like a dog. Boy runs off, taking trowel*) Haven't

I told you, over and over, not to talk to strangers and ragged little boys? You don't know what sort of things you might pick up—germs and bad language.

RECORDER : (*to Mother*) Have a care, my good woman. You lay yourself open to a criminal charge. The reference is to Micah's judgment in the case of the Lord versus Samaria: "From their young children you take away my glory for ever." This court takes a very grave view of offences against minors.

MOTHER : (*to Recorder*) I'm sure you agree that a mother knows best. (*to Eve*) Eve, dear, you must learn to be a lady. You must give up grubbing in the garden and behave as I do, move in society.

EVE : Mother, dear, what is society?

MOTHER : A masked ball, darling, where we learn the proper steps to dance with proper persons; foxtrot flirtations, the waltz of courtship, the minuet of marriage, the PTA polka, and the Square Dance divorce.

EVE : I love to dance. Can I wear a mask too, and gloves, and a hat, and high-heeled shoes? How do you dance in high-heeled shoes?

MOTHER : As you grow up I'll show you how to do it, and your partner will be a suitable young man: someone your father thoroughly approves of.

(*Mother takes Eve off. Father and Adam enter from Juror's benches.*)

FATHER : You understand, Adam, we love our daughter.

ADAM : So do I, sir.

FATHER : She's had the best of everything, all we could give her—has wanted for nothing.

ADAM : I understand, sir.

FATHER : I'd like to think she was nicely settled. It's all very well to marry for love but when you've been used to a comfortable existence it's hard to cut down your standard of living . . .

ahem . . . in other words . . . ahem . . . what's your income?

ADAM : Oh, as to that, sir, you needn't worry. Dad is the president of several corporations—Blue Chip, Uranium, and Oil Unlimited.

FATHER : And you, young man? What's your occupation?

ADAM : I wanted to be an archaeologist. . . .

FATHER : Digging up pots from a dusty past? Not much of a job for a bright young man.

ADAM : So my father said. Myself, I saw it as a way of reaching truth, the facts of history buried with the artifacts which wait to be found dark in the tombs, deep in the sand.

FATHER : Very interesting. But there's no future in digging up the past.

ADAM : So my uncles said. Anyway, sir, I was finally persuaded to keep the archaeology just as a hobby and take a junior executive position. . . .

FATHER : Yes? Yes? What is it?

ADAM : I'm a vice-president of Eldorado Holdings.

FATHER : Ah, well, in that case, no more need be said. You are obviously an ideal husband for my daughter.

ADAM : I think she loves me . . .

FATHER : Of course she loves you! Any girl of sense would find you irresistible . . . a hardworking man with an interesting hobby. I'm proud to welcome you, son. Shake hands! (*They shake hands. Father walks downstage center*) I'll give my little girl the wedding of her dreams. (*Takes out notebook*) Let's see . . . orchestra . . . caterers . . . champagne . . . Better get imported. Some snob will check the labels. Flowers . . . a wedding-dress . . . half-a-dozen bridesmaids. (I ought to buy their outfits; this is no time for scrimping.) What else? I suppose I'll have to rent a preacher—I wonder how much it would cost to hire a bishop? (*Exit Father*)

(*Music—prelude to wedding march. Psychiatrist turns his collar around, holds his notebook like a prayer book, moves downstage center. He is now the Minister. Wedding March full blast. Adam fingering tie. Mother is escorted by Miss Much and Mrs. More in flowered hats. Eve, veiled, enters on her father's arm. Bride and groom stand before Minister, others symmetrically arrayed on each side. Recorder looks on from his bench. Music low.*)

MINISTER : Dearly beloved, we are met today (*Congregation bows heads*) in solemn congregation, on a festive occasion, before us these delightful young people (*Adam and Eve bow*) the children of well-respected families (*Mother & Father bow*) living in this model town of Middletown (*More & Much bow*) in the United States of America. (*All bow deeply*) Here we are; to sanctify a union which has already been approved by Society; blood test certified, licence ratified, appropriate invitations issued and answered, and the necessary costly gifts presented. All has been arranged with tasteful elegance and all that remains is to stamp the occasion with clerical approval. Give me your hands. (*Adam and Eve join hands. Minister raises his in blessing*) Bless you, my children. Be fruitful and multiply. Fill the earth and subdue it.

(*Mother rushes forward, tosses back Eve's veil and kisses her*)

MOTHER : Very nice, darling. How well you studied everything I taught you. I couldn't have danced it better myself.

(*During the following speeches, everyone is moving around Adam and Eve who stand as if in receiving line, shaking hands*)

MRS. MORE : Such an addition to our local society.

MISS MUCH : You'll find the country club has just about everything!

FATHER : Welcome, son, as one of the family.

MINISTER : Very pleased to have you in our little community.

MOTHER : The west room will make a perfect nursery.

MRS. MORE : Such a lovely house! And a two-car garage!

MISS MUCH : The country club is only a twenty minute drive.

FATHER : What's the latest word on Eldorado Holdings?

MINISTER : I'll look forward to seeing you both on Sunday . . .

MOTHER : (*sobbing*) So happy . . .

MRS. MORE : Such a charming couple . . .

MISS MUCH : Such a lucky couple . . .

FATHER : Bless you, my children.

MINISTER : Bless you, young people.

MOTHER : Bless you, my darling.

(*All go off. Father hands Minister an envelope. Adam and Eve, alone at last, look at each other.*)

RECORDER : (*reading from Bible*) ". . . make the heart of this people fat and their ears heavy, and shut their eyes . . ." (*To audience*) The judgment is from the case of Isaiah versus the Principality of Judah, in the year that King Uzziah died.

EVE : The garden's getting chilly. Let's go in, Adam. Let me show you the presents—the silver tea service, the linen and the crystal from Great-aunt Sarah. Did you like the wedding?

ADAM : I like being married to you.

EVE : Darling Adam, you say the nicest things. Will you always say them?

ADAM : Always.

EVE : For ever and ever?

ADAM : (*very solemn*) For ever and ever.

EVE : I'm cold in this garden. Let's go in.

(*They walk off together. Stage darkens. Lights up on Recorder alone behind his bench.*)

RECORDER : I'd like to record a satisfactory ending for this prince and princess, a charming couple, gilded youth in a golden age, but the usual formula—"happy ever after"—may not, in this case, be entirely applicable. I find I have insufficient evidence to justify a judgment. You see, although I am in theory a friend of the family I was not invited to this wedding. (*Hammers with his gavel.*) The Court will come to order. (*Jurors file in to take their places. Eve comes in last, sits on her stool in same disconsolate attitude as we first saw her.*) Pray proceed with your evidence, young lady.

EVE : (*walking about stage as she speaks*) I loved my world of the glossy magazines; looking crisp at breakfast, elegant at evening, dedicated daily to the art of gracious living. I moved in such a whirl that I never even guessed there was nothing at the center. Then the rhythm changed; spun me ever faster in a new direction.

MOTHER : Darling, I'm so happy . . .

PSYCH. : I can't overemphasize the absolute importance of utter relaxation . . .

DOCTOR : combined with my patented maternity diet.

ADAM : Put your feet up, darling.

MOTHER : Let the hem down, darling. Then the skirt won't rise so much in the front.

MRS. MORE : A pair of pink bootees . . . I know you want a girl.

MISS MUCH : I knitted it in blue, for of course you want a boy.

ADAM : Let's call him David . . .

MOTHER : Of course you'll call her Sarah . . .

PSYCH. : The psychic satisfaction of natural nursing . . .

DOCTOR : my patented formula builds bonny babies and comes in the giant economy size.

ADAM : Why not call her Angela, after your mother?

(*The hubbub stops, and Eve takes her hands from her ears*)

EVE : We called him Kenneth, after my father. A lovely baby. I held him in my arms and laughed as he pommelled me with dumpling fists. He cried at his christening, my wilful son.

RECORDER : He was baptized, then?

EVE : Oh, yes. We took all the usual precautions. He was vaccinated, and inoculated, and father took out an endowment policy to pay for his college education. Afterwards he did the same for Billy, my second baby, born two years later. I'd hoped for a daughter. What did I get? Another snub-nosed hellion in dirty bluejeans, and a classic case of sibling rivalry!

(*Enter Billy and Ken, running*)

BILLY : Bang! Bang! I got you. You're dead!

KEN : Nuts! I've got a bullet-proof chest.

BILLY : Mum! Mum! Tell Ken he's dead. (*Enter Adam, carrying briefcase.*) Dad! Dad! Tell Ken he's dead.

KEN : I'm not dead. I'm not dead. Wait till I get you.

EVE : Now Billy. Now Ken. Run off and kill each other and leave Mummy to finish what she is doing. Grandma and Grandpa are coming for supper (*Billy and Ken run off. Eve calls after them*) so be sure and wash your hands.

ADAM : From the blood, I suppose.

EVE : Don't be silly, Adam. They are only playing. If you took a little more interest in the children you'd know it's a natural show of aggression.

ADAM : So is the atom bomb. All I ask is a little peace and quiet when I come home after a hard day's work at the office.

EVE : And how about me? I don't work, I suppose. The dinner cooks itself, and guest towels just happen in the downstairs bathroom.

ADAM : I don't invite guests. Heaven knows, I see enough people all day in the office.

EVE : So you come home just to sleep. Well, how about me? I spend the day cooped up in the house talking to people who are three feet high. There are times when I like a little adult conversation.

ADAM : Then why invite your parents? (*Enter Mother*) Ah, good evening, Mother. How nice to see you.

(*Enter Ken and Billy, still running*)

BILLY : Bang! Bang! Got you, Grandma. You're dead.

KEN : No, I got her. Grandma, lie down.

MOTHER : No, dear, I can be perfectly dead standing up.

BILLY : Aw, shucks! Then I'll get Grandpa when he's finished parking the car.

KEN : I'll get him first. Race you! (*Children run off*)

MOTHER : Such high spirited children. You must find them very . . . challenging. You were always such a quiet child, Eve, always such an obedient child. I really don't know what things are coming to.

(*Enter Father*)

FATHER : Who doesn't know what things are coming to?

EVE : I don't know what my life is coming to!

FATHER : Perhaps you need a holiday?

MOTHER : Perhaps a tonic?

ADAM : Perhaps we should go out dining and dancing?

EVE : Not one of you understands me. (*She bursts into tears. Mother and Father gather round at once, crowding Adam out. He walks back to his Juror's bench dejected.*)

FATHER : There, there, my dear.

MOTHER : It's not your fault; you always were sensitive. Like me, you are very highly strung.

FATHER : It takes a specialist to care for my daughter. I know just the man. (*He walks over to the Psychiatrist*)

MOTHER : We know just the man. Leave the arrangements to your father and me.

(*Father returns to his seat and Psychiatrist joins Mother. They stand each side of Eve's stool and talk over her head.*)

PSYCH. : I find a lot of my patients suffer from the same delusions of claustrophobia. They feel shut in, cooped up, put away—

MOTHER : My daughter wants taking out of herself.

EVE : No, Mother, not that. I'm already out of myself. I want to be put back in.

PSYCH. : Well, well. That's an interesting switch of hallucination. A little psychotherapy is indicated. Now, how about Art? Or Bridge? Or Tennis? (*Eve shakes her head at each suggestion*) Something, perhaps, a little more constructive? (*Eve looks up hopefully*) I have it. The very thing. A charity committee. Emotional involvement with the underprivileged is just what you need.

MOTHER : And I know the chairman of such a charming group . . . a Mrs. More. Her husband is in banking.

(*Mother leads Eve across stage to where Mrs. More and Miss Much, sitting behind benches, are primping*)

EVE : Mother, what does the committee do?

MOTHER : It publishes cookery books for campers.

MRS. MORE : (*correcting her*) Recipes for Refugees—a duly registered non-profit enterprise. So glad to meet you. . . . Mrs. er . . . and Mrs. er . . . We think it important that those poor people should have a varied diet and learn how to eat the food of other nations on the chance that one day they may be resettled. One must start the orientation process early. (*To Miss Much*) How many books did we print last year?

MISS MUCH : Twenty thousand in basic Arabic, after some very careful research on the dietetic value of shrimp chow mein.

MRS. MORE : Miss Much is our most efficient secretary. Quite remarkable. One of the Boston family, you know, an intellectual of the old tradition. So glad you are joining us. We'll look to see you three-thirty next Tuesday at my Snob Hill residence. (*Mother and Eve go off*) I suppose I might have asked them to stay?

MISS MUCH : My dear, I was just so relieved you didn't. The society photographer for *Vogue* is due and it might have been awkward if they had stayed. I know it sounds a tiny bit fussy, but one can't have just anyone photographed with one. After all, to be on our Charity Committee, one must have good breeding. . . .

MRS. MORE : Or a great deal of money.

(*The two ladies hold their pose a moment, as if for a photographer.*)

RECORDER : It certainly seems that one does not need charity. One can head this committee without a heart.

(*As Recorder speaks, Ken and Billy settle themselves in front of his bench, one sprawled on floor, one sitting. Jurors and Recorder look on with interest.*)

KEN : Channel Two is "Slaughter."

BILLY : Channel Four is "Revolution."

KEN : Nah, that's corny. Let's watch Channel Seven—"Murder and Mayhem"—six to six-thirty. (*Enter Adam*)

ADAM : Where's your Mother?

KEN : (*not turning to look*) Out.

ADAM : I know that, but where?

BILLY : She went to tea with those committee ladies.

ADAM : Damn the committee! She ought to be home. (*Enter Eve*)

EVE : I *am* home.

ADAM : Must you go traipsing off this way? Can't you keep some charity for us at home instead of teaching the refugee Chinese how to toss pizza pies in Australia?

EVE : Don't be silly, Adam. You know I'm only trying to take a responsible place in the world.

ADAM : I've nothing against your tender heart; it's just that you need a harder head to tell the true from the imitation. Your job is here, not on a committee. The children need you . . . they're getting out of hand.

KEN : (*to Billy*) There, what did I tell you?

BILLY : What did you tell me?

KEN : Whenever Mom and Dad get into a row it's always us who've gotten out of hand.

EVE : Stop it, all of you. Let me alone. Whatever I do is sure to be wrong. (*Adam and the Boys slink out. Eve sits, head in hands*) Surely there must be a way to do right? (*Enter Psychiatrist*) Perhaps you have the answer?

PSYCH. : It seems to me that your problem is one of family adjustment and could be helped by some social institution designed to cement the family bonds. Have you tried your friendly neighborhood church? (*Eve shakes her head*) Then I'd recommend it. Just walk around the block.

(*As Eve walks round the stage, Psychiatrist once more reverses his collar, becomes Minister. Martha and Dorcas join him. They are older and dowdier versions of Mrs. More and Miss Much. Eve returns, and Minister introduces them*)

MINISTER : I'd like to introduce you. Our newest member and these two ancient pillars of my church—Miss Martha, Miss Dorcas. You'll find they can tell you absolutely everything you ought to know about our congregation. I leave you in good hands.

(*Minister makes his escape, returns to bench. Martha and Dorcas stand one each side of Eve*)

MARTHA : The women's circle meets on Wednesday.

DORCAS : Then of course, on Monday, there's the Church Business Meeting . . .

MARTHA : We like members of the circle to attend this—

DORCAS : So good for the men to feel we take an interest.

MARTHA : Thursday is choir practice, from eight to ten-thirty

DORCAS : and Tuesday afternoon we hold the junior Bible reading.

MARTHA : Friday night is social—

DORCAS : the Couples Club

MARTHA : and the Young Adults group

DORCAS : and the Older Youth.

TOGETHER : We all have fun in the Church Hall together

MARTHA : though of course we occupy separate rooms.

DORCAS : On Saturday the Men's Association has breakfast—

MARTHA : So good for the men to cook their own waffles.

DORCAS : And every month there's a family church supper,

MARTHA : the tasty casserole of tuna macaroni!

TOGETHER : And then there's Sunday—

DORCAS : there's always Sunday—

MARTHA : the day of rest. (*short pause*)

DORCAS : It starts quite early—

MARTHA : Communion at eight-thirty,

DORCAS : Sunday school at ten,

MARTHA : Worship at eleven, and the minister's sermon timed to finish on the stroke of noon.

DORCAS : He's always so considerate, and understands the problem of getting home in time to cook the family luncheon

MARTHA : before the nursery children have a jolly hymn-sing

DORCAS : at three-fifteen

MARTHA : so that church can be cleared for the evening service

DORCAS : at seven-thirty.

MARTHA : And that's our Sunday—

DORCAS : Such a *religious* day.

TOGETHER : Sunday starts the week so well.

ADAM : (*shouting offstage*) Eve! I'm ready!

EVE : Excuse me. My husband. He needs his breakfast coffee.

(*Martha and Dorcas back to their seats. Enter Adam, getting into his jacket*)

ADAM : I hope you brewed it strong and black. Yesterday's day of rest exhausted me.

EVE : You shouldn't speak like that.

ADAM : (*yawning*) It's just that I'm tired.

EVE : Then think how I feel.

ADAM : You'd have more sympathy if it hadn't been your idea in the first place.

EVE : That's a lie. It was yours.

ADAM : I haven't time to argue before the train. There's a conference at ten. I'll be back at seven with the overseas manager and his wife and maybe some others. I'll give you a ring. What are you going to give us for dinner?

EVE : How like a man! You might have warned me.

ADAM : I told you a week ago. . . .

EVE : You did not.

ADAM : I did. I distinctly remember . . .

EVE : It doesn't make much difference whether you told me or not. I didn't know until this moment. Now I'll have a rush to polish the silver, and iron the dinner mats, and whip up a souffle. It used to be fun to entertain friends. I liked to cook then. But now we have expense accounts and business people and very dull evenings.

ADAM : You know these evenings are part of my job. It's the way to get on.

EVE : Do you think it's worth it?

ADAM : Isn't it what you want?

EVE : I don't know what I want. (*She gets his briefcase and hands it to him.*) Will you stop at the appliance store on Main and ask the repairman to call today. The Duomatic has broken again.

ADAM : Goodbye, my dear. When you know your heart's desire I'll get it for you.

(*Adam puts on his hat, walks back to his bench. Eve switches on an imaginary radio, gets out an imaginary vacuum cleaner, and sweeps across the stage. Vacuum noise and radio playing rock and roll continue under following scene. Eve looks at her watch.*)

EVE : There might be time to fix that marvellous dessert Mrs. More described. Now where is that recipe . . . "Take a quart of cream . . . ten eggs . . . one lemon . . ." (*Phone rings. Eve goes to answer it.*) Hullo . . . Hullo . . . oh, good morning, Miss Much. No, I can't manage Tuesday . . . this afternoon? That's worse. We have people coming . . . no, nobody you know. A most important client from overseas . . . consulting Adam . . . I believe his wife is charming . . . from Paris . . . no, from France. So sorry I can't help you. Please ask me again and thank you for ringing.

(*Eve starts to whip imaginary eggs. A commercial starts on the radio. Noise of vacuum and music still continue under . . .*)

COMMERCIAL : . . . no ordinary hair dye. The blue black of beetles' wings, distilled just for you in my up-to-date laboratories . . . You owe it to yourself to try my blue-black beetle burnish rinse . . . It's fabulous!

(*Phone rings again. Once more Eve answers it.*)

EVE : Hullo . . . Hullo . . . Good morning, Miss Dorcas. No, I can't manage Tuesday . . . This afternoon? I'm sorry . . . (*Doorbell rings. Radio and vacuum noise increase. Doorbell rings again.*) Sorry, I can't hear you. Hold on! Hold on! I think she's gone. . . .

(*Into the hubbub walks the Repairman—the Recorder in jeans and shirt, carrying a toolkit. He walks to stage front and turns an imaginary knob off in mid-air. Complete silence.*)

EVE : How did you do that?

REPAIRMAN : I turned the knob.

EVE : It's wonderful.

REPAIRMAN : It's only commonsense. Always surprise me the way some folk will listen to anything. They never choose. Guess they're afraid of missing something. Me, I like silence.

EVE : How do you get it?

REPAIRMAN : Turn off knobs. Keep still. Go fishing. I go fishing. Marvellous quiet down by the lake; like the quiet in your yard where you used to plant things.

EVE : How did you . . . ? Why, you're the boy from across the tracks who used to go fishing.

REPAIRMAN : Yup, that's me.

EVE : And your father was a carpenter.

REPAIRMAN : Yup, that's right. Dad liked to fix things and so do I. Now let's have a look at the Duomatic. (*Together they push the imagined machine forward. He pretends to open and look into it. Eve looks over his shoulder.*) Looks okay to me. What seems to be the matter?

EVE : It just doesn't work.

REPAIRMAN : It's a nice machine you got. Maybe you treat it wrong. Let's take a look. (*He kneels and pretends to open back of machine.*) Okay . . . okay . . . ah-hah.

(*He sits back on his heels, deliberately takes out book of matches, lights one, holds it in front of him a moment, shakes match out. Eve watches closely.*)

EVE : What's that little light?

REPAIRMAN : That? Why that's the pilot. It burns all the time, and keeps the dryer ready so that it works when you turn the knob. Your pilot was jammed, but it's okay now. You can go ahead, lady, any time you care to. Just check from time to time that the jet is lit.

EVE : Isn't it wonderful that it's always there ready to work when you turn the knob. It reminds me of a seed. . . .

REPAIRMAN : How come?

EVE : A seed stays alive although it looks dead, and when you plant it, it begins to work at growing.

REPAIRMAN : That's about it. Talking of planting things reminds me I've got something of yours. (*He opens his tool kit*) I always figured your ma didn't like me, so I didn't come back to give you this. (*He hands Eve the trowel*)

EVE : My trowel!

REPAIRMAN : I kept it safe. Thought we might meet some day. Figured you might need it. Did your cherry tree grow?

EVE : We moved from the house and I never went back again to look in the garden. I'd like to know. I wish I could go back. Sometimes I think if I could find that garden and walk under the trees again, in the cool evening, I'd find what I most want.

REPAIRMAN : What's that?

EVE : I wish I knew. But I seem to remember I knew it in the garden, when a seed sprouted, or a flower burst its calyx. Do you think I can go back?

REPAIRMAN : No.

EVE : Never?

REPAIRMAN : No, never. You can't cheat time by putting a clock back; you can't go back. But there are other gardens; I've been in quite a few. You could learn to work them. Might do more good with your grown-up hands than you did as a child. Thing is, you have to know what you're doing: where to dig, and what to plant.

EVE : How can I learn?

REPAIRMAN : I can give you a book. (*He looks in his tool kit*) No, sorry, haven't got it. I remember now, I gave it away to the man who tore into my store this morning—young commuter chap in the devil's own hurry, wanting to catch the eight-forty-two. I made him late, so I drove him to the depot just as the eight-twenty-eight pulled in. He caught that instead. He was in such a hurry to be fourteen minutes up on his day's routine he hadn't even time to buy a paper so I gave him my book. Might slow him down a bit. When you see him, ask him to read it to you.

EVE : And when shall I see him?

REPAIRMAN : When you get to that garden.

EVE : And when will that be?

REPAIRMAN : All in good time; or maybe out of time altogether. It all depends. . . .

EVE : Depends on what?

REPAIRMAN : On whether you look with all your heart and soul and mind and strength.

EVE : I'll try. (*He looks to see if she really means this*) I really will try.

REPAIRMAN : Okay. Then try the knob. (*She looks questioningly at him*)

EVE : The radio? The Duomatic?

REPAIRMAN : (*smiling*) More simple than that. There's a door to the garden. First you must turn the knob.

EVE : Thank you. (*As she reaches out her hand to turn the knob, lights go up on the garden. Adam is sitting there, reading.*)

EVE : Adam, is it you?

ADAM : Yes, Eve.

EVE : How did you get here?

ADAM : It's really very odd. I was reading this book, which a stranger gave me—(*reading*): "Behold I have given you every tree . . . with seed in its fruit: you shall have them for food . . ." and suddenly I was here . . . sitting under a tree with a handful of cherries as if I were ten years old. Try a cherry . . . they're wonderfully sweet.

EVE : Why, that's my cherry tree! The one I planted when I was little.

ADAM : It wouldn't surprise me. Although it looks so different I have the feeling we've been here before, that we belong. How did you find the way?

EVE : The repairman sent me. He mended the Duomatic. It was something to do with the pilot jet. He lit it. (*There is a moment of friendly silence. Adam is reading, his head against Eve. She is stroking his hair.*) Adam, where do you think we are?

ADAM : Well, the archaeological evidence would seem to indicate somewhere east of Eden, but I doubt if it matters exactly so long as we're together. Why do you want to know?

EVE : I want to be sure this is the right garden.

ADAM : It's a lovely place. . . .

EVE : Yes, and you're in it, and my cherry tree. But there should be something more . . . someone I want to meet here . . . something I have to learn . . . something to do with children. . . . Adam, can we bring the boys?

ADAM : I don't think so, Eve; they have to come alone as you and I did.

EVE : But how will they get here?

ADAM : Don't worry. I expect they're here already. Children know the way by heart. It's we who lose it. Finding it grows harder as we grow older; the world closes in and covers the path. There's a man in this book I'm reading who says we must learn to become like children before we can stay here. . . .

EVE : How can we learn? What does it say about that in your book?

ADAM : (*reading*) "To all who received him and believed on his name, he gave power to become children of God."

EVE : Who must we receive? What is his name?

ADAM : Perhaps he's the one you want to meet, the man in the garden. To judge by the story he must know all about being a child because he himself was one twice over—a child of God and a child of man.

EVE : Adam, let's read it now.

ADAM : Where shall I begin?

EVE : Begin at the beginning.

ADAM : (*reading*) "In the beginning was the Word . . ."

EVE : Why, I remember saying that! When was it? Just this morning. Adam, stop! Stop! I have to go back.

ADAM : Back where? To the charity committee? A Dorcas meeting? A cake in the oven?

EVE : Something more serious. I left my trial. I summoned the Court, so I must go back. There was a judge, and jurors—you were one of them—and a charge against me, and sentence still to come. Adam, suppose they send me to prison!

ADAM : You've been in prison already, I think.

EVE : Suppose they send me away from you, away from this garden. I shall never hear the story and I want to, so much.

ADAM : Is that your heart's desire?

EVE : (*as it dawns on her*) Yes . . . Yes, it is. How strange that it should have been so hard to discover when I knew it all the time. This is what I want: to be a child of God, to stay in the garden. (*bitterly*) And now I must go back. (*pleading*) Adam, come with me.

ADAM : I shall be there, but I cannot go with you. You must go back alone, as you came here alone. Justice and grace are personal matters; all I can do is send you my love, my heart and my love to give you courage.

(*As he speaks, Adam is backing away from Eve into darkness. Spotlight on Eve. Rest of the stage dark.*)

EVE : Justice and grace are personal matters . . . But between which persons? Eve . . . and who else? Whom shall I meet? Perhaps that someone who walks in the garden under the trees in the cool of evening. Perhaps that child, the carpenter's boy. . . . perhaps a gardener . . . perhaps a man, human as I am, who prays for grace and waits for judgment, alone, in the dark. (*Suddenly resolute*) Summon the Court again!

(*Lights go up on the Court and assembled Jurors. Eve squares her shoulders as she turns to stand and face the bench.*)

RECORDER : You have heard the charges, listened to the evidence. You have seen how this woman, a child of God, raised in the comfort of a settled home was taught how to dance to the tune of society. She stands here, self-accused, of failure to live and love as she should. Consider your verdict. (*Jurors confer together*) Now, do you find her guilty or not guilty?

JURORS' CHORUS : Not Guilty!

EVE : (*astounded*) Not Guilty?

CHORUS : Of course she isn't guilty!

JURORS 2 & 3 : She has raised her children by the book—

PSYCH. : Gessel and Ilg

DOCTOR : and Doctor Spock.

WOMEN JURORS : She has paid attention to the Decalogue—

MISS MUCH : fashion's ten commandments

MRS. MORE : in next month's *Vogue*.

MEN CHORUS : She has followed the established paths, the ways of old,

FATHER : a good girl!

MOTHER : She has always done what she is told.

CHORUS : Of course she isn't guilty! The charge is untrue.

EVE : No, I am to blame. And so are you—and you—and you. (*She points to each set of Jurors in turn, then to audience*) In the beginning was the Word. In the beginning was Light. In the beginning we knew the way to heaven. For what we have not seen, for what we have not heard, for what we have forgotten, may we be forgiven.

RECORDER : Good girl! Good girl! (*Hammers with his gavel*) The Court can stand adjourned.

EVE : Not yet, oh, not yet. Because I haven't learned what happens to me.

RECORDER : According to the rules under which you called this Court in the first place you have been tried by a jury of your peers; you've heard their verdict.

EVE : Yes, but it isn't true. I did fail to live and love as I should; I really am guilty.

RECORDER : I know, my dear, I know. If it makes you feel better, I can put you on probation.

EVE : What does that mean?

RECORDER : We usually prescribe some suitable form of remedial labor.

EVE : (*eagerly*) Would gardening do?

RECORDER : An excellent idea! But remember, the work takes more than your hands; it takes all your heart and soul and mind and strength.

EVE : I understand.

RECORDER : That's settled then. I'll read the terms of your probation. Paul writes to Ephesus: ". . . once you were darkness, but now you are light in the Lord; walk as children of light (for the fruit of light is found in all that is good and right and true), and try to learn what is pleasing to the Lord." (*He closes the book ceremonially*)

Eve : And is that all my sentence?

Recorder : No, my dear, you already have another to run concurrently with the first. One might call it a life sentence . . . that's pretty good! A life sentence . . . You must learn to live with yourself as long as you both shall live.

Eve : But how do I begin?

Recorder : (*Rising and suddenly impressive*) Begin at the beginning.

Jurors : (*Speaking as darkness deepens around them. At the end of their Chorus, the light is concentrated in a spot on Eve*)

Jurors Men : Now is the time for all good men—

Women : Now is the time,

Men : Now and forever . . .

Women : In the beginning—

Men : Start now,

Women : Here and now . . .

Men : In the beginning is the everlasting,

Chorus : In the beginning was the Word.

Adam : (*reading*) ". . . and the Word was with God, and the Word was God. In him was life; and the life was the light of men."

(*As Adam reads, the other Jurors file out. Adam joins Eve. Together they walk to center stage. Eve puts out her hand to turn the doorknob, and they walk through together. Lights up on Ken and Billy who are examining the trowel in the garden. Adam and Eve join the boys, and the family go off together. Recorder gathers up his gavel and his book, and walks downstage center. He gives the audience a little nod of recognition, then follows the family off, as lights dim and the play ends.*)

by
Helen Kromer

VERDICT OF ONE

The Setting

The stage is hung with a plain backdrop, against which is set a three-foot-high, six-foot-wide platform—extending across upstage right to left. A flight of steps just right of center and another at stage left make it accessible from the stage floor and may be used for additional playing levels.

Just left of center on the raised platform is placed a wooden armchair, surrounded on three sides by a railing to simulate a witness box. It is set at an angle toward down right, as if to face the Judge's bench, which would appear to be offstage down right—but which in actuality is never seen. All the courtroom scenes are to be played as if to the Judge—i.e., to down right. The Judge, in his high bench, appears only as an elongated shadow, thrown at strategic moments for emphasis on the backdrop. (This effect can be achieved by masking a light with a cutout form.)

To the right of the witness box on the platform is placed a small rectangular table, with three straight chairs, where the two lawyers and the Defendant sit. To the left of the witness box, angled to face toward down right is a double row of straight chairs, placed in precise order—two on the front row, three on the back—for the rest of the participants in the trial.

Lighting arrangements should include provision for four spots: one on the witness box, and three on the downstage area—right, center, and left—for the interpolated scenes. The courtroom area —i.e., the platform area—should also have general lighting.

Production Notes

Within the body of the script, the set and lighting directions have been kept as simple as possible. However, more effective use of the play will be made if the maximum facilities of the stage are employed. Thus, a cyclorama will make possible the use of rear projections; and a multi-level stage connected by ramps and steps, will allow fluidity of movement and a wider variety of scene placements.

The interpolated scenes which were plotted contrapuntally will be most effective if the lighting equipment permits each to be spotted and blacked out following the pattern of the interrupted action—thus eliminating the necessity of freezing the actors and more quickly and completely focusing the attention of the audience.

The final scene of massive destruction would be aided enormously by a rear projection or silhouetted shadow of collapsed walls, sagging roofs, helter-skelter twisted beams, etc.; the use of a color wheel to simulate flickering flames; and a blue spot centered on the actors themselves.

Throughout the script, a skillful use of lighting can add immeasurably to the desired impression that we are not quite placed in time and situation.

THE CHARACTERS

THE JUDGE	Offstage Voice
THE PROSECUTOR	
THE DEFENSE ATTORNEY	
EDWARD ROE COX	A college senior
RICHARD KEITH COX	Father of Edward
MARTHA HODGE	16, crippled by polio
JIM HODGE	17, brother of Martha
MARION HODGE	Mother of Jim and Martha
SHORTY TAYLOR	17, undersized
JACK TAYLOR	Father of Shorty
ALMA TAYLOR	Mother of Shorty
THE "COUNT"	18, leader of the Champion Gang
MARGARET PARKER	Welfare Worker
PAUL BARNES	Policeman
DR. KRONHEIM	Psychiatrist
DAVE MEEKER	Newspaper Reporter
PROFESSOR RAYMOND HARTFORD	Educator
THE REV. RALPH CLELAND	Minister of First Church
THE REV. SYNGMAN CHONGJU	Korean, Director of Youth Activities at First Church
SHIRLEY	A college sophomore

Time : The present.

The scene : The curtains part on a dark stage. Upstage left center, on the raised platform, seated in stiff formation along the straight row of chairs—their backs to the audience—are the participants: Richard Cox, Syngman Chongju, Professor Raymond Hartford, the Rev. Ralph Cleland. Seated in similar silent tableau at the rectangular table, are the Prosecutor and the Defense. Standing stiffly at attention, down center front— his back to the audience—is Edward Cox. Light comes up slowly silhouetting the outline of the Judge at the bench on the backdrop, so that his shadow becomes the impressive and dominating presence in the courtroom.

OFFSTAGE VOICE : *(Over public address system, so that the voice seems all-pervasive and yet disembodied).* Hear ye, hear ye, the Superior Court is open for session. All persons having business before this Court are hereby summoned to appear. The People versus Edward Roe Cox!

(Spot hits Edward, as he stands, back to the audience—a solitary figure in a pool of stark white light)

JUDGE : *(Offstage voice on microphone)* Edward Roe Cox, present yourself before this Court!

(Edward turns to face stage right)

"The Grand Jury, by this indictment, accuses the Defendant of the crime of Manslaughter, committed as follows: that Edward Roe Cox, on the night of October 24, (insert year), did comply and assist in the violation and murder of Martha Hodge." How say you? Guilty or Not Guilty?

EDWARD : *Not Guilty!*

JUDGE : The prisoner will turn and face the Jury.

(Edward turns and faces the audience. During the following speech, the center spot dims slowly)

53

The People have heard the indictment. The prisoner is of the People. The crime was committed against the People. I charge the People to judge his innocence or guilt!

(*The stage goes to black. Light comes up full on court area. Edward walks to the table and takes a seat. The Prosecutor stands. The Defense opens a brief case and takes out a sheaf of papers. The various participants shift in their chairs and whisper to one another, as there is a sudden general relaxation*)

JUDGE : The Prosecution may present its case!

(*The Prosecutor moves swiftly to the witness box, and with a broad gesture, points to Edward seated at the table*)

PROSEC : I call the Accused to the stand!

(*The Defense leaps up in agitation*)

DEFENSE : Objection! (*Turning toward down right as if to face the Judge*) My client cannot be made to testify against himself!

JUDGE : (*Sternly*) Prosecution knows full well he cannot examine the Accused, unless the Defense puts him on the stand!

PROSEC : (*Moving to down right as if to address the Judge*) The request, Your Honor, I admit is most unusual, but actually no more so than the case itself. The charge here is complicity and responsibility for Manslaughter. My learned colleague, the attorney for the Defense, thinks he has a perfect case, since it is an admitted fact that Edward Cox was two miles away from Martha Hodge at the moment of her death. With such an airtight alibi, the Defendant should be willing—even eager—to take the stand. Cooperation with the Prosecution should be his best defense!

JUDGE : What does the Defense say?

DEFENSE : Your Honor, the Prosecution's involved paradoxes do not impress me; and I resent his attempt to take over my job. However, to show our confidence in our position and our firm belief that the evidence is so obvious my client has nothing to fear, I consent to the Defendant's being called at this time.

JUDGE : The Defendant will rise. . . . (*Edward does so*) You understand that if you refuse to testify, that fact will not be to your prejudice?

EDWARD : I understand that, Sir, and I wish to testify.

JUDGE : The Court grants the request.

PROSEC : The people call Edward Roe Cox!

(*Edward goes to the stand*)

Raise your right hand. Do you solemnly swear to tell the whole truth, so help you God?

EDWARD : I do.

PROSEC : State your name, address and present occupation.

EDWARD : Edward Roe Cox, 2365 Beekman Drive. I'm a senior at State University.

PROSEC : Where were you on the night of October 24?

EDWARD : I was at home studying.

PROSEC : Will you construct for the Court, as nearly as you can, exactly what you did on that evening?

EDWARD : I came in after football practice around 6:00. Had dinner with the family and began studying. A little before 8:00, my father interrupted me . . .

(*As he speaks, light dims out on the court area. Bring up sound of jazz left stage. There is a brief moment of darkness, and a spot comes up on Edward, who is lying on the floor down stage left, his elbows braced on a pillow, a book open before him. A telephone and a portable radio are on the floor beside him. He turns to adjust the radio and get a different program of jazz, as Richard Cox walks into scene. He is dressed casually in shirtsleeves, is smoking a pipe and carrying a slip of paper*)

RICHARD : For heaven's sake, turn that thing off . . . !

(*Edward reaches over and turns the radio down*)

EDWARD : I think better with it on . . .

RICHARD : Nobody could unless he had two heads!

EDWARD : (*Grinning*) I've got two—just look at me cross-eyed . . .

RICHARD : (*Holding out the paper he carries*) Well you're going to need *both* of them to explain the extra on here . . .

(*Edward takes the paper and glances at it quickly, then holds it out to his father*)

EDWARD : They always add that to September's bill . . . It's for rushing . . .

RICHARD : (*Retrieving the paper*) Twenty-five dollars for rushing!? It jumps every year. That fraternity's cost more than your education!

EDWARD : (*Soberly, a little aggrieved*) I'll pay it, Dad . . .

RICHARD : No—I'll pay it . . . I just want to know *what* I'm paying for! I hope you pledged the cream of the crop at those prices!

EDWARD : We always do! (*Grinning*) After all, they got me, didn't they?

RICHARD : You're a prize package?! You and that noise box . . .

(*He turns and starts out*)

EDWARD : (*Calling after him*) You're just not "with it"—you *know* that!

(*Edward takes up his textbook and freezes in studying position, as light comes up down stage right. Martha Hodge comes hobbling awkwardly into the light and sits down with complete dejection on a small stool. Her brother, Jim, has followed her on*)

MARTHA : Let me alone, Jim! I don't *want* to go!

JIM : You've got to *make* yourself do some things, Martha . . .

MARTHA : I make myself do things all the time. You don't know what it's like . . .

JIM : I do, too! I know darned well how tough it is . . . But you can't just drop out of everything . . .

MARTHA : (*Sullenly*) Nobody wants me around. They just asked me because everybody in Home Ec was asked . . .

JIM : I don't *care* why they asked you! The point is you can go to that meeting and be a part of things!

MARTHA : I'm *not* a "part of things" . . . and *that's* not going to change it! I have to go alone and I just sit there alone . . .

JIM : Well call somebody . . . Call Judy and ask to go with her . . .

MARTHA : She goes with Jane all the time . . . and afterward they meet some of the boys, I think . . .

JIM : (*Growing increasingly impatient*) All right! Stick around! Join in!

MARTHA : I don't have anything to say to them! They talk about the dancing club and going skating . . .

JIM : There's no reason why *you* couldn't dance, if you'd let me teach you . . .

MARTHA : What'd be the use of it? Who wants to date somebody crippled . . .

JIM : Plenty of people—if the girl has enough personality! *You* go around with a long face and a sad-eyed expression . . . Nobody likes a sour puss!

MARTHA : Oh thank you! *That* makes me feel just fine!

JIM : (*Feeling increasingly helpless and irritated*) I don't care how you feel! You get so wrapped up in yourself . . . you can't see beyond your own nose!

(*Marion Hodge, their mother, comes into the light, wiping her hands wearily on her apron*)

MARION : Oh Jim—stop nagging her . . .

JIM : (*Reacting angrily*) O.K.! She can just sit here and mope for the rest of her life!

MARION : Aren't you ashamed of yourself . . . after all that child's been through . . .

JIM : A *lot* of people go through a lot, Mom! That doesn't mean they stop living . . . *You* don't help any!

MARION : I don't want her hurt any more!

JIM : She can get hurt just sitting around *not* getting hurt! She can wind up an old maid!

MARTHA : (*Reacting painfully*) Well that's what I'm going to be all right! You don't need to rub it in . . . I hate the way I am . . . I wish I were dead . . .

MARION : *Now* aren't you sorry!

JIM : (*Beside himself*) No, I'm not! I don't have to feel sorry for her . . . she feels too sorry for herself!

MARTHA : I know you wish you didn't have me for a sister . . .
(*This makes Jim remorseful, and he bends down and puts his arm around her*)

JIM : Oh Martha—that's not so. Would I rant and rave if I didn't care about you? I think you're a swell egg. Why, sometimes around here, you're funny as the dickens . . . I want other people to know you like that . . .

MARTHA : (*Mollified*) I don't *feel* funny around other people . . .

JIM : You would if you stuck with it . . . that's the only reason I keep pestering you to go to things . . .

(*The group freezes, as light comes up center stage. The Count comes into the light, mincing comically, as he holds up a lady's slip before him. Shorty Taylor follows nervously, watching as the Count parades back and forth*)

COUNT : Now ain't that purty! Lace'n all . . . who'd a believed ya'd do it, Kid . . .

SHORTY : (*Desperately*) I ain't no kid! I told ya—I steal as good as anybody! I took a lady's handbag once . . . an' I've broke into cars . . .

COUNT : Where'd ya get this?

SHORTY : Hogan's Department Store. (*Pleading*) Come on . . . ya said if I did it, ya'd give me a chance . . . *try* me!

COUNT : It ain't that easy, Taylor—I got the rep a the Champions to think of . . . You're a baby . . . a runt . . .

SHORTY : I *ain't* no runt! I been fightin' since I can remember . . . Once I hit a teacher wit' a two by four an' almost broke his head . . .

COUNT : (*Impressed*) Yeah?

SHORTY : Yeah. An' I done time for stealin' in the Youth House . . .

COUNT : (*Slyly*) That don't make ya a man, Kid. Ya gotta be a *real* man to belong to the Champions . . .

SHORTY : I already tole ya . . .

COUNT : Naw . . . I mean ya ain't never had a girl . . .

SHORTY : (*Defensively*) I have too . . . I had a lotta girls . . .

COUNT : Who wuz they . . . midgets?

SHORTY : I ain't afraid a no girl!

COUNT : Well no girl's gonna be afraid a you . . . that's for sure! You ain't big enough to take one on . . .

SHORTY : Lissen—I know all about that under-the-stairs jive . . .

COUNT : Yeah, I'll bet! Any girl you got'd have to have a handicap . . .

SHORTY : You jus name her . . . jus name her . . . I'll prove it to ya . . .

COUNT : You *do* that, Runt! I got just the dog for ya . . . a crippled kid name a Drag-leg Hodge . . . She's got a handicap . . .

SHORTY : (*With disgust*) Aw—*that* one! She'd turn my stomach . . .

COUNT : Now that's no way to talk about a lady . . . You're
gonna do her a big favor, Boy . . . yes sir . . . a real big
favor . . .

(*A telephone rings down stage left. Shorty and the Count
freeze, as Edward, holding his book, rolls over on his back, and
lazily picks up the phone with his free hand*)

EDWARD : Hi, Shirley! . . . Oh, I knew it was you . . . I'm just
so irresistible . . . No—I finished the math . . . I'm reading
Crocker . . . Yeah, I'm learning something . . . (*Reading
from the book*) "A lighted match idly thrown away can cause
deforestation which will change the rainfall and climate. The
course of certain atoms and elements in the *physical* world can
be directly determined by a mental decision . . ."

(*Edward freezes, as downstage right, Martha gets up slowly
and turns to Jim*)

MARTHA : What if I'd go to the *next* meeting after this one, Jim?

JIM : That's just putting it off, Martha!

MARION : You don't have to go to *any* you don't feel like . . .

JIM : It won't be any easier the next time! (*He puts his hands on
her shoulders and forces her to straighten up*) Come on—
straighten your shoulders . . . put a smile on your face . . .
go on out there and give 'em the old one two! (*He pretends to
sock her on the chin. She smiles uncertainly*)

(*They freeze briefly in the Hodge scene, as—center stage—the
Count flicks an imaginary speck off Shorty's jacket*)

COUNT : Gonna be a big night for you, Boy! Maybe I better come
along . . . show ya how . . .

SHORTY : (*Fiercely*) I don't need no help . . .

COUNT : (*Disgustedly, hands on hips*) Brush down your hair! Ya
wantta make a good impression, don't ya . . . !

MARION : (*To Martha, pointing offstage*) Go put your scarf on
. . . I'm not going to have you catch cold . . .

JIM : She's not going to catch cold this kind of weather . . .

MARTHA : (*With fright*) Oh Jim, do I *have* to go?

JIM : (*Driving her out*) *Yes,* you do! Go on—get out of here!!

(*Dim center and down-right spots slowly, as Martha starts hobbling reluctantly toward up left. The Count gives Shorty a shove toward stage right. Shorty stumbles, collects himself, starts up right and circles around to intercept Martha. Down left, Edward—still holding the telephone, sits up and hugs his knees, as if he were looking out the window of his room*)

EDWARD : Look at that moon, Shirley! What a night to ride down to the bay . . . hold hands . . . drink sea water . . . go crazy . . .

(*Shorty approaches Martha*)

SHORTY : Hi, old Hobbledy Hodge . . .

MARTHA : (*Frightened*) What do you want? (*She stands frozen as Shorty advances on her*)

(*The music on the radio changes*)

EDWARD : Listen, Shirl—they're playing our tune . . .

(*Light dims on Edward as he flops over to turn up the radio. Shorty grabs Martha's arms and she starts to struggle*)

MARTHA : Let me alone! Please let me go!

(*The radio comes up full, as Martha begins to scream. Shorty forces her back into the shadows off right, and Martha gives an agonized wail as the stage goes to black*)

DEFENSE : (*Shouting*) I object! I object!

(*Light comes up on the court area. Edward has returned to the stand. Richard has returned to his seat. The Defense has risen angrily*)

The tactics of the Prosecution are an outrage on the dignity of these proceedings!

(*The Prosecutor turns to face down right, as if addressing the Judge*)

PROSEC : Please the Court—I have reconstructed the movements of the persons involved on the night of the crime: the victim, her assailant, and the man accused of complicity and responsibility. I submit that nothing could be more relevant!

JUDGE : Objection overruled.

(*The Prosecutor turns back to face Edward on the stand*)

PROSEC : Will you tell the Court what you were studying on the night of October 24?

EDWARD : Physics.

PROSEC : You plan to be a physicist?

EDWARD : I'm told I have the qualifications to make a scientist.

PROSEC : What does that involve? (*Edward hesitates*) Don't be modest; just answer the question.

EDWARD : A good mind. An understanding of science and mathematics. The ability to look at life with reality.

PROSEC : And you believe you have that ability?

EDWARD : Yes, I believe I do.

PROSEC : Have you ever heard the sentence: "All the progress of mankind to date results from the making of careful measurements"?

EDWARD : Yes, I think . . . somewhere . . .

PROSEC : You should! It's the first sentence in your physics text. Now, would you say likewise, that all the failures of mankind result from *the lack of careful measurements?* Can you not, in fact, subtract from man's progress as well as add?

EDWARD : I suppose that is the implication.

(*The Prosecutor goes to the table and collects a map, a record book and three pins: a church fellowship pin, a fraternity pin and a science honorary. He moves to the witness box and hands Edward the map*)

PROSEC : I hand you this document and ask you what it is . . .

(*Edward studies it for a moment*)

EDWARD : It's a map . . . of this city.

PROSEC : Will you please point out where you live?

EDWARD : (*Indicating with his finger*) Right there . . . on Beekman Drive . . .

PROSEC : As you can see, I have marked your address in red. I have also marked the area in which the crime occurred. Have you ever been in this area—known as Queensbridge?

EDWARD : No. I have not.

PROSEC : Yet it is only two miles from your home. Is it not a fact that to get to the State University each morning, you must drive through this area?

EDWARD : Yes. But why would I have any reason to stop there?

PROSEC : You are positive you have never been there?

EDWARD : Positive.

(*The Prosecutor hands Edward the record book and takes the map from him*)

PROSEC : Can you tell me what this is?

EDWARD : (*After a moment's study*) It's the "Membership Record of First Church."

PROSEC : Does your name appear there?

EDWARD : Yes. I joined when I was 14 or 15.

PROSEC : Do you remember what kind of promises you made when you joined this church?

EDWARD : No, not exactly.

PROSEC : But you consider yourself a Christian?

EDWARD : Certainly.

PROSEC : As a Christian, what do you believe?

EDWARD : (*Hesitantly*) Well—I believe in God and Jesus Christ. I believe in helping others . . . There's a sort of basic commandment—"Thou shalt love the Lord thy God with all thy heart and with all thy mind . . . and thy neighbor as thyself . . ."

PROSEC : And who is your neighbor, Edward Cox? The family who lives next door? (*Holding up the map*) Two miles away? Two thousand miles away?

EDWARD : Well, I've always thought . . . (*His voice trails off as he realizes he's contradicted himself. The Prosecutor takes the record book from Edward and hands him the fellowship pin*)

PROSEC : I hand you this emblem. Can you identify it?

EDWARD : (*Surprised*) It looks like my Fellowship pin from my youth group at church . . .

PROSEC : Are you in the habit of wearing it?

EDWARD : Oh well, no.

PROSEC : As a matter of fact, hasn't it lain in the top drawer of your bureau since the day you got it—six years ago?

EDWARD : Well—that's kind of a childish thing, wearing a pin like that.

PROSEC : (*Handing Edward a second pin*) Do you ever wear this one?

EDWARD : Oh well sure—that's my fraternity pin. During rushing I wear it.

PROSEC : (*Handing him a third pin*) And how about this one?

EDWARD : That one, too—that's the science honorary. You're supposed to wear anything that adds prestige to your house and helps impress the rushees.

PROSEC : And that would not include the church emblem?

EDWARD : (*Shrugging*) No. It just wouldn't count for anything.

PROSEC : It . . . just . . . wouldn't . . . *count* . . . for anything?!

EDWARD : Not in that situation. People pledge to a house because of the campus credits and the social rating. They're not interested in religion.

PROSEC : But how about *you*, Mr. Cox? When you promised to love the Lord thy God with all your heart, mind and soul, did you make clear that you were reserving a certain category that would not be His province at all?

EDWARD : (*Nettled*) Listen—I think it's a childish thing to wear any kind of pin—but you're required to.

PROSEC : Required?

EDWARD : It would be frowned upon if you didn't.

PROSEC : Then *realistically* (and you have told the Court that you consider yourself a realist) you *care* what your fraternity brothers think but you do not care what God thinks? So—the Court can conclude that you care about your professional career and the social stratum in which you will move, but you do not care about your religion!

EDWARD : (*Irritated*) I didn't say that!

(*The Prosecutor holds out his hand for the pins. Edward returns them. The Prosecutor looks at the pins, then at Edward*)

PROSEC : (*Dryly*) Thank you.

(*He moves back to the table and deposits the five articles, and then turns toward the Defense*)

(*Gesturing toward Edward*) Your witness. . . .

(*The Prosecutor sits down at the table as the Defense rises to question Edward*)

DEFENSE : (*Quietly, reasonably*) Mr. Cox, why do you want to be a scientist?

EDWARD : I think that's the way I can best help mankind.

DEFENSE : You are aware that science has given us the atom bomb, the hydrogen bomb, intricate developments in biological warfare?

EDWARD : Science has also given us unlimited power for the *peaceful* uses of atomic energy.

DEFENSE : And you intend to limit your scientific research to those uses which will be peaceful?

EDWARD : You do not "limit" in science. You explore . . . on *any* frontier!

DEFENSE : But your ultimate aim is to be of good use during your lifetime?

EDWARD : Yes. That is true.

DEFENSE : Will you tell the Court how you apportion your time?

EDWARD : Well, I've got classes five hours every day; I study about five. During the fall I play football . . .

DEFENSE : In the light of your plans for the future, can you justify the use of that time?

EDWARD : I think I can. I would say that a healthy body will be a most valuable asset for the future . . . Life in a research lab is pretty sedentary . . .

DEFENSE : Do you study weekends?

EDWARD : I certainly do! Though—I usually have a date Friday and Saturday nights. Sometimes there's a party or a dance at the fraternity house . . .

DEFENSE : And can you justify the use of that time?

EDWARD : Well—sure. You need to relax some to be able to do a good job. The more adjusted you are, the better you get along with everyone else, and I think the better you do over the long haul.

DEFENSE : So you joined a fraternity for the social opportunities it gave you?

EDWARD : Everyone I run around with joined a fraternity! You need a group to which you can belong. And the contacts are important. Some of our alumni are among the most outstanding professional men in this city. That opens up a lot of opportunities for the future!

DEFENSE : Now how do you spend your summers?

EDWARD : I work as a bellhop in a summer hotel, to help pay my way . . .

DEFENSE : In other words, you spend your summers working at menial labor, to help pay for your education?

EDWARD : Well . . . I wouldn't say that exactly . . . My folks pay for that—but there are a lot of other expenses—dates . . . fraternity assessments . . . and then I needed a car to get back and forth to the campus. I was wasting a lot of time traveling by bus. And I figured time saved one place could be put to good use somewhere else . . .

DEFENSE : Would you say that you have been taking steps as a responsible person to further your study, to keep your life well-balanced, to make good contacts—all with an eye to serving society in a beneficial way in the future?

EDWARD : Yes. I would say so.

(*The Prosecutor rises*)

PROSEC : Mr. Cox—to put it another way—as you see it, the *end* justifies the *means*?

(*The Defense whips around angrily*)

DEFENSE : Objection! Irrelevant and immaterial!

(*The Prosecutor turns to face down right as if to the Judge*)

PROSEC : We believe the question has a direct bearing on the issues in this case, Your Honor . . .

JUDGE : I must sustain the objection . . . *until* such issues are properly raised . . .

PROSEC : May it be understood that the witness—then—may be *re*called for examination?

JUDGE : It may be so understood and I so rule.

DEFENSE : (*To Edward*) You may step down . . .

(*Edward returns to his chair; the Defense attorney returns to the table*)

PROSEC : The People call Mr. Richard Cox . . .

(*Richard takes the stand*)

Raise your right hand. Do you solemnly swear that you will tell the whole truth, so help you God?

RICHARD : I do.

PROSEC : You are the father of Edward Cox?

RICHARD : I am.

PROSEC : Can you give the Court any idea why your son would be involved in a crime of this nature?

RICHARD : (*Exploding*) He *wasn't!* The boy was at home with us! This whole thing is incomprehensible. . . . That my son should be dragged in here, when there is not a shred of evidence against him . . . ! He's innocent of any connection with this crime!

JUDGE : The Court will decide that.

PROSEC : You have stated, Mr. Cox, that your son is innocent of *any connection* with this crime. Yet you say he is your son . . . ?

RICHARD : (*Controlling himself with great effort*) Yes. I have said so.

PROSEC : He is of your flesh? Your blood runs through his veins . . . ?

RICHARD : (*Close to the edge again*) What are you getting at? The boy was *not* adopted. He is my legitimate son!

PROSEC : I see. How long have *you* lived in this city?

RICHARD : All my life. My father settled here when he was a young man.

PROSEC : What do you know of the area called "Queensbridge?"

RICHARD : It's a weak spot . . . the poorest section of the city . .

PROSEC : Has it always been like that?

RICHARD : No. Back in the old days it was a fine residential district

Then we got the foreign influx . . . and the section began to run down. It's gotten steadily worse . . .

PROSEC : What have you done about it?

RICHARD : I've paid my taxes. My taxes provide police protection in there . . . send in welfare workers . . . support the relief rolls, maintain the mental institution . . .

(*Light goes out on the Court area, as it comes up downstage right. Marion Hodge is sitting in a straight-backed chair. She has a numb and vacant expression, as if she neither sees nor hears. Bending over her is the Welfare Worker, Margaret Parker, who is wearing a hat and coat. Jim Hodge, looking worn and troubled, stands by watching silently*)

MARGARET : (*Calling gently*) Mrs. Hodge . . . Mrs. Hodge . . . It's Margaret Parker . . . from the Welfare Department . . . You remember me . . .

JIM : It's no use, Miss Parker . . . She doesn't hear . . . She won't eat or dress herself or anything . . .

MARGARET : (*Concerned*) Have you been managing with her alone?

JIM : I've been feeding her and getting her up and things . . .

MARGARET : How long has she been like this?

JIM : Since the night it happened . . . We had to go . . . identify my sister . . .

MARGARET : (*Shocked*) Oh my . . .

JIM : I didn't want her to . . . but she was set on it . . . and when she saw what—well, my sister'd fought so hard . . . she didn't look like herself at all . . . (*He gets a haunted expression on his face*). I can't tell you how . . . (*He breaks off speechless*). Mom just sort of crumpled up . . .

MARGARET : What a ghastly thing!

JIM : She didn't come to for a whole night and a day . . . and then she was like this . . .

MARGARET : They should have kept her in the hospital!

JIM : The doctor said she might come back faster if she was around things she knew . . .

MARGARET : Do you think she knows you?

JIM : No . . . But I don't think she wants to . . . See, I was to blame for it.

MARGARET : (*Astonished*) For your sister? How were you to blame?

JIM : I *made* her go that night . . . I just thought somebody had to make her do things . . . *Mom* wouldn't . . . See, the thing is my Mom nursed my sister all the time she had polio. . . . Sometimes the pain got so bad Martha'd cry all night, and Mom would just hold her and talk to her until it got daylight . . . Well, what I mean is—she just watched her suffer so much, she didn't want her to be hurt any more . . . And I didn't either . . . only I worried about what was going to become of her . . .

MARGARET : But that's natural for a brother . . . You were doing right . . .

JIM : (*With fierceness*) No, I wasn't! I should have just let her do things she felt like doing . . .

MARGARET : But that wouldn't have been best for her . . .

JIM : She'd be alive, at least! The way she died . . . well, some days I hope my Mom never gets any better so she won't remember . . . (*Anguished*). My sister'd never even had a date, Miss Parker! She was *afraid* of boys! I go over and over what she must have felt . . . She had such a hard time . . . and then she died . . . like that . . . and it's my fault—it's my fault!

(*The characters in the Hodge scene freeze, as light comes up down left. Shorty Taylor is seated on a small stool behind a simple set piece of bars, placed at an angle to simulate a jail cell. The policeman, Paul Barnes, is bringing Shorty's father, Jack, from off left to face Shorty through the bars*)

BARNES : Your Father's here to see you, Taylor . . .

SHORTY : (*Reacting with violence*) I don't wanna see him! (*He looks up, gives his Father a long sullen look and then stares down at his hands*)

JACK : (*Deadly*) I wantta see *you*, Boy . . . I wantta see what a two-legged polecat looks like . . . Come on over here, where I kin get my hands on you . . . I'll break every bone in your body . . .

(*Shorty turns his head away*)

Don't you try ignorin' me, you cheap no-good bum! I didn't come here to take no more crap from you! I come 'cause your Ma made me . . . You know what you done to her? You got any idea what you done? She's cryin' all the time! Night an' day she's cryin' . . . won't go outta the house, she's so ashamed . . . Ain't you proud ya gone an' done it at last . . . ?

SHORTY : Get outta here!

(*The boy gets up and turns his back on his father*)

JACK : (*Oily, taunting*) I don't have to, Boy . . . I'm your *Pa* . . . I got a legal right . . . Yeah, an' your Ma ain't here to take up for ya this time, is she? If she'd let me beat some sense into ya, like I wanted to . . . (*Suddenly shouting furiously*) Why'd ya do this crazy thing? Ain't you always had a roof over your head . . . clothes on your back . . . Answer me! By God, you *answer* me!

(*Shorty ignores him. The father turns to the policeman*)

(*With disgust*) Ah-h-h-h, he wuz born bad . . . looked like a monkey . . . (*Shouting in at the boy*) Never had no more brains 'n a monkey, either! *I* knew you wuz crazy a long time ago . . . I tole your Ma when they sent ya back from the West side . . . them doctors didn't know what they wuz doin' . . . I said then, you wasn't fit to be runnin' around loose . . .

(*The boy's silence drives him to fury*)

How come you're still livin'? How come you ain't drowned yourself in that toilet?

(*With a swift movement, he unfastens his belt and whips it off, holding it through the bars toward the boy*)

Here—hang yourself . . . save the State the trouble . . .

(*As Shorty turns around and shrinks at the sight of the belt, the policeman reacts quickly, pulling the father away from the bars*)

BARNES : Hey you! You outta your mind? Get away from there! (*He starts hustling him off*) Come on . . . you've had it, Sonny-boy . . .

JACK : (*Screaming over his shoulder, as he is forcibly ejected*) Kill yourself—you hear me! Kill yourself!

(*The boy runs to the bars to watch his father being dragged off left. His knees crumple and he slips down—his face full of hatred. Barnes returns to take up his post by the boy's cell. The two freeze, and light comes up down center as Dr. Kronheim—the Psychiatrist—walks into position, followed by Dave Meeker—the newspaper reporter. Meeker has his hat pushed back on his head and, as the interview progresses, he makes notes with a pad and pencil. Kronheim wears a white belted medical smock*)

MEEKER : Dr. Kronheim?

KRONHEIM : That's right.

MEEKER : I'm Dave Meeker from the Evening Standard. My paper wants a statement from you . . . Guess you know the whole city's up in arms about the Hodge case . . . Everyone's asking why you let the Taylor boy out of here in the first place . . .

KRONHEIM : Well, that's not too hard to answer . . .

MEEKER : How long have you been head psychiatrist here?

KRONHEIM : I came with the State Institution nine years ago.

MEEKER : Then the Taylor boy was your responsibility?

KRONHEIM : He was sent here for observation . . . yes. He had been convicted of stealing and the Juvenile Home transferred him to us.

MEEKER : And how long did you keep him?

KRONHEIM : A little over six months. We gave him a number of tests . . . the usual medication . . . and a period of therapy . . .

MEEKER : Now why'd you let him go? Did you think he was cured?

KRONHEIM : No—we did not. We felt that he had responded sufficiently to treatment that he might make a reasonable adjustment.

MEEKER : But obviously he didn't, so it would seem to have been a serious error on someone's part . . .

KRONHEIM : (*Growing increasingly irritated*) What you people don't seem to realize is that we've got a waiting list of over a thousand! We do the best we can—but we have to make relative choices! This boy's stealing—well, it was simply a way of getting what he hadn't been given. He was an unwanted child. We helped him understand that! That's as far as we could go . . .

MEEKER : Were you aware that if he was returned to his normal situation, the problem might open up again?

KRONHEIM : Certainly! Most of the people we get come from families who have no idea how to live together! We can do one of two things: remove the child from the home—in which case a healthy foster home must be found, and that's another risk— or we must work to correct the home itself. That may mean therapy for as many as 3 to 12 persons. Almost always a deeply disturbed child comes from a deeply disturbed family! We're struggling against overwhelming odds. We can't remake a third of the human race!

MEEKER : Are you saying a third of the human race needs psychiatric help?

KRONHEIM : I'm saying approximately a third of the people in this country need help at one time or another . . . I have no reason to suppose the figure for other countries is less—it may be more!

MEEKER : That presents a pretty hopeless picture, doesn't it? Psychiatry will never be equipped to handle that load . . .

KRONHEIM : Of course not! We try to do what we can, along with all the other agencies society has set up to protect itself . . . the Welfare Department, the police . . .

(*Kronheim and Meeker freeze, as Barnes takes a step downstage and speaks out front, as if answering them, though he never turns toward them*)

BARNES : Oh come off it! What can *we* do with a kid like that? Scare him—sure . . . Keep an eye on him . . . Lock him up —so he comes out worse'n he went in! You got nothin' to work with—there's no substance. He's a lost cause by the time we get him!

(*Margaret Parker, down right, also takes a step downstage and speaks out front in a similar manner*)

MARGARET : A family like the Taylors, well . . . I spent time with that boy . . . worked with the mother and father, too. Helped them get relief funds on two different occasions . . . But that doesn't get at the root of the problem! We're *always* limited in what we can do . . . Take this Hodge situation: I'll get a visiting nurse in here to help look after Mrs. Hodge . . . I'll get enough money so Jim can go back to school . . . But I can't make sense out of a senseless crime! I can't give this family *faith,* or hope! . . . any more than I could build *character* into the Taylor home, when all the basic ingredients are missing!

BARNES : And when it's missing in the home, it's missing in the kid! You got no place to begin, if he don't know right from wrong . . .

KRONHEIM : (*Turning to speak out front*) The boy *knows* right from wrong! He's *incapable* of acting upon his knowledge! To act rightly is to act out of love, and a child learns love from his parents. If he doesn't get that experience—he concludes he's unlovable, so why should he love anybody?

MEEKER : Then the parents are to blame . . . ?

KRONHEIM : (*Turning back to Meeker*) No—not altogether. It follows that *they* were incapable of loving because *they* had no experience of love. Adults set the same pattern in the home that was set for them as children. A man who beats his child, for example, was probably beaten by his parents! *His* children become the victims to even up the score. That malice runs its vicious course right down through the generations. I suppose, in a sense, that's what is meant by the Biblical "sins of the fathers being visited upon the sons . . ."

MEEKER : But isn't the very purpose of psychiatry to break that pattern?

KRONHEIM : Psychiatry is "limited" like everything else! We helped this boy recognize his need for love, and the reasons for his defenses against it—but psychiatry could not *give* him love!

(*Light comes up in the Court area as the Prosecutor rises in his place*)

PROSEC : Then LOVE is the missing ingredient!

(*Kronheim looks startled, then turns to answer him slowly, agreeing*)

KRONHEIM : Yes, you can say it that way. . . .

(*The three spots down front go out. The characters in the scenes quietly leave the stage. The Prosecutor turns back to Richard*)

PROSEC : Now Mr. Cox—when I asked you what you had done about this area, you said: "I've paid my taxes. My taxes provide police protection in there . . . send in Welfare workers . . . support the relief roles . . . maintain the mental institution . . ." *But,* by the testimony of those *who are supported* by your taxes, not one of them provides the necessary ingredient to prevent this crime!

RICHARD : If that is true, then that is *my* problem as a taxpayer! What has this got to do with the guilt or innocence of *my son!*

PROSEC : Mr. Cox, the situation in which your son is implicated was *made* by your miscalculation. I shall prove that he is guilty —in part—simply because he *is* your son!

(*To Defense, with exaggerated politeness in the face of Cox's astonished look*)

Your witness . . .

(*The Prosecutor returns to his seat at the table, as Defense moves to question Richard*)

DEFENSE : Mr. Cox, you are a member of several service organizations. Could you name those for the Court?

RICHARD : Yes. I'm a Mason, an officer in the local chapter of the Rotary Club, and a committee member of the International Red Cross.

DEFENSE : Did not the Rotary Club provide a dozen scholarships to the State University for underprivileged students?

RICHARD : Yes—they've done that for the past three years.

DEFENSE : And aren't those scholarships available for qualified students from the Queensbridge area?

RICHARD : They are.

DEFENSE : Is it not true that you also served on the central Red Cross Committee?

RICHARD : Yes. I was chairman of the annual fund drive.

DEFENSE : During the floods of 1958, were not funds from the Red Cross used to aid the families along the river in Queensbridge?

RICHARD : I think more than $6,000 was allocated to that area.

DEFENSE : As a Mason, are you not supporting a number of hospitals and homes for underprivileged children?

RICHARD : Yes. I think the number of those institutions is well into the thousands.

DEFENSE : Are you a member of a church?

RICHARD : I am. I belong to First Church.

DEFENSE : Do you make a regular pledge?

RICHARD : As a family, we've tried to tithe.

DEFENSE : And did not First Church help start a church in Queensbridge a number of years ago?

RICHARD : Yes, we did help support one there for a time.

DEFENSE : So then—as a matter of fact—*you* working through community organizations and through your church, have done everything in your power to help in this area.

RICHARD : I feel that I and my family have done what we could.

DEFENSE : Thank you. No further questions. (*He turns to the Prosecutor*) Back to you, Mr. Prosecutor.

(*The Prosecutor moves to question the witness, as the Defense returns to his place at the table*)

PROSEC : Mr. Cox, what happened to that church you started in Queensbridge?

RICHARD : We had to give it up. It didn't grow fast enough and the minister was needed elsewhere. There is a shortage of ministers.

PROSEC : Have *you*—as a member of First Church—ever gone into this area?

RICHARD : I'd have no reason to. I have nothing in common with those people. As a matter of fact, no one *wants* to go into a situation like that. For a while we had student pastors in—but they get paid too little and it's just a dirty job without rewards. That's no kind of a career for a young man.

PROSEC : What do you consider a "good" career for a young man, Mr. Cox? What, for example, do you want for *your* son?

RICHARD : The same things any father wants. I want him to be healthy and happy.

PROSEC : How do you define happiness?

RICHARD : A happy man is a successful man. He's usually a secure man. He's adjusted. We've tried to make him a well-rounded, adjusted boy.

PROSEC : Adjusted to what?

RICHARD : To life around him. To our society. . . .

PROSEC : Have you ever questioned that society to which you want him adjusted?

RICHARD : (*Self-righteously*) No! There has never been a society in history that gave a better life to a greater number of people . . . this country is unique!

PROSEC : What do you think has made it unique?

RICHARD : Our belief in freedom and our faith. . . . This country was founded by a religious people who were determined to worship as they pleased and to govern themselves. . . . They rebelled against the Old World ways and started a new thing here.

PROSEC : Did I hear you say "rebelled" against the Old World ways? Then they weren't exactly "adjusted" to their society, were they? Or successful . . . or secure. . . .

RICHARD : They were secure—*in God*. They were successful in His sight . . . They obeyed a higher law—and that has been this country's strength and the source of its freedom.

PROSEC : Ah—but Mr. Cox—security with God and with society are two very different things! For a man obeying God, if he sees something in his society which runs counter to God's purposes, may be forced to take up the *un*popular cause—the *un*successful, *in*secure, *mal*adjusted position! You didn't say anything about obedience to a higher law when I asked you what you wanted for *your* son. I ask you how strong a nation "rooted in obedience" can be—if it does not ask *first* for obedience from its sons?! (*He pauses for an answer. Richard shifts uncomfortably. He turns to the Defense*) That is all . . . your witness. . . .

DEFENSE : (*Abashed*) No questions.

PROSEC : You may step down.

(*Richard leaves the stand*)

PROSEC : The People call Raymond Hartford!

(*Professor Raymond Hartford takes the stand*)

Raise your right hand. Do you solemnly swear that you will tell the whole truth so help you God?

HARTFORD : I do.

PROSEC : State your name, address and present occupation.

HARTFORD : Raymond Hartford, 302 Campus Boulevard. I am Professor of Physics at State University, and Supervisor of the Research Department financed by the Federal Government.

PROSEC : Can you tell us what you know of the Defendant?

HARTFORD : Unusually fine mind. Inquisitive, hard-working, articulate. As fine a mind as we have in the class of '__ (insert year).

PROSEC : You have urged him to go into scientific research, have you not? Will you tell the Court why?

HARTFORD : Yes. He is thoroughly qualified; there is a particular need for scientists at the present time. We're in a race with the Russians. We need every good mind we can get. Whoever gets to the moon first will control the earth.

PROSEC : In other words, if America wins the race, the world will be in better hands than if the Russians get there first?

HARTFORD : I would say so. We're the more humane and responsible nation, certainly.

PROSEC : Would you tell the Court what kind of research you have been directing on State's campus?

HARTFORD : I can't talk about our present project—it's top-secret. But I can say we contributed to smashing the atom, reducing it for the bomb . . .

PROSEC : So you helped make this "humane and responsible" nation *first* with the bomb?

HARTFORD : Well—we were in a race *there,* too. It was us or the Fascists.

PROSEC : But the "more humane and responsible" nation was *first* with the *bomb*.

HARTFORD : Well, you had two nasty choices there. It was the Japanese or more American soldiers. . . .

PROSEC : But "the more humane and responsible nation . . ."

HARTFORD : (*Interrupting*) Just a minute, Sir. I suffered a great deal when the bomb was dropped on Hiroshima. But the hard facts were—you had two irreconcilable moralities proceeding from two different readings of man's fate and future. We're in the same spot now!

PROSEC : You are saying that our morality is superior to that of either a Fascist or a Communist State?

HARTFORD : I think the morality inherent in the religious tradition on which this country was founded *was* superior—yes!

PROSEC : So then you would say that the basic problem is a spiritual one?

HARTFORD : Certainly. Man is moving forward technologically faster than he is spiritually. The lag is going to mean chaos unless we close the gap.

PROSEC : So—as a matter of fact, then—the crisis of the spirit is greater than the crisis of science?

HARTFORD : Well—yes. I believe that is true.

PROSEC : And you honestly believe the world can be annihilated by the products of science, but saved by the development of man's spirit?

HARTFORD : I think that development is our only hope.

PROSEC : Then how can such a spiritual growth take place?

HARTFORD : Well, I'm not sure I know . . . I suppose . . . (*Pause*) I remember after the First World War, there was some Y.M.C.A. leader who kept warning that if we didn't send 100 missionaries to Japan, the day would come when we'd send 100,000 soldiers. I think he probably put his finger on it . . .

PROSEC : So then you believe it's a question of extending the Christian faith?

HARTFORD : Something like that. . . .

PROSEC : And who recruits, trains, gives conviction to those "missionaries"?

HARTFORD : That's a problem for parents, educators, preachers. . . .

PROSEC : Educators? But that's *your* field, isn't it? Yet, Professor Hartford, by your own testimony, you selected one of the finest minds in the class of '__ and encouraged, yes, urgently appealed to Edward Roe Cox to go into a profession which you believe *may ultimately bring the world to its own destruction!*

HARTFORD : (*Angrily*) "May," I said—doesn't necessarily *need* to! The scientist can do just as much or more for the spiritual welfare of humanity as the next man can!

PROSEC : Are *you?* In your discipline as an educator, are you dealing with the things of the spirit? With the humanities? Are you taking any responsibility for the end results of scientific progress?

(*There is a pause. Hartford is silenced. The Prosecutor turns to the Defense*)

Any questions?

DEFENSE : No questions.

(*Hartford gets up heavily, leaves the stand, and returns to his seat*)

PROSEC : The People call the Rev. Ralph Cleland!

(*Ralph Cleland goes to the stand*)

Raise your right hand. Do you solemnly swear that you will tell the whole truth so help you God?

CLELAND : I do.

(*Cleland sits*)

PROSEC : You understand that you've been called as an expert witness?

CLELAND : (*Nodding*) I do.

PROSEC : Will you state your name and present position.

CLELAND : Ralph E. Cleland, pastor of First Church here in the city.

PROSEC : How long have you been in the ministry?

CLELAND : Thirty-two years.

PROSEC : Will you tell us where you were educated and list the various positions you have held . . .

(*The Defense rises and interrupts*)

DEFENSE : Mr. Cleland's eminent qualifications are admitted!

(*The Prosecutor nods to the Defense and continues*)

PROSEC : Mr. Cleland, what does it mean to be a Christian?

CLELAND : (*Slowly, thoughtfully, as he feels his way*) It is . . . to belong to a company of people God called into being in the name of Christ.

PROSEC : What is its primary belief?

CLELAND : That Jesus Christ is the Lord of all life.

PROSEC : What is its purpose?

CLELAND : To speak and live that piece of news, as Christ demonstrated through the pattern of his own life.

PROSEC : I see. Did that pattern involve a "successful career"?

CLELAND : On the contrary. It began with success, then it moved to hostility, rejection, betrayal, and at the end to death by execution on a cross.

PROSEC : Did that pattern involve "security" in terms of the world's goods?

CLELAND : No. Christ said we were to seek first the "Kingdom of God"—not the world's rewards.

PROSEC : Did that pattern include peace of mind? Adjustment?

CLELAND : It did not. Christ brought no peace but a sword. In a profound sense, He taught that we have to die into life rather than assert ourselves into it.

PROSEC : Can you give us any idea why a man would choose such a Lord?

CLELAND : We did *not* choose Him. He is precisely what we would *not* have chosen! *He* chose us! *Out of love!* He clothed Himself with flesh. He came to live with us, to endure what we endure. And by that act, He taught us a better way. He changed and transformed the direction of human life!

PROSEC : How?

CLELAND : Because He loved us, because He found us *worthy* of love, we can love . . .

PROSEC : So! We are back to the missing ingredient . . . LOVE. Now, think carefully before you answer, Mr. Cleland. Are you saying that what psychiatry, the Welfare Department, various philanthropic organizations, the police force—and by inference, the whole governmental apparatus of this country—*cannot supply,* Christ can?

CLELAND : I am saying exactly that. *But* that love must be incarnate in a human being. Whatever unites us in fellowship with Him and one another continues the Incarnation which began in Jesus!

PROSEC : So—on the night of October 24th, when Martha Hodge was violated and murdered in Queensbridge, the missing ingredient was Christ's love incarnate in a human being?

CLELAND : I'm afraid, Sir, that is true . . . not only on that night, but in all the time before in the lives of Shorty Taylor, his parents, the gang of Champions. . . . It's even possible Martha Hodge need never have been crippled if love had been at work. . . .

PROSEC : But isn't this love the Church's business? Why isn't it "at work" in your congregation?

CLELAND : (*With great sadness*) It is . . . at times. . . .

PROSEC : Why no more?

CLELAND : (*Almost to himself*) Perhaps I do not make it clear enough . . . perhaps I do not live it enough . . . perhaps my faith is not sufficient. I know *Christ* is sufficient, and His love is sufficient. It is *we* who fail. . . .

(*There is a brief pause. Then the Prosecutor looks at the defense who shakes his head negatively*)

PROSEC : Thank you, Sir, that's all.

(*Cleland steps down*)

The people call Syngman Chongju!

(*Chongju goes to the stand and raises his right hand*)

Do you solemnly swear to tell the whole truth so help you God?

CHONGJU : I do.

PROSEC : State your name and present position.

CHONGJU : Syngman Chongju. I am Director of Youth Activities at First Church.

PROSEC : Where did you receive your theological education?

CHONGJU : At the Central Seminary in Seoul, Korea.

PROSEC : Then you are not a native American?

CHONGJU : No. I came to this country four years ago as a fraternal worker.

PROSEC : Do you know the Defendant?

CHONGJU : Yes. He was a member of the College Club at First Church.

PROSEC : Did you ever discuss the Queensbridge situation with him?

CHONGJU : I did. I talked it over with the Youth Cabinet one Saturday morning, when Edward Cox was president. That was . . . three years ago . . .

(*The light goes out on the Court area. There is a brief moment of darkness, and a spot comes up down left, where Edward and Shirley are talking. Shirley is seated cross-legged on the floor. Edward is squatting nearby*)

EDWARD : Why couldn't we adopt one of those kids Syngman worked with in Korea? (*As Chongju walks into the scene, Edward stands to speak to him directly*) Everybody certainly got steamed up when you told about that home for delinquents . . .

SHIRLEY : That's a marvelous idea! We could send one of them food packages . . . things like that! We might even raise money and help put him through school . . .

EDWARD : (*Enthusiastically*) What's wrong with that idea, Syngman?

CHONGJU : Nothing. Only why go all the way to Korea? Why not pick a job closer to home?

EDWARD : (*Shrugging*) We just don't have problems big enough to get everyone excited . . .

CHONGJU : We certainly do! Two miles south of here we've got an area where the juvenile delinquency rate rose 6% just last year . . .

SHIRLEY : (*Astounded*) Where?

CHONGJU : Queensbridge . . .

SHIRLEY : Good night! I didn't know that . . .

EDWARD : Well I knew it wasn't getting any *better!* But I didn't know it was *that* bad . . . Seems to me our church tried something down there once . . . It didn't work out . . .

CHONGJU : I know . . . but this time we could try a different approach . . . (*He squats down to talk more directly to Shirley*) Supposing we'd go in there this summer—that's the worst time because the kids don't have anything to do—and . . . well . . . maybe build a recreation center—something like that . . .

EDWARD : (*Settling himself on the floor near the other two*) You mean . . . *actually* build it?

CHONGJU : Yes—run a regular workcamp . . .

SHIRLEY : (*Incredulously*) Where they live with the people and start a whole program?

CHONGJU : Well, we wouldn't live down there because we're so close. But we'd spend the days there—maybe work until 3:00, then have some kind of recreation . . . and in the evening lead discussion groups . . .

SHIRLEY : You think that would work in that neighborhood?

CHONGJU : It has everywhere they've had one of those camps! People get drawn in when they see what's happening . . .

SHIRLEY : Glory—that'd be something to tackle!

EDWARD : (*Annoyed*) Well sure—but who's got the time for it? Everyone I know works all summer!

SHIRLEY : That's right, they do—or they go away for vacation . . .

EDWARD : Well it isn't a question of "vacation" with me! I just plain need the money I can earn! My folks are teed off all the time about what it's costing me on campus . . . The fraternity soaks me every time I turn around . . . (*Companionably needling Shirley*) You take me to the cleaners . . .

SHIRLEY : (*Reacting with mock anger*) I'm a cheap date and you know it!

EDWARD : (*Grinning*) No—but it all adds up! Heck, they're all kinds of things . . . I want to get a car of my own this fall . . . Then there's football camp the last two weeks of August . . . I just don't know where we'd get the people . . .

CHONGJU : (*Thoughtfully*) People *find* a way to do things when they become convinced the need is great enough . . .

EDWARD : But it isn't as if it's a question of life and death down there! Those people aren't starving . . .

(*They freeze in position, as light comes up downstage right. Martha is lying on a narrow single cot, placed at an angle. She is dressed in pajamas and has obviously just wakened. As she pushes back the covers and swings her legs over the side of the bed, we note that she is not crippled, but moves easily. As she starts to get to her feet, her legs crumple and she falls*)

MARTHA : (*Calling, frightened*) Mother . . . ! Mother . . . !

MARION : (*Running in from off right*) What's the matter, Honey?

(*Jim follows quickly*)

JIM : What happened?

MARTHA : I can't stand up! My legs won't hold me . . .

MARION : (*Reassuringly*) Oh now, Honey—you probably slept on one the wrong way and it's gone to sleep . . .

MARTHA : No . . . it doesn't feel like that . . .

(*Marion moves to get Martha up. Jim goes to the other side of her to help, and together they lift her*)

MARION : *Now* try . . .

(*Martha's legs give way*)

MARTHA : I can't . . . I told you! They hurt . . .

(*They ease her back onto the cot*)

I hurt all over . . .

(*Marion puts her hand on Martha's forehead*)

MARION : Why, I believe you have fever! Are you sick to your stomach?

MARTHA : (*Shaking her head*) But my throat's sore . . .

JIM : You got a headache? (*She nods "yes"*)

MARION : Open your mouth, Honey . . .

(*Martha opens her mouth and her mother moves her head to get a proper light on her throat. Martha suddenly pushes her hand away*)

MARTHA : Ow! My neck hurts, too . . .

MARION : Well, your throat's inflamed all right . . . Is your cold worse?

MARTHA : I coughed a lot in the night . . .

(*Marion moves to tuck her in*)

MARION : Well, Honey—you've just got the flu, that's all! We're going to have to keep you in bed a few days . . .

MARTHA : Oh darn it! I miss everything! Jane and I were going skating . . .

MARION : I wouldn't let you do that anyway with that cold. You just lie quiet today and read some. Maybe Jim'll play Scrabble with you . . .

JIM : Mom—I think we ought to get a doctor . . .

MARION : We'll see—if she isn't better in a couple of days . . .

JIM : But that's not so hot—that business with her legs . . .

MARION : Oh, flu can do that—make you weak as a kitten!

JIM : But it might be something serious!

MARION : (*Aggravated*) Jim, we can't just call a doctor every time one of us gets a sniffle! They charge terrible prices to make a house call, and I have to think of a lot of things—keeping a roof over our heads . . . keeping you two fed . . . who's going to do it if I don't? We haven't got anybody to fall back on! Anyway, I know what to do for this . . . I'll give her some aspirin and we'll watch her temperature . . . You take it every few hours . . .

(*They freeze in position in the Hodge scene, as light comes up down center stage on Shorty Taylor, squatting on his haunches. He is surreptitiously emptying the pockets of his trousers and studying their contents: candy, cigarettes, a pocket knife, a copy of* Mad Magazine. *He gets so absorbed in the magazine, that he does not notice his father, who comes in from off left and moves to stand over him—arms akimbo*)

JACK : What ya doin' there, Shorty? What ya got there? Pretty big haul, huh?

(*Shorty—with a panicked movement—drops the magazine quickly to cover the other things*)

SHORTY : I didn't steal 'em! I paid for 'em!

JACK : Yeah? With whose money?

SHORTY : Mine! My own! I earned it off a lady . . .

JACK : I'll bet! Doin' what . . . ?

SHORTY : (*Improvising rapidly*) Carryin' some stuff for her . . . She was kind of old, an' she had all these packages . . . groceries and things . . . like . . . *heavy* things—cans of paint, maybe . . .

JACK : (*Snorting*) Cans of paint!

SHORTY : An' she asked would I help her . . .

JACK : God—you're not even a good liar!

SHORTY : (*Frantic*) I don't *know* what they wuz! I didn't ask her!

JACK : (*Taunting him*) So this little old lady drops right down outta the blue an' gives ya some money . . .

SHORTY : That's right! She give me a dollar . . .

(*Jack pushes the magazine aside with his toe and kicks at the articles*)

JACK : Don't gimme that! A dollar wouldn't half pay for that crap! That knife alone there's worth . . .

SHORTY : I *traded* that with a guy . . .

JACK : You're lying! I seen them down there at Curie's Drug Store! You been in an' helped yourself . . . You stole them things . . .

SHORTY : No I didn't . . . I didn't!

JACK : (*Grabbing his collar*) You *stole* them . . . admit it!

(*He starts to shake the boy. Shorty breaks loose and lashes out in a fury*)

SHORTY : Yeah, I stole 'em! How else'm I gonna get anything? *You* don't gimme nothin' . . .

JACK : (*Advancing on him*) I'm gonna give ya a taste a somepin you ain't had near enough of, Boy . . .

(*Shorty starts to whimper, covering his head with his hands in a protective gesture*)

SHORTY : Don't hit me . . . don't hit me . . . please don't hit me . . .

(*As his voice rises, his mother, Alma, comes running in from off left, in time to see Jack start to slap and beat the boy*)

ALMA : (*Screaming*) Stop it! Let him alone, Jack!

(*She grabs his arm and hangs on until he flings her away and turns from the boy on her*)

JACK : (*Furiously*) Sure—I'll let him alone! He's *your* problem anyway—ain't he! (*Pointing to the boy*) Take a look at him! Take a real good look! Could any son a mine look like that? . . . a snivelin' snot-nose crybaby nobody wants around . . . (*He grabs her wrist*) *Answer* me . . . I had an answer comin' a long time . . . He *ain't* mine, is he?

ALMA : (*Horrified*) Oh Jack . . . Jack . . .

JACK : That year I wuz on the road . . . you wuz foolin' around, wasn't ya . . . ?

ALMA : No no no . . . I never did . . .

JACK : Sure ya did . . . He's the kid a some tramp—an' ya stuck *me* with 'im!

(*Jack twists her arm, and she goes down to her knees as he releases his grip in scornful rejection. Shorty lets out a guttural cry of shock and anguish as he watches. Then the three freeze in position, as Chongju suddenly rises impatiently*)

CHONGJU : People can starve to death in a lot of different ways— Ed . . . if nobody cares about them, for instance! And it's the worst kind of starvation! They grow up deformed and you don't see it, until they take it out on society . . . (*Thoughtfully, almost to himself*) But the tragedies don't need to happen . . . I've seen just plain ordinary people perform miracles because they were in the right spot at the right time and Christ was working through them . . . Someday somebody's going to write the story of all the things that could have happened that *didn't* because the Church was there . . .

SHIRLEY : (*Ruefully*) And all the things that *did* happen, because it wasn't . . .

(*They freeze, as—in the Hodge scene—Marion rises from her seat on Martha's bed*)

MARION : (*To Martha*) You help me by being a good, brave girl, Honey . . .

(*Martha grabs her mother's hand*)

MARTHA : Oh Mom . . . I feel just *awful* . . . Stay home just this once . . .

MARION : (*Stricken*) Martha, I *can't!* We need the money too bad . . . Jim'll be here with you, Honey . . .

JIM : What about my papers?

MARION : I'll be home 'fore you have to go carry your papers. Maybe Mrs. Cox'll let me skip the windows today . . .

(*She turns toward the wings, her shoulders slumped, depression in every movement*)

I don't know . . . I hope *someday* things'll be easier for us . . .

(*As she exits off right slowly, the spot goes off on the Hodge scene. Chongju moves to squat down again by Shirley and Edward*)

CHONGJU : When you're a pastor . . . you see all the secret griefs and you share in all the transformations—that's one of the wonderful things! You learn that Christ can change any

situation wherever there are people who will put him first
. . . He can even change human nature . . .

(*They hold in position, as Shorty suddenly makes a dive toward
the articles lying on the floor, grabs the knife and switches open
the blade*)

SHORTY : (*To Jack*) You lay one more finger on her, I'll kill
you . . .

JACK : (*Sneering*) You ain't got the guts, Boy! I'd like to see you
with that much spunk, but you ain't got it . . .

ALMA : (*Moaning*) Oh God . . . God . . . *stop* this!

(*Jack lunges and knocks the knife from Shorty's hand*)

JACK : *Now* what're ya gonna do, Big Mouth?

(*He starts slapping and beating the boy about the head and
face*)

Go on . . . cry for Mama . . . run to Mama . . .

SHORTY : (*Gasping out between the blows*) I hate you . . . I
hate you . . . I hate you!

(*His voice goes to a wail, as the scene blacks out. Edward
jumps up restlessly*)

EDWARD : (*Aggrieved*) Wow, Syngman! You sure put us on the
spot! I'd like to do that workcamp thing—but you have to
decide in the long run what's best for you! Heck, I waste hours
riding that bus up to the campus. If I work this summer, I'll
get the money to buy a car, I'll save time coming and going to
the University, I'll study more, I'll be better educated, I'll wind
up a better citizen, and I can do more as a Christian later on,
can't I?! It's all *relative* . . .

(*The stage goes to black. There is a moment of darkness and
light comes up on the court area. Chongju is again seated on
the stand, as if the scenes never took place*)

CHONGJU : Well . . . Edward made a choice. To him it was the
only sensible choice: (*scornfully*) the *end* justified the
means . . .

PROSEC : So! We are back to the question of ends and means. Why do you quarrel with Edward's decision?

CHONGJU : Because that is the Communist way . . . the Fascist way . . . the way of the materialist. But it is *not* the Christian way! Edward believes in Almighty Man—in the standards that he sets and the patterns that he makes. The Communist, too, believes that man is the masterwork of creation and man's mind is his fate. Edward believes that his "career" justifies any sacrifice along the way. The Communist, too, believes that whatever means he can use to impose his rational will on history is justified by the end result.

PROSEC : And how is it different for the Christian?

CHONGJU : The Christian believes that man is nothing without Almighty God! In Korea, we saw this difference . . . The Communists came and ravaged my country and my people. But they believed themselves to be—not monsters—but *doctors* of the human race. "You must cut out the cancers of society," they said; "rid men of their age-old shackles and set them free." And I thought perhaps they were right. Christianity seemed a failure. My father had been a Christian pastor. What had he achieved in his life? He had let himself be murdered by them without lifting a hand to save himself . . . and I was ashamed. So I joined them . . . and worked for them. Until one day I was ordered to poison the milk supply for a group of refugees. In that group was a boy from our village . . . I had played with him, I knew his family. I found myself incapable of harming this one boy. Faced with the reality, I saw very clearly; his life was precious to me simply *because I knew him!* How much more precious must all life be to God, who knows *every* human heart! I had been ordered . . . not to a moral use of man's reason, but to a terrible crime; for if both my soul and that boy's soul were God's property—to violate them was to deny Him! In that moment, I became useless to the Communist cause, for I saw that if the means are not in accord with God's will, there can be no peace or order at the end! True freedom lies *only* in Jesus Christ!

PROSEC : Are you saying that Edward—in preferring the end over the means, acted as a Communist?

CHONGJU : Ah no! For the Communist would have sacrificed the car and organized the workcamp. For the wrong reasons and in the wrong way—but he would have seen the *necessity* of doing it! He at least has a sense of history. He knows he is *in* history! He believes he can remake it! For him, "career" does not exist—only historical necessity exists!

PROSEC : Then why do you relate Edward's decision to the struggle against Communism?

CHONGJU : It's not just a struggle against Communism! It's a struggle against Evil! *Whoever* denies God does evil; for wherever God is denied, violence is done to the human spirit. That violence done to a single life is just as evil as violence done to thousands. *Whatever* name it goes by—materialism, Fascism, Communism—its inevitable result is *always*—the rape of the body and soul!

PROSEC : Then Edward's choice relates him directly to the crime?

CHONGJU : The crime *is* Edward's! "In the day when heaven was falling, he was for neither God nor Satan—but only for himself . . ."

(*Edward leaps up at his place at the table—completely beside himself*)

EDWARD : No! No! That's not true! I've done the best I knew . . . You're turning everything around . . . You make me feel guilty for something I did not do . . . I was nowhere near the scene of that murder.

(*The Prosecutor turns swiftly and points for emphasis*)

PROSEC : That is the whole point! You were nowhere near the scene of that murder—or the others . . . the endless others . . .

JUDGE : (*Rapping sharply*) Order! Order in the Court!

EDWARD : (*Unheeding—to the Prosecutor*) But I'm not six people! How many am I supposed to be responsible for? I've only got one life to live . . .

JUDGE : Order! Order! If the Prosecutor wishes to examine the Defendant let him put him on the stand . . .

PROSEC : (*To Chongju*) You may step down . . .

(*Chongju leaves the stand and returns to his seat*)

Edward Cox—take the stand.

(*Edward moves quickly and decisively to the stand*)

The oath taken by you is still binding, Mr. Cox.

EDWARD : Yes, Sir.

PROSEC : You have stated that you have only one life to live . . . ?

EDWARD : Yes! And how much can one person do . . . ?

PROSEC : How long do you expect to live?

EDWARD : (*Impatiently*) I don't see what that . . . I don't know . . . 67 or something . . . That's the life expectancy now, isn't it?

PROSEC : I'm asking you. You give yourself about 67 years?

EDWARD : I suppose so . . . give or take a few . . .

PROSEC : But in that creed to which you subscribed when you joined First Church, there are these words: "I . . . believe in the Resurrection of the body and the *life everlasting* . . ." Do you really believe that?

EDWARD : Well sure . . . that's the whole point of Christianity.

PROSEC : But there's nothing there about age 67, is there?

EDWARD : Oh well . . . no . . .

PROSEC : "Life everlasting" is a very long time, Mr. Cox! Are you spending your days into eternity in the garb you shall wish them to wear forever?

EDWARD : (*Hesitantly*) Well that's a big thought . . . I . . .

PROSEC : How does your "career" look to you in the light of your "everlasting life"?

EDWARD : Well, for the time I've got on earth . . .

PROSEC : . . . which will remain to be contemplated through all eternity . . .

EDWARD : . . . it seemed to me . . . that . . . since I have a natural bent for science and mathematics . . . that my first responsibility probably lay in the field of physics . . .

PROSEC : Your *first* responsibility? Did you not state that as a physicist, you must be realistic?

EDWARD : That's right. You've got to deal with the facts as they are. You've got to make careful measurements . . .

PROSEC : But what *are* the facts, Mr. Cox? Professor Hartford tells us that the crisis of faith on earth is greater than the crisis of science . . . Now statistics don't really tell us much about the Church—but you're used to them, so let's try measuring by your standards. How many Christians are there in the world today?

EDWARD : I don't know . . . but it's spreading all the time, isn't it?

PROSEC : Is it? In 1952, there were 850 million Christians! Today there are 691 million . . .

EDWARD : (*Astonished*) You mean there are *fewer* Christians now than there used to be?

PROSEC : That is correct. The Christians are becoming a steadily dwindling portion of the human race.

EDWARD : But this country is more Christian than it used to be!

PROSEC : Is it? There are more on the church rolls. But the volume of crime in the United States has more than doubled since 1950. We're giving nearly 5 times as much for alcohol and 3 times as much for cigarettes as we are for Christian causes. *Realistically,* what conclusion can we draw?

EDWARD : (*Slowly*) Well I . . . I . . . guess that we think we're one thing, when we're really another . . . Everybody's confused . . .

PROSEC : Indeed! And in the midst of that confusion, other forces are gaining! The Communists now control one-third of the human race. New forms of nationalism claim one-fourth. *Materialism* has obviously made great gains in this country! And—mark you—these incredible changes have taken place in less than fifty years. How long have the Christians been at work, Mr. Cox?

EDWARD : (*Small voice*) About 2,000 years.

PROSEC : So—what do the "measurements" tell us?

EDWARD : (*Disturbed*) The Christians are losing—fast!

PROSEC : That, Mr. Cox, is the "mathematics" of time! Now—let us consider the "science" of human relations. All these people who are trying new forms of government . . . what do you think they want?

EDWARD : They want what we have—freedom!

PROSEC : Do you think they are going to get it?

EDWARD : Well the Communists certainly aren't. They just trade one kind of tyranny for another.

PROSEC : Isn't that true of the nationalists as well? Doesn't "my country, right or wrong" produce another kind of tyranny?

EDWARD : Well there you get into the whole question of a higher loyalty and what freedom really is.

PROSEC : Indeed you do! Mr. Chongju tells us that the only *true* freedom lies in Christ. You yourself—when you joined First Church—said these words: "I believe in God, the Father Almighty, and in Jesus Christ *His only Son,* our Lord . . ." What do you think that means?

EDWARD : Well . . . that Christ is the Lord and Saviour of the world.

PROSEC : That no one shall find God *except* through Christ! That is very definite, is it not?

EDWARD : Yes. I guess it is.

PROSEC : Now if Jesus Christ *is* the "only name under heaven given among men by which they can be saved," why do not all men everywhere invoke that sacred name?

EDWARD : Because, obviously, enough people haven't been reached to hear it!

PROSEC : Exactly! "How shall they call on Him, in whom they have not believed, and how shall they believe in Him of whom they have not heard—and how shall they hear without a preacher?" *Realistically,* Mr. Cox, what is the primary job to be done at the present time?

EDWARD : Well, I see where you're leading all right—but why me? Why me?

PROSEC : "Measuring carefully" does it not make sense to select the most qualified men for the jobs of first importance?

EDWARD : Sure it does. But that doesn't mean everyone has to be a professional clergyman. Laymen can sometimes do more.

PROSEC : But do they? Will *you,* as a scientist? As a science student you've consistently put second what the measurements show must be first. And, Mr. Cox, how good a scientist do you think you will make if you begin by denying the scientific process? You have made the careful and realistic measurements, you have drawn the inevitable conclusions—but if you do not act upon them. . . ?

EDWARD : (*Slowly, thoughtfully*) You mean science itself dictates that something besides science has a prior claim on my life. . . .

PROSEC : Doesn't it?

(*The Defense jumps up furiously*)

DEFENSE : Objection! Objection! The prosecution has consistently put words in the mouth of this witness! In all my experience I have not seen a Defendant so misused in a courtroom! I protest in his defense . . .

PROSEC : (*Interrupting angrily*) . . . "in his defense"? Can my learned colleague be serious? Has he heard the testimony in this courtroom? Can he believe in good conscience that he is serving as this boy's *defense*? Does he understand the meaning of the word?

DEFENSE : (*Angrily*) To defend my client is to act on his behalf, to protect him, to repel danger, to keep him from harm . . .

PROSEC : Precisely! And that is what you cannot do by defending his actions. As long as he *is* defended, he shall be pursued relentlessly for redress and punishment on this earth: he shall *be* prosecuted throughout his lifetime! But *I* by prosecuting him for his actions, can repel the danger and enable him to act on his own behalf. Thus—you—by defending him become his prosecutor; and I—by prosecuting, *become* his defense!

(*Edward gets up, bracing himself on the railing and leaning forward to cry out in bewilderment*)

EDWARD : What kind of Court is this—where the prosecution is my defense and the defense my prosecution . . . where I never set eyes on the Judge? Where *am* I?

PROSEC : (*Turning on him swiftly*) In the Court of Humanity, sitting under the judgment of God!

EDWARD : But how did I get in here?

PROSEC : You were *born* . . . in the Twentieth Century!

EDWARD : But why was I put on trial?

PROSEC : You were not "put" on trial . . . You *are* on trial . . . for your LIFE! If a man lives in the midst of corruption and refuses to do anything about it, his very inaction is a form of participation in that corruption . . . and the victory of that corruption is only a question of time . . .

(*The entire company freezes, all turned toward Edward as full recognition comes to him with shock and comprehension. Light dims out during the following speech*)

OFFSTAGE VOICE : (*Over public address system*) How long does it take for the evil to build? How many years till the violence mounts? How much time till time runs out and the murder strikes *your* home?

(*Blackout on stage, and in the darkness flashes of red and amber light begin to flicker on the backdrop: simultaneously, distant reverberations of heavy explosions can be heard*)

EDWARD : (*Calling frantically, as if he were searching*) Shirley! Shirley! Are you in there? Can you hear me? Answer me! Shirley—where are you?

(*Light begins to come up down center stage on an older disheveled Shirley, sitting on a low stool. She waits in a dumb and helpless grief, cradling a baby in her arms. Her clothing is torn and her face is partially blackened, as if by an explosion. Edward comes stumbling toward her. He, too, is disheveled and distraught. Shirley does not look up*)

EDWARD : (*With wild relief*) Thank God you're safe! Thank God . . . thank God! I made it in time! I've got to get you out of here—fires are starting all around us . . .

(*Shirley gives no indication that she has heard him. He stoops beside her*)

Darling, are you all right? Can you walk? We haven't a minute to lose . . . I'll take the baby . . .

(*Shirley clutches the child to her and recoils from him*)

Shirley! You've got to help me! I can't carry you both . . .

(*As she does not react, he suddenly reaches out and slaps her sharply. She draws in her breath with a long shuddering sigh, at the same time releasing her hold on the baby, so that he rolls back in her lap to rest there, as her arms go limp. Edward speaks gently, as he lifts the baby from her*)

I had to do that. You were hurting him.

SHIRLEY : (*Dead, flat voice*) He can't be hurt any more . . .

(*Edward looks into the baby's face with sudden panic*)

EDWARD : He isn't breathing . . .

SHIRLEY : No. He isn't breathing . . .

(*Edward puts his mouth to the baby's mouth to breathe into it*)

That won't help. I tried it. I tried to breathe my life into his. And then I remembered that the air was polluted. My lungs are filled with death—as yours are. And I let him die to save him the death that will come to us . . . more slowly . . . more painfully . . .

EDWARD : (*Drawing the baby to him gently, with a great despair*)

I thought . . . I had made it . . . in time . . .

SHIRLEY : (*Half-laughing, half-sobbing*) . . . made it . . . in time! When would you have to have started . . . to have made it . . . in time . . . ?

(*The spot on center stage dims out, as the flashes of red and amber strike more vividly on the backdrop, and the sound of heavy explosions grows louder: then the stage goes to black. There is a moment of darkness, then light comes up again slowly on the court area. Edward is once again seated on the stand, his eyes riveted on the downstage area where the scene took place. The Prosecutor turns toward down right as if to face the Judge*)

PROSEC : (*With finality*) Your Honor, the Prosecution rests. . . .

(*He turns toward the Defense*)

Your witness. . . .

(*Edward suddenly breaks out of his own private nightmare. He gets to his feet with a firm intensity and purpose*)

EDWARD : No! *My* witness! *My* witness! I will bear witness!

CURTAIN

by
Darius Leander Swann

THE CIRCLE BEYOND FEAR

The Circle Beyond Fear, Darius Leander Swann. Friendship Press, New York. © 1960. Used by permission. Acting copies available in sets of six for $1.25 from denominational bookstores.

THE CIRCLE BEYOND FEAR

The Circle Beyond Fear is designed to be staged as a choral drama, though it may be done as a simple choral reading. It employs a chorus of which all twelve participants (six men and six women) are a part. All of the action, therefore, develops out of the chorus. From time to time members of the chorus assume briefly individual roles and afterwards become a part of the chorus again. Man 3's role is somewhat more individualized than the others, for he represents Cain throughout Parts I and II.

The chorus itself represents at various times different groups and if possible should be composed of persons of varied racial and ethnic backgrounds. In Part I it represents humanity in general. In Part II it represents the church, and this can be made clear by the use of specifically Christian symbols carried among the chorus as this section is presented and by adding such symbols to the costumes.

As for the costumes themselves, a wide latitude is possible, provided that there is uniformity or harmony in the group. Quiet colors and simple designs are suited to the style of the drama.

No scenery is required, especially if the drama is presented in a church. In a hall, a very simple setting may be used. Platforms of various levels may be used to advantage for the arrangement and distribution of the chorus.

THE CIRCLE BEYOND FEAR

PROLOGUE

ALL : In the beginning,
      In the beginning there was only God;
      And with God was the Word and the Word was
         God.
      Through him were all things made.
      In the beginning
      God created the heavens and the earth.
      Through the Word were they made,
      For without him was nothing made.
      And the earth was formless and void
      And upon it a great darkness rested.
      And the Spirit of God brooded upon the waters
      Until he called forth the light.
      That was the first light.
      And God filled the earth with every living thing
      That inhabited the woods and the waters and the
         skies.
      And on the sixth day God made man.

(soft drums)

MAN 4 : God made man and set him in a garden.
WOMAN 1 : He gave him dominion over every living thing,
MAN 2 : And for food the fruit of every tree
WOMAN 2 : Save one in the midst of the garden.
MAN 3 : And man from full obedience fell—
ALL : He took the fruit which God forbade
      And marred the perfect thing he was.

(loud fanfare of trumpets and drums)

ALL : We stormed the gates of Eden
To pluck the tempting fruit;
Knowledge was our motive
But pride lay at the root.

MAN 1 : God decreed the day half darkness;

ALL : We have made it light.

MAN 2 : God set man on earth to walking;

ALL : We have given him flight.

MAN 1 : We've harnessed nature,

WOMAN 1 : Split the atom,

MAN 3 : Put aloft a moon or two,

WOMAN 2 : We've turned the wastelands into gardens,

WOMAN 3 : Made new noses, too.

ALL : We've tidied up this earth of ours,
Set right a few things here and there.
Give us time—we'll make an Eden
In this earth that once was bare.

(*Musical bridge while the lights die. When the lights come up again, the Chorus has divided in two, Semi-chorus I being made up of Men 1, 2, and 3 and Women 1, 2, and 3; and Semi-chorus II of Men 4, 5, and 6 and Women 4, 5, and 6.*)

SEMI-CHORUS II : We are troubled by darkness;
Life is full of shadows.

WOMAN 5 : The darkness of disease lingers in the corners of our houses.

WOMAN 4 : The darkness of ignorance casts shadows upon our faces.

MAN 4 : The darkness of sin waits by the door of our hearts.

WOMAN 6 : We are troubled by darkness;

MEN OF
SEMI-CHORUS II : Give us this light.

WOMEN OF
SEMI-CHORUS II : We are troubled by hunger;

MEN OF
SEMI-CHORUS II : Give us this garden.

WOMEN OF
SEMI-CHORUS II : There are too many people;
MEN OF
SEMI-CHORUS II : Give us space.
SEMI-CHORUS I : Stand back!
SEMI-CHORUS II : We are poor.
SEMI-CHORUS I : Keep off!
SEMI-CHORUS II : We are hungry.
SEMI-CHORUS I : This is mine!
SEMI-CHORUS II : We are dying.
SEMI-CHORUS I : There are too many of you.
SEMI-CHORUS II : Can't you understand?
We are human beings.
SEMI-CHORUS I : Get back! I warn you.
I'll destroy you!
(*screaming*) Get back, I say!
I'll kill you!

(*a crescendo of music, a crash of drums and then
perfect silence*)

ALL : We stormed the gates of Eden
To pluck the tempting fruit;
Knowledge was our motive
But pride lay at the root.
The God who made us we defied
And sin possessed the world through pride.

(*The light fades out slowly, then comes up again
to find Semi-chorus I upstage center and Semi-
chorus II downstage R. and L. sitting and half-
lying in attitudes of dejection and despair.*)

SEMI-CHORUS I : God is too slow.
MAN 1 : We cannot wait upon his everlasting time.
WOMAN 1 : Men sink beneath the galling loads.
WOMAN 2 : Men fall beneath the cruel goads.
MAN 2 : Men die upon the dusty roads.
SEMI-CHORUS I : God is too slow!

MAN 3 : When will he curb the rich man's greed?

WOMAN 3 : When will he fill the poor man's need?

MAN 1 : When will he lift the tyrant's heel?

SEMI-CHORUS I : God is too slow!

WOMAN 2 : We cannot wait upon his creeping justice.

WOMAN 1 : Half the world in bondage sighs,

MAN 1 : Half the world in hunger dies,

MAN 2 : The rest in sinful luxury lies.

SEMI-CHORUS I : God is too slow!

SEMI-CHORUS II : We plead to man, strong and free.

Into the swinging balances

Man must thrust his hand

And right the wrongs God will not see.

MAN 1 : Here, you. Take this man's load.

MAN 2 : And you, give him your coat.

WOMAN 1 : You have too much.

WOMAN 2 : And you too little.

MAN 1 : You work.

MAN 2 : You rest.

MAN 1 : Faster!

MAN 2 : Slower!

SEMI-CHORUS I : Obey!

SEMI-CHORUS II : You make us slaves

And we were born free.

SEMI-CHORUS I : Trouble makers, eh? Philosophers.

(*strikes with the whip*) Well, philosophize about
that.

SEMI-CHORUS II : Better to die than crawl on the belly,

Better death than this death of the soul,

Better to die—

SEMI-CHORUS I : Then die!

(*loud drums, fading away*)

ALL : We stormed the gates of Eden

To pluck the tempting fruit

But with the light of knowledge

A sickness, too, took root.

The God who made us we defied
And sin possessed the world through pride.

(*The light fades slowly on the Chorus, standing
with bowed heads. When it comes up presently,
the six women are grouped on one side of the
stage and the six men on the other.*)

ALL : And God created man.

MEN : Male

WOMEN : And female.

WOMAN 1 : He set them in families.

WOMAN 2 : And the meaning of a family
Is mutual love and responsibility;

WOMAN 3 : And the meaning of responsibility
Is the discipline of love.

MAN 1 : The gifts of woman were not made to hide;
Let her beauty kindle man's desire.

MAN 2 : Array her.

MAN 3 : Display her.

MAN 4 : Make all men want her.

MEN : This is why God made her.

WOMEN : Who made the rule that there should be just one
And chained us to boredom when love is done?

WOMAN 1 : Free man must break the chain and claim his
feast.

WOMAN 2 : Beauty was made for love,

WOMAN 3 : And love was made for joy,

WOMAN 4 : And love is sweet in the heat of the flesh.

MAN 1 : (*taking Woman 3 by the arm*)
This woman pleases me.

MAN 2 : Cast off the bonds and take her.

MEN : (*except Man 3*)
The free man breaks no laws,
For only his will is his law.

MAN 3 : Hands off! The woman's mine.

MAN 1 : And I want her. She's mine.

MAN 3 : I spent my money on her.

WOMAN 3 : Tightwad! You got your money's worth; I'm not your slave.

MAN 3 : Why you cheap little chiseler—I warn you,
You'll not make a fool of me.

WOMAN 3 : (*laughing*) I don't need to. Nature took care of that.

MAN 3 : I'll break your cheap little neck. (*He seizes her.*)

(*loud music, then silence*)

ALL : The logical act is to kill
When man lives by the force of his will.
We stormed the gates of Eden
And ate the tempting fruit,
But with the light of knowledge
A sickness, too, took root.
The God who made us we defied
And sin possessed the world through pride.

(*The light dies and comes up presently upon the two semi-choruses rearranged on opposite sides of the stage.*)

MAN 1 : God made of one blood all peoples to dwell upon the face of the earth.

SEMI-CHORUS I : God made the races and the nations,
Gave them times and special places,
Callings, gifts, and dispensations,
And to each some saving graces.

MAN 1 : But of one blood he made them all.

MAN 5 : I don't believe it. Science doesn't prove it.

WOMAN 4 : Type A cannot be mixed with Type B.

WOMAN 5 : Type B abhors AB.

MAN 4 : Each rejects the other two.

MAN 1 : But O can substitute for all.
It's universal.

SEMI-CHORUS II : It's confusing.
It disturbs us that in nature
We find such mongrelization.
Now take the races and the nations—

We have remedied God's obvious omissions
And classified the world according to our new
    traditions.

WOMAN 6 : Take the color of his eyes
And the way he ties his ties.

WOMAN 4 : See the color of his hair
And the way he breathes the air.

MAN 4 : Note the shape of his head
And the height of his bed.

MAN 6 : Judge the curve of his nose
And the width between his toes.

SEMI-CHORUS II : Oh, we have a wonderful classification.

(*The two semi-choruses shout epithets at each other, at the same time drawing closer together and becoming more violent.*)

SEMI-CHORUS I : Gentile!
SEMI-CHORUS II : Jew!
SEMI-CHORUS I : Wop!
SEMI-CHORUS II : Hun!
SEMI-CHORUS I : Jap!
SEMI-CHORUS II : White devil!
SEMI-CHORUS I : We have an adequate classification.

VARIOUS
VOICES : Gringo! Boche! Christ killer! Chink!
Wetback! Darky! Donkey! Jackass! Owl! Turtle!
Dog! Snake! Pig!

(*trumpets*)

SEMI-CHORUS I : We stormed the gates of Eden
And ate the tempting fruit,
But with the light of knowledge
A sickness, too, took root.
The God who made us we defied
And sin possessed the world through pride.

(*Trumpets and drums slowly fading. Lights out as chorus assumes formal position for beginning of Part I.*)

PART I

ALL : And man from full obedience fell;
He took the fruit which God forbade
And marred God's perfect image.

(*Chorus breaks from its formal position to informal clusters.*)

MAN 5 : That was a long time ago.
In the cool of the day God walked in the garden.
In the quiet garden he found Adam with his question.
Adam, where are you?

WOMAN 1 : He is always asking questions.

WOMAN 2 : He is good at asking questions.

WOMAN 3 : He never speaks without a question.

MAN 3 : He knows we cannot answer,
In a hundred thousand days never answer.

MAN 1 : Perhaps there is no answer.

MAN 2 : Perhaps there is only the question.

MAN 3 : And God alone who can answer it.

MAN 4 : And God alone who can answer it.
(*pauses*) Could it be he asked in mercy
That night in the desolate garden?
That the words fell in compassionate anguish?

ALL : But now in our stubborn disobedience
They fall like a hail of pebbles upon an iron skillet.

MAN 4 : Now I see that it was not a geographical question.
I knew myself in God's question;
I knew that I was naked and wanted covering.
I knew what it is to be known.

ALL : We are always covering our nakedness,
Covering inadequacy with fate:

WOMAN 2 : Well, I suppose it just wasn't to be.

ALL : Covering our failures with excuses:

MAN 2 : Believe me, it was a thoroughly impossible situation.

ALL : Covering our selfishness with a false nobility:

WOMAN 4 : Of course I had to think of the good of the children.

ALL : We say that we are too busy
When in truth we are too empty.
We dare not answer the questions
Lest we know ourselves and despair.

MAN 5 : But even so,
As long as things were as they were
There was still a small hope
That the breach might be healed
And God's anger would relent
And we might again have Eden—

WOMAN 1 : But Cain ended all that.

MAN 5 : Where Adam blundered into sin
Cain flung the mercy of God upon the ground
And quenched his wrath in the blood of his brother.

WOMAN 1 : His deed was not an accidental error;

MAN 1 : It was rebellion,

MAN 4 : Since God was not pleased with what he grudgingly offered
He would slay the thing that pleased God
And whom God pleased,
And set his banner of defiance high
That all might see that man is free.

ALL : Cain defied God that man might be free.

MEN 1 AND 5,
WOMEN 2 AND 3 : Only they still hope for Eden
Who have not known the sin of Cain.

MAN 1 : This is the story of Cain:

(*The lights go down and a spot picks up Man 5.*)

MAN 5 : Cain found his brother and slew him,
And the world is filled with God's question.

(*The lights come up on a scene suggesting a courtroom, with the men grouped in the trial*)

area. The women watch the action from the op-
posite side of the stage and comment upon it.)

WOMAN 1 : The case of Cain, son of Adam, versus God and
man.

WOMAN 2 : But it is only against God, not man.

WOMAN 1 : If it is against God it is against man.

WOMEN : Now the trial begins.
Now the judge puts the question;
Ominously he puts the question.

MAN 6 : Where is thy brother?

WOMAN 3 : Now the accused prepares to answer.

MAN 2 : Objection, your Honor, the judge cannot also be
prosecutor.

MAN 6 : Objection overruled.
The prisoner will answer the question.

MAN 3 : I have forgotten the question.

MAN 6 : The question is about your brother.

MAN 3 : Am I my brother's keeper?

WOMEN : He has not answered the question.

MAN 6 : The prisoner will answer the question.

WOMEN : The judge has ruled in the matter;
The prisoner must answer the question.

MAN 6 : Where is thy brother?

MAN 3 : I do not know.

MAN 6 : Enter it in the record
That the prisoner does not know.

MAN 3 : (*breaking out suddenly*) Dead! He is dead.
Somewhere his blood blackens in the dust.
Let it be a fit sacrifice to the God he worshiped.
Enter this in the record, too:
I, Cain, a free man, killed him.
Let this be notice on you that I am free.
God, do you hear? I'm free and I killed him.

MAN 2 : (*interrupting hurriedly*)
Your Honor, my client wishes to plead guilty to
the charge,
But I beg permission to show

That the crime was committed under extreme provocation.

MAN 6 : The defense has permission to state its case.

WOMEN : The defense will state the case for Cain.

MAN 2 : My client lived under extreme provocation.

In a world where there is no observable government,

Where order and justice are subject to human prejudices,

Where evil prospers and good languishes,

Where corruption is rewarded and virtue scoffed at,

Where might is almost always right,

And where men laugh behind their hands at innocence—

In such a world my client felt justified in taking steps.

It is admitted that his acts may have introduced

Certain additional elements of injustice and harshness into the world,

But in the light of these extenuating circumstances

I ask that the court find the acts of my client justified

And give him his freedom.

MAN 6 : Has the jury reached a verdict?

MEN 1, 4,

AND 5 : We have, your Honor.

MAN 6 : The jury will render the verdict.

MEN 1, 4,

AND 5 : The jury find the accused guilty as charged.

MAN 6 : Is there a recommendation of mercy?

MEN 1, 4,

AND 5 : The jury does not so recommend.

MAN 6 : The prisoner will stand and hear the sentence.

WOMEN : The prisoner stands without recommendation of mercy.

WOMAN 3 :   The judge must render the sentence.

MAN 6 :   As freedom was what he sought

The prisoner is hereby sentenced to freedom forever.

He will not be bound to any law or loyalty or relationship,

Neither will he be required to give allegiance to God or his fellow human beings,

Nor shall any group or person force any relationship upon him.

Go in freedom and wander in the ways you have chosen.

ALL (EXCEPT

MEN 3 AND 6) :   And may God have mercy on his soul.

WOMAN 1 :   The court has pronounced the sentence.

WOMAN 2 :   The prisoner has heard the sentence.

WOMAN 4 :   We who have heard the sentence

Do not guess how heavy it is.

MEN, 1, 2,

4, AND 5 :   The face of God is hid from Cain;

The world is waste and void again.

ALL :   The cloud of our defiance

Blots out the face of God;

We wander in a wilderness

Naked, unhoused, unshod.

WOMEN :   Cain goes forth, an exile and a wanderer

Over the dry salt flats of existence.

He turns in the eye of the unblinking sun

Without purpose or direction.

Every oasis becomes an illusion

In a dry and thirsty land

Where the only truth is death.

Cain is stripped of his inheritance;

Cut off from his fellow man.

WOMAN 2 :   He cannot speak.

WOMAN 3 :   He has forgotten what to say.

WOMAN 4 :   He is alone and his burden grows.

MEN : (*coming down stage to address the audience*)
Though a million spinning wheels
On the highways and the speedways,
On the throughways and the freeways,
Bring us together at the ball parks and the beaches,
Though mass communication
Brings strange voices and new faces
Into the quiet houses which used to be our homes.
The walls of our isolation still remain.

WOMEN : Men still bear their private agonies alone.
The hidden wounds are fresh in the ulcerated flesh
And we dare not show the sorrow that we bear.

WOMAN 1 : It would be improper.

WOMAN 4 : It would be imprudent.

WOMAN 2 : It would be embarrassing.

WOMAN 3 : It would be inconvenient.

WOMEN : We have armored our private worlds
For we dare not be vulnerable to each other.

(*They gather in a group and chant.*)

MAN 4 : If the man's about to fall

MEN : Face the wall.

WOMAN 2 : If in distress someone should weep,

WOMEN : Pretend to sleep.

MAN 2 : If a person's going to be sick

MEN : Get out quick.

WOMAN 3 : If someone's about to die

WOMEN : Avert the eye.

ALL : Don't get involved.
Don't get involved.

WOMAN 4 : Let them go to the Salvation Army.

ALL : To be safe never meet the eyes of a stranger,
For the eyes of a stranger will break into your world,
And it will be destroyed forever.

WOMAN 4 : Let them go to the Salvation Army.

(*At the end of the chant the Chorus break from their positions and re-form as a Chorus.*)

MAN 3 : The hand of every man is against Cain,

MEN (EXCEPT

MAN 3) : For Cain deserves to die.

MAN 3 : And the hand of Cain is against every man,

MEN (EXCEPT

MAN 3) : For who deserves not to die?

MAN 3 : (*coming out of the group*)
I read murder in the eyes of men.

ALL : There is none to protect him
He has rid himself of every tie—
Family, tribe, region, creed.
Cain, the free man, is a prey of every man.

MAN 3 : No man is my friend;
All men seek to slay me.
What is there now but flight?

ALL : But in an alien, friendless world
Where shall Cain flee?
Death waits at every turning.

MAN 3 : Lord, now is my punishment heavier than I can bear.

MEN (EXCEPT

MAN 3) : Now then, Cain, run.

WOMEN : Run!

ALL : Run!

(*Man 3 stumbles off stage.*)

ALL : (*after a pause*) This is the world then, this is the world.
Cain is the blind, rebellious, sinning world.

WOMAN 1 : Wherever men organize their lives without God,

ALL : There the world comes creeping in
And the spirit of Cain is born.

WOMAN 2 : And life without God is flight

MAN 1 :   And loneliness
WOMAN 3 :   And brokenness
MAN 2 :   And a terrible sickness of the heart.
ALL :   In God's questions the terror falls upon us;
            It seizes us; it drives us running and stumbling
                before it.
MAN 1 :   Where are you?
MAN 2 :   Where is thy brother?

            (*lights out*)

PART II

(*The spotlight picks up the Chorus at center
stage.*)

ALL :   The cloud of our defiance
            Blots out the face of God;
            We wander in our wilderness,
            Naked, unhoused, unshod.

            (*musical bridge*)

            In the circle of his fear,
            'Neath the sun's unblinking eye
            Cain will fly and fly and fly
            In a hopeless, helpless circle
            Where God is dead
            And men have but to die.
            In a world shaped to his will
            He can only run and kill, kill and run,
            Run and kill,
            Until he die.

            (*The lights go out. The Chorus arranges itself in
            a semicircle around the stage. A spotlight picks
            up Man 3, who enters in flight and exhaustion.*)

MAN 3 :   Now I am run out;
            There is no sanctuary within this wilderness,
            All around I sense hovering malevolence

And the presence of many enemies,
And I am desolated by the hand of God.

(*He detects a movement in the shadows R. He draws back in fear.*)

Who's there? (*peering into the shadows*)
There is a form within the shadows;
Could it be, could it be
That I've reached the desert's end,
And the form that looms before me
Is not hostile but a friend?
(*hopefully*) Who's there, I say?
Who are you?
How desperately I need this knowledge.
Has someone threaded the mazes of this wilderness
Where I wandered in a solitary fear?
If so, this is the beginning of my destruction
(*with dawning realization*) And the beginning of my birth.
(*eagerly*) Who goes there?

MAN 1 : A friend.

MAN 3 : I have roamed the wilderness alone
And I have yet to find a friend.
In this world where God is not
Friendships are replaced
By mutually convenient relationships.

MAN 5 : What is your name?

MAN 3 : (*with suspicion*)
What's that? Who asks my name?
Against this revelation I must take care.
When I am known then am I lost.
Why do you ask me?
Leave me alone; I will not tell my name.

(*He starts off L., but realizes there is another person there.*)

(*with growing fear*) Who's there?

(He turns in one direction, then another, only to be blocked each time by a member of the Chorus who steps forward slightly to the edge of the light.)

VARIOUS
  VOICES : Who are you? Your name? Who are you?
  MAN 3 : *(backing away in terror)*
    Keep off! I warn you!
    I am Cain, do you hear me? *(drawing his dagger to hold them at bay)*
    Stay your distance!
    This is Cain speaking,
    Cain, do you hear?

(The remaining members of the Chorus now step forward so that they are visible, but not clearly. Man 3 is closed in this semicircle.)

  ALL : Where is thy brother?
  MAN 3 : Now it has come,
    Now they have found me.
    I am caged in a narrow cell
    And the question is a swinging sword
    Held by a tenuous thread above my head.
    And it was held by the effort of my will
    But now I know the thread must break.
    Now must I stand and answer
    For I can run no more.
  MAN 1 : The name of the man is Cain.
  WOMAN 1 : See the mark of God is upon him.
  WOMEN
  1 AND 2 : In his hands
  MEN 1 AND 2 : In his eyes
  WOMEN
  1 AND 2 : On his head
  MEN 1 AND 2 : In his face—
  ALL : The mark of God is upon him.
  MAN 3 : My brother is dead, a sacrifice to my pride.
    With the clear judgment of my mind

I smote him down, for this I knew;
In smiting him, I smote God, too.
And now you are come to slay me.
Many times I sensed your presence in the wilder-
    ness,
And I evaded you. Now before I die
Tell me who you are.

MEN : We are they who ask God's questions;

WOMEN : We are here to cut the string that holds the
    sword.

ALL : We are here to help Cain die.

MAN 3 : I understand.
I stand before the executors of his wrath,
The hounds that corner the Divine prey.
Now is the death of my hope.

ALL : Now is the birth of your hope.
We are here to tell you of the desert's end
And the place where life begins again.
We tell you of God's mercy.
The eye of God is upon Cain in love;
God cares about Cain.

MAN 3 : *(in wonder)*
If God cared about Cain
The world would begin again,
Life would begin again!
(dismissing the possibility) But I know this can-
    not be.
He has followed me with his question,
With his everlasting question.

ALL : God cares enough to ask the question;
He cares enough to answer it.

MAN 3 : I do not understand.

ALL : In our person we bear the mark you bear,
The self-same mark.

MAN 1 : We were exiles and wanderers.

MAN 2 : We have sojourned in strange places.

WOMAN 1 : We have dwelt in the wilderness of cities,

WOMAN 2 : And in the desert places of the mind,

MAN 4 : And in the slippery pits of fleshly lust.

ALL : From these God claimed us
And upon us set his mark.

WOMAN 3 : We are beggars made rich,

MAN 5 : Blind men who see,

MAN 1 : Lame men who walk,

MAN 2 : Prisoners set free.

MAN 3 : But I am a murderer.

MAN 1 : We are all murderers,

WOMAN 1 : And the blood of just men is upon us all.

MAN 3 : I did to death one who served God well,
Because he served him well.

ALL : We did to death upon a cross
Him that was God's very Son
Because he was God's Son.

MAN 3 : Come out of the shadows;
Let me look into your eyes when you speak.
Let the light fall upon your faces
In the telling of what seems an idle tale,
For if this be true, then this is life indeed.

MAN 4 : This circle now is the arc of his love.

ALL : And in that love we are claimed.

WOMAN 1 : By an infant in a stable,

WOMAN 2 : By his ministry of mercy,

WOMAN 3 : By his agony on Calvary,

WOMAN 4 : By his joyous resurrection,

WOMEN : By his blessed Holy Spirit.

MEN (EXCEPT
MAN 3) : God would claim you, too.

MAN 3 : I am willing to be claimed.

*(The Chorus moves forward again. Now the full
light is upon them and Man 3 sees them clearly.)*

ALL : Look upon us, Cain.

*(Man 3 is startled at the appearance of the
Chorus made up of many races and nations. He
stiffens into his old attitude of defense, his hand
on the dagger he carries.)*

ALL : Do you recognize us, Cain?

MAN 3 : But no, no. This cannot be.
You have deceived me;
In the shadows I could not see you.
You are not my kind.
There are foreigners among you—

MAN 1 : Wherever life is organized without God
All men are foreigners.
To themselves and to each other.

MAN 5 : But when God claims us then we know
That no man is a stranger, but every man a
brother.

WOMAN 1 : The word has gone out from stranger to stranger.

MAN 1 : From Paul, a Pharisee of the Pharisees, to the
Greeks.

WOMAN 2 : From Philip, a Jew, to an Ethiopian traveler.

WOMAN 3 : From Livingstone, intrepid Scot, to Africans of
the interior.

MAN 4 : From Sundar Singh, Indian mystic, to the people
of Tibet.

ALL : The word has gone out from stranger to stranger,
For all men stand in the same place,
We stand eternally in the same place
Until God claims us.

MAN 3 : But old enmities still stand;
Bad blood is passed from fathers to children.

MAN 6 : God has torn down the dividing wall.

MEN 1 AND 2 : (*joining*) In the agony of his flesh
He has made one new man.

ALL : And we are that man.
We are the Cains of all the earth
Who have ceased to run.
Look closer, brother.

MAN 3 : You—you are like Abel—and me.
And each of you bears a resemblance to the other.

ALL : It is the mark, Cain, God's mark.
And the urgency of God's question,
"Where is thy brother?"

Drives us into the wilderness
Among the rocky crags of desolation,
For we know what the answer must be:
Our brother must be with us.

(*The Chorus divides, making a place for Man 3 in their ranks.*)

Come into the circle, brother.

MAN 3 : (*going in*)
The mercy of God has conquered Cain;
Now the world begins again.

ALL : The end is not rest but joy.
We shall not leave the wilderness
For there are many coming and going.

MAN 6 : We are sent together into all the world
To the places where men still run in fear:

MAN 1 : Beyond the hills and into the outer seas,

WOMAN 6 : We declare his act in the shadows of splendid temples,

WOMAN 1 : And where the altar stones have fallen,

ALL : To the uttermost parts of the earth.

MAN 5 : It is not only a geographical world
Where the good news is not yet preached
But in all the places where men live
In foreignness to their true nature,
The world without and the world within.

MAN 1 : Where the pursuit of knowledge ends in destruction,

WOMAN 2 : Where the passion for justice ends in tyranny,

MAN 3 : Where natural love ends in lust and perversion,

MAN 4 : Where awareness of differences ends in discrimination.

ALL : In these wildernesses we proclaim God's mercy.
Here we declare that his mark upon Cain
Is the measure of his grace and love.
The mark upon Cain is the mark of a cross.

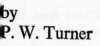

by
P. W. Turner

CHRIST IN THE
CONCRETE CITY

© 1960, P. W. Turner. Published in 1961 for the Religious Drama Society of Great Britain by the Society for Promoting Christian Knowledge. Acting copies may be obtained from the Walter H. Baker Company, 100 Summer Street, Boston 10, Mass. Permission for an amateur stage performance may be obtained from Baker's at a rate of 15.00 each showing.

This play attempts to portray the passion of Christ from three points of view: 1) a story of something that actually happened, 2) a story of universal significance, speaking timelessly to all mankind, and 3) events of personal significance, speaking intimately to the individual in the secret places of his own soul, and urging him to action here and now.

Thus the action moves in three guises: 1) historical characters from the Gospel narrative (there is no necessary continuity between the various characters played by one actor), 2) a chorus suggesting a formal presentation both in speech and movement, and 3) contemporary persons, frequently caricatures.

It is of great importance to keep these three themes clear in production. Modern costumes are appropriate although large cloaks may be thrown across the shoulders during the historical scenes. No scenery, other than varying levels, is wanted.

In the following version the editors have made minor changes in the text to replace British with American allusions, some of which were first suggested by Tom F. Driver.

The players enter, taking up their formal positions as chorus.

MAN 4 : Christ in the concrete city.

MAN 1 : In the city square of the heart,
The heart of the city,
Stands the arrogant, soot and sin stained,
Uncompromising bronze bulk of the Black Prince,
Self's effigy, which dominates the heart.

MAN 2 : Beside it, white clad, watches
The Christ.

MAN 1 : And the hurrying, traffic-dodging, job driven
Passers-by on the pavement
Make choice of the one or the other.
Before the last bus of all takes them home.

MAN 3 : And that is the subject of this play.
Not that incident
But the truth contained in the frame of that incident,
The calvary in your backyard.

WOMAN 2 : The whiplash hung on your kitchen door,

MAN 1 : And the resurrection in the local cemetery.

MAN 4 : From the beginning God has interfered.
His word has challenged to action in a particular situation.
Our story is the drama of God gate-crashing the petty concerns of men. The story of which I am the narrator.

(Pause.)

In the beginning God created heaven and earth.
The spirit of God moved on the face of the deep,
And God said "Let there be light," and there was light.

129

> And God saw everything that he had made,
> And behold, it was good.

MAN 3 : In the beginning God created us.

WOMAN 1 : Male and female he created us

WOMAN 2 : After his own likeness,
And in his own image.

MAN 2 : And he stood back and surveyed that which he
had created,

ALL : And behold, it was very good.

MAN 3 : But the man and the woman deface the image of
God
Of their own free will.

MAN 1 : Of their own free will,

MAN 2 :   turn,

MEN 1, 2,
   AND 3 :   and strike their
Creator in the face.

MAN 1 : Sin is born
And our story has its origin.
For, in order that sin might be conquered,

MAN 2 : And with sin, its partner, death,

MAN 1 : The Word became flesh
And dwelt among us.
And we beheld his glory.

MAN 3 : Glory as of the only son of a father.
Full of grace and truth.

MAN 2 : (*harshly*) And because we could not bear his
glory, you and I murdered God. Which is why
we each have a part in this story.

MAN 1 : If you ask me, it's a matter of looking after
"number one."
Nobody will do it for you.

MAN 2 : Is that so? Well, who asked you in the first place?

MAN 3 : The idea is to stay out of trouble. Don't get
mixed up in anything.

MAN 1 : That's it. We know how we like it.
We go out for an evening's entertainment,

To the ball game,
Or to the drive-in,

WOMAN 1 : Or we stay at home and watch television.

MAN 1 : We sit back, and are amused,

MAN 2 : Or entertained by the shadow of sorrow.

WOMAN 1 : Wasn't it lovely!

WOMAN 2 : Ooh yes! Ever so lovely!
I cried and cried. Specially when he said he couldn't live without her.

WOMAN 1 : And when she said, "Let's run away together." Do you remember that bit? But I liked him better in "Love for Sale." He's so handsome.

WOMAN 2 : Do you remember when he went off with the slave girl in "I Belong to You"?

WOMAN 1 : Yes. But I liked the cartoon.
Wasn't it funny!

WOMAN 2 : Ooh yes! Ever so funny.

WOMEN 1
AND 2 : We are the viewers.

MEN 3 AND 1 : We are the audience.

WOMEN 1
AND 2 :   Untouched,

MEN 1 AND 2 :   Uncommitted,

MEN 3 AND 1 : We watch things happen.

MAN 1 : Whispering to one another above the crackle of popcorn. (to Woman 1) Well, what do you think? How do you like it?

WOMAN 1 : Isn't Caiaphas good?

MAN 4 : (loudly and decidedly) No! Caiaphas is not good.

MEN : Caiaphas is a sinner.

MAN 4 : And that really is the crux of the matter. You see, as entertainment this play could never be justified.

MAN 2 : As entertainment it would be blasphemy.

MAN 3 : For this play deals with something that really happened in history,

MAN 1 : Like the Normandy landings, or the French
Revolution.
Something that God did, and bloodily suffered,
In the city of Jerusalem,
When a man called Pilate was commissioner for
Galilee.

MAN 4 : But more than this,

WOMEN 1

AND 2 : Much more than this,
And much more important,

MAN 1 : This play deals with something that happens
now.

MAN 2 : In the lives of each one of us. In the brief light
and warmth of human existence, between the
darkness of birth and the coldness of death,
while man-made satellites orbit the earth.

MAN 3 : The Son of God is crucified.
Both by us, and for us.

MAN 4 : And because this is so,
None of us can stand acquitted.
This is not a religious play

MAN 2 : But a re-enactment of the bloodiest murder
You and I ever committed.
Thus I act at times the part of Caiaphas, the high
priest,
Symbol and type of spiritual pride,

WOMAN 2 : And blindness and hardness of heart,

MAN 1 : And the expedience of the politician,

MAN 2 : But also the pride, and blindness, and hardness,
that is behind the front door of each one of us

MAN 3 : Sometimes we are Pilate,

MAN 2 :   And Caiaphas,

MAN 1 :   And the crowd,

MAN 2 : On a certain Friday and Sunday, round about
the year thirty.

WOMAN 1 : And sometimes we are plain you and me, at
Coney Island on the Fourth of July, or
wherever it may be.

WOMEN 1
  AND 2 : So we represent what happened once,
          And was done by certain people.
   MEN : And we represent what is being done now,
          By ourselves and all people.
  MAN 3 : That being so, let's get under way.
WOMEN 1
  AND 2 : Yes, let the story begin.

(Man 4 moves to the narrator's position.)

  MAN 4 : In the fifteenth year of the reign of Tiberius
          Caesar, Pontius Pilate being governor of
          Judaea, Herod tetrarch of Galilee, Philip of
          Iturea, and Lysanias tetrarch of Abilene;
          Annas and Caiaphas being High Priests.
  MAN 1 : After the years of chairmending, and learning
          the art of plane, chisel and saw, under the
          instruction of Joseph,
  MAN 3 : Jesus-bar-Joseph, as he was known in the village,
          set out from Nazareth on a mission to the lost
          people of the house of Israel.
  MAN 2 : A meteoric career of three years' duration.
  MAN 1 : Healing the diseased,
  MAN 2 : And damning the spiritually proud.
WOMAN 1 : Preaching the love of God to the penitent sinner,
WOMAN 2 : And pronouncing his judgment on sin.
WOMEN 1
  AND 2 : Cheered as the savior of the world,
MEN 1 AND 2 : And cursed as having a devil.
  MAN 4 : So down to the last night, a certain Thursday,
          where we take up the story in a garden in the
          suburbs of the royal city of Jerusalem. Geth-
          semane. Here he has come to pray, bringing
          with him his three closest friends,
  MAN 1 : James,
  MAN 2 : Peter,
  MAN 3 : and John.
  MAN 4 : Leaving them his instructions.

(Men 1, 2, 3 move for the Gethsemane scene.)

MAN 2 : "Wait here while I go and pray." Why does he tell us to wait?

Is there nothing to do but wait?

MAN 3 : No, nothing. How suddenly this agony has come upon him.

It's the valley of the shadow of death, a horror we can't begin to understand.

MAN 1 : "Watch and pray that you do not enter into temptation."

That's what he said.

Watching is hard work when you do not know what you are watching for.

MAN 2 : Praying is hard work when you do not know what you are praying for.

MAN 1 : And cold work, too, here in the darkness.

MAN 3 : And in the loneliness.

How far away God seems when you are dispirited

MAN 2 : And tired

MAN 1 : And afraid.

(*1 and 2 huddle together. 3 is a little apart.*)

MAN 4 : And being in an agony, Jesus prays, "My Father, if it is possible, let this cup pass from me. Nevertheless, not my will, but yours be done."

MAN 3 : Always that same awful prayer, over and over again. And the sweat gleaming on his brow, and falling like drops of blood. I am afraid.

MAN 1 : We desire to escape into sleep

MAN 2 : From the terror

MAN 3 : From the agony

MAN 1 : Which we do not understand.

(*All three huddle together.*)

MAN 4 : And yet again, being in agony, he prostrates himself, and prays, "Father, if this cup cannot pass without my drinking it, thy will be done."

MAN 1 : We desire to escape into sleep,

MAN 2 : Because we are caught up in that which is greater than ourselves.

WOMAN 2 : When the Preacher calls at our house, we invite him in.

WOMAN 1 : Hoping he will not see the emptiness where our smile does not fit.

Nor hear the sound of our escaping husbands.

WOMAN 2 : We sit on the edge of chairs in the front room, and talk elaborately of the weather.

WOMAN 1 : And of our families, and the political situation,

WOMAN 2 : And of the weather; how hot it is for the time of year.

WOMAN 1 : Or, for the time of year, how cold.

WOMAN 2 : Building a wall of the banal, lest he should be so indiscreet as to mention God.

WOMAN 1 : We desire to escape from the embarrassment,

WOMAN 2 : From the fear of discussing that which we do not wish to understand.

MAN 4 : But the time for sleeping is past. The traitor has arrived with an armed guard to carry out the arrest of Jesus.

MAN 3 : (*Starts up*) Wake up! There are lights in the garden!

MAN 2 : Weapons in the garden!

MAN 1 : Voices! Hostile voices,

MAN 3 : Angry voices and confusion.

The Son of God is betrayed,

Betrayed in the garden.

MAN 4 : The disciples break and run in the dark. The arrest is effected without much difficulty. Christ is taken and marched away under the armed guard, brought for the purpose by his former friend, the traitor, Judas.

WOMAN 1 : Yes, my dear, by Judas,

Judas, who kept the money,

Judas, the treasurer to the company.

WOMAN 2 : Well what do you know! Judas!

Who'd have thought it!

(*They reform as chorus.*)

MAN 4 : From the treachery of Judas,

WOMEN 1

AND 2 : Good Lord deliver us.

MAN 4 : But not only from the treachery of Judas.

MAN 1 : We desire to escape into sleep
From that which is greater than ourselves,

WOMAN 2 : And from that which we do not wish to understand.

MAN 1 : We desire to escape into the movies or the magazine story,

MAN 2 : Or the sports page of the evening paper,

MAN 3 : Or—if we're frightfully highbrow—into the
technique of the ballet or the comparative
study of religions.

MAN 2 : Alternatively, if you prefer it,
We desire to escape into too much beer in the
neighborhood bar.

MEN : Turn away the head,

WOMEN : Close the eyes,
Shut out the agony,

MEN : The agony of God in the garden.

WOMAN 1 : We desire to put off till tomorrow
The moment of decision.
Put up the shutters of the mind.

WOMAN 2 : Hide ourselves from the vision,

MAN 4 : The urgency of God in the garden.

MAN 1 : Until the moment for conviction,

MAN 2 : Until the moment for action

MAN 3 : Is past
And the Son of God is betrayed.

MAN 1 : We desire to escape into sleep from the terrible
humility of God

ALL : Which we fear to understand.

MAN 4 : That which remains for Christ is action. Things
to be done, and things to be suffered.
The news of his arrest spreads through the city
like wildfire or the news of war.

MAN 1 : Have you heard the latest? Have you heard the
news?

WOMAN 1 : What news?

MAN 3 : What news?

MAN 1 : They've arrested the trouble-maker,
The Jew carpenter,
Jesus of Nazareth,

MAN 3 : The King of the Jews!

MAN 1 : What did I tell you? Some king he'd make! Just what I said to Mabel on Sunday when he came into town and they made all that fuss—three cheers for the Son of David and all that stuff about coming in the name of the Lord—"A king on a blasted donkey?" I said. "Take it from me, they'll be playing a different tune by the end of the week." That's what I said, didn't I, Mabel?

WOMAN 2 : You sure did, Joe. He was starting to get all excited like everybody else, and then all of a sudden he turns to me and screws up his face and says, "A king on a blasted donkey? He's not making any fool out of me!" Just like that.

MAN 1 : And now look what they've done!
I told you so. But what a story!
What a scoop for the papers!
You can read all about it tomorrow,

WOMAN 1 : Over bacon and tea and toast
In the Mirror or Times,
Or Morning Post.

WOMAN 2 : A million papers at breakfast-time
Will carry the story,
The latest sensation,

WOMEN 1
AND 2 : The greatest murder of all,

ALL : The execution of the Son of God.

MAN 4 : The party who had arrested Jesus led him away to the palace of the High Priest, Caiaphas, where the rulers and legislators had hastily assembled. Now it was Caiaphas who had pointed out to the Jews that it was to their advantage that one man should die for the people.

(*The Chorus take up their cloaks for the trial before Caiaphas.*)

MAN 3 : My lord, this is a most unusual hour to call a meeting of the supreme court. Irregular, most irregular.

MAN 2 : I regret the inconvenience, but the national emergency makes some slight irregularity necessary.

MAN 3 : My lord, as I came through the streets there seemed to be great excitement among the people whispering at the street corners. Ugly words were being bandied about. I heard the word "murder" mentioned.

MAN 2 : Murder? Why murder?
Don't be absurd.
This is justice.
The majesty of law uncorrupted,
You use quite the wrong word.
The innocent have nothing to fear from the absolute impartiality of our legal system.
Meanwhile, we await the return of the officer detailed to effect the arrest.

MAN 1 : My Lord, the prisoner waits your convenience.

MAN 2 : Good. Bring him in.

(*Pause.*)

Your evidence, officer.

MAN 1 : Acting on information received from one, Judas of Kerioth, former friend of the accused, at two A.M. this morning I proceeded with a detachment of police to the orchard known as Gethsemane, beyond the Kidron valley on the east side of the city. There I effected the arrest of the accused, who himself offered no resistance. Two of his accomplices drew weapons and attempted to obstruct the police in the execution of their duty, before taking to flight and escaping into the darkness.

MAN 2 : The accomplices do not concern us. The body dies without the head. What are the charges against the prisoner?

WOMAN 1 : He claimed the power to forgive sins.
Only God can forgive sins.

MAN 3 : He claimed authority over the law.
Only God is over the law.

WOMAN 2 : He gave sight to the blind,

WOMAN 1 : Voice to the dumb,

WOMAN 2 : And life to the dead. He raised a corpse. I saw him do it—it's wrong—it's against nature I tell you. Only God can give life—

WOMAN 1 : Or speech, or sight, or straight, sound legs to the hideous cripple.

MAN 2 : That, then is the charge. That he claimed the power and privilege of Almighty God for himself.

Has the prisoner anything to say?

(*Pause.*)

WOMAN 1 : (*quietly, rather awestruck*) He doesn't answer.

WOMAN 2 : (*quietly, rather awestruck*) He ignores our accusing.

(*Shouts*) We want none of your goodness.

MAN 1 : Keep your fancy religion to yourself.

WOMAN 1 : Let us alone, can't you?

ALL : Let us alone, to spend our lives as we want to.

MAN 2 : What need have we of further witnesses? To claim the power and privilege of God is a capital offense. The judgement of this court is that the "Son of God" be nailed by hands and feet to the gallows, there to hang until he is dead.

Take him away to the military governor for confirmation of our sentence.

MAN 4 : The judge of all is judged by men and found
wanting. Because he does not conform to the
established pattern of religion and authority
it is found expedient that one man should die
for the sake of many people.

(*They reform as chorus.*)

MAN 1 : There is a sin that is without forgiveness.

WOMAN 1 : What is that?

MAN 1 : The sin against the Holy Spirit of God.

WOMAN 2 : What is that?

MAN 1 : The coat of humility turned inside out,

MAN 2 : To raise up a God in the image of self—
To build a working model of the Almighty from
the blue print of our own character.

MAN 3 : Look! Here is the god you have made, bow down
and worship.

MAN 1 : Glory to man in the highest,
For man is the maker of gadgets.
Hail to the Unholy
Who gives us—
That which we wish to get.

MAN 3 : I am the god with the plastic face.
The Average Man!
Behold and worship.

MAN 2 : O thou who makest no demands,
Who winkest the tolerant eye
At our adultery
And understandest our great need
To get rich quick,

ALL : We worship and adore thee.

MAN 3 : I am the god with the indiarubber face,
Your grandfather in heaven.
Behold and worship
My avuncular benevolence.

MAN 1 : Thou art the god who disguisest thyself
As a pumpkin at the harvest festival,

WOMAN 1 : And as Santa Claus
At the Kiddies' festival of Christmas.

MAN 2 : Thou art Mars, god of war,
To whom we turn,
During the period of the national emergency.

MAN 1 : And when all else has failed
Let us fall to our prayers.
O Lucifer, son of the morning,
Image of man on the mirror of God,

ALL EXCEPT

MAN 3 : We worship and adore thee.

MAN 1 : This is the sort of God we like.

WOMEN 1

AND 2 : This is the sort of God we can worship.

MAN 3 : His face is our face.

MAN 2 : Because we made his face to our image.

WOMEN 1

AND 2 : This is the sort of God we can worship.
But from this other—

MAN 1 : From this God who is a person,
Breaking and entering our lives,

MAN 2 : From this God who meddles
With details that do not concern him:
Passing judgement on habits, on thought,
And speech.

MAN 1 : Our practice in sex, sleep and labor,
Entering the innermost being.
From this meddling God,

MAN 3 : From this interfering God,

ALL : Good Lord, deliver us!

MAN 2 : And should he enter our lives
In the final sense,

MAN 3 : Commit the ultimate indiscretion of taking flesh,

MEN 2 AND 3 : Of becoming man,
Our sins will take that to its logical conclusion.

MAN 2 : We will re-enact the bloodiest murder we ever
committed.

MAN 4 : God's mill grinds on.
The enormous wheels of murder-by-jury
Groan to life.
The Christ,

MAN 1 :   interrogated,

MAN 2 :   struck in the face,

MAN 3 : And condemned to death,

MAN 4 : Now is led through the early morning streets of Jerusalem where the shops are hardly open, to the grandiose, white-pillared palace of Pontius Pilate, Roman Governor of the occupied territory of Judaea, there to await the convenience of the commander of the forces of occupation.

(*The chorus take up their cloaks for the trial before Pilate.*)

WOMAN 2 : Hello, Liz! Come for the big trial? What about the store?

WOMAN 1 : The store? I left it for once—I broke out of prison. I'm startin' to go out and he says, "Who's gonna look after the front counter?" I said, "Who cares? They're havin' a nice, juicy execution today and I'm not gonna miss it. And if you don't like it—you know what you can do!"

WOMAN 2 : Good for you. I don't know why you married that guy. He's not a man, he's a walking cash-register. You shoulda caught some good-looker, like the prisoner.

WOMAN 1 : (*eagerly*) The prisoner? Do you think he'll get it?

MAN 1 : Get it? Of course he'll get it. Caiaphas sentenced him, didn't he? All regular and official. All Pilate's got to do is say "yes."

WOMAN 1 : And he wouldn't dare do anything else. He knows the score.

MAN 1 : He's nothing but a rubber stamp. A rotten Roman rubber stamp, that's what. But where is he? . . . Trust a Roman to keep us waiting.

WOMAN 2 : Yeh, why doesn't he hurry up?

WOMAN 1 : Perhaps his lordship is having his morning bath, or powdering his Roman nose.

WOMAN 2 : Quiet now, here he is.

MAN 2 : Good morning your excellency, my lord Pilate. (*Deep bow.*)

MAN 3 : Well, Caiaphas, what's all this native nonsense, eh? Why can't you bring your prisoners at a civilized hour? What's the charge against this man?

MAN 2 : If he was not a criminal we should not have brought him to you.

MAN 3 : Judge him by your own fantastic laws, then.

MAN 2 : By our laws he has been sentenced to death.

MAN 3 : Oh, you're after blood are you, you old fox? (*He sits down.*) Well, what is the charge?

MAN 1 : He sets himself up as the Son of God.

MAN 2 : The military governor can hardly be expected to worry over a religious offense. Say rather, he sets himself up as—the king of the Jews.

MAN 3 : King of the Jews? The charge then is one of treason, of inciting to rebellion?

MAN 2 : That is so.

MAN 3 : Hmm. I've heard something of this man and of his teaching.—Oh, yes, the authorities know most of what is going on in this damned city of yours—How if this kingdom is not a political one at all, but a kingdom of righteousness and peace and the—er—love of God, whatever that may mean? Suppose he were that sort of king?

MAN 2 : Then those of us who care for the truth would listen to him.

MAN 3 : Truth? What is truth?

But this is a court of law, not a philosophic discussion. (*He stands.*) By Roman law I see no crime against the prisoner. By your Jewish standards he is guilty. Very well. I propose a compromise. It has been my custom on national holidays to release a prisoner. I propose today to release the "King of the Jews," thereby satisfying Roman mercy and Jewish "justice."

(*Silence.*)

Well? That is my decision. You either have this man or Barabbas.

MAN 1 : Barabbas the murderer. (*Shocked that it has come to such a crude choice.*)

MAN 2 : Barabbas with blood on his hands.

MAN 3 : Barabbas or Jesus, who is called the Christ. Which is it to be?

WOMAN 1 : Give us Barabbas, his ways are our ways.

WOMAN 2 : Give us Barabbas, we understand him,

MAN 1 : And he understands us. Good old Barabbas!
Our lives are not condemned by his holiness,
Not like this other. Give us the murderer.

ALL : Barabbas! Barabbas! We want Barabbas!

MAN 3 : Very well. The murderer shall be released and this Jesus shall be flogged. Blood you want and blood you shall have.

(*He sits down while the flogging is carried out.*)

MAN 1 : Hands lashed to the post.

MAN 2 : Back stripped for the lash.

MAN 1 : Flesh waits.

MAN 2 : Whip raised.

ALL EXCEPT
MEN 3 AND 4 : And whines down with a slash.

(*The two women turn away.*)

WOMAN 1 : I can't bear the sight of blood. It turns my stomach.

WOMAN 2 : There, there dear; you needn't look. You'll be all right in a minute.

MAN 1 : The crack of leather on flesh.

MAN 2 : Blood on the lash.

MAN 1 : Bruised flesh waits.

MAN 2 : Whip raised.

MEN 1 AND 2 : Down on the back.

WOMAN 1 : Oh why doesn't he scream? It's not human to be so silent.

WOMAN 2 : I don't know about that. These criminals don't feel like ordinary people. That's why they weight the lashes with pieces of lead. They've finished now, so you can look again, honey.

MAN 1 : The lash lies in the dust,
The flogging is done.
And we have seen blood.

MAN 2 : The sight of blood breeds the desire for more blood—have you never watched a crowd at a boxing match?

MAN 1 : And we have seen blood.
But first the crowning of our king.

WOMAN 1 : The soldiers are making a garland for his head.

WOMAN 2 : A garland of thorns, barbed like wire.

WOMAN 1 : Now they're putting on a tattered old purple cloak,

WOMAN 2 : And a wooden sceptre in his hand. What a clown he looks!
Oh your majesty, your holy majesty, have mercy on us!

WOMAN 1 : Will your gracious majesty forgive us our trespasses?

MAN 1 : Hurrah for king Jesus! Three cheers for the king of the Jews!

MAN 3 : (*standing up*) Enough! Pilate wearies of this sordid mockery. Justice has been done. Behold the man!

MAN 1 : (*quietly*) We have seen blood.
And we will see more.

MAN 2 : We demand the death penalty for this man.

WOMAN 2
AND MAN 1 : Yes, let him be executed.
MAN 3 : Why? What harm has he done?
MAN 1 : Harm enough. He will not leave us alone.
WOMAN 1 : He will not leave us as we wish to be.
MAN 1 : He wants to make us what we are not and we are afraid.
Execute him.
MAN 3 : Shall I execute your king?
WOMAN 1 : We have no king but Caesar,
No king but the crowd.
WOMAN 2 : No will, no purpose but the will of the majority.
MAN 1 : The will of the majority to protect us
From the terror of thought,
WOMAN 2 :   Action,
MAN 1 : And decision of our own.
Take from us this reproach on our sinfulness.
MAN 2 : (*deliberately*) Let him be crucified.
ALL EXCEPT
MEN 3 AND 4 : Crucify! Crucify! Crucify him!
MAN 3 : Very well, I wash my hands of the whole affair.
I am innocent of the blood of this just man. It is your own responsibility.
MAN 2 : His blood be upon us, and upon our children.

(*They reform as chorus, slowly and deliberately.*)

MAN 4 : The sin of Pilate,
MAN 3 : Cowardice and political time-serving.
MAN 4 : The sin of Caiaphas,
MAN 2 : Spiritual pride and ecclesiastical time-serving.
MAN 4 : The sins of the soldiers,
And of the crowd,
MAN 2 : Brutality.
WOMAN 1 : The lust for blood,
WOMAN 2 : And blind following the majority.
MAN 4 : These sins are not museum pieces, impaled on pins in glass cases, to be examined at leisure by those interested in religion.

MAN 2 :   Strange reactions of long ago people
          In far away places.
MAN 4 :   No. Far from it. They are the sins
          Of Maple Avenue and Oakwood Drive;
          Neat, comfortable sins
          Of respectable citizens
          Living on respectable streets,
          The sins of the milkman
          And the neighbor who borrows your mower,
          And the man who sits next to you on the eight-
          fifteen.
MAN 1 :   They do not know why their children say this or
          that,
WOMAN 2 : Why teen-agers act as they do these days,
MAN 2 :   Why some people get so worked up over politics,
WOMAN 1 : What to do if the neighborhood changes,
MAN 1 :   Or why they are so bored.
WOMAN 2 : It is these, ordinary people,
          Never in trouble
MAN 2 :   And never out of it,
WOMAN 1 : Loving the community dirt they have got used to,
MAN 1 :   Whose little, unrecognized, wishy-washy sins
          Catch fire from one another from a fester in the
          heart.
MAN 4 :   And flame in the heat of the moment, to the
          hate-blinded murder of God.
          The mockery of trial is past,
          The scorn and spitting are done.
          The flogging administered,
          And suffered, blow by gasping blow, in silence,
          And Jesus takes up his cross.
WOMAN 1 : Why do they make him carry his own cross?
          Why should a man bear the gallows on which he
          is to die?
MAN 1 :   It is hard.
MAN 2 :   It is heavy.
WOMAN 1 : The weight he bears is heavier than we can tell.
WOMAN 2 : In the enlightenment of the twentieth century it

is not customary to crucify the political prisoner.

MAN 3 : On the contrary our methods are marked by a
comparative lack of physical violence.

MAN 2 : Some unpleasantness, of course, is unfortunately
necessary in the interests of psychological re-
conditioning.

MAN 1 : Shortage of sleep,

MAN 2 : A minimum of food, the use of drugs,

MAN 3 : And many hours of incessant questioning.

MAN 1 : It is an unnecessary crudity to crucify the body if
the mind is capable of readjustment.

The weight he bears is heavier than we can tell.

(*The chorus breaks for the Via Dolorosa. Women
1 and 2 look on. Man 2 is with them to start
with. When he becomes Simon of Cyrene he
joins the procession. The procession consists
of Man 1, the centurion, Man 3, the sergeant
of the guard, and later, Man 2.*)

MAN 2 : Step on step,
Down the Main Street.

MAN 3 : Step on step,
On his last slow journey.

MAN 1 : Crowds silent on the pavement,

WOMAN 2 : Crowds pushing to see,
Crowds craning the neck for a better view.

MAN 1 : With a military escort to look to the execution
of justice,
Under the command of a Roman officer,
To carry out the sentence,
And keep back the crowd.
Stand back there! Make way there! Must I get
a whip to you? Make way for the Roman
army!

WOMAN 2 : He can never last out to the end.

WOMAN 1 : The agony in the garden,
The betrayal, then the trial,

WOMAN 2 : And the questioning,
And the long standing,
And the mockery,
And the bone-stripping bite of the lash.

WOMAN 2 : And now the dead weight of the cross.

MAN 3 : Step on step.

WOMAN 1 : It is too long.

WOMAN 2 : Too long drawn out for flesh and blood to stand.
Oh, he has fallen!

ALL : Ahh! etc. (*The procession breaks while Man 3 investigates.*)

MAN 1 : Hey! Take care, that cross is government property.

MAN 3 : Come on, now! No time to stop and say your prayers, we've got an appointment. (*Pause, and then more gently.*) Well, they did lay it on a bit thick. Too strong on that whip, that corporal!
(*Pause.*) That's right. You're a plucky one, anyway.

WOMAN 1 : Look, he's trying to get up again.

WOMAN 2 : No, he's fallen again.

MAN 3 : It's no good. Prisoner's done, sir.

MAN 2 : Of course it's no good, you Roman vultures. Why don't you carry the thing yourselves?

MAN 1 : Sergeant, arrest that man.

MAN 3 : Now then, come here you! What's all this about vultures, eh? You'd better come and tell the commander about the little birdies. Come on then. (*Man 3 lays hold of Man 1.*)

MAN 1 : Let's have a look at him! Now then, who are you handing out orders to the Roman army?

MAN 3 : (*twisting his arm*) Come on, bud, answer the officer.

MAN 2 : (*sullenly*) Simon of Cyrene.

MAN 3 : (*twisting*) Vultures! I'll vulture you! Where's yer manners!

MAN 2 : Simon of Cyrene—sir.

MAN 3 : That's better. I should think so, too. Look who's telling the army what to do!

MAN 1 : All right, sergeant, that's enough.

Well, Simon of Cyrene, you're quite right about one thing. The prisoner's done. Exhausted apparently. And someone's got to carry his cross. And that someone's you.

MAN 2 : What, me? Carry a gallows? I'll be damned if I do!

MAN 3 : You'll be damned if you don't. And what's more, you'll get a taste of a Roman flogging. Come on, pick it up. This is your lucky day. That's it. This is the day you were born for.

MAN 2 : That's enough. Let's get a move on now. And keep an eye on the prisoner in case he falls again.

(*The procession reforms, with Simon carrying the cross.*)

MAN 1 : Step on step,
To Calvary.
Step on step,
To the place of execution.

WOMAN 2 : See the wounds on his back,
The wounds of our giving.

WOMAN 1 : See the crown, and the blood on his brow,

MAN 1 : Blood shed for our sins.

(*They reform as chorus.*)

MAN 2 : The hot salt sins of the dark places
Of the city and of the mind.

MAN 3 : The dirty lusts of our darkness,
The pornographic magazine,
The mind's debauched lechery.

MAN 1 : The yellow sins of our cowardice,
Coldness, and couldn't-care-less treachery
To the strong faith of our fathers.

MAN 3 : The blind desertion of our destiny,

And the gross sins of our gluttony.
More ease,

MAN 1 :   Less rest;

MAN 3 : More efficiency,

MAN 1 :   Less accomplishment;

MAN 3 : More pleasure

MAN 1 :   Less joy.

MAN 3 : Wanta watch TV, Joe?

MAN 2 : Nah, the programs are no good tonight, let's go to the movies.

WOMAN 2 : "The Seven Deadly Sins" is on at the Plaza.

WOMAN 1 : We can go from there to the Palace and rock n' roll, get some pizza at the corner place, have time for a quick one at the Blarney Stone and still be back in time for the big show.

MAN 2 : We mustn't miss the big show.

MAN 1 : No, we must be in at the kill,

MEN 1, 2,
   AND 3 : At the killing of the Son of God.

WOMAN 2 : The priests say he is to die for sin.

MAN 1 : Whose sin, his or mine?

WOMAN 1 : Well, it can't be his, because he was a good man.

MAN 1 : And it can't be mine,
Because I always lived a good life,
And never did anyone any harm,
And I'll slug the guy who says I did.

MAN 4 : The sullen echo of our emptiness
And the deadly sins of our enormous pride.

WOMAN 2 : If the Joneses have two cars, we must have two cars—one newer than the Smiths'.

MAN 3 : And we must see that little Willie gets a good schooling, so that he can get on in life.

WOMAN 2 : That is, earn more money than the Joneses or the Smiths.

MAN 3 : Keep his wife in the luxury far grander than the Joneses or the Smiths.

MAN 2 : And then die, full of wealth, circumstance, and indigestion,

WOMAN 2 : And be buried in a casket more sumptuous by far
than the Joneses' or the Smiths'.

MAN 4 : The stupid sins of our enormous pride
Send the Son of God,

WOMAN 1 : Brow bleeding,

MAN 1 : Slow treading,

MEN 1 AND 2 : The stony road to Calvary.

MAN 4 : And he was followed by a large crowd of towns-
people and of women who beat their breasts
and wailed for him.

WOMAN 2 : How tired he looks! And how young,
Why he's only a lad after all.

WOMAN 1 : How could they do such a thing?
How could they be so cruel?

WOMAN 2 : Jesus, don't you remember us?

WOMAN 1 : We knew you when you were only quite a little
boy in Nazareth.

WOMAN 2 : And now it has come to this.
Oh, your poor mother! What must she be feeling?

MAN 3 : These maudlin women! They'd cut their grannies'
throats so they could bawl at her funeral.

MAN 4 : And Jesus turned to the daughters of Jerusalem
and said, "Weep for yourselves and for your
children, not for me. The days are coming
when they shall say blessed are the barren, and
the breast that never gave suck; for if they do
these things in the green tree, what shall be
done in the dry?"

WOMAN 1 : (*highly offended*) Well! Do not weep for me!

WOMAN 2 : (*highly offended*) But weep for yourselves.

WOMEN 1
AND 2 : What does he mean?

WOMAN 1 : Weep for yourselves and your children,
And happy the sterile woman,
And the breasts that never suckled.

WOMAN 2 : It's hardly decent,

                  But whatever does it mean
                  If they do this when the wood is green,

WOMAN 1 : What will happen when the wood is dry?
WOMAN 2 : We only wanted to show our sympathy,
WOMEN 1
    AND 2 : And we do not like to be answered
                  In words we do not understand.

          (*They reform as chorus.*)

MAN 4 : This day the green wood is kindled,
MAN 3 : Revealing the timeless pattern of innocent suffering,
WOMAN 1 : The key to the mystery of all pain,
WOMAN 2 : And of those who get what they do not deserve.
WOMAN 1 : The fierce pain of the mother in labor,
                  The unmeaning pain of death in the family.
WOMAN 2 : Why should this happen to us?
MAN 1 : We never did anyone any harm,
                  Why should we lose our son?
WOMAN 2 : Our only son—he was so young,
                  His life had scarcely begun.
MAN 1 AND
WOMAN 2 : Why should this happen to him,
                  And to us?
MAN 3 : The savage suffering of war
                  And its hideous aftermath,
MAN 2 : The shell of the gutted city.
WOMAN 1 : What mothers would have daughters
                  In an enemy occupied city?
MAN 1 : The wire,
                  Barbed wire.
                  The whip of the concentration camp,
                  The face drained of pity,
MAN 2 : And the hopeless misery of the political prisoner.
MAN 3 : Sudden death on the road.
WOMAN 1 : The accusation
                  Of a million, million faces,
                  The holy innocents of all places,

MAN 1 : Here, in this which is done today
Both by us and for us,
Here is the answer,
Your answer and mine.

MAN 4 : By thine agony and bloody sweat,
And by thy Cross and most holy Passion,

ALL : Good Lord, deliver us.

MAN 4 : Thus they brought him to the place Golgotha,
Which means the Place of a Skull.

WOMAN 1 : The stony journey is done,
The cross carried to its appointed place.

WOMAN 2 : The journey now begun
Is stonier yet,
The crucifixion still to face.

WOMAN 1 : There is no rest?

WOMAN 2 : No rest yet.

*(The chorus now break for the crucifixion.
Women 1 and 2 and Man 4 watch, while the
rest carry out the crucifixion. Man 1 becomes
a soldier.)*

MAN 4 : And it was the third hour. And they crucified
him.

MAN 1 : Right. You can lay the cross there. Got your
ropes?

MAN 3 : Sir.

MAN 1 : Get him trussed up as quick as possible. We don't
want to be here for ever.

*(Man 2 lays down the cross and the roping is
carried out.)*

MAN 1 : This is a rotten business, sergeant.

MAN 3 : Yes, sir, you never quite get used to it. It's too
cold-blooded.

MAN 1 : Quite. Too cold-blooded.
Tools ready.

MAN 3 : Sir. Hammer and nails.

MAN 1 : Right hand first, sergeant.

MAN 3 : Right hand, sir.

MAN 2 : Palm open,
The point of the nail in the palm.

MAN 4 : The open palm
Of the free-giving hand of God.

MAN 3 : One blow,

MAN 2 : One blow,

MAN 3 : Hammer blow on nail head.

MAN 4 : The right hand of God
Transfixed for our sins.

MAN 1 : Left hand, sergeant.

MAN 3 : Left hand, sir.

MAN 2 : Palm open,
The point of the nail in the palm.

MAN 4 : The open palm
Of the free-giving hand of God.

MAN 3 : One blow,

MAN 2 : One blow.

MAN 3 : Hammer blow on nail head.

MAN 2 : Hand nailed to the wood.

MAN 4 : God's open arms
Transfixed in beseeching
For our sins.

MAN 1 : Now the feet.

MAN 3 : Feet together, sir.

MAN 2 : Nail poised on the foot.

MAN 3 : One blow.
Hammer blow on nail head.

MAN 2 : Hammer blow on nail head.

MAN 3 : The nail in the wood.

MAN 2 : Ready to raise the cross, sergeant?

MAN 3 : Ready, sir. (*gently*) This is where it really **hurts,**
son.

MAN 1 : Ready, sir.

MAN 2 : Right. Up,

MAN 1 : Up,

MAN 3 : Up, and down in the socket.

(*They stand back and gaze in horror at what
they have done.*)

MAN 4 : And Jesus said, "Father, forgive them . . ."

MAN 2 : What was that he said?

MAN 1 : It sounded like . . . "Father, forgive them, for they don't know what they are doing."

MAN 2 : (*slowly*) What have we done?

(*Pause.*)

MAN 3 : Done, sir? (*He is watching the officer closely.*) We've done our duty, that's what. We've done the job we get paid for, and a poor sort of job it is too. Army of occupation! Government butchers more like! Give me active service every time. (*Pause.*) But our standing here won't help. (*He again looks at the officer, who pays no attention.*) The world's got to go on, execution or no execution, and that's just about it.

(*to Man 1*) Come on, there's his clothes to divide. I'll roll you for the coat, it's a pity to spoil it.

(*They go downstage to prepare to throw for the coat.*)

WOMAN 1 : My son is dying.

WOMAN 2 : The light is going out of the world.

MAN 1 : Who are you that we crucify in the day's work?

MAN 2 : A five and a four. Your throw.

MAN 1 : We only do our job. Why should we need forgiveness?

MAN 3 : (*throws*) Oh well, I couldn't care less. The coat's yours. I never did have any luck with dice.

(*Men 2 and 3 stand up.*)

MAN 2 : Look, sergeant, there's his mother.
Who's the other one?

MAN 3 : (*surprised and deliberate*) It's Mary of Magdala. She used to sing in that joint down by the barracks. What's she doing here?

MAN 4 : Now there were standing by the cross of Jesus, his mother, and Mary Magdalene.

(*Woman 1 and Woman 2 move forward.*)

WOMAN 2 : May we come closer, sir?

MAN 1 : Why? Have you a special interest in the condemned?

WOMAN 1 : I am his mother.

MAN 1 : (*taken aback*) Oh, I see. But—madam—would it be wise? I mean . . . (*Unable to put into words what he wants to say.*)

WOMAN 1 : He is my son.

MAN 1 : Very well. Come closer—the end is very close. He hasn't moved for some time now.

(*Pause.*)

WOMAN 2 : O God, why have you forsaken us?

(*Pause.*)

MAN 2 : Look! (*Pointing*) He's raising his head.

MAN 3 : That means it's finished.

WOMAN 1 : It is finished indeed, my son.

MAN 1 : Truly this was the Son of God.

(*Pause.*)

MAN 4 : And there was darkness over the whole land until the ninth hour.

WOMEN 1
  AND 2 : Darkness.

MAN 2 : How dark it is.

MAN 3 : And how cold.

MAN 1 : Will it never be day again?

(*They rise and reform as chorus.*)

MAN 4 : No. For the final deed is done. Christ murdered.

MAN 1 : Pilate's word is true,
That which is written,

MEN 2 AND 3 : Is written.

MAN 1 : And it may not be erased.

MAN 4 : It is too late.

WOMAN 2 : Too late.

The evil days have come.

MAN 1 : We welcome them,

MAN 2 : And now we have no pleasure in them.

MAN 4 : But for the grace and mercy of God, our story is done. The play played out, and the chain of cause and effect traced, link by doomed link, from the sins of the cobbled streets of the North to the judicial murder of the Son of God.

MAN 3 : Murder by jury! Pretty slick when you think about it.

MAN 1 : But it was a dirty piece of work. A typical example of the narrowminded intolerance of religion.

MAN 3 : The preacher chap—what was his name?

MAN 1 : Caiaphas.

MAN 3 : Caiaphas! There's an oily swine if ever there was one!

I wouldn't trust him with my wallet.

You might know there would be a parson at the bottom of it.

That's religion!—you can keep it for me.

MAN 1 : Religion! The opiate of the people. A handrail for the weak-minded. The politicians' "Aid to Government in Three Easy Lessons."

MAN 4 : All deeds of shame and the self-satisfaction near the heart of each one of us culminate in the deed we have re-enacted. And that is the end of the story—but for the mercy of God. Late in the day, Joseph of Arimathea, a councillor of good standing, begged the body from Pilate. He took Jesus down from the cross, wrapped him in linen, and laid him in a tomb, rolling a stone across the entrance.

WOMAN 1 : (*eagerly*) And early on the Sunday morning the women went to the tomb. . . .

WOMAN 2 : Oh yes, and when they got there, they found the stone rolled back, and the body gone, and a young man or an angel or something there. Isn't that right?

WOMAN 1 : And he told them that Jesus had risen from the dead.

(*Pause.*)

MAN 1 : Oh! So it all ended happily!

MAN 4 : No, triumphantly! When Jesus was risen early on the first day of the week, he appeared first to Mary Magdalene, and she ran and told the others.

(*They take up their cloaks.*)

WOMAN 1 : (*hysterical and out of breath*) Peter! John! He's alive! He's alive! I've seen the Lord.

MAN 1 : You must be mad!

MAN 2 : Where? When? What do you mean?   (*all*

MAN 3 : You've what?   *together*)

WOMAN 2 : Mary, what are you talking about?

WOMAN 1 : Just now, in the garden. I saw Jesus.

WOMAN 2 : When you were with Peter and John?

MAN 2 : But we were with you in the garden. } (*together*)

MAN 1 : It's this business of the empty tomb coming after the strain of everything else. She needs a good rest.

WOMAN 1 : Wouldn't you like to lie down, dear?

MAN 3 : We ought to get her away for a holiday before she goes off her head altogether.

MAN 2 : Not necessarily. Perhaps she's not mad. Perhaps we're just stupid. The tombstone rolled aside. Those graveclothes so— so— undisturbed. Things he used to say that we never understood. Remarks that come back after the event —remarks about the rising of the dead. Mary, tell us what happened.

WOMAN 1 : (*She is quite quiet now.*) After you went away I stayed beside the grave. I was crying because they wouldn't leave him alone even after they'd killed him. Then I turned away. And there was—a man—standing there. I suppose I thought he was the gardener. And he asked me why I was crying. And I asked him to tell me where he had taken the body. I—I wanted to go and do what I could for him.

And then he said, "Mary," and I realized who he was. It was the Lord. (*Her control breaks.*) It was the Lord, and I've seen him and he isn't dead any more. He's alive, and his hands and his feet bear the wounds from what they did to him.

WOMAN 1 : Yes, that's it—he said, "Mary," didn't he? And he said it with the old inflection of voice,— and then—she just knew.

MAN 1 : Yes, that is how it happened.

WOMAN 1 : And how it happens.

(*They reform as chorus.*)

MAN 4 : For Christ is risen indeed, and goes before you into Galilee.

MAN 2 : Your Galilee,
The Galilee of the modern industrial city,
Of the neon lights, and the department store.

MAN 4 : Where you jostle Christ on the pavement
Among the plate-glass windows.

MAN 2 : Galilee Street,
The street in which you live,
And where he waits to move in,
Fulfilling his promise to be with us,
Always,
Even to the end of the world.

WOMEN 1
    AND 2 : Arise, shine,
    MEN : Thy light is come,
    ALL : And the glory of the Lord is risen upon thee.

by
Dennis J. Winnie

A VERY COLD NIGHT

THE CHARACTERS

THE FIRST MAN
THE SECOND MAN
THE VOICE

The Setting: A railroad station

The Time: A night in winter. The year does
not matter.

A man in his late thirties is sitting by the stove, his hands close to the metal, wanting desperately the slight heat that comes from it.

FIRST MAN : The heat—the heat—so little of it. There's such little warmth here.

A second man appears. In appearance he is very much like the man at the stove.

FIRST MAN : Friend, there isn't much heat here.

SECOND MAN : So? (*He smiles.*) So?

FIRST MAN : I'm not moving from here. If you can get some heat, all right—but I'm not moving from here.

SECOND MAN : I haven't asked you to move, have I?

FIRST MAN : No—but I know what you're thinking.

SECOND MAN : You only know what you believe I'm thinking. No—I don't want your stove—your precious stove.

FIRST MAN : This cold is like being crucified.

SECOND MAN : No it isn't.

FIRST MAN : I say it is. Yes—it's like being crucified.

SECOND MAN : It's nothing like being crucified. Nothing at all like being crucified.

FIRST MAN : A lot you know about it.

SECOND MAN : Indeed—I do know about it. (*He holds out his hands.*) See the scars? The round, red, ugly scars?

FIRST MAN : (*He laughs and holds out his hands, showing identical scars.*) I, too, have the scars.

SECOND MAN : You've impressed me.

FIRST MAN : I'm glad. I've impressed you and I'm glad.

SECOND MAN : What happened to the other one—you remember —the one in the middle?

FIRST MAN : I've heard many strange things about Him.

SECOND MAN : You know—I really would like to have a little heat. (*He moves closer to the stove.*)

165

FIRST MAN : Don't get any smart ideas, friend—keep your distance.

SECOND MAN : Just a little heat—

FIRST MAN : Keep away! First thing you know I'd be out in the cold and you'd be nice and warm in here.

SECOND MAN : You don't trust me?

FIRST MAN : No!

SECOND MAN : Congratulations. (*He smiles.*) The Man in the middle—He would trust me.

FIRST MAN : Yes—I've heard that He trusted everyone.

SECOND MAN : A kind man.

FIRST MAN : Kindness is a foolish thing—and yet, He wasn't a foolish man—

SECOND MAN : You said you've heard many strange things about Him. What kind of strange things?

FIRST MAN : Nothing.

SECOND MAN : Tell me. Please—tell me.

FIRST MAN : No! (*He looks angry for a moment, then smiles.*) Forgive me.

SECOND MAN : Of course—but about this Man—

FIRST MAN : Don't ask me! Please—I'm not able to tell you.

SECOND MAN : Not able?

FIRST MAN : I don't have a big enough soul. (*He nods.*) Yes—my soul isn't big enough.

SECOND MAN : (*Softly.*) Summertime.

FIRST MAN : Summertime?

SECOND MAN : Yes—summertime. I wish it was summertime—I wish I could feel the warmth of the summer sun.

FIRST MAN : Don't talk about it.

SECOND MAN : It's painful to think about it, isn't it?

FIRST MAN : Yes—it's like when I think about the Man on the middle cross.

SECOND MAN : They were brutal to Him.

FIRST MAN : Yes—nailed Him to the cross they did—and stabbed Him with a spear—

SECOND MAN : Yes.

FIRST MAN : The Romans did that.

SECOND MAN : No—not just the Romans—not just the Romans
—no one group did that.

FIRST MAN : No?

SECOND MAN : No. All of man crucified Him.

FIRST MAN : And did all of man crucify us?

SECOND MAN : No—we crucified ourselves. They—we—crucified
the Man on the middle cross.

FIRST MAN : You know much.

SECOND MAN : And there are strange stories about Him?

FIRST MAN : Yes.

SECOND MAN : When did these stories start?

FIRST MAN : I can't say. I really don't know. (*He shakes his
head.*) He died a happy death.

SECOND MAN : He died a horrible death.

FIRST MAN : Certainly. It was horrible but He was happy in
dying that way.

SECOND MAN : Then He was mad.

FIRST MAN : If goodness is madness then yes, He was mad.

SECOND MAN : We're here—but where is He?

FIRST MAN : They—the stories—say that He is everywhere.

SECOND MAN : No man can be everywhere.

FIRST MAN : Who said He was just a Man?

SECOND MAN : What does that mean? Are you trying to confuse
me?

FIRST MAN : I'm not interested in confusing.

SECOND MAN : Then explain what you meant by suggesting that
He was not just a man.

FIRST MAN : Some say that He was—(*He stops.*) Please—don't
talk to me. Just let me alone.

SECOND MAN : Did He die?

FIRST MAN : Yes—in a way.

SECOND MAN : In a way?

FIRST MAN : Yes—in a way—no please—don't talk any more.
I'm very tired.

SECOND MAN : Where is He now?

FIRST MAN : Perhaps everywhere.

SECOND MAN : Perhaps nowhere?

FIRST MAN : Yes,—perhaps nowhere.

SECOND MAN : I believe you're mad.

FIRST MAN : I don't care what you believe.

SECOND MAN : Don't you?

FIRST MAN : It's very cold.

SECOND MAN : Don't you care what I believe?

FIRST MAN : No.

SECOND MAN : It's very cold—won't you let me come closer to the stove?

FIRST MAN : No!

SECOND MAN : You're very cruel.

FIRST MAN : Yes—yes, I'm very cruel. I know that—and now you know it.

SECOND MAN : And if He comes?

FIRST MAN : Who?

SECOND MAN : The Man on the middle cross. Will you let Him near the stove?

FIRST MAN : No—

SECOND MAN : Will you let Him near the stove?

FIRST MAN : I don't know—No!—I won't let Him near the stove!

SECOND MAN : I don't believe you.

FIRST MAN : I don't care.

SECOND MAN : I think you'd let Him near the stove. I think you'd let Him warm Himself.

FIRST MAN : I'm too cruel for sentimentality.

SECOND MAN : I think you'd let Him have your place at the stove.

FIRST MAN : (*He laughs.*) That shows how little you know me. I wouldn't let my own mother near this stove to-night. It's too cold.

SECOND MAN : I've got a confession to make.

FIRST MAN : I'm not interested.

SECOND MAN : Yes you are.

FIRST MAN : All right! All right—confess—confess—

SECOND MAN : I know those stories about Him—the stories you mentioned.

FIRST MAN : You know them?

SECOND MAN : Yes—I know all of them.

FIRST MAN : And do you believe them?

SECOND MAN : Yes.

FIRST MAN : All of them?

SECOND MAN : Yes, every one of them. Every detail of them. (*He smiles.*) Yes—I believe.

FIRST MAN : He's coming—isn't He?

SECOND MAN : (*He nods.*) Yes, He's coming. He's very cold, and He's coming here to ease His great discomfort.

FIRST MAN : When?

SECOND MAN : (*He glances at his watch.*) Very soon.

FIRST MAN : I won't let Him near this stove! Not even Him!

SECOND MAN : You're a good man.

FIRST MAN : I'm a cruel man! I hate with great hates!

SECOND MAN : Yes, you're a cruel man—and yes, you hate with great hates, but you'll let Him have your place at the stove.

FIRST MAN : No!

SECOND MAN : You're not that bad, my friend. You may think you are—but you're not.

FIRST MAN : He'll be here?

SECOND MAN : Yes—in just a little while He'll be in this room.

FIRST MAN : The thought frightens me—it frightens me—

SECOND MAN : Don't be afraid. He doesn't want fear. He only wants love.

FIRST MAN : But He wants my place at the stove—

SECOND MAN : Only if you want to give it to Him.

FIRST MAN : He won't demand my place?

SECOND MAN : No.

FIRST MAN : And wouldn't it be a great kindness if I gave Him my place?

SECOND MAN : A very great kindness.

FIRST MAN : Listen—(*They listen to the footsteps on the gravel path outside.*)

SECOND MAN : That's Him.

FIRST MAN : Are you sure? How can you tell?

SECOND MAN : I can tell.

FIRST MAN : May I—may I open the door for Him?

SECOND MAN : If you like.

(*The First Man goes to the door, listens for a moment and then opens the door slowly.*)

THE VOICE : It's a cold night.

FIRST MAN : Yes—please—please come in out of the cold.

THE VOICE : I remember you.

FIRST MAN : I'm glad you remember me—and sir—

THE VOICE : Yes?

FIRST MAN : Please take my place at the stove. (*He adds after a slight pause.*) It's a very cold night.

by
Don A. Mueller

EYES UPON THE CROSS

CHARACTERS:

	The Narrator
A Man He Looked At	The Shrew
	The Mother of the healed boy
	Priest
	Barabbas
The Man Who Denied Him	Sarah
	Leah
	Peter
The Man Who Believed Him	Woman (The Shrew)
	The Mother of the healed boy
	The Man (Judas)
The Man Who Tried Him	Joanna
	Claudia
	Pilate
The Man Who Gave the Order	The Man (Centurion)
	A Boy (Wine-Seller)
The Disciples in Secret	Joseph
	Nicodemus
	A Young Boy
Two Mothers	Salome
	Mary (Jesus' mother)
	John (The Disciple)
The Woman Who Loved Him	Jacob
	Mary of Magdala
The Man in the Linen Sheet	John
	A Woman who gives myrrh to the dying
	Mary (John's mother)

NARRATOR : A time of quiet is settling across our nation in this hour. It is a time when the people who call themselves Christians remember how the man they call Christ met his death.

History tells us that Jesus was killed. But the gospels, and the church, and the testimonies of Christians in every century since that time, tell us that he who was killed is not dead, that he lives. What was it that they saw, that led them to believe, that made them base their lives on this belief?

Perhaps we can answer that best by looking at him through the eyes of persons who followed him, who betrayed him, who condemned him, who watched him die. Imagine that you are part of a crowd that has gathered on a skull-shaped hill as three men carrying crosses start their weary climb, and a fourth drags painfully behind.

THE EVENT

(In this prologue, some of the players are seen in the characters they will later assume. Others may appear simply as anonymous members of the crowd, the women changing their costumes by use of a different headpiece. The speeches come very quickly, often overlapping.)

SARAH : Oooh! Would you look at the size of those crosses!

MARY OF MAGDALA : Oh, no, no, no, no, no!

BOY : Where? I don't see nothing!

A WOMAN : (*She who gives myrrh to the dying*) What is a child like you doing here? What in the world were your parents thinking of to let you come?

THE SHREW : On your knees, everybody! Here comes the King of the Jews!

WINE-SELLER : Wine? Sweet, cool wine! Wine? Right here for your wine!

BARABBAS : (*Jovially*) Good morning, sir! Lovely day, isn't it? Good morning, lady!

A WOMAN : (*Played by Mary the mother*) Aaron! What are you doing here? I told you to stay home. This isn't the sort of thing (*She continues under the next speech*)

JUDAS : Save yourself, Master! Save yourself! Why doesn't he do something?

MARY OF MAGDALA : You can do it, Master! You saved others!

THE MOTHER OF THE HEALED BOY : Save yourself, Jesus! Oh, Jesus!! . . .

SHREW : Yeah, save yourself, if you're really the Son of God. Son of God, are you?

THE PRIEST : Messiah, are you? Tear down the Temple, will you? Re-build it in three days, will you? Let them take a good look at you now!

BOY : Mother, why are they going to kill those men?

MOTHER : Two of them were wicked, son.

BOY : Why are they going to kill the other man, Mother?

MOTHER : God only knows, son, God only knows.

BARABBAS : Good morning! Beautiful day, isn't it? (*She gives him a cool nod.*)

SARAH : Ooh! Look at those nails! I can't look! (*She does, however.*) I wonder what's keeping that Leah?

(*The people crowd to one side of the playing area. The Centurion appears.*)

CENTURION : Get back, will you? Out of the way! What are you people doing here, anyway? Get back, now! Back, I say! (*He tries to push them backward, but the people want to watch. He disentangles himself from the crowd and then Mary of Magdala rushes forward, falls to her knees, clasps him by the legs and implores him.*)

MARY : Don't! Please don't! He's innocent!

CENTURION : (*Pushing her away*) Let go! Get back now! Out of the way! (*She starts toward the cross, but he stands in her way.*) Back, I say. Get back, you.

BARABBAS : Good morning, officer. Wonderful day, isn't it?

MARY : He's innocent! He's innocent!

SHREW : Yeah, save him! Save the King of the Jews! Maybe he's got some more bread and fish!

WINE-SELLER : (*Without conviction or heart*) Wine! Cool, sweet wine. Wine, here . . . (*To the priest.*) Wine, sir?

PRIEST : (*Angrily*) No!

MAN : (*Actually Joseph*) Here, boy, over here.

MAN : (*Actually Nicodemus, though neither is recognized*) How much, boy?

WINE-SELLER : Three shekels, sir.

MAN : (*Nicodemus*) Three shekels? Are you crazy, boy?

WINE-SELLER : (*Defensively*) It is good wine!

SARAH : Leah! Lee-ah! Oh, Leeeeeeee-ah??? Where is that silly girl? Leah! I knew she'd miss the most exciting part!

JUDAS : Save yourself, Master! Save yourself!

SHREW : Hey, King! Haven't you forgotten something? Where's your crown, King?

MOTHER OF THE HEALED BOY : (*To Centurion*) Couldn't we do something? Couldn't we ransom him? I've heard that sometimes they—Jesus, I mean. Maybe we could take a collection . . .

CENTURION : From *these* people? Stand back, now, lady, please. All right. (*He looks offstage, then raises an arm. A hush falls as he drops his arm and a woman screams while the other women, except for the shrew, cry out with lesser force. We hear the sound of a hammer—pound, pound, pound. The Wine-Seller doubles up and sits. The women turn to each other for strength and consolation. The little boy tries to look; his mother shields his eyes from the view with her body.*)

BARABBAS : Beautiful day, isn't it? (*His voice trails off in the middle of the question.*)

(*There is another pause, all look at the Centurion. He says to the offstage soldiers,*)

CENTURION : I gave you the signal. Get on with it.

(*We hear the hammer again—pound, pound, pound. Then the crowd shifts, leaving the Priest and Barabbas in the center of the playing area.*)

NARRATOR : There are more nails to be driven, but let's not hear them. Let's choke off memory until the nails are in and the cross with its quivering burden has been dropped into its hole in the ground, in the scar cut in the crest of the hill called Golgotha. Let's take new positions on the hill, so we don't have to watch the cross, but only those people who do. Like that priest. Like that confessed murderer they call Barabbas . . .

A MAN HE LOOKED AT

(*Barabbas and the Priest stand at a distance from one another. For a while Barabbas surveys the unseen crowd, swaying just slightly as he stands. The Priest is absorbed in the drama upon the cross. Occasionally he clouds over, frowns; once he shrugs; once he winces; once he allows himself an uncertain smile. Several voices are heard from offstage. They are the women who figure in the drama of Judas.*)

THE SHREW : (*From offstage*) Hey, silent one! Destroyed any temples lately? (*Barabbas looks in the direction of the voice with anger; the Priest, quizzically.*) Come on down, king! It must be hot up there! (*The Priest wipes his brow.*)

THE MOTHER : Jesus, Jesus, save yourself! You can do it, master! Come down! You saved others, save yourself, master! Come down!

PRIEST : (*Muttering*) Crazy woman! (*Shouting, not too boldly.*) Hold your tongue!

BARABBAS : (*Seeing him*) Oh, it's you.

PRIEST : What? Oh, good day.

BARABBAS : *Good* day? It's a wonderful day! I'll bet you didn't think you'd see me today, did you? Not standing here, big as life, you didn't . . .

PRIEST : Sh! Not here. I'll talk with you later. People are watching!

BARABBAS : You were glad enough to talk with me when you thought you could use me. (*Looks up at the cross.*) Who is this man that you got to take my place?

PRIEST : *I* didn't *get* him! I had nothing to do with it. The crowd chose *you*, Barabbas. Now hold your peace. I'll discuss it with you later.

BARABBAS : You'll discuss it with me now, or I'll tell everybody on this hill whose bloody hand nailed him there. Now, who is he, and why do you want to kill him?

PRIEST : He's nobody, Barabbas, nobody at all! A fanatic! (*The Priest speaks in a low voice, nervously watching to see if people are listening. He hopes that Barabbas will lower his voice, too. The hope, however, is to prove vain.*) He's a—a vagrant from Nazareth, of all places. A gypsy sort that went around stirring up the rabble. That's all there is to it. Now will you let me— (*He starts to leave.*)

BARABBAS : (*Casually stopping him with one great hand on the shoulder*) And since when do the priests of Jerusalem get so excited about gypsies and vagrants that they dirty the fringes of their garments attending crucifixions? You wanta see that he's really dying, or just enjoying the view?

PRIEST : (*With distaste*) You're drunk, Barabbas.

BARABBAS : Not too drunk to know that you wanted to see him killed. You didn't do it because you liked me.

PRIEST : What's causing you such tender concern about him, anyway? A man who has spilled as much blood as you have, Barabbas, shouldn't be bothered by one man's death. Just why are you so interested?

BARABBAS : Because he's up there and I'm down here, that's why! (*Drunkenly, as though delivering a great truth.*) I have a *right* to know who's taking my place!

PRIEST : That's very touching, I'm sure. But all that I can tell you is that the crowd asked for you.

BARABBAS : You're lying. There's more to it.

PRIEST : (*Annoyed, obviously improvising*) You—you're a popular figure, Barabbas, that's all. (*With irony that is wasted on Barabbas.*) You appeal to the popular imagination. Every red-blooded beggar, pickpocket and thief in Jerusalem looks at you and says, "My, now! There's a fine figure of a man!"

BARABBAS : Save it! I want to know why, flabby one, why they chose me insteada him.

PRIEST : Because you hate Rome and the rabble hates Rome, that's why.

BARABBAS : What about him? They loved him. When he entered the city—

PRIEST : I know all about it.

BARABBAS : —They shouted. Shouted! I thought they were going to knock the old Praetorium right over with their shouting.

PRIEST : Rabble, that's all they were, rabble waving stolen branches. Lepers, cut-throats, tax-collectors, trampling every garden in sight, stripping every respectable man's trees of their branches and—

BARABBAS : (*Grabbing the Priest by his lapels and dragging him forward to an eye-to-eye position*) Then why, if they loved him so much, did they ask for me, not him? Why did they shout, "Crucify him!"?? Why or I'll break your dirty neck!

PRIEST : Certain—expenditures were made. (*Fear forces this out of him.*)

BARABBAS : There were 50, 60—two hundred people there! You can't bribe a whole crowd.

PRIEST : (*Cynically*) One doesn't need to.

BARABBAS : (*With contempt*) You—rat! (*He gives the Priest a shove and sends him reeling, stumbling.*)

PRIEST : (*Furious, trembling with indignation*) You—you'll regret that, Barabbas!

BARABBAS : I don't think so. I've got *friends*, Aaron Bar Esau. Lift a hand, say a word against me, and you'll be afraid of every footstep in the street behind you, every board that creaks at night, every whisper that you hear outside your window. And in time—(*He makes a gesture of slitting the throat.*)

PRIEST : I don't understand you. How many men have you killed, Barabbas? Yet you're concerned about one man's death.

BARABBAS : He was a good man. Have you ever known a good man, Aaron?

PRIEST : Well, I know *him*. He was an impostor.

BARABBAS : He was a good man! And he loved me.

PRIEST : What? (*It is a little whoop of delight.*) He loved you? Who could love *you*, Barabbas?

BARABBAS : He could, that's who.

PRIEST : How do you know? Tell me; I'm interested.

BARABBAS : I know, that's all I know. (*He pauses.*) I know because he looked at me! (*He stops, remembering the look.*) Did he ever look at you?

PRIEST : (*He, too, stops, remembers*) He—looked at me.

BARABBAS : What was it like?

PRIEST : (*Remembering, telling himself almost, rather than telling Barabbas*) He looked right through me, right—right into me! It was as though he were seeing my thoughts, reading my mind. . . . He—he made me ashamed.

BARABBAS : And so you hated him. And so you decided to take his life.

PRIEST : What? (*Focusing on the present with an effort.*) No, no —so I saved yours. (*Sighs.*) I should think you'd be grateful.

BARABBAS : I wonder why I'm not.

PRIEST : Gratitude comes hard to some people. Or could it be that you're a convert? (*The thought arrests him.*) You wouldn't be a convert, would you, Barabbas? YOU?

BARABBAS : (*Stubbornly*) He was a good man.

PRIEST : Perhaps, then, I should arrange for the soldier to take him down and put you in his place!

BARABBAS : Try it and see what happens to you.

PRIEST : Then you wouldn't die for him.

BARABBAS : Would any man? No, if it's a choice of him or me, let him stay there.

PRIEST : Have no fear, gentle Barabbas, he will . . . he will . . . I thought for a moment he might have influenced you.

BARABBAS : All he has done is to make me sick to the stomach of the sight of lice like you. Get away from me. Go back to your temple and your prayers. Maybe you can pray away your guilt.

PRIEST : Of what am I guilty? Of saving your life? Or guilty of saving Israel from the destruction of the law, the defilement of the faith, the ridiculing of the tradition?

BARABBAS : It's strange how men can find the best of reasons for the worst of deeds.

PRIEST : You should know, Barabbas, you should know. Now, if you'll excuse me—

BARABBAS : One thing before you crawl back under your stone. You were there at his trial. How did he stand up under the questions? What did he say in his own defense?

PRIEST : Nothing. He ignored the questions, or else he asked some irrelevant question in return.

BARABBAS : He was fighting for his life and didn't defend himself?

PRIEST : I'd hardly call just standing there "fighting for one's life." He obviously realized that he was wrong and that we were right and gave himself up.

BARABBAS : "He realized that you were right." Don't make me laugh. (*He stops, then asks in a mood of wonder.*) He didn't put up a fight? (*The Priest shakes his head primly.*) And there he hangs, and here I stand.

PRIEST : That's right, Barabbas. In a way he died for you. Now, what are you going to do for him?

BARABBAS : What can I do? He's dying. I can't pull the nails out or— And yet . . .

PRIEST : Yes?

BARABBAS : If there were something, I think I'd do it.

PRIEST : Provided it isn't too much trouble.

(*But Barabbas isn't listening. He continues to look at the cross.*)

BARABBAS : A man is dying for me. What will I do about it?

PRIEST : Let me know if you ever make up your mind. (*He exits.*)

BARABBAS : A man is dying for me. What will I do about it? (*He is still looking at the cross as the lights fade.*)

NARRATOR : Go your way, Barabbas; you are lost to us now. But, Barabbas, you are more right than you know. He died for you.

*

It's a strange day, isn't it? It's so dark for midday! Maybe it's going to storm. This hill is no place to be if that's the case. What are you doing here today, anyway, you who usually ride in cars or sit upon upholstered chairs? Why have you come here?

SARAH : (*Starting down an aisle toward the chancel*) Leah! Leah! Excuse me, please. May I get through here?

NARRATOR : You've come to church many times during Holy Week, year after year, just as she has come to crucifixions many times. She's hardened to brutality. I'm not so sure about her friend Leah over there. They're servants. Servants . . . Wasn't there a maid who spoke to Simon Peter?

THE MAN WHO DENIED HIM

SARAH : (*Calling*) Leah! Leah! (*To herself*) Well, she can't say I didn't try. I'm hoarse from shouting. It's no wonder I can't find her in a crowd this size.

LEAH : (*Entering*) Sarah! I've been looking all over for you. How long have you been here?

SARAH : Long enough to grow hoarse with calling your name. Let me tell you, Leah, people *looked* at me, shouting as I was, all about this here hill! (*She nods significantly. This is a momentous thing she has endured.*)

LEAH : Did you have any trouble getting away? I simply said we were all out of oil and went right out the door, bold as you please. My, this *is* a crowd.

SARAH : I saw the most handsome soldier a minute ago! He looked at me as though he weren't really looking at all, but I went right on! Imagine!

LEAH : The nerve of these Romans! What's in the basket?

SARAH : A bit of fruit, some bread, and—look!

LEAH : My, aren't we eating fancy these days!

SARAH : The master was so upset. People were coming and going all evening. He hardly got a chance to eat a bite. Here, have a leg!

LEAH : Ooooh! This is good!

SARAH : It ought to be! After all, it's been blessed by a high priest! Just think, Leah, me! Working for a high priest! Imagine!

LEAH : It staggers the imagination, Sarah, it really does. When did it begin?

SARAH : You know. I've been there for almost—

LEAH : No, the crucifixions.

SARAH : About an hour ago. I remember my first crucifixion. I was so upset I could hardly eat.

LEAH : Things like this are upsetting to a sensitive person.

SARAH : I'm still very sensitive, but I can eat. It's a shame, isn't it?

LEAH : What?

SARAH : Killing three perfectly good men, and us without husbands.

LEAH : I guess they're not perfectly good, or they wouldn't be up there.

SARAH : Well, you know what I mean. One of the women who was here from the start said it was just awful the language they used.

LEAH : Really! Oh, I'm glad I wasn't here, then. (*Pause.*) The one in the middle doesn't look the type.

SARAH : No, it was the other two. They screamed and swore something terrible. But not the one in the middle. He's hardly made any noise at all.

LEAH : Have they had the drug yet?

SARAH : The other two have. The middle one refused it.

LEAH : Imagine! I'd never refuse it! Oh, Sarah, how do you suppose it feels?

SARAH : Just terrible, that's how. I feel sorry for them, even if they were wicked.

LEAH : What did they do?

SARAH : Those two were thieves. (*She points with her chicken leg.*)

LEAH : And the other?

SARAH : Wait till I tell you about him! *He* was brought to our place last night. He was so close to me as they took him upstairs, I could have reached out and *touched* him!

LEAH : No!

SARAH : Yes! And something else! Two of his men came with him. One of them was a big bruiser, and the other—

LEAH : Yes????

SARAH : He wasn't so broad in the shoulders, but he didn't need to be!

LEAH : Good-looking?

SARAH : Was he!

LEAH : Did he notice you?

SARAH : I'll say he did. I'm the one who let him in.

LEAH : Imagine!

SARAH : Have another piece of chicken?

LEAH : Just a bit of bread, if you have some.

SARAH : Good, isn't it? Well, I actually spoke up to the one with the broad shoulders. I said to him, "You were with him, weren't you?" And he denied it.

LEAH : Sarah, you didn't!

SARAH : I did! And we all spoke to him and accused him of it. I could tell right off by the way he spoke. You know how funny they talk around Galilee, dontcha? He couldn't tell *me* he wasn't one of them!

LEAH : Sarah, you are the one! What happened?

SARAH : Well, something interesting, believe me. When they brought the prisoner back—the one in the middle there, Jesus, they call him—this Jesus just gives old blustery a look.

LEAH : What kind of look, Sarah?

SARAH : I can't rightly say. It made me sorta think of my mother, when one of the neighbors had caught me doing something wrong. She was angry that I'd done it, but at the same time, she let me know nobody was going to lay a hand on her daughter but her! Loving, kinda.

LEAH : No!

SARAH : That's how it struck me. And then old grizzly-beard turns around and runs to the gate. Well, it was barred, naturally. He just beat on it till I showed him how to get out. And, Leah—

LEAH : Yes????

SARAH : He was crying! Like a baby! That grown man was crying!

LEAH : Sarah, if you weren't telling me yourself, I'd never believe it from anyone else. A big man, too!

SARAH : I'll say. See that fellow over there? About that size.

LEAH : (*Touches Sarah's arm and leans toward her*) Oh, Sarah, that—that Jesus one is saying something.

SARAH : (*After they listen*) Poor fellow. But you can't blame his father for *not* being there. This would be enough to make anybody—Leah?

LEAH : Yes, Sarah?

SARAH : That one over there. The one I said was the same size as Old Grizzly? *That's him!*

LEAH : No! Oh, Sarah, I'm frightened. Do you suppose he'll do anything?

SARAH : Not him! I think I'll go speak to him!

LEAH : Sarah, you mustn't! Everyone will think you're that kind of person.

SARAH : Not if I speak respectfully until everybody knows we know each other socially.

LEAH : Oh, Sarah, what do you want to do that for?

SARAH : I just do. That's all. Come with me.

LEAH : Oh, no!

SARAH : Do you want to stand here all alone?

LEAH : Don't leave me, Sarah! (*They cross to Peter.*)

SARAH : May I wish you a good afternoon, sir! You'll recall we met last night at the home of the high priest!

PETER : We—met? (*He doesn't remember her. He is distraught.*)

SARAH : I let you in. You're the one who said you didn't know him.

PETER : I didn't know him . . . Yes, I said that . . .

SARAH : Oh, you knew him all right. You're one of his followers!

PETER : I was one of his followers, but I didn't know him . . . I wanted to, and thought I did, but I didn't really know him.

SARAH : You were pretty sad last night, weren't you? (*Her triumphant look to Leah says, "Didn't I tell you?"*)

PETER : You baited me last night. Wasn't that enough?

(*Sarah ignores this; her audience is the crowd.*)

SARAH : I suppose that's why you *cried*. Or was it because you were afraid?

LEAH : (*Worried, quietly*) Not so loud, Sarah. People are looking!

SARAH : Let them look.

LEAH : You're not being kind to this man, Sarah. Sir, Sarah doesn't mean to be unkind.

SARAH : I'll thank you, Leah, not to—

PETER : Don't quarrel. Let her say what she likes about me. It's true.

SARAH : See? I was not being unkind. Just truthful.

LEAH : But you practically called him a coward. Is that kind?

PETER : I have been called many things. He called me a rock.

SARAH : Hmph! A rock that weeps and runs away! He didn't know you very well.

PETER : He knew me, all right. He knew my strength—and he knew my weakness. He—he prayed for me.

LEAH : Sir, was he really such a wonderful man? I have heard some things about him—that he was kind and good, and that he could do things. Wonderful things.

SARAH : Leah, you never told me that!

PETER : He was very kind and very good. You should have seen him with little children. Or the sick and the hurt. He was kind even to the very men who arrested him. I used my sword, last night when they came for him, but he stopped me. And calm as the hills, healed the wound with his fingers.

LEAH : (*Timidly*) Sir, this friend of mine said that he was—the Son of God!

PETER : (*He looks at her long and hard and then nods.*) I thought so. I believed it with all my heart. But—we were wrong.

SARAH : (*Loudly, for the benefit of all within earshot*) Yessir! A grown man! Crying in the courtyard!

LEAH : You've said that before, Sarah. Everyone knows all about it. Now stop drawing attention to yourself!

SARAH : (*Flabbergasted*) *Well,* Leah!

LEAH : Tell me more about him.

PETER : All I can think about now is last night. I—I saw him last night, as they were taking him away. And he looked at me. He wasn't angry, just sad. I think my heart stopped beating when he looked at me.

LEAH : I wish *I* had known him.

PETER : Don't wish that. Don't. To have known him, and then to see him now . . . I loved that man, as I have never loved parent or brother, wife or friend. I once said that I'd die for him. I wish I could! I . . . (*He turns his back to conceal his emotion and leaves.*)

SARAH : Well, Leah! A fine friend you are! I think you owe me an apology!

LEAH : I didn't mean to hurt your feelings, Sarah. But I didn't want to hurt him either. Sarah, couldn't you see how he was suffering? How could you be so unkind?

SARAH : Chaff and thistles, Leah! If he was such a good friend of Jesus', why didn't he do something for him when they arrested him?

LEAH : Maybe he was frightened, Sarah. That doesn't mean—

SARAH : I heard what he said about dying for him. I'd like to see him! Let it happen all over again, and he'd run and cry, just like before, that's what he'd do!

LEAH : I don't think so.

SARAH : (*Shrugs*) Believe what you like. (*Reaches into basket.*) More chicken?

LEAH : (*Shakes her head no, deep in thought*) No, Sarah, he wouldn't run away. Not again.

(*They take a final look at the figure on the cross, then exit Sarah as jaunty as ever, Leah, still lost in thought.*)

NARRATOR : Return to your jobs, girls; hurry back before your employers miss you. You had no part in this; you didn't cause it; you couldn't have stopped it. But now that it's happened, what are you going to do about it? Will you come to more crucifixions with your picnic basket and roast chicken? Or will you be different somehow?

*

It takes all kinds to people a hill during a crucifixion! There's one kind (*he nods toward a woman, not one of the players in the following scene*). She wouldn't harm a fly! She keeps a little sparrow in a wooden cage at home and each day she feeds it and sings it happy songs. It's her second bird; she cried a day when her first bird died. But she has been here for over an hour and hasn't wept a tear yet!

Now the woman over there—she's a widow. Jesus healed her boy, they say, the apple of her eye! Give her half a chance and she'll tell you all about him.

That man over there is a puzzle. Some say he's one of the daggermen who live in the hills and talk revolution and revolt, armies and killing. You'd better not get too close to him; there's something desperate about him.

You can't miss the one with the swagger; she'll bump right into you if you don't get out of her way.

They're citizens of three different worlds, yet just a few steps apart during the grim, black hours when the Romans crucify.

THE MAN WHO BELIEVED HIM

WOMAN : (*Jeering, calling loudly*) Hey there—King! Yer highness! How are ya feelin' today, yer highness? (*The mother looks at her sidewise and recoils, ever so slightly.*) How does your throne feel, king? Is that peg comfy now? (*She turns to the mother, proud of her knowledge of the details of crucifixion.*) They take this peg, see, and they make 'em—

MOTHER : (*Cutting her off, not unkindly, just anxious not to have it spoken*) I know.

WOMAN : Oh, y'do, huh? (*Disappointed*) Most people don't. They think it's just the nails. They use nails, all right, but they also take this here peg—(*She indicates size with her fingers.*)

MOTHER : (*With some emotion*) I know!

WOMAN : Oh. (*Looks at her suspiciously. Rocks a bit, hands on hips, then calls out again.*) Which one o' them apes is the queen, King?? (*She emphasizes each reference to royalty with bitter sarcasm. To the mother:*) Called himself the king of the Jews. Only the Jews didn't want no King.

MOTHER : (*Softly*) Thank you.

WOMAN : Yeah? What're you so proud about?

MOTHER : Excuse me. I—see a friend I would speak to. (*Starts to move away.*)

WOMAN : Too good to talk to me, eh? Maybe you're a *friend* of his? (*Stops the mother with a restraining hand.*)

MOTHER : I have nothing to say to you. Release me, please.

WOMAN : (*Mimics*) Release me, please! Well, now, what a fine lady this is! Maybe you're one of the princesses! (*Laughs. Raises her voice.*) Hey, now! Looka here! This is one of the princesses—daughter to the king up there! Watch this, princess. I wonder how the king would like a present from one of his royal subjects! (*She stoops, picks up a stone, throws it. She registers delight as it strikes; the mother winces. She stoops for another.*) I've got another, your highness!

MOTHER : (*Lays a hand on her arm to restrain her*) No! Don't.

WOMAN : (*Shakes her arm free*) Why not? He's a phony! That's what he is!

MOTHER : Why do you hate him so? What did he do to you that you—

WOMAN : (*With a haughty toss of the head*) I know his type. I even went to hear him once. I'd heard all about him. Feeding everyone with bread and fish. But the day I went, he got scared and turned tail and hid in the hills. I never even seen him!

MOTHER : So you stone him for that!

WOMAN : Why are *you* so interested in the king of the Jews? Could it be that—

MOTHER : (*Steps back, but the woman grabs her by the arm*) Please. I cannot look any longer. I feel ill. I must leave.

WOMAN : (*Loudly*) Oh! Tch, tch, tch. The princess feels sick! She doesn't want to see the king any more!

MOTHER : Please stop!

WOMAN : Oho! This here princess—

(*A man moves swiftly toward her, something concealed in his hand by the folds of his robe. She stops in the middle of her speech with a look of wide-eyed surprise.*)

THE MAN : (*Whispers*) Do you feel that, daughter of a mule?

WOMAN : I— What's the big idea? Who do you think you're—

THE MAN : Quiet. I'd just as soon stick it right through you. Shut your arrogant mouth.

WOMAN : I was only trying to—

THE MAN : Well, stop trying.

WOMAN : I have friends in this crowd. If they found out that you're threatening me—

THE MAN : And I have friends in this crowd who hate loud-mouthed women. And if you so much as say another word, you'll learn how sharp our knives are.

WOMAN : (*Looks covertly around to see if she can see any of these "friends" of her threatener*) I was only—

THE MAN : Go, and not another word, if you value that loud tongue of yours.

WOMAN : (*Muttering*) Bully! (*As she leaves*) Probably one of 'em hisself!

MOTHER : Oh, thank you. I can't tell you how grateful—

THE MAN : (*Watching the woman's retreat*) If she so much as *looks* at another stone—

MOTHER : How could she possibly do it? How could she bring herself to throw even a pebble at him?

THE MAN : You knew him?

MOTHER : (*Proudly, sadly*) He healed my son.

THE MAN : He healed many. (*Then, as an afterthought.*) . . . I have heard.

MOTHER : Others tried to heal him and failed. The physicians—one after another—they could do nothing. Then Jesus laid a hand upon him and looked into his eyes, and smiled. And my boy—

THE MAN : He was made well. (*Almost involuntarily he completes her sentence.*)

MOTHER : How could anyone hate him? And yet they did! Men came to me after the healing. They said my son had not really been ill. They tried to tell the mother who had nursed him since infancy, I, who had spent all I ever had on physicians, that he had not really been sick!

THE MAN : They were jealous of him.

MOTHER : They were hateful! They actually hated him! I don't see how anyone could hate him. Whenever he spoke, wherever he went, there were crowds of people who loved him. . . .

THE MAN : (*Under his breath*) Or else loved the loaves and fishes.

MOTHER : Pardon me?

THE MAN : It was nothing. You were saying . . .

MOTHER : They actually offered me money to say he had not been sick. Oh, they did it subtly, but it was there, just the same . . . the offer to pay me if I'd lie, if I'd deny that the healing had really happened.

THE MAN : You refused, of course.

MOTHER : I had never before ordered anyone to leave my home. But I did that day. I didn't care what happened to me—I told them to leave!

THE MAN : They think they can buy anybody.

MOTHER : They must have succeeded in buying a great many people. How else could this have happened?

THE MAN : (*Forgets himself*) But it wasn't for the money— (*Stops.*)

MOTHER : Yes?

THE MAN : (*Recovering*)—that I would say that he was betrayed. Men can have other motives.

MOTHER : How could men be so wicked?

THE MAN : Maybe it wasn't wickedness. Some say he wanted to be king. Some say he could have been king, and they might have tried to force his hand.

MOTHER : Who could have been so foolish? (*Looks cautiously about.*) Since when have kingship and kindness ever gone hand in hand?

THE MAN : But he could have been king! He could have done so much for the people, his people, if he'd only tried!

MOTHER : He *could* have? What more could he have done than he did?

THE MAN : He could have raised an army!

MOTHER : (*Looks about in fright.*) This is no place and no year for talk like that! The Romans—I must go. Good day to you, and thank you again.

THE MAN : Don't go.

MOTHER : (*Looks at him curiously*) Why—?

THE MAN : I—there may be something a woman can do. (*He is groping for an explanation.*) His mother might come.

MOTHER : Oh, I hope not! I hope not!

THE MAN : But she might, just the same.

MOTHER : You're more involved in this than you admit. Are you a follower—?

THE MAN : (*Evasively*) Many followed him. Multitudes, once.

MOTHER : But you were more than a part of the multitudes. You knew him personally. (*This is a trial balloon on her part.*)

THE MAN : I—yes, I knew him.

MOTHER : Did you try to help him? Why didn't somebody prevent this? Who condemned him? Who accused him?

THE MAN : The priests! The filthy, lying, grasping priests! They hated him. Because he turned over the tables in the Temple! Because he saw dishonesty and called it by its name; because he saw their corruption and told what he saw!

MOTHER : But this is a Roman crucifixion! Do the Romans interfere with Jewish affairs now? Do the Romans so love the priests they they crucify the man who criticizes them?

THE MAN : (*Wildly*) I don't know, I don't know. All I know is that he doesn't have to hang there! He didn't lift a finger to defend himself!

MOTHER : Doesn't have to hang there??? You believe in him!

THE MAN : He has such tremendous power in his fingertips, all he would have to do is say the word and legions of angels would come, even now, and take him—

MOTHER : Shh! He's speaking. (*They pause to listen.*) I didn't hear all of it. Just the end of it—". . . for they know not what they do."

THE MAN : That's it! I didn't know what I was doing! I didn't mean for him to die! (*He speaks with a sob.*)

MOTHER : (*Raising a hand to silence him*) He may speak again. (*Though they listen, nothing more is said.*) Those may be the last words he'll ever speak. The man who healed my son! He spoke, and I didn't hear what he said! What did he say? I want to know *all* of what he said.

THE MAN : I'm sorry. I'm sorry I kept you from hearing.

MOTHER : He might have said something that *you* wanted to hear! (*She scans the crowd on tiptoe.*) Oh! There's one! I recognize him. He was one of the disciples! I'll ask him. Maybe he heard.

THE MAN : One of—the disciples?

MOTHER : Good day, sir. And thank you again. (*She gives him a dubious look, then leaves, glad to get away from him.*)

THE MAN : (*His voice is hollow, empty*) "He might have said something that you wanted to hear!" What could any man say that I would want to hear—now? (*He turns, and as he does, something that he has held coiled and concealed, now falls. He picks it up but the end of it trails behind him as he leaves. It is a rope.*)

NARRATOR : So . . . You betrayed him. Whether it was to force his hand, or to put thirty pieces of silver in yours, you betrayed him! We'd never do such a thing! We might hedge a little, or compromise a bit, or tolerate some things in our businesses and communities that he wouldn't approve of, but we'd never betray him! We'd never do what you did. But you make us uneasy, just the same.

THE MAN WHO TRIED HIM

NARRATOR : Let's get away from that hill for a while. It's much nicer here. And the people . . . well, you just naturally find a better class of people in palaces, don't you? There's a state luncheon going on somewhere in this one. Not in this room, however; these are the private chambers of Pilate and his wife, Claudia.

(*The interior of a palace. Upstage is an altar; downstage, audience right, is a table with a wash basin upon it. Enter Claudia, and her maid, Joanna.*)

JOANNA : Was the wine not cool, mistress? Was the food not good?

CLAUDIA : The food was good, Joanna; the wine was cool. I have no appetite.

JOANNA : Mistress, the master glowered when you left the table. He seemed distressed by your leaving.

CLAUDIA : He is often distressed, Joanna. Say no more about it.

JOANNA : Should I draw the curtains, mistress? Could you sleep for a little?

CLAUDIA : If I only could!

JOANNA : Last night—the dream came back?

CLAUDIA : I dreamed again, yes; but this was a new dream. Still again I saw his face; again I heard his voice.

JOANNA : What did he say, mistress? Was he talking to you?

CLAUDIA : It was a strange dream. In it my husband offered him bread, but he refused to eat. He offered him wine, but he refused to drink. Then my husband took a basin of water and flung it at him. The basin clattered loudly in the corridors of my dream, but the Nazarene did not move. He spoke and said, "You will flee, but you cannot lose me. You can hide, but you cannot escape me. Sooner or later you must deal with me. For I am part of you."

JOANNA : It was a *strange* dream! Were you in the dream?

CLAUDIA : Yes . . . I seem to remember that I was holding something; a thorny branch, I think. And when I awoke, my finger was bleeding!

JOANNA : Poor mistress!

CLAUDIA : Is there any word—from outside?

JOANNA : None. It was all done so quickly! His followers are bewildered, scattered, frightened. His men weren't soldiers; they do not think as military men.

CLAUDIA : No, and yet if they were but loyal—as men sometimes are to men—they would do something.

JOANNA : What can they do against the legions of Rome, mistress? We—*they*—are but a few and weak; Rome is great and strong.

CLAUDIA : They would do *something*. (*Enter Pilate, striding angrily.*)

PILATE : Well, wife, that was becoming behaviour!

CLAUDIA : He was a man of little consequence. It did not matter.

PILATE : He was a guest of Pontius Pilate!

CLAUDIA : It is done. And I have said he does not matter. You will see that I am right.

PILATE : Your great wisdom in the matter of politics tires me, Claudia.

CLAUDIA : My great wisdom in the matter of politics brought you to your present position, my lord.

PILATE : (*To Joanna*) Well?? What are you waiting for? Out!

JOANNA : Yes, master. (*Scurries away.*)

PILATE : You may find it was a mistake.

CLAUDIA : You should recognize mistakes by now. They are close friends.

PILATE : Jerusalem is quiet today, is it not? Where are the threatened riots? Answer me. I have averted the riots, haven't I?

CLAUDIA : The day is not over.

PILATE : Always a helpful bit of encouragement for your husband, haven't you?

CLAUDIA : You should not have done it.

PILATE : Done what?

CLAUDIA : You may well ask. The list is long. For now I mean your verdict against the Nazarene.

PILATE : Bah! Another stupid Jew!

CLAUDIA : A Jew, yes. But not just another Jew. No, he has a different kind of wisdom.

PILATE : The Jews are wise, are they?

CLAUDIA : They made Pontius Pilate take down the Emperor's image, did they not, by praying for six days around your palace? You beat them with staves, but *you* were rebuked by the Emperor. The Jews are wise.

PILATE : I despise them.

CLAUDIA : I know.

PILATE : They tried to force my hand again last night.

CLAUDIA : They succeeded.

PILATE : They did not!

CLAUDIA : They did not? Then why was my lord dressed and ready to receive the prisoner at six in the morning today?

PILATE : I have a sixth sense for these things. I could smell trouble.

CLAUDIA : And why did you deny him a fair trial? Because you did, my lord!

PILATE : I tried him fairly.

CLAUDIA : Your mind was made up! They refused to try him, because they could not sentence him to death! But you! You tried him and gave them the decision they wanted!

PILATE : You presume, wife. You seem to forget that—

CLAUDIA : There sometimes comes a day when truth must be spoken, regardless of consequences. For me that day has come. Pilate! The sky! The sky grows black and sickly green!

PILATE : The gods are angry that a wife should upbraid a husband!

CLAUDIA : This is a judgment on a crime, not a custom! Nature in its loathing at the day's injustice seeks to hide its face. The heavens cloud over to blot this spectacle from the eyes of the gods.

PILATE : Rot! It is going to rain, that is all.

CLAUDIA : Pilate. When was it to take place?

PILATE : What?

CLAUDIA : The crucifixion. When?

PILATE : It would be now in process. Some two or three hours ago it began.

CLAUDIA : Pilate, what have you done? The man was innocent!

PILATE : Would you rather have the entire city shaken with riot, or have one man die?

CLAUDIA : (*There is a rumbling noise. Claudia and Pilate sway slightly. A greenish light shines upon them now*) Do you feel that? The very earth utters its protest!

PILATE : Where is the incense? *Joanna!* (*He thunders her name.*)

CLAUDIA : It is a judgment on you, Pilate!

PILATE : You are mad, Claudia. I am not on trial for what I did with Jesus.

CLAUDIA : All men are on trial for what they do with Jesus!

(*Enter Joanna, trembling.*)

JOANNA : Yes, master?

PILATE : Incense! Mars and Jupiter are angry! Quickly, fool!

JOANNA : Yes, master! (*Exits.*)

CLAUDIA : You see, I was right. The upheaval of the earth itself cries out against this deed!

PILATE : Your fantasies no longer amuse me! Your dreams no longer irritate me—they infuriate me! It is not enough that you send me a message in the middle of the trial—

CLAUDIA : They were true words. He *was* a righteous man! And in my dreams I suffered much because of him! You should not have done this! And you will suffer.

JOANNA : (*Re-entering*) The incense, master.

PILATE : (*Throws it in brazier. It explodes with a puff of smoke*) Great Mars, god of war; mighty Zeus, god of blood, accept the worship of this humble slave and hear his fervent petition. Cease thy rumblings; end thy warfare; still the quaking earth! (*To Claudia and Joanna.*) On your knees, fools! Kneel!

CLAUDIA : (*Calmly, to Joanna*) You may leave us.

PILATE : On your knees! Your knees! (*But Joanna flees in terror.*)

CLAUDIA : I no longer kneel to the name of Mars and Zeus.

PILATE : Down, down!

CLAUDIA : No pinch of incense clears these skies! No muttered prayer will calm this earth. Perhaps it is that so little blood is innocent that the spilling of a single drop as pure as his has put the world in such a frightened state.

PILATE : (*Rises*) I washed my hands of him! I said it was their affair.

CLAUDIA : One does not wash one's hands of such a man. One is not free of such a crime.

PILATE : They sentenced him, not I. *I* called him king! I wrote it at his head.

CLAUDIA : It was a taunt! It was a paper triumph over the Jews! As he haunts my dreams, Pilate, he will haunt yours. You will not soon be free of this man.

PILATE : (*Quite shaken; as in a dream, he crosses to a basin, and dips his hands in*) I am innocent of the blood of this righteous man!

CLAUDIA : (*Looks at his hands*) Then why do you wash? (*Crosses to window. The greenish light fades.*) The skies have cleared. The earth is stilled. It is like the silence of a parent who has wept, and wept, and can weep no more for a son that is dead.

PILATE : I am innocent of the blood of this righteous man.

CLAUDIA : The blood remains.

(*She leaves him. As the light fades, he is still dipping his hands in and out of the water.*)

NARRATOR : You're wasting your time, Pilate. They won't come clean. You're imprisoned in the pages of history, redhanded in your guilt. Oh, but if you only knew, Pilate! The blood that makes your white hands scarlet with guilt has made scarlet hearts white with forgiveness. But you'll never know that, because you are too proud to admit your guilt; to say that you have sinned; to ask forgiveness. So you wash your hands instead. What is it your wife said to you? "One does not wash one's hands of such a man." Sooner or later, Pilate, you will have to deal with him.

THE MAN WHO GAVE THE ORDER

NARRATOR : There they are again, the three wooden crosses and the three dying men. Don't look at them! Human eyes were never intended to look at such suffering. Look somewhere else.

Look instead at that man over there. They call him a centurion. He's a Roman soldier, an officer—he commands a platoon of one hundred men. Think how he felt when he gave the order to the men to lie down on their crosses. Think how he felt when he told his men to drive nails through the strong but gentle hands of the one in the center. Or maybe he didn't know. Maybe he didn't know until the order was given and the deed was done that the one in the center was different. And if he had known, could he have refused to give the order? That would have been treason!

This heat makes a man thirsty. That boy over there with the jug—he's doing a lot of business with whatever it is he's selling. Wine, it looks like.

I wonder what a young boy like that will make of all this brutality . . .

(*The centurion, designated man, is seated on a pile of soldier's gear. He watches the crowd, occasionally glances up at the crosses, mops his brow and then spies the boy with his wine-skin.*)

MAN : Boy! (*He pauses. More imperiously.*) Boy!!

BOY : (*Entering*) Yes, sir?

MAN : What do you have there?

BOY : Wine, sir. *Cool* wine, sir. Feel for yourself. (*Man puts hand on skin.*) I keep it in a stream during the night. It's good wine too.

MAN : Give me some.

BOY : Yes, sir. (*He pours a cup of wine.*)

MAN : Will this do? (*He extends a coin. The Boy slowly examines the coin, then looks up in surprise.*)

BOY : Why, yes, sir. It is much more than enough. (*The Man sips.*)

MAN : Good. It is good wine.

BOY : Thank you, sir. (*Starts to leave.*)

MAN : Wait.

BOY : Yes, sir?

MAN : This is no task for a lad of your age. How old are you?

BOY : (*In an I'm-not-so-young voice*) I'm seventeen.

MAN : Is this the sort of place you usually work?

BOY : Men grow thirsty at such a place, sir.

MAN : And the brook not far from here?

BOY : There is a saying, sir, that a demon inhabits the brook. All who drink of it grow sick.

MAN : Did you ever drink of it?

BOY : Once.

MAN : And did you grow sick?

BOY : No, but that was before I knew about the demon.

MAN : The demon is good for business.

BOY : (*Grins*) I'm thinking of making him a partner.

MAN : That's an idea. Still, this place is no spot for a boy your age.

BOY : My people believe a boy becomes a man at the age of 13.

MAN : You are a Jew, then?

BOY : (*Somewhat proudly*) I am a Jew.

MAN : What do you think of the one there in the middle? He's a Jew, too, isn't he?

BOY : (*Innocently*) I am sure he is guilty, or Rome would not kill him.

MAN : (*Looks at the Boy suspiciously, but the Boy maintains his pose*) Guilty of what, boy?

BOY : Of whatever charge was made. Now I must go, sir, I've still got half a skin of wine to sell.

MAN : Stay! (*It was a command.*) Why are you so anxious to leave?

BOY : My business, sir, is selling wine—

MAN : And not talking to a Roman centurion, right?

BOY : My business is selling, not talking, just as you point out, sir.

MAN : Sharp tongue for a lad of your age, haven't you?

BOY : (*Frightened; after all, this is Rome, personified, that he has addressed*) I meant no disrespect, sir. Honest I didn't.

MAN : Easy, lad. Just watch the tongue a little more closely.

BOY : Yes, sir. I didn't mean to—

MAN : I know. (*Returning to a subject which interests him.*) Do you know what the charge was against the one in the center?

BOY : I heard many versions of the charge. One said he threatened to destroy the temple.

MAN : Did you believe it?

BOY : Him??? Destroy the temple?

MAN : What else did you hear?

BOY : That he claimed to be the Messiah. Ha!

MAN : Why do you laugh?

BOY : Does he look like a Messiah now?

MAN : Did you hear any other charges?

BOY : Another as foolish. That he was the king of us Jews! We have no king but Caesar.

MAN : And prefer no king at all. Do you think the punishment fits the crime?

BOY : Sir, I may be a man in years, but you ask me questions that would stump a rabbi. Why do you question *me,* sir, about these matters?

MAN : Because you are a Jew, boy. Because I'm interested in the reaction of a Jew who sells wine at the feet of a dying Jew— at the feet of a crucified Jew.

BOY : My father says it will teach me something about life!

MAN : He employs a hard teacher.

BOY : Life teaches a hard lesson.

MAN : You speak well for a boy—a man—of your age.

BOY : My father says I think and talk like a fool!

MAN : No evasions, boy! *Why* did your father want you here today?

BOY : (*Shrinking back*) Why do you ask me?

MAN : Because I've been watching you. You're not like the rabble who come to these things to be entertained. You're not standing here with tears streaming down your face, like some of the women here and there, or just standing with a look of suffering, like some of the men. You can hardly bear to look in the direction of his cross. And once, when one of them jeered, you winced, as though you had been struck in the face.

BOY : I—thought he was a good man.

MAN : Thought, boy, thought? You think so no more?

BOY : If he were innocent, Rome would not—

MAN : I am not about to arrest you for treason against Rome, boy. I want to know what you think.

BOY : I don't know what to think. My father says—

MAN : I don't want to know what your father thinks. What do *you* think?

BOY : I'm not sure! He can't be the Messiah. Moses said, "Cursed be he who hangs upon a tree." And the rabbi says—

MAN : Forget the rabbi! Was he a good man?

BOY : He did kind deeds. He healed! He taught! He—he was wise.

MAN : Then why does your father dislike him so? Why do the rabbis hate him?

BOY : Not all of them do, sir! Rabbi Gamaliel—

MAN : He was convicted by the leaders of your people, boy. Why? (*A pause.*) Have you heard anything from him?

BOY : No, sir. I haven't . . . the others are so—

MAN : He hasn't cried out like the others, has he . . . He hasn't cursed . . . and screamed and blasphemed and dirtied the air with filthy words . . .

BOY : Oh, he wouldn't—

MAN : No, he wouldn't, would he . . . He's different, all right. Why did you follow him, boy?

BOY : I didn't follow him, sir. I only heard him speak. (*Pause.*) But I felt he was strong and when he spoke, he spoke as though he knew what he was talking about.

MAN : What *did* he talk about?

BOY : (*Hesitates*) About God.

MAN : About God. And he knew what he was talking about, hmmm? That's a different tune than the one you sang a few minutes ago, when you said they charged him with being the Messiah.

BOY : He is not the Messiah! The Messiah will be a warrior.

MAN : No, this man is no warrior. Is that what your father and the priests have against him?

BOY : They're against him because he said God expects difficult things from us. Forgiveness and honesty and he even said—

MAN : What?

BOY : (*Smiling*) That we were to love you Romans!

MAN : (*Reaches out and tousles Boy's hair*) Impudent rascal! (*Looks up at the cross, sobered.*) Well, that's what his love got him.

BOY : Oh, sir, if you could only have heard him . . .

MAN : I heard him. For about an hour, once. A year ago or so. And I heard him, boy, when we dropped the cross into its socket. That's when they feel the pain, *all* the pain, for the first time. I heard him. . . . I've heard many at such a time.

BOY : What did he say?

MAN : He said, "Father, forgive them, for they know not what they do."

VOICE : Boy! Wine!

BOY : They are calling me, sir. . . .

MAN : You may go.

BOY : Thank you, sir. (*He starts out, then hesitates and returns a step or two.*) Sir, what do *you* think of him?

MAN : (*Turning to look the boy in the eyes*) I think he is the Son of God.

VOICE : Boy!! Wine! Over here!

BOY : (*Calling uncertainly*) Coming. (*He starts out, torn between two fires, finally runs unwillingly out of sight.*)

NARRATOR : So you think he's the Son of God, do you? What difference will that make in your life? Move away, out of the spotlight, off the stage. You have spoken the single line in this drama that gives you your immortality in the memory of Christian man. But move along a changed man. Changed for the better? Who knows? But you are changed, that is certain, for you gave the order that crucified him. And we in our pews —we never gave an order that crucified Christ.

Did we?

THE DISCIPLES IN SECRET

NARRATOR : Well, it's over now. The earthquake is stilled and the midday darkness departed. The daylight came back for a while, but it was a sickly, tentative thing that changed its mind again, and surrendered to twilight. The hazy sun, retreating from this grim scene, is making long shadows stretch from those three gaunt crosses and the three dead bodies upon them. The curses and the cries of the thieves are silenced. The agony of the bodies is over. No more words of grief, or concern or hope or even despair will fall from the blackened lips of the one in the center. It's nearly nighttime and we're all alone on Calvary with three dead bodies.

No, that isn't quite true; I hear footsteps. It's Joseph, the one from Arimathea. He's very well-known in Jerusalem. A member of the Sanhedrin. He seems to be meeting someone. Of course. Nicodemus. The one who came to Jesus "by night, for fear of the Jews," the learned one who couldn't see how a man could be born again. He's on the Sanhedrin, too; two judges of the Supreme Court. I wonder what they will make of Roman justice?

(*Joseph enters and looks this way and that for Nicodemus, but it is night and he sees nothing. Then Nicodemus enters with a young boy carrying a crudely wrapped box, large enough for Nicodemus to sit on. The boy stands deferentially to one side for a moment.*)

JOSEPH : Ah, Nicodemus, you come at last.

NICODEMUS : Peace, peace, friend, and patience. Forty pounds is a heavy weight for a lad as young as this. And it is a long way.

JOSEPH : Many miles have been traveled this day. Not all were as easy as yours.

NICODEMUS : Easy or not, I am tired. A man of my age—I don't take this sort of exercise often. Or well. Here, boy! Bring them over here. (*The boy, with some difficulty, brings the box closer to Nicodemus, who settles himself upon it with obvious relief at being able to sit again.*)

JOSEPH : Your servant looks tired. Perhaps *he* should sit on the spices . . .

NICODEMUS : Really, Joseph, your humor is ill-timed. (*But he recognizes the truth in what Joseph has said.*) Sit, sit, sit, boy. Don't stand there. This isn't appropriate for a man my age.

JOSEPH : Things were out of joint today, yes. Death was not appropriate for a man of his age. (*Nods toward the cross, offstage.*)

NICODEMUS : You have the ladder?

JOSEPH : (*A faint trace of a smile*) I have the ladder.

NICODEMUS : What amuses you, Joseph? Really, this is no time to smirk so.

JOSEPH : *We* amuse me, good Nicodemus, you with your spices and I with my ladder. What did you pay for the spices? A goodly sum, to get so many. And what did I pay for the dead body? The price of a live slave. So here we come, when the danger is past, to tell a lifeless body we believe the words spoken by the spirit that once dwelt therein.

NICODEMUS : The danger is not past, Joseph, and I resent your implication. What could I have done that I did not do?

JOSEPH : I said we, good friend. You had your chances, and I, mine. And we turned our backs.

NICODEMUS : Don't preach! Be explicit.

JOSEPH : Nicodemus! (*In loving remonstrance*) Have you deceived even yourself? Through the years, when you shared your secret hopes with me, you pictured the Kingdom of God, as you devoutly wished it would be, as you swore you would help to make it.

NICODEMUS : My Kingdom hopes hang crucified there.

JOSEPH : And you helped to crucify them.

NICODEMUS : I did not! I went to him, one night, to learn what I could, to promise my support. But all I received was vague answers, vaporous evasions, impossible pictures.

JOSEPH : Saw right through you, did he?

NICODEMUS : This mood, Joseph, is unbecoming to you.

JOSEPH : It grows out of grief, my friend. I have wept until my eyes can weep no more. Now I must laugh—sadly, but laugh.

NICODEMUS : You would take the body down with a "Ho, ha, ha!"? This is not like you.

JOSEPH : I will weep again, I doubt not, once I touch the cold and mangled flesh. But still, now, as I survey the two of us, we are a sorry pair. And I smile at our courageous pretenses.

NICODEMUS : Really, Joseph! I like neither your poetic language nor your accusations. Pretenses, indeed! (*He rises angrily.*) Every moment we are here, we are in danger! This man was hardly the favorite son of Rome! Rome crucified him. His every friend must be suspect in the eyes of the imperial eagle.

JOSEPH : And yet we could have done something worthwhile when he was living. Do you know why I stayed away from the trial? Because it was illegal! The law does not provide for the Sanhedrin to be summoned at night! The law *does* allow for an innocent man to be crucified. But I turned over in my bed, and he turned over on a cross!

NICODEMUS : Turned over on a cross! How can a man turn over on a cross?

JOSEPH : Words, Nicodemus. What words did you ever employ in his behalf?

NICODEMUS : You know very well, Joseph, that when they first tried to arrest him, and the officers came back without him, I was the one who spoke up for him.

JOSEPH : And I recall that deathless utterance, Nicodemus. "Does our law judge a man without first giving him a hearing and learning what he does?" *There's* a valiant defense to set the ears of the court a-burning!

NICODEMUS : I at least— (*Stops.*) It wasn't much, was it? (*With emotion.*) But what could we have done?

JOSEPH : We could have warned him!

NICODEMUS : Would he have then run away? (*There is a pause.*)

JOSEPH : (*Quietly*) He would not have run away.

NICODEMUS : So you see, there was nothing we could have done.

JOSEPH : There was much we could have done! We could have joined him!

NICODEMUS : How would that have helped?

JOSEPH : God knows how, or even if. I don't. I don't know that our mustard-seeds of influence would have tipped the scales in his favor. Nor do I know what our poor abilities might have counted for had we placed them in his hands. But I do know that scales *have* been tipped, battle-tides turned, great victories won through the influence of smaller factors. And I do know that, had I joined him, I would not be standing here, weighted with self-reproach for what I might have been, but kneeling here, thanking God that I was at least all I could have been.

NICODEMUS : But your family! We had our families to consider!

JOSEPH : Always and always there is some excuse to shield us from the reaching fingers of responsibility. For excuses there will always be. But there will be responsibility, too.

NICODEMUS : This was not the time, Joseph! When the time comes—

JOSEPH : This was not the time, Nicodemus? For what event or circumstances do you save yourself? What cause is there great enough to make you give yourself if not his? You make these compromises that you may live until you can die in a great cause—significantly! But these compromises do not lead to significant dying. They lead to meaningless living. You rust to death, Nicodemus, waiting for a cause of significant greatness to command your littleness.

NICODEMUS : What about you, Joseph? Were you, then, so brave and noble? What fearless word did you speak? What daring deed did you do?

JOSEPH : I did none, dear friend, and the hard reproach I heap upon you is but an echo of the contempt I have hurled upon myself.

NICODEMUS : Really, Joseph, you are too hard on us.

JOSEPH : I'm not trying to hurt you with words, old friend. But I could no more hold them back than hold back the Jordan at its flood.

NICODEMUS : (*After a pause*) This is all very well, but it is not getting the body down.

JOSEPH : For me the body will never come down. Come, let us pull out the nails, and wonder which ones we drove in, in absentia. . . .

(*But Joseph has not said this to Nicodemus. Without looking at his friend, he walks toward the cross. Nicodemus signals to the lad, and points to the spices. They follow.*)

NARRATOR : Pull out the nails, Nicodemus. Pull out the nails, Joseph. Pull out the ones that you hammered in, and pull out the ones that we hammered in. We didn't hold the hammer; we didn't feel the quivering flesh—but we pounded just the same. Business is business, we said, and in went a nail. Well, you wouldn't want one of them marrying your daughter, we said, and in went another. We've got to be practical, we said: nail number three. What thanks do you get? we complained: pound, pound, pound. Pull out the nails, Nicodemus; pull out the nails that kept his hands from reaching out in compassion. Pull out the nails, Joseph, that kept his feet from walking our streets. Pull out the nails. What we could have done, we didn't. I wish we could help you, for some of them are ours.

TWO MOTHERS

NARRATOR : Come down the hill with me now. The hill is shrouded in darkness; the light has all gone out of the skies. Some will say that the light of the world has gone out. Come down the hill.

Come down the hill and let Friday's darkness be dissolved in Saturday's sunlight. Maybe it was all a dream, that grim show we saw outside the city. There's Salome, the mother of James and John. She isn't crying, though her eyes are red. Maybe she has the right idea—keep your hands so busy that your heart can't take time to remember. Good old Salome, trying to make the best of everything. Like the time that her boys left her to follow Jesus. She tried to put the best face on the situation, but her smiles didn't fool anybody. They knew she hated to see them go.

(*A knock on the door.*)

Answer the door, Salome; a person can't give up living just because somebody died. . . .

(*A table and a chair, or perhaps a bench, suggest the interior of a home. The room is empty, until a knock is heard. Then Salome, a woman of some 50 years of age, enters, crosses, and opens the door a crack to peer cautiously out.*)

SALOME : Mary! (*She opens the door all the way.*)

MARY : Peace, Salome. I had to stop. We're on our way— (*She enters, carrying a basket.*)

SALOME : Come in, come in, and sit down. You didn't come alone, did you?

MARY : John came with me. Not your John, the other one. He is watering the donkey.

SALOME : You poor dear! You should never have made such a trip after—

MARY : Salome, I want to ask you something. That is, if I can.

SALOME : That's right, dear. Have a good cry. It always helps. When my Zebedee died . . .

MARY : I didn't think I could cry any more. And yet more tears come from somewhere, every time I remember . . .

SALOME : You must be hungry. When did you eat last?

MARY : What? Oh, I don't know, Salome. I don't recall. But I don't think I'm hungry. Thank you. (*She sits.*)

SALOME : He was so sweet. Would a sip of wine . . . ?

MARY : Salome, your sons knew him better than the others. You knew him. He must have said something, sometime . . . What I want to know is, what did I do wrong?

SALOME : Wrong, Mary? You never did a wrong deed in your life! A sweeter, kinder mother no man ever had. My James once said to me that the mother of his master was so full of love, she would give away the roof right over her head, if it would help him.

MARY : If it would help! Nothing I did seemed to help! I couldn't understand.

SALOME : Could anyone? I went to him once—just once! with a very civil request. He brushed me aside as if I hadn't spoken a word—acted as if my boys, not I, had asked him! And then what he *did* say made no sense! Talked of a cup and a baptism. He knew they were baptized when they were following that John!

MARY : (*Only half listening*) No, I didn't understand him. I tried to, oh I tried! I gave him love and kindness, ever since that day that—ever since he was a child. I had special reasons. . . .

SALOME : He was your first, wasn't he? The first one is always the dearest. Until the last one . . . Until the last stirring in your body. The last little miracle that you will bring forth . . .

MARY : Salome, did you ever feel he was—strange? Different from other men? Did you wonder if he were—well, if he thought the same way that we do?

SALOME : Think the same as we? Not him! Talk to him about putting aside for a rainy day and he'd talk about sparrows. Say that they didn't build any barns. Well, I'm not a sparrow, I felt like telling him and I nearly— There, now, I'm sorry! I didn't mean that he was wrong. He just had greater faith than I had, I guess, that's all. Don't cry. I didn't mean to—

MARY : Don't apologize. It makes him still seem real, somehow, to know that his teachings are remembered. To know that the things he said still have the power to stab and sting a little . . . (*She rises and paces a step or two.*)

SALOME : And yet he spoke his tender words . . .

MARY : Yes, yes! Warm words! Good words! Beautiful words! Words that fell like a benediction upon your heart. If he had only spoken these words always, and not been critical of the rulers . . .

SALOME : Sit, Mary, you pace too much. (*She guides Mary gently to a chair.*)

MARY : Salome, do you remember when his brothers and I went to him? Maybe it was wrong. So many times I've asked myself, what did I do wrong? The words we heard, the tales they brought to Nazareth—well, we just had to go! Tales of miracle and power, and strangeness!

SALOME : I know. I heard them, too.

MARY : He was beside himself, they told us, imagining great things of himself, speaking glory-dreams aloud. While things at home —no work. No bread. The *real* carpenter has left, they told us. The others don't build as well. Let us know when Jesus comes back. And so we went, to bring him back, to take him home.

SALOME : I know. I wish you had.

MARY : But when they told him we were there, Salome, he didn't even come out to see us! "These are my brothers and sisters —and mother," he said, and pointed to them. "Whoever did the will of God," he said, was part of his real family.

SALOME : It makes me boil just to think of it! A fine welcome, I must say.

MARY : His own family! His own mother! Salome, was I wrong? Did I presume too much that day in thinking I, who loved him so well, might better see his destiny, might know what was best for him? Was I so wrong, Salome?

SALOME : Hush, now. You were only doing what every mother would have done. Yet there comes the time in each man's life, to some the sooner, to others, late, when they alone must choose their paths and leave behind the ways of home.

MARY : But he mustn't leave home! Don't you see, Salome, he mustn't go away! He's made enemies, powerful enemies! They'll hurt him, Salome! They'll destroy him. He must stay home— with his family! (*Mary starts to rise at the word "destroy," but Salome pushes her gently back on the chair.*)

SALOME : Mary, you're forgetting.

MARY : What? Oh, yes. And it's good to forget—the hill, and the crowd. But I won't forget the tenderness.

SALOME : The tenderness? There was tenderness?

MARY : Even amid the insults and the jeers, Salome, above the noise of the crowd he spoke to me—to us. John was with me; I couldn't have borne it without John. And he looked at us and said that John was to be as a son to me, and I was to be as his mother. He asked the man he loved best to take care of me . . .

JOHN : (*From outside*) Mother!

MARY : (*Answering*) Coming, son. (*She smiles.*) You see? We're practicing. It almost seems—natural, already. (*She reaches for her basket.*)

SALOME : You're leaving?

MARY : John wants to reach Nazareth before nightfall. But I had to stop.

SALOME : I'm glad you did, my dear.

MARY : But you haven't told me what I came to find out. What did I do wrong?

SALOME : Perhaps—just perhaps—you tried to hold what never can be held. What the Almighty gives us, He gives us as a loan—gives to us in trust! Never does He give to own, to keep . . .

MARY : But he was my child, Salome, my firstborn child.

SALOME : I know, dear. (*They walk toward the door.*) The Lord bless you and keep you, Mary . . .

MARY : (*Still protesting*) He was my child!

SALOME : The Lord give you peace, Mary. (*Mary exits.*)

NARRATOR : What did you do wrong, little woman, maiden-mother of the Bethlehem babe? Why ask, for whatever it was, you would do it again . . .

Go now; take your place with the disciples. Learn with them that the story isn't over; take your place with the Jerusalem followers of the Way. Let Luke find you worshipping in an upper room when he writes his Book of Acts. Take your place in the Church, weeping mother, and let every child in need take the place of the child who grew up and left and died. And know that inasmuch as you do kindness to one of the least of these who climbed upon his friendly knee, you do it to the one you named Jesus.

THE WOMAN WHO LOVED HIM

NARRATOR : There's one more place we should visit before we quit Jerusalem tonight. This place is a shop. The Sabbath is over, but there's no business here, from the look of things. Old Jacob is about to turn in (*A sharp knocking is heard.*) or rather, he's about not to turn in, I'd say, from the sound of that knocking.

(*Jacob is taking off his outer robe when the knocking begins. He pauses, debating whether to put it back on and answer the door, or to go to bed. When he decides to admit Mary, he may light a small oil lamp, or lacking that, a candle.*)

JACOB : At this hour! (*Raising his voice.*) The shop is closed!

MARY : (*Through the door*) Please! It is urgent!

JACOB : The shop is closed! This is the Sabbath! (*To himself.*) Besides, I'm dead tired.

MARY : (*Pounding, now*) Please, Jacob!

JACOB : (*Sits on the pallet, about to lie down*) I wonder how long she'll persist. Probably hasn't a coin in her pocket.

MARY : (*Pounding again*) Jacob!

JACOB : Then again, perhaps she has! (*To her.*) I'm coming. Peace, peace! (*He opens the door.*) What is it?

MARY : I want to buy spices. For embalming. I'm sorry to disturb you but it is urgent.

JACOB : Do you have any money?

MARY : I have money.

JACOB : This is the Sabbath, and I am a Jew. I cannot do business on the Sabbath.

MARY : It's because you are a Jew that I come to you. Please, may I enter?

JACOB : (*With resignation*) Come in, come in. Now, who are you, and what do you want?

MARY : I want to buy spices.

JACOB : If you come from the high priests, tell them I do not do business on the Sabbath. I obey the law.

MARY : I don't come from the priests. I'm a friend of the Galilean —the man they—they killed . . . He was a Jew, like you. That's why I come to you.

JACOB : (*In surprise, more interested*) Jesus—of Nazareth? The one they crucified yesterday?

MARY : Yes.

JACOB : A friend, eh? Don't I know you? Haven't I seen you before?

MARY : If you have stood with a crowd and listened to him speak, I, too, stood in such a crowd.

JACOB : No, I never stand in the streets with the rabble and the pick-pockets. It must have been somewhere else. (*He peers at her.*)

MARY : I want to buy spices.

JACOB : The Sabbath forbids—

MARY : The Sabbath has ended. Will you sell me—

JACOB : I know you! How different you look from when you swept through the town with your train of slaves, all dressed in your fine clothing! You had no eye for me then. Only for your Marcus Lucius. You are Mary, of Magdala!

MARY : What I was, I am not now. Will you sell me—

JACOB : (*Steps toward her, perhaps to touch or pinch her cheek*) Where is the scarlet color now, scarlet woman? Where is the—

MARY : (*Recoiling in repugnance*) There are other shops. (*She turns.*)

JACOB : But will they do business with such as you?

MARY : My coin is as solid as any. And it has not come from soiled hands such as yours, Jacob bar-Aaron.

JACOB : Wait! Now that you are here, now that I have put off my hour of retiring—I might just as well accommodate you.

MARY : I seek no favors.

JACOB : You have grown haughty since you have joined the ranks of the great impostor.

MARY : No, Jacob, I was once proud. Now I have so little pride, I come to a shop like yours to do business.

JACOB : Is that the tongue that delighted the Roman soldiers so?

MARY : It is the tongue that— (*She stops herself, and again turns to go. Jacob bars her way.*)

JACOB : I will sell you what you want. The price will be somewhat higher, of course, because of the Sabbath—

MARY : The Sabbath ended when the sun went down—and left blackness on the earth. The blackness of greedy hearts and evil minds.

JACOB : The price for spices sufficient to embalm the body of a man of average size is ten and two.

MARY : Half of that is the usual price!

JACOB : Do you want to go to another shop, and *there* announce you are a friend of a crucified outlaw? The ears of Rome are sharp!

MARY : I am not going to argue with you.

JACOB : It is a fair price!

MARY : It is unfair! And I don't have that much!

JACOB : How much have you?

MARY : Eight, no more.

JACOB : I would be taking a chance—

MARY : The Sabbath is ended.

JACOB : Very well. I am a fool—

MARY : You are as foolish as the serpent in the tree . . .

JACOB : How proudly you talk, you who—

MARY : If I talk with pride, I sin. *He* was humble.

JACOB : (*Begins to measure spices in a sack, or ointments into a jar*) You *have* changed.

MARY : (*Simply*) I am changed.

JACOB : What, may I ask, changed you?

MARY : You may ask. But it is not part of the bargain that I answer you. Hurry, please.

JACOB : You are ashamed of him. (*This is a calculated remark.*)

MARY : No.

JACOB : Others are not ashamed. I heard a beggar once, he claimed he had been blind from birth, and that your *friend* healed him.

MARY : You who do not stand in crowds with rabble and pick-pockets . . .

JACOB : (*Shrugs*) I who have business in other shops like any man. He believed *his* healing was real. (*Mary turns away from him. He peers after her, then taunts.*) Perhaps that was all he was—a healer.

MARY : (*Involuntarily*) He was more than that! He told me I was forgiven, and I was.

JACOB : (*Pounces*) How were you forgiven, scarlet Mary of Magdala! How?

MARY : (*Emotionally, defiantly*) By his touch! By his look! By his words! By his faith in me! He told me to sin no more, and I felt the stain of sin wash off. In a way you'll never understand.

JACOB : How could he do that, Mary of Magdala? How? How?

MARY : Because he was the Son of God! Give me the spices!

JACOB : The Son of God, Mary?? But surely one could not kill the Son of God!

MARY : He was the Son of God! I will not argue with you!

JACOB : How could he be when he could not save himself? Maybe he is not dead? Maybe you buy these spices for someone else?

MARY : He was the Son of God! I do not know how or why, but I know that he was. I know that I was forgiven! Now let me go!

JACOB : By whom, Mary? The Son of God? But they couldn't have killed the Son of God. You were forgiven by an ordinary man, who had no power to forgive!

MARY : I am forgiven! I have changed!

JACOB : You only think you are! You go to bury the body of a failure, Mary. But you do more! You go to embalm your dreams! You anoint dead hopes! You go to bury your forgiveness!

MARY : No, no it is not true. Give me the spices! Take your precious money and let me be gone!

JACOB : Before you go, Mary, let me tell you Marcus Lucius will be here tomorrow. He is in Jerusalem for a few days. The handsome Marcus Lucius, Mary. They said he was the only one of your—friends—you ever really cared for! (*Mary stiffens at the name of Lucius.*)

MARY : The spices. Give me the spices. Here is your money.

JACOB : Will I see you again, Mary? Tomorrow?

MARY : You will not see me again, ever!

JACOB : He is very handsome, Mary. And very rich.

MARY : Then *you* go see him! (*She is near the door.*)

JACOB : (*A final thrust*) Go, Mary, go, bury your false forgiver.

MARY : (*She is close to tears*) I bury my true Saviour. (*Exits.*)

JACOB : (*Recounts the coins*) 6, 7, 8! A nice profit for so late at night. (*Starts to take off his robe*) She will be back. (*Thinks about it.*) No, maybe not. (*Shrugs.*) Maybe she *was* forgiven. Who knows?

(*If the cycle is to be given before Easter, it may end with the preceding play and the following speech by the Narrator.*)

NARRATOR : Who knows? Everybody who has ever sinned and has found forgiveness, that's who, Jacob. And our number is legion.

Blow out your candle and go to bed. Go back into your places in history, all of you, centurion and serving girl, disciple and betrayer, weeping mother, pardoned murderer, Roman procurator and Jewish judges. We have glimpsed what Christ meant to you; we know deep in our hearts what Christ means to us. Perhaps we have thought of how much more he could mean to us, if we let him. For we know what you didn't: that he who was killed is not dead, but alive in the world, where every man must deal with him. So may we meet him, and know him and love him.

And now may the Lord bless you and keep you; the Lord make His face to shine upon you and be gracious unto you; the Lord lift up His countenance upon you, and give you peace. Amen.

(When the entire cycle is to be given, the following speech should replace the preceding speech to introduce the final play-let.)

NARRATOR : Who knows? Everybody who has ever sinned and has found forgiveness, that's who, Jacob. And our number is legion.

Mary will know, too, at the end of the Sabbath, when it begins to dawn, when she takes her spices and goes to the sepulchre. We won't go with her to intrude on her sacred moment with the risen Christ. She must meet him as we must, by herself.

Besides, we have other business, back at the hill. Nicodemus and Joseph have done their work; one cross stands empty. The other two still bear their grim reminders that the Roman empire shows no mercy to thieves. It wasn't a pleasant sight on Friday, and the passing of time hasn't improved things. Why should a woman like that be in this terrible place?

Or that young man?

THE MAN IN THE LINEN SHEET

(A middle-aged woman enters. She walks with eyes downcast until she stands where she can get a good view of the cross as it presumably stands over the audience's heads. She fidgets, steels herself, then lifts her eyes to the cross. It is a painful sight; she immediately looks down and looks away. She tries it again. As she does, a young man enters quietly, stands behind her, silently observing her strange performance. She buries her face in her hands for a moment, then lifts her head, her

eyes closed. She is about to open her eyes when he takes a step in order to observe her better. She hears him, and, startled, looks at him briefly before beginning to leave. She has taken only a step or two before he speaks in a kindly way.)

JOHN : Don't go.

WOMAN : (*Her words are incoherent*) That's all right, I mean, I wasn't doing anything. . . .

JOHN : Peace be unto you.

WOMAN : (*Dubiously*) And unto thy house.

JOHN : I wish you wouldn't go. I didn't mean to chase you away. I'm sorry if I frightened you.

WOMAN : That's all right, I'm sure. I mean, no harm done.

JOHN : May I ask what you were doing?

WOMAN : (*She is uncertain whether to be friendly*) Well. . . .

JOHN : (*Earnestly*) I don't mean to pry. What you were doing is your own business. It's just that I came here for a purpose. I thought maybe you came here for the same reason.

WOMAN : Why did *you* come here?

JOHN : Just to stand here and to see it. It was the one in the middle, wasn't it. . . .

WOMAN : They used all three of them. It was dreadful, dreadful.

JOHN : I know. Or I can imagine.

WOMAN : No, you can't. Not unless you were here. You just can't imagine.

JOHN : You *were* here, then.

WOMAN : Not very long, I wasn't. I thought I could do it, but, oh, dear, I'm afraid I'll just have to tell them I can't.

JOHN : I don't understand.

WOMAN : No matter. Good day to you, son. (*She starts to leave.*)

JOHN : Please stay and tell me why you came here. I want to know I have a *reason* for wanting to know.

WOMAN : Oh? What reason could you have? You don't know me.

JOHN : I have some news. But it would be of concern only to—to certain people.

WOMAN : I don't want to get mixed up in anything. I don't think it concerns me. I must be getting home.

JOHN : Please, won't you just tell me why you came here? I mean unless it's personal.

WOMAN : Why do you want to know?

JOHN : I want to find out more about one of the men who were killed.

WOMAN : Well, I don't know anything about any of them.

JOHN : You know something.

WOMAN : (*With her first show of spirit*) No, I don't!

JOHN : You know the one in the middle was different from the other two, don't you?

WOMAN : How do I know that? I never saw any of them before in my life.

JOHN : But you saw them that day, didn't you. . . .

WOMAN : I saw them. The good God knows I tried not to. . . .

JOHN : Tell me why you came here.

WOMAN : (*Suspiciously*) You aren't connected with the Temple, are you? Or with the priests?

JOHN : Not I, thank you! Not with them!

WOMAN : I came here because I thought I'd have to give up my job with the society. It was my first time, and I was nearly sick at the sight.

JOHN : The society?

WOMAN : There's a group of women who come to these things with wine. It has myrrh in it. It's to help them. It makes them forget the pain a little.

JOHN : And Friday was your first time to come to a crucifixion.

WOMAN : It was dreadful, dreadful. . . .

JOHN : And I had to call it all to mind! I'm sorry! I apologize.

WOMAN : No need for that. I came here to remember. To see if I could look at crosses again and not get sick. To see if I thought I'd ever be able to serve again. Or whether I'd have to give up before I started.

JOHN : (*Uncertainly*) I see.

WOMAN : I didn't want to go to them and say, I'm sorry. You'll have to find someone else. Or else just let them suffer. I just couldn't do that. Oh, the suffering!

JOHN : I'm not sure just what it is you do. . . .

WOMAN : We bring the drugged wine, put it on a sop, and then raise it on the end of a reed or a pole. If the—the victims want to, they can suck it out of the sop. We do it again and again until they have had enough.

JOHN : What a blessing you must be to them. . . .

WOMAN : No one called me a blessing on Friday.

JOHN : They didn't want the wine?

WOMAN : I was thinking about the ones watching. They jeered and cursed at us. "Whattaya want to do that for?" they kept asking. "Let 'em suffer!" I hate to think of it, even. It was terrible. You're not like them.

JOHN : No. I couldn't be like that. I . . . You never met the one in the middle?

WOMAN : The one they called Jesus? No. We've had so many Messiahs . . . I don't want to get mixed up in revolts and the like. . . .

JOHN : He was different.

WOMAN : All I know is, he didn't take the wine.

JOHN : He didn't?

WOMAN : He said he was thirsty, but when he tasted it, he didn't want it.

JOHN : He didn't?

WOMAN : No. He just smiled, ever so faintly, and shook his head. Poor man, he was so weak, he could hardly hold his head up. I don't know how he could pray at such a time. . . .

JOHN : He prayed? You heard him? Oh, tell me, tell me!

WOMAN : Please, what is this all about? I don't like to remember it. I just came here to look at the crosses—or to see if I could. I don't know anything about the man you're talking about.

JOHN : I do. I know so much! So little, but so much. And *he's* why I'm different. You said I was different.

WOMAN : Please, I don't want to get involved in anything. . . . Just let me go home, now.

JOHN : You must be involved, you *are* involved! You've seen him; you've done something for him. Don't you want to know about him?

WOMAN : Why should I want to know more? So I could feel worse than I do that they killed him? So I could hate the Romans even more? So I could get sick at the thought of the suffering? He's dead; he's out of it. That's all I want to know now; he's dead; he's through suffering.

JOHN : But that's it, he isn't dead! He isn't! He's alive! He's still living!

WOMAN : (*She looks at him long and hard, then speaks*) Please, I've got to go now. This isn't the sort of place I like to be. It's terrible, even when you know they aren't suffering any more.

JOHN : Listen to me. The one in the middle—Jesus—was buried. They put his body in a tomb. They rolled a tremendous stone in front of the tomb—it took five Roman soldiers to do it. They put the seal on the tomb—the seal of Rome. But he wasn't in the tomb. The earthquake rolled the stone aside and he wasn't there!

WOMAN : Well, I'm not responsible. We don't do anything with the bodies once they're dead. . . .

JOHN : Don't you understand what I'm telling you? He rose from the dead!

WOMAN : I don't believe it.

JOHN : It's true. We've seen him.

WOMAN : You were one of his followers, weren't you? I heard he had some. I didn't see any of 'em, however, when they might have done some good.

JOHN : I know . . . I tried . . . I was there when they arrested him, but well, I had an accident. . . .

WOMAN : You look well enough. . . .

JOHN : I wasn't hurt. One of the soldiers snatched my clothes away. Well, not my clothes really. They had supper at our house, Jesus and his friends. And then, late at night, when I heard them leave, I decided I'd follow. But I didn't have time to get dressed, so I just wrapped a sheet around me . . . You should have seen him, when they arrested him. Calm and proud and straight, and unafraid.

WOMAN : I'm sorry he wasn't scared to death. I'm sorry he didn't get so frightened that he ran away.

JOHN : Oh, he wouldn't have done that! He would never run away. There was something about him. I thought so then. Now I *know* it.

WOMAN : Son, will you accept this word of advice from someone old enough to be your mother? Keep your ideas to yourself. Don't tell people. You say he's alive. But nobody's very likely to believe it. Well, you believe it, if you like, but don't tell others. Wicked, cruel things happen to people these days; they could happen to you. You saw what happened to Jesus. . . .

JOHN : But that's it! I know what happened to him, but I know that's not the end of the story! I know he's alive!

(*His mother, a woman named Mary, enters. She is enough unlike the other woman named Mary that she will not be mistaken for her by the audience.*)

MARY : I thought I'd find you here.

JOHN : Mother, this is one of the women who—who do kindness to the dying. She is the very woman who gave Jesus the wine.

MARY : (*In pleased surprise*) No! Everyone who has ever met Jesus would say what I say if they could—God bless you.

WOMAN : It isn't much, really, but someone has to do it. Poor things, they can't just be allowed to hang there and suffer. . . .

MARY : If only more people felt like you do. . . .

JOHN : I told her, mother, about Jesus not being dead.

MARY : Did you know Jesus?

WOMAN : I never saw him before—that day.

MARY : Then you couldn't understand.

JOHN : Why not, mother? Why shouldn't everyone understand? Why shouldn't I tell everybody?

WOMAN : Begging your pardon, madam, I hope you tell him just what I told him. Believe what you like, but don't say it out loud. It isn't safe. Not with those Romans around; not when we have the priests we have.

MARY : Thank you for your concern for my boy, and for what you did for Jesus.

JOHN : And you're not going to give it up?

WOMAN : I hope that they can find someone else, but if they can't, I suppose . . . God go with you both.

THEY : God bless you and your house. (*She exits.*)

JOHN : She didn't believe me, mother.

MARY : No, dear. You didn't expect her to, now, did you?

JOHN : But she saw him die. She knew he wasn't like the others. She must have known!

MARY : Not everyone who saw him knew, son. Otherwise they wouldn't have killed him.

JOHN : Oh yes, they would have. They knew, all right. They knew
he was different; good, kind, honest. They knew he was holy.
He was so pure he made their foulness look black by com-
parison. Men that evil just have to hate goodness when they
see it. Especially goodness like his.

MARY : (*Understandingly*) Yes, dear.

JOHN : Well, you don't have to agree with me. (*His tone implies
that she does not.*) Mother, I *have* to tell people!

MARY : She didn't believe you. There will be others like her, John.

JOHN : She didn't want to get "involved." That's what she kept
telling me.

MARY : Yet she is a good woman, son. You know that. The thing
she does for the dying men takes courage and determination. It
isn't easy to be in the middle of the kind of crowd that goes
to a killing. The language—the threats—she is a good woman,
and a brave one.

JOHN : But why didn't she let me tell her? She didn't even seem
to want to know what I was talking about. How can anyone
say, "Yes, that's very nice," and ignore what you're saying?

MARY : There will be many, I fear, my son, many who will nod
and smile and never hear what you say. There will be others
who will *not* be so unmoved by what you are saying, but, alas,
my son, they will not believe you, either. They won't smile and
say, "How nice!" They'll reach for a stone or pick up a club.
And neither will be any nearer to believing you or your message than the other.

JOHN : Then I should say nothing? Shall I close my mouth and
keep my peace and say nothing? Shall I forget there ever was
such a man? Shall I forget the day we were all in the room
together and he came to us? Shall I forget that thing we felt,
that thing we couldn't even tell about, just as though it hadn't
happened? Mother, don't you see that. . . .

MARY : No, son, no. Never lose your vision! Never forget what
you have seen. Never forget the tingling of your pulses or the
leaping of your heart! You are our hope, son; you who have

the kind of heart that can dream and hope and believe what men call unbelievable! You have the vision! You must never let it die!

JOHN : How can I keep it alive unless I tell about it?

MARY : You must keep it alive, my son, but telling is only a part. You met him once; meet him again! You remember how he appeared to the disciples by the lake?

JOHN : Yes.

MARY : We have heard from other followers, he appeared to them. At the same hour. Miles away.

JOHN : I didn't know that!

MARY : I learned it only today.

JOHN : How, mother, how? Are you sure it was the same time?

MARY : It was daybreak, son. One does not mistake the sunrise.

JOHN : But how could he have?

MARY : How could he be dead and yet alive? Something is happening to the world these days, my son; what happens to us happens to all mankind. I know this somehow, even as you know that he was in your midst, and that it was none other than Jesus.

JOHN : Then what shall we do about it? I want to tell everybody; I want to—I don't know what I want to do. But I want to do something.

MARY : I know, my son. I feel it, too, this same urgency. God will tell us what He wants us to do. Till then we must be ready.

JOHN : Mother, if he could be at both ends of the country at the same time, he could be somewhere else, too.

MARY : He could be everywhere.

JOHN : Only God is everywhere.

MARY : (*Quietly, significantly*) Only God. . . .

JOHN : (*He looks at her*) Mother, do you believe . . .

MARY : God will tell us what he wants us to believe, my son. Till then we must be ready.

JOHN : What if God doesn't tell me what to do, mother? And how will I know what it is he wants me to do?

MARY : You knew that it was Jesus in the room, didn't you?

JOHN : (*Not quite sure he understands*) Ye-es. . . .

MARY : You will know, my son.

JOHN : Mother, I just can't seem to get it all through my head. I want to stretch my arms out and—and—

MARY : These are giant days, my son. What happens to us here in this small country happens to all mankind.

JOHN : Yes, mother, I think I see that much. . . .

MARY : Then you see a great deal. Come, John. His cross is empty. He is not here with the dead; he is at work among the living. That's where we'll find him. That's where we'll serve him. (*They look at the cross and turn. Behind her son, Mary takes a final look at the cross, looks at the youth, and closes her eyes in a moment of silent prayer, before they both leave.*) Come. . . .

NARRATOR : That's where we've found him; that's where we serve him—on the streets where we live, at the places where we work. That's where we go now, back to our accustomed places, but changed, perhaps, for we have thought about one whose business still is the changing of lives. We have glimpsed what he meant to those who saw him in the flesh; perhaps we have thought what he can mean to us, when we encounter his spirit. More than he meant to them, for we know what they did not —that he who was killed is not dead, but alive in the world where each man, in Claudia's word, must deal with him. So may we meet him and know him and love him.

And now may the Lord bless thee and keep thee; the Lord make His face to shine upon Thee and be gracious unto Thee; the Lord lift up His countenance upon thee, and give thee peace.

Amen.

by
Alan Poole

THIS ROCK

Published in 1948 in a volume entitled *Six Short Religious Plays* for the Religious Drama Society of Great Britain by the Society for Promoting Christian Knowledge. Acting copies of *Six Short Religious Plays* may be obtained from Walter H. Baker Company, 100 Summer Street, Boston 10, Mass. *This Rock* is not published separately. Permission for an amateur stage production may be obtained from Baker's for a royalty fee of $5.00 for each performance.

CHARACTERS
IN ORDER OF APPEARANCE:

MARY MAGDALENE

MARY   The mother of Jesus

JAMES
JOHN
ANDREW   The Apostles
PETER

SCENE. An upper room of a house in Jerusalem. There is one entrance and a window overlooking the street; the room is scantily furnished.

It is the evening of the first Good Friday and Mary the Mother and Mary Magdalene are sitting weeping silently. John is sitting with his head in his hands and James is standing by the window, looking down into the street.

JAMES : There they go, hundreds of them, just as if nothing has happened.

MARY MAGDALENE : Nothing has—to them.

JAMES : Listen to their chatter—they're like a lot of magpies.

JOHN : (*Joining him at the window*) A few days ago they threw palms before His ass and shouted Hosanna. Hosanna indeed! Today they crucified Him. Oh, the fools, fools!

MARY MAGDALENE : Don't, please!

There is a pause.

JAMES : The sky is very red tonight—blood red.

JOHN : The whole day has been strange. God is angry.

Another pause.

JAMES : Andrew is a long time.

JOHN : He won't come back till he finds Peter.

JAMES : Oh, this eternal waiting! Why doesn't he come? Where are the others—Philip and Thomas and Bartholomew?

MARY MAGDALENE : James, please! Have some pity for us, for—

(*She indicates the Mother sitting with bowed head. James controls himself with difficulty.*)

JOHN : You will be going to the sepulchre with spices after the Sabbath?

MARY MAGDALENE : I should like to, but there's the guard, and the stone is sealed.

JOHN : We must see Joseph; he may be able to influence Pilate.

JAMES : I was surprised to hear what Joseph had done; I never thought he would dare to ask for the body.

MARY MAGDALENE : We knew he was a disciple in secret.

JAMES : Yes, but I'd begun to doubt it; I thought he was afraid because of his position.

MARY MAGDALENE : Well, there's no doubt now. He's a brave man; his action is sure to bring him disfavor.

Slight pause.

JOHN : I don't think I told you, the centurion spoke to me after the—(*checking himself*) afterwards.

JAMES : The centurion? What did he want?

JOHN : When the crowd had gone he marched the soldiers a little distance away and came up to me. He said he was sorry but he had only carried out his orders.

JAMES : (*With contempt*) Orders! I expect the earthquake scared him.

JOHN : I don't think it was that. He was standing very close to the cross when the Master died, and I heard him say something which struck me as rather strange.

MARY MAGDALENE : What was that?

JOHN : (*Quietly*) "Truly this man was the son of God."

JAMES : (*Unconvinced*) They're a superstitious lot, these Romans.

JOHN : He said he would speak to the men and try to get his coat back—he thought we might like to have it.

MARY MAGDALENE : I should like to—(*looking around*) that is, if—

JOHN : It should go to the Mother.

JAMES : If it ever turns up at all.

MARY MAGDALENE : Yes—I didn't think; I'm sorry.

(Slight pause.)

JAMES : It's getting dark now. I hope Andrew's all right.

JOHN : He's well able to take care of himself.

JAMES : I'm not so sure. The Master has been taken, it may be our turn next. Perhaps it would be as well to keep out of the way for a little while.

MARY MAGDALENE : I shan't! If they want me they can take me. I'm not ashamed of being a disciple.

JAMES : Do be reasonable, Mary.

MARY MAGDALENE : Reasonable! What do you mean? Is reason your excuse for cowardice? You weren't afraid when the Master was alive, not even when they threatened Him.

JAMES : It was different then. He had power; when He was near us we felt safe; we never thought they would take Him.

MARY MAGDALENE : And now they have, you want to run away and hide; you want to desert Him.

JAMES : No, I don't; but what can we do by ourselves? What are we?—just ignorant fisher folk, strong in body but as helpless as children.

MARY MAGDALENE : At least we can die bravely, as He did—unashamed.

JOHN : I don't think they'll bother about us. Now the Master is dead they have nothing to fear from us, and they know it.

JAMES : *(Suddenly)* Here's Andrew at last.

They all look up hopefully.

JOHN : Is Peter with him?

JAMES : *(Craning his neck)* I can't see, there are so many people. *(With a note of disappointment in his voice)* No, he's alone.

MARY MAGDALENE : Oh, that means he hasn't found him.

JAMES : We shall soon know; he's just come in.

Slow footsteps can be heard on the stairs and then Andrew enters. They look at him inquiringly. He shakes his head. John buries his head in his hands.

ANDREW : Not a sign of him. I've searched everywhere.

JAMES : Oh, this is intolerable! Deserting us like this just when we need him. Is he the leader or isn't he?

ANDREW : He is a servant of the Master, as we are. Only the Master can help us now, not Peter.

MARY MAGDALENE : What do you mean?

JAMES : You talk like a fool. You know as well as any of us the Master is lying in the tomb. What can He do now?

ANDREW : I don't know; but we believed He was the Messiah.

JOHN : Yes, we believed that.

JAMES : Our prophets said the Messiah would come to deliver His people, but—

ANDREW : (*Pressing his hands to his forehead*) I know, I know. I can't think clearly, but I saw a man in the street tonight who used to be blind—doesn't that mean anything?

JAMES : It might have done, but not now.

ANDREW : I wonder if—(*he stops.*)

JOHN : Yes?

ANDREW : Perhaps we are blind—perhaps— Oh, I don't know what I'm thinking. (*Changing the subject*) I've seen Philip and Thomas.

JAMES : Where?

ANDREW : On the outskirts of the city. I told them where they could find us. They haven't seen Peter since yesterday.

JAMES : (*In exasperation*) Has no one seen him? Has he left the city?

ANDREW : Peter wouldn't do that.

JOHN : Is there any other news?

ANDREW : Judas has hanged himself.

MARY MAGDALENE : (*Rising, horrified*) Oh!

ANDREW : He went to the priests this morning and gave them back their money. He told them he had betrayed the innocent blood.

MARY MAGDALENE : I can't understand Judas—he was so enthusiastic at first—why did he do it?

JAMES : I suppose things turned out differently from what he expected—from what we all expected.

MARY MAGDALENE : I don't understand you.

JAMES : Our prophets said the Messiah would lead us to victory over our enemies. Instead . . . (*He shrugs his shoulders helplessly.*)

MARY MAGDALENE : How can you talk like that? The Master was kind and gentle, He wouldn't hurt anyone, not even a Gentile. You believed in Him when He was alive and now He's dead you want to desert Him. You don't care!

JOHN : We do care, Mary.

MARY MAGDALENE : It can't be all over, I just won't believe it! Andrew's right; what of the lepers who were cleansed, the deaf who can hear, the lame who can walk again? That must mean something; everywhere He was triumphant over pain and ugliness. This can't be the end—it just can't!

JOHN : Yes, everywhere He was triumphant. He saved others but —He couldn't save Himself. Remember how they mocked Him and challenged Him to come down from the cross.

MARY MAGDALENE : (*In anguish*) Oh, why didn't He?

JOHN : (*gently*) Because He couldn't, Mary. He was beaten.

MARY MAGDALENE : (*realizing it*) No, I see now He couldn't; they'd beaten Him. Oh, how horribly cruel. He could save others, but—Himself— (*She buries her face in her hands.*)

ANDREW : Why not lie down for a while and try to sleep? You'll feel better then.

MARY MAGDALENE : (*not hearing*) I can't realize it yet; it just doesn't seem possible we shall never see Him again. If only I'd been there when you kept the Passover, just to have heard Him speak to you; John says He told you many things.

ANDREW : He did, but we only understood a little. Most of it I've forgotten now, so much has happened since.

MARY MAGDALENE : Can't you remember anything?

ANDREW : My mind is so confused, I just can't think now.

JOHN : There's one thing He said which I shall never forget.

MARY MAGDALENE : Oh, do tell me.

JOHN : (*slowly*) "These things I have spoken unto you that in me you might have peace. In the world you shall have tribulation, but be of good cheer, I have overcome the world."

MARY MAGDALENE : There's comfort in those words. I don't know why, but there is.

ANDREW : It was almost as if He was in this very room speaking to us.

JAMES : You're imagining things.

The door opens silently and Peter enters. He closes it behind him and leans against it. His face is ashen; his eyes weary yet tormented.

JOHN : Peter!

JAMES : At last.

Andrew goes to Peter and helps him to a seat. The others look inquiringly at him but he makes no attempt to speak. The silence becomes intolerable.

JAMES : Well?

Peter does not reply.

JOHN : (*gently*) Peter. (*Peter looks at him*) We've been looking for you. Where have you been?

PETER : (*dully*) Everywhere.

JOHN : Everywhere?

PETER : Tramping the streets.

Mary Magdalene comes forward and puts her hand on his shoulder.

MARY MAGDALENE : What is it, Peter?

There is a silence, and then with a kind of sob Peter turns his head and leans against her.

PETER : Mary, He was forgiving, wasn't He?

MARY MAGDALENE : (*quite simply*) Yes.

PETER : Would He—could He—forgive anything?

MARY MAGDALENE : He forgave me.

PETER : Yes, I know, but—

ANDREW : Tell us, Peter.

PETER : I denied Him.

JAMES : (*amazed*) You denied Him?

PETER : (*His head in his hands*) Three times—before the cock crew twice. He warned me.

ANDREW : When was this?

PETER : After He was taken in the Garden. I was frantic—I couldn't let Him go alone—so I followed them to the High Priest's palace. They took Him into the hall and I crept in and sat down among the servants.

JAMES : Go on.

PETER : Then they brought witnesses to prove His blasphemy, but they couldn't agree. After a while the High Priest stood up and asked Him if He was the Christ.

JOHN : (*eagerly*) What did the Master answer to that?

PETER : "I am. Hereafter shall you see the Son of Man sitting on the right hand of God and coming in the clouds of heaven."

MARY MAGDALENE : Oh, what a glorious answer! (*She hides her face suddenly*) I'm so ashamed of myself.

PETER : Then the High Priest said He was condemned out of His own mouth and guilty of death, so they all set upon Him and beat Him and spat in His face—and I sat there and said nothing.

(*There is a pause*)

A little later, a serving woman came up and asked me if I was one of His followers. Everyone began to stare at me and I was afraid and denied it. Then someone else said he was sure he'd seen me in the Garden. I turned on him and told him he was a liar, but at once another joined in and said he knew I was a Galilean by my speech. (*Getting excited*) I couldn't stand any more of it—they were all staring at me and wherever I looked I met angry eyes! I began to curse and swear and denied Him again, then— (*He buries his face in his hands.*)

MARY MAGDALENE : Yes?

PETER : The cock crew. (*After a little while he continues*) As they led the Master away He turned and looked at me. His eyes!—Oh, our Father in heaven! All night long I walked the streets trying to shut out those eyes, but it was no use. I was in the crowd that followed Him to the hill this morning. After they crucified Him I stayed and watched from a distance. I didn't dare come too close lest I should see His eyes again. Later, I came back to the city and went to the Garden. I found the place where He prayed last night—there were two marks in the earth where He knelt.

MARY MAGDALENE : Peter, don't torture yourself any more.

PETER : But I can't help it. What can I do?

ANDREW : Nothing now. We are all to blame; we all forsook Him when He needed us most.

PETER : But I professed so much, and I've failed Him more than any of you! I denied Him!

JAMES : Calm yourself. What are we going to do now? That's the point.

PETER : Do? What can we do? The Master's lying in the tomb; it's all finished now.

ANDREW : We are fishermen; this place is foreign to us. We can go home.

PETER : There can be no home without Him. Everywhere we go He will haunt us. We shall see Him sitting on the hillsides among the spring flowers; when we are fishing He will be with us in the boat; every time we see a field of corn waving in the sunshine, or hear the song of a bird, or look upon the smiling face of a child, we shall remember; we cannot shut Him out, we who knew Him.

JOHN : No, we cannot forget, but we must go on and face the future bravely together—serving one another as He would have us do. (*He looks at Mary the Mother.*)

JAMES : Andrew's right; we must go back to our work.

PETER : I can't go back. We are fishers of men now; he made us so.

JOHN : Well, what are you going to do?

PETER : (*helplessly*) I don't know.

JAMES : There's no other way, we must live. We can begin again, all of us—except Judas.

PETER : Judas? What of him?

JAMES : He's dead. He hanged himself.

PETER : When?

ANDREW : This morning. He went to the priests and gave them back their money, but it was no use.

PETER : Judas dead. He was a traitor; he deserved to die.

ANDREW : The Master would not have said that.

PETER : He was a traitor, he had to die. He took the only way out. (*He pauses, then slowly*) I, too, am a traitor—

ANDREW :   (*quickly*) What do you mean?

PETER :   (*rising*) Nothing. I'm just going out for a little while.

MARY MAGDALENE :   Stop him! Don't let him go!

PETER :   (*turning to her and speaking soothingly, unnaturally*) It's all right, Mary. Everything's all right.

John and James stare at him, not quite grasping the significance of the situation. Peter turns to the door and finds Andrew barring the way.

ANDREW :   You're not going out, Peter.

PETER :   I am; let me pass. (*Andrew does not answer, does not move*) Let me pass, I tell you!

ANDREW :   (*quietly*) No.

PETER :   You've got to; I must go out!

ANDREW :   It's no use, Peter.

PETER :   But I must! Don't you see? I can't go on living now; it's the only way out—I want to die!

ANDREW :   Listen, man; you are Peter, the Rock; the Rock. Do you hear that? That's what He called you. Remember the story of the house built on the rock—the wind and the rain couldn't shake it. You are the Rock; on you He said He would build His Church.

PETER :   Stop it! Stop it!

ANDREW :   Do you remember?

PETER :   Yes, yes! Are you trying to torment me?

ANDREW :   We all feel the same; none of us can see ahead; but we must go on, however hard it is. You want to take the coward's way out, you want to deny Him again.

PETER :   I can't hurt Him any more now. What's the use of going on? What can we do? It's the only way out, I tell you!

ANDREW :   And you are Peter the Strong! You are the fighter, the one who would never desert Him—never—while there was a breath left in your body. You want to crawl away and die, like a sick animal in the undergrowth!

MARY MAGDALENE : Andrew, don't!

PETER : At least I'm not afraid to die! Get out of my way I tell you. Let me pass! (*He falls on Andrew and beats upon his chest with his fists.*)

MARY THE MOTHER : (*speaking for the first time*) Simon Bar-Jona. (*Peter's hands fall to his sides when he hears his old name; he neither turns nor answers, but stands with his head hanging on his breast*) Simon.

PETER : (*almost inaudibly*) Yes?

MARY THE MOTHER : Many years ago, your Master was presented in the Temple. There was a very old man, Simeon was his name. He took the child Jesus in his arms and blessed him, and then spoke to me. He told me that my son was set for the fall and rising again of many in Israel, and that a sword would pierce through my own soul also. I was very young then and I did not understand, but now I know. That sword has fallen on me today. Come here, Simon. (*He goes over to her and kneels at her feet*) We are all passing through the valley of the shadow of death, perhaps we have to go down even deeper yet into the valley. Maybe we shall never come out into the sunlight again. There is no light in our darkness, we only have our memories—those they cannot take away. I know your grief, Simon, it is as mine; I know your remorse, too, but you are forgiven.

PETER : If only I could believe that.

MARY THE MOTHER : You cannot believe me?

PETER : But how can you know?

MARY THE MOTHER : Because He was my son. Look at me. (*Peter raises his head*) You say that as He was led away He turned and looked at you. (*Peter nods*) Why did you want to shut out those eyes? Why couldn't you bear to meet them again?

PETER : Because I was ashamed.

MARY THE MOTHER : Yet it was more than that.

PETER : I don't understand.

MARY THE MOTHER : What did you see in His eyes?

PETER : I don't know.

MARY THE MOTHER : Think.

PETER : (*springing to his feet and pacing to and fro*) I don't want to think. I can't bear it!

MARY THE MOTHER : You must, Simon.

PETER : If only there'd been reproach—blame—disappointment— but there wasn't! It—it was Hell!

MARY THE MOTHER : The hell of being face to face with absolute love.

PETER : (*stopping short*) Face to face with—why yes—that's what it was—absolute love!

MARY THE MOTHER : He forgave you—Peter.

PETER : He forgave me! (*He stands for a moment with a light of realization suffusing his face, then falls on his knees in prayer. The others bow their heads*) Our Father which art in heaven, hallowed be Thy name, Thy kingdom come, Thy will be done, in earth as it is in heaven. Give us this day our daily bread, and forgive us our debts as we forgive—

SLOW CURTAIN

by
Henri Ghéon
adapted in English by
Eric Crozier

CHRISTMAS IN THE MARKET PLACE

Published by agreement with J. Garnet Miller Limited, 13 Tottenham Street, London W. 1, England. Permission for an amateur stage production may be requested from Walter H. Baker Company, 100 Sumner Street, Boston 10, Mass., at a royalty fee of $10.00 for each performance. Acting copies may be obtained from Baker's.

CHARACTERS

A band of strolling players, of gypsy extraction, consisting of:

OLD MELCHIOR, who plays The Reader
The Angel appearing to the
    Shepherds
King Melchior, the Magus
Herod
Old Simeon
A Doctor

OLD COLOMBA, his wife,
who plays The Old Woman who expected
    the Messiah
The Neighbour who didn't
    expect him
Elisabeth
A Roman Lady
A Farmer's Wife
Anna, the Prophetess

JOEY, their son aged 40,
who plays A Jew of the Advent
Joseph
A Doctor

MARIA, their daughter-in-law,
        who plays   Mary
BRUNO, their grandson aged 12,
        who plays   The Angel of the Annunciation
                          and the Visitation
                          A Young Shepherd
                          The Child Jesus

And a whole pack of children, but we see only one, who is JESUS
      in the cradle, in the shape of a doll.
      Lastly, the ASS, but he is only heard braying.

Scene : *The players' camp in a village market-place. A caravan. A
        miserable platform. Two poles for stretching a curtain.
          Down stage, a fire with a pot boiling on it. An acetylene
        lamp on a perch. Stools. A drum, etc.*

PART ONE

THE ADVENT AND THE ANNUNCIATION

I

TIME: Night. There is light from the fire, moon and stars, and perhaps the reflection of a nearby street-lamp. The acetylene lamp is not lit.

(Melchior, Colomba, Joey, Maria and Bruno are sitting round the fire, eating their soup. Some of the villagers are watching them eat, but we do not see them: they are the audience. Silence. Then Joey turns round to them. Ironically.)

JOEY : Funny, isn't it?—Oh, very funny! People eating!—Haven't you ever seen people eating before? Perhaps you don't know what eating is? Next time you have a meal, put the table in front of a mirror! (*He laughs. A pause.*) What a dumb lot! Just look at them! That big chap there with whiskers—and cauliflower ears! And the skinny one with a cold in his nose. There's enough flour on his coat to feed a flock of sparrows! And the little old woman in a black hood—she wobbles her head like a pendulum! And Sweet-and-Twenty with her kiss-curl, giggling into her shawl! We can't move an inch without bringing up a whole crowd of shop-keepers, kids, and women with nothing better to do. We aren't Red Indians. . . . We aren't Eskimos. . . . We're honest gypsies, and we eat just like everybody else. This is how you eat soup. One, fill your spoon. Two, blow on it. Three, slip it down your gullet. One . . . two . . . three. . . . Then you start again. One . . . two . . . three. . . . Three movements, that's all! Have you got it? (*He laughs, and goes on eating.*) Oh, the soup isn't all it might be, you know! Although I wouldn't tell the cook that. It will be better to-morrow, with a nice boiling fowl in the pot. Heaven has sent us a chicken! Did you know that, Dad?

253

MELCHIOR : Joey, if you don't mend your ways, my boy, you will be hung.

JOEY : What, for that? For one runaway chicken? Hung for one giddy fowl, revolting against the laws of the hen-roost? Justice shall be done! Pssshut! (*He mimes wringing a chicken's neck.*) How else could we celebrate Christmas?

COLOMBA : You talk too much, son!

JOEY : Don't worry! The police are busy over a few bottles up at the Brown Bear or the Crown. Besides, the rebel belonged to the next town.—You wouldn't give me away, would you? Eh, Missus? They're too busy watching the show. Just eat a bowl of soup and keep them amused! (*Eating his soup—and the others imitate him.*) One . . . two . . . three! One . . . two . . . three! To finish with, lift the bowl to your mouth. (*Which they do.*) But that's not done in the best circles. (*Getting up.*) And there you are! The show's over. You can go home now. Sleep well! (*He goes to fetch a stool which has been left on the platform. Turning round.*) No, no! We are not playing this evening. There is a dance on at the Brown Bear, so we couldn't have the room. It is no good playing out of doors, you'd catch your death of colds, and so should we. Besides, there are preparations to make for celebrating the Holy Birth. You thought we were heathens, eh? Oh, no! We go to Mass once every year—on Christmas Eve. You will see us there—all five of us.

MELCHIOR : It's sacred.

COLOMBA : It's sacred.

JOEY : The dog and the donkey will look after the kids. Oh yes, and we go to Mass in the summer, too, in honour of Saint Colomba, the patron saint of the Gypsies.

COLOMBA : *My* patron saint, sonny. (*Mumbling a prayer as fast as she can.*) Saint Colomba, our patron saint . . . (*The rest is unintelligible.*)

THE OTHERS : Amen.

JOEY : Are you satisfied? You have seen our family prayers. I wasn't down in the programme. Now we are going to have forty winks before Mass. You had better do the same.—Go on, hop it!—I said, hop it! Can't you understand plain English?

(*Maria has got up, and is collecting the bowls.*)

Go and have a drink . . . warm yourselves up . . . call on your young ladies. What's the good of standing there like lamp-posts?

MARIA : Sing them a song. They'll go away then.

JOEY : That's an easy way of shifting them! But I don't know anything suitable. You can't sing just any old song on Christmas Eve. "The Girl with Three Husbands and a Corporal"? Not respectable enough. "Hootenanny Hoedown"? A bit too lively. "Ten Nights in a Barroom"? Might put ideas into their heads. —Well, what shall we give them, Grandpa?

MELCHIOR : If I had a bit more voice, I should sing them the song of the Three Kings. Perhaps they don't realize that I am descended from one of the Three Kings? I was named after him —that proves it. Melchior! Yes, Melchior! And I received an heirloom—a great book with pictures, in which my ancestor collected everything about the Child Jesus. That is all I read, good people, since I have had time to read. While the others give our donkey a hand to pull the caravan along—he isn't very fat—or weave baskets, or go out on the prowl—you can't stop them: it's in their blood—or while they are entertaining the villagers, I study—all alone. I try to teach myself something about the world, and when they are tired out in the evening, I tell my children what I have learnt. Oh! It's beautiful! Beautiful!

MARIA : Sing them the song, Grandpa.

COLOMBA : Him? He can't do it! There's not a drop of wind in him!

MELCHIOR : (*Trying to sing*) "We-e-ee . . . three kings . . . of Orient . . . are . . ."

COLOMBA : Don't you see, you old fool?—it's impossible.

MELCHIOR : (*Excited*) Then—then—I will explain my book to them—tell them the story—and you shall act it for them.

THE OTHERS : What?—Us? Act it?

MELCHIOR : Don't you remember the year when you acted it in the crypt for our Saint Colomba?—In honour of the Child Jesus! It will be a magnificent gesture, Joey! We owe Him something. He may pardon that chicken.

JOEY : And all the others!

MELCHIOR : Yes, and the others, you bad lad. Suppose you died before Mass, would you like to go down to Hell?—Come on! see what you can remember. Use your imaginations! Make it up! I'll keep you to the story with this. (*His book.*)

MARIA : Oh yes! Do let us do it! I love acting the Virgin Mary.

JOEY : We may as well have a shot . . . (*To the audience.*) Well, what do you think? Is it a good idea? Don't all shout at once! You won't go to sleep standing up? Or get frozen into snow-men? You promise not to laugh at us?—Come on, then! Let's go! On the stage . . . Brr . . . Brr . . . it is cold. (*He beats his arms. To Bruno, who has dropped off to sleep.*) What about you, sonny? Are you asleep? (*He shakes him.*)

BRUNO : What's up?

JOEY : We are giving a show. Put the stools round. Get the costumes, and light the flares.

BRUNO : What are we playing?

JOEY : Whatever we like. In honour of the Child Jesus! (*Thinking better of it. To the public.*) But we don't start until we get enough in the kitty! Open up your pockets . . . undo your purses . . . empty your handbags . . . springclean your wallets. I'll take the collection straightaway!

MELCHIOR : Joey! Joey! You can take the hat round afterwards Let them give what they like. If you do this for money, tha' chicken won't be forgiven. You will have to give it up.

JOEY : Give it up? Oh, no! Not me!—Well, let us begin, goo people! We are doing this for the glory of it!

MELCHIOR : The glory of God, son!

COLOMBA : (*mumbling her prayer*) Saint Colomba, our patron saint . . . (*The rest is lost.*)

MELCHIOR : (*to Joey*) Bang the drum. If we are going to play, everyone should know.

JOEY : What shall I announce?

MELCHIOR : "The Sacred Mysteries of the Childhood of Our Lord." That is the title of the book. (*Drum.*)

JOEY : Silence, good people! A few minutes ago you were only ten. Now you are thirty. You will be a hundred soon. The moon is shining. It's piercing cold. It will freeze hard to-night. But our hearts are warm, good people . . . and yours will soon be warm, too. Heavenly fire will kindle them . . . the flame of love for the Child to be born at midnight. We shall play for you, as clearly as we can, one of the masterpieces of King Melchior the Magus, in a revised version by his great-great-great-great-grandson, who is on my right. (*Melchior salutes.*) "The Sacred Mysteries of the Childhood of Our Lord"! May the splendour of the subject keep you from laughing at its interpreters. We'll begin at once. Just one moment while we light the lamps.

(*Bruno has dragged on an old hamper overflowing with stuffs. He lights the acetylene lamp. Melchior has a chair placed for him under the lamp, and installs himself with his book. Then he signs to the others to go into the wings, and to Bruno to ring the little bell announcing the beginning of the show. Bell. They dress themselves.*)

II

MELCHIOR : (*alone: reading, with a prophet's gestures*) "In those days the people were waiting: for centuries and centuries they had waited. For the prophets had foretold the coming of an all-powerful King, who should save them, lighten their burdens, and dry their tears—and this King should be their God."

THE OTHERS : (*off*) Their God!

MELCHIOR : "Each morning and evening, they scanned the horizon and the sky, lest He should rise through the gates of day on the chariot of dawn, or appearing among the clouds, fly like a bird to earth."

(*Enter Colomba, leaning on Joey. They scan the horizon from left to right, and stare at the sky above them.*)

"But they saw nothing, and they lamented among themselves."

JOEY : What a life! What a cursed life! When will this cursed life end?

COLOMBA : When we go to our graves, my son.

JOEY : I don't mean that. Graves? What's a grave? A grave isn't an end. I mean . . . when will it end without ending? When will the curse of it end? The poor aren't happy . . . the rich aren't happy . . . and the middling sort of people aren't happy either. They all wind up in a grave, with a few shovelfuls of earth on top. The poor man loses his poverty and his dreams of being rich: the wealthy man loses his riches for ever. What good is there in being rich or poor? . . . in starving on the roads, or drowsing life away in an armchair? If there is nothing afterwards . . . nothing *final?* (*Looks at the sky.*) I see nothing. No one comes . . .

COLOMBA : Remember what the Ancients said, my son . . . the Ancients of the people.

JOEY : I remember . . . but you can't fool me with that. I was born a Gypsy, and a Gypsy I'll stay, until my time comes to be just another Gypsy pushing up daisies.

COLOMBA : The Ancients prophesied . . .

JOEY : The Ancients give me a pain. Ancient folk talk drivel, Granny. Like you.

COLOMBA : Thank you, my lad. (*Inspired.*) But the hour draws near! The wolf has howled thrice! . . . the owl has circled thrice! . . . the viper has hissed thrice! . . .

JOEY : Oh, yes, yes, yes! That doesn't cut any ice with me, old girl. Tell it to the porters and the charwomen, and watch them flap their ears. I'm going in for a sleep. (*He moves to go. Softly.*) Still, something must come. Something . . . or some-one. . . .

COLOMBA : (*going out with him*) To-morrow, perhaps?

JOEY : (*laughing*) That's right! To-morrow and to-morrow and to-morrow! Another instalment in our next!

(*They disappear.*)

III

MELCHIOR : (*reading*) "She who waited most patiently was a Virgin called Mary. She watched throughout the day in her garden, and was not weary."

(*Maria enters as Mary. She bends over a bush, smells a flower, looks around her, listens, strains to hear: then, sitting on a bench at the left, takes her work and sews. Enter Colomba, as a neighbour.*)

COLOMBA : Good evening, Mary.

MARY : Good evening, neighbour.

COLOMBA : Whew! It is hot! What are you doing, Mary?

MARY : Nothing. I am just here.

COLOMBA : I can see that for myself.—Any news?

MARY : I haven't heard any.

COLOMBA : How is Joseph?

MARY : Very well. He is working.

COLOMBA : And when will the wedding be?

MARY : Nothing is fixed yet, but it will be soon.

COLOMBA : Does he come to see you often?

MARY : Oh, yes. When he can manage it.

COLOMBA : You must be impatient!

MARY : I am—and I'm not. I am learning to be patient. I am just here.

COLOMBA : I'm just here, I'm just here! But I can see that! What a queer girl you are!

MARY : We must stay where God sets us. God set me here, and here I stay.

COLOMBA : Yes, we know you're there!—Did you know that Jehu, the saddlemaker's son, had left the district?

MARY : No, I didn't know.

COLOMBA : Or that old Crœsus had disinherited his sons?

MARY : He must have had reasons for it.

COLOMBA : Oh no, he did not! Not a reason in the world!

MARY : I am not in touch with things . . .

COLOMBA : And Methuselah . . .

MARY : Who is he?

COLOMBA : Don't you know Methuselah? They say he is going to marry again. At his age! And guess who! Deborah!

MARY : Oh?

COLOMBA : It's all the same to you.

MARY : I don't know either of them.

COLOMBA : (*breaking off*) Good night, Mary, my dear. It is no good talking to you. Nothing interests you.

MARY : Yes, it does. Everything interests me more or less. But, above all—

COLOMBA : What?

MARY : I cannot say. No, I must not say. You would laugh at it. I am waiting.

COLOMBA : Waiting? What for?

MARY : The world has awaited Him for centuries . . .

COLOMBA : Ah! The Messiah!

MARY : Please do not laugh, Colomba. You have not heard anything, have you?

COLOMBA : Of the Messiah? (*She laughs.*) No. Not a thing. You will have to wait a long time for Him. We shan't see Him.

MARY : Don't you believe He will come?

COLOMBA : Of course I do—but it doesn't worry me, because *I* can't do anything about it. Good night, Mary.

MARY : Good night, neighbour.

COLOMBA : (*going out*) The Messiah! The Messiah!

(*She goes out.*)

IV

MELCHIOR : It was then that the Angel arrived.

(*The Angel, who is Bruno, approaches downstage, carrying a basket of flowers, in which a dove is supposed to be sleeping.*)

ANGEL : (*to himself and to the public*) Yes, this is it! I nearly went in the wrong door. I am a little absent-minded—it's emotion. (*Stopping.*) Oh! My heart is beating like a bird you hold in your hand—like the dove in my basket. . . . (*He strokes the dove.*) Sweet! Sweet! She's sleeping among the flowers . . . (*A pause.*) It is the first time the Heavenly Father has given me a job of this sort. Carry to a young girl—to a completely pure young girl, the purest of all—she was created for this—the news that she will be a mother—that she will bear a little boy. Without marriage. Without a lover. And this tiny creature will be God. No more, no less—God! But flesh and blood, like a little man. What a mystery! What a mystery! Although I'm an angel—and one of the more intelligent angels—oh! I am not boasting about it—God made me an angel, an archangel, a super-angel!—Well, all the same, I can't understand it. The Heavenly Father is cleverer than I am. It is His business.

(*A pause. He takes a step to mount the platform.*)

She does not move. She does not realize. She is listening to that fat blackbird singing among the leaves. He sways the branch, shaking the tiny stars of jasmine. The jasmine smells sweet. See how she breathes the scent, scarcely widening her nostrils. (*A pause.*) There she is: waiting. The world is so lovely to her that she waits for its salvation. He who made it lovely shall save it. But how can she dream that she could help Him in the saving? She thinks herself insignificant among created things. What use would she be to Him? God does not need men: it is men who need God. (*He mounts the platform.*) Shall I warn her, or take her by surprise? I might cough or sing . . . (*He coughs gently.*) Hum! . . . Hum! Hum! . . . No, she does not hear. I will stand under the jasmine, play my flute, and wait till she sees me.

(*He moves to stand opposite Mary and plays several notes: "Ave, ave, ave Maria." A pause.*)

MARY : What a lovely song! Oh! the perfume! The light! (*She sees the Angel.*) Ah! someone is there! (*She rises.*)

ANGEL : Hail, Mary, full of grace . . .

MARY : (*aside*) How did he get in? Who is he?

ANGEL : The Lord is with thee.

MARY : (*softly*) With me?

ANGEL : Blessed art thou among women. (*He comes nearer and salutes again.*)

MARY : He is beautiful! And he greets me! He is not made of flesh —that is impossible. (*A pause.*) Am I dreaming?—No, I am not dreaming. He comes near. (*She recoils a little.*) Why does he salute me? I am ashamed. (*A pause.*) I am frightened.

ANGEL : Fear not, Mary . . . (*moved*) for . . . for . . . thou hast found favour . . . with God. (*Aside.*) This is the moment to tell her—— Courage! I dare not! Little dove, help me. (*Aloud.*) Behold, thou shalt conceive in thy womb—and bring forth a child, Mary—a son—and shalt call His name Jesus. He shall be great, and shall be called the Son of the Highest: and the Lord God shall give unto Him the throne of His father

David: and He shall reign over the house of Jacob for ever—
and of His kingdom there shall be no end.

MARY : (*softly*) There shall be no end. (*Aloud.*) I do not understand—I am amazed—and do not understand. May I sit down?
—I am trembling. But is it for fear or happiness? (*softly.*) The
Messiah . . . the Messiah . . . in me? (*A pause.*) How shall
this be—seeing I know not a man?

ANGEL : (*taking the imaginary dove in his hand*) The Holy Ghost
shall come upon thee, and the power of the Highest shall over-
shadow thee: (*he raises the dove above Mary*) therefore also
that Holy Thing which shall be born of thee shall be called the
Son of God. And, behold, thy cousin Elisabeth, she hath also
conceived a son in her old age: and this is the sixth month with
her, who was called barren. For with God nothing shall be
impossible.

(*A pause. Mary slowly bows down.*)

What reply shall I give Him, Mary?

MARY : (*prostrating herself*) Behold the handmaid of the Lord.
Be it unto me according to thy word.

ANGEL : (*releasing the dove*) See! The dove has flown! To God!
. . . The Lord is with you, Mary. I leave you my basket of
flowers.

(*He puts down the basket in front of her, and goes out gently.
A pause. Mary lifts her head.*)

V

MARY : He has gone. But I am not alone . . . I shall never be
alone again, O God. For I carry in my womb the predestined,
the elect, the King—Christ, the ransom of earthly sin. (*Seeing
the basket.*) He has left his flowers. (*Taking, and looking at
them.*) They smell of Paradise. White roses . . . white roses
. . . so many white roses. Ah! One red rose—red as blood!
(*She pricks herself.*) Ah! it pricks . . . I pricked my finger—
and my blood stains the flower. The white ones are lovely. But
I prefer the red . . . although it pricked me.

(*She holds it in her hand, rises, carrying the basket in the other hand, and goes out smelling it.*)

A child—from God. A child—from God.

MELCHIOR : Pray! Go on, all of you, pray! (*Beginning.*) Hail, Mary, full of grace . . .

THE OTHERS : (*around her: continuing*) The Lord is with thee. Blessed art thou among women, and blessed is the fruit of thy womb, Jesus.

COLOMBA : (*as before*) Saint Colomba, our patron saint . . . (*The rest is lost.*)

THE OTHERS : Amen!

JOEY : (*to the public*) Hooray! Hooray! Hooray! Well, why don't you clap? That's right! Louder! It will warm you up.—They did it well, didn't they? Did you hear me prompt anyone? Oh, very little—hardly at all. The Holy Ghost prompted most of the time.—And now we are having an interval. Popcorn, peanuts, soft drinks. The stand is open! If you can't find it, take a sharp run three times round the market-place to wish us luck. Brr. . . . Brr . . . Curtain! Cheerio for the present!

CURTAIN

PART TWO

THE VISITATION AND THE NATIVITY

I

SCENE: The same place. Colomba and Bruno are changing. Maria is resting. Melchior moves back to his place. Joey darts towards the public.

JOEY : We are beginning! Take your places, everybody! That's a good idea—you have fetched some chairs. Hi! . . . you in the corner . . . yes, you, sir! I know you don't mean to interrupt us when we are playing, but that graveyard cough of yours is very distracting, you know. Try shoving a handkerchief in your mouth, will you? What's that? You haven't got a handkerchief? . . . Oh! you *have* got one! Fine! You don't mind my mentioning it, do you?—Not at all, thank you! We must keep our dignity, mustn't we! I certainly must. I am playing Joseph this time—a very dignified man. (*To the players.*) Ready? On the stage! Off we go. . . .

(*Joey retires to the back. Bell. Melchior opens his book.*)

MELCHIOR : "And the Angel appeared also in a dream to Joseph, saying: 'Joseph, fear not to take unto thee Mary thy wife: for that which is conceived in her is of the Holy Ghost. And thou shalt be his adopted father—the adopted father of the Messiah. Let this content thee, for it is a splendid title and a great honour."

Soon after this, Joseph took Mary to visit her cousin Elisabeth, who had conceived in her old age and whose child should be John the Prophet, that should baptize with water.

II

(*Heavy and tired, Colomba, as Elisabeth, mounts the platform, and goes to sit at the left.*)

ELISABETH : I am old to bear a child. You realize that, Lord? . . . But I wanted it—I begged for it, and so did Zacharias. We were taken at our word. How strange! (*A pause. She sits.*) I shan't have any milk, I know. Zacharias will have to buy a cow or a goat. A goat would be better. Cow's milk upsets babies. (*A pause.*) Ah! the little chap leaves me in peace . . . until he quickens! He doesn't keep me awake at nights. But will he live? Will he be born alive? He will be the child of an old couple. I wonder sometimes . . . it's wrong to worry . . . but it is strange that this should happen to me. And I'm not the only one with worries! There is my cousin, Mary. There have been rumours—rumours. What can have happened to her?

(*She takes her head in her hands. The Angel arrives, and stands behind her.*)

III

(*Mary and Joseph come on from the right.*)

MARY : Here we are! This is the house.

JOSEPH : You need a good rest.

MARY : I am not tired, Joseph. You would think I was not carrying Him—that He was carrying me. I feel light—like a bird. (*Seeing Elisabeth.*) Ah! Elisabeth! (*She goes nearer and greets her.*) Good-day, Cousin. I came with Joseph. We did not warn you—we wanted to give you a surprise. Ah! such a surprise!—Are you well?

ELISABETH : (*rising: transported*) Mary!—it is you, Mary! No—no, I will come to you. Do not come to me!

MARY : Why not, Cousin?

ELISABETH : Because—because, Mary—blessed art thou—among women—and blessed is the fruit of thy womb.

ANGEL : Blessed, blessed, blessed!

MARY : Who told you, Elisabeth?

ANGEL : (*aside*) I did.

ELISABETH : Ah! Whence is this to me, that the mother of my Lord should come to me?

MARY : Receive her quite simply. She is your cousin and friend. How did you know?

ELISABETH : When you greeted me—at that moment, at that instant—the babe leaped in my womb for joy. I, who was barren, feel the living joy! My mother spoke often of that first stirring that tells a woman: "I am in you. You are not alone. You carry another life in yours." But my babe's joyful cry was a greeting, too. "I greet my Lord! My Lord visits me!" Blessed is she that believed, for those things which were told her from the Lord shall be performed.

(*She has bowed down before Mary, who raises her up and takes her in her arms. Joseph falls on his knees.*)

MELCHIOR : (*moved*) Beautiful! Beautiful! (*He wipes aways a tear.*) "Then Mary, in reply, sang, inspired by the Holy Ghost."

(*Mary straightens herself, lifts her eyes to heaven, and recites, between Elisabeth, who bows, and Joseph, kneeling. Bruno, as the Angel, might play softly on the accordion.*)

MARY : My soul doth magnify the Lord,
And my spirit hath rejoiced in God my Saviour.
For he hath regarded the low estate of his handmaiden:
For, behold, from henceforth all generations shall call me blessed.
For he that is mighty hath done to me great things:
And holy is his name.
And his mercy is on them that fear him
From generation to generation.
He hath showed strength with his arm;
He hath scattered the proud in the imagination of their hearts.
He hath put down the mighty from their seats,
And exalted them of low degree.
He hath filled the hungry with good things;
And the rich he hath sent empty away.
He hath holpen his servant Israel,
In remembrance of his mercy;
As he spoke to our fathers,
To Abraham, and to his seed for ever.

MELCHIOR : (*lyrically*) Glory to the Father, and to the Son, and to the Holy Ghost: as it was in the beginning, is now and ever shall be, world without end, Amen.

COLOMBA : (*as Elisabeth: as before*) Saint Colomba, our patron saint . . . (*The rest is lost.*)

(*Elisabeth and Joseph rise. The Angel retires.*)

MARY : I feel better. I was bursting with joy, Cousin: it would have stifled me if I had not sung. (*Embracing her again.*) My son greets your son. (*Simply.*) What shall your son be, Cousin?

ELISABETH : A roadmaker, I hope.

JOSEPH : A roadmaker?

MARY : I understand, my dear. He will build the road that our son shall follow.

ELISABETH : You must rest now. Come!—I will show you your room. The best room, with curtains.

MARY : Oh, Cousin!

ELISABETH : For the King of Heaven! (*Leading her off.*) I hope you will stay for a while. We will work together at our babies' linen. (*She goes out with Mary.*) Coming, Joseph?

JOSEPH : I am coming. (*But he stays where he is. A pause.*) Lord, I am just a poor man. You have shown me that, I might say, in everything about me. Oh! I am not complaining! You say "Go!" and I go. I go—I stay—I don't try to understand. I know now that You are with me. You hold me by the hand . . . *in* Your hand. Don't be afraid—I obey You. I shall guard Your son, take care of Him, and bring Him up well. He will be a credit to You.

MARY : (*off*) Joseph!

JOSEPH : Coming, Mary! I'm coming. (*He goes out after them.*)

IV

MARIA : (*in the wings*) Quick, Bruno—hurry up! Put your shepherd's things on! Give me your wings. Here is your sheepskin. (*To Colomba.*) You must be quick, too, Granny!

COLOMBA : It's no good fussing me. I am being as quick as I can.

(*She is changing into the clothes of a fine lady, and goes on mumbling as she does so.*)

MELCHIOR : (*to shut her up*) Hum! Hum! Hum! Hum! (*Reading.*) "Mary abode three months with her cousin, but John the Baptist was born when she had departed. Now, at this time there went out a decree that all the world should be taxed. And all went to be taxed, everyone into his own city. And Joseph went up from Galilee, unto the city of David, which is called Bethlehem (because he was of the house and lineage of David): to be taxed with Mary his wife, who was great with child, and it was near the time that she should be delivered."

(*Bruno comes on the stage, as a shepherd. He moves up and down, pretending to cross a busy crowd with his equally imaginary flock of sheep.*)

V

SHEPHERD : Goodness, what a crowd! I've never seen anything like it! Talk about a squash! Thousands and thousands and thousands of human beings!—Sheep! Sheep! Sheep!

JOEY : ⎫ (*imitating the bleating of sheep, in the wings*) Baa! . . .
MARIA : ⎭ Baa! . . . Baa!

SHEPHERD : Don't get excited . . .

JOEY : ⎫
⎬ Baa! . . . Baa! . . .
MARIA : ⎭

SHEPHERD : These people won't eat you! Anyway, not yet. Though it would be funny if someone out of all that crowd wasn't to have one of your cutlets, or a slice off the leg.

JOEY : ⎫
⎬ Baa! . . . Baa! . . . Baa! . . . Baa! . . .
MARIA : ⎭

SHEPHERD : We must get across. There's nothing else for it. We simply must get across. Don't you recognize the great square of Bethlehem? Nor do I. But the fold is at the other end of the town, so either you cross the square, or you'll have to sleep out. You'd rather sleep out? I wouldn't! It is going to freeze. The stars are twinkling already.

JOEY : ⎫
⎬ Baa! . . . Baa! . . . Baa! . . .
MARIA : ⎭

SHEPHERD : Sorry, mister!—Excuse me, madam! . . . Keep to the right! Keep to the right, or you will be trodden on!

JOEY :

MARIA : } (*frightened*) Baa! . . . Baa! . . . Baa! . . .

SHEPHERD : Yes, they are my sheep! Well, what can I do? I'm taking them home.—Sheep! Sheep! Sheep!

(*At this moment, Colomba, dressed as an elderly Roman lady, in a glorious hat, with umbrella and gloves, emerges from the right, opposite the young Shepherd.*)

VI

LADY : Oh! This is the last straw! Sheep! . . . A chariot threatens from the right . . . a cab runs me down on the left . . . a horseman splashes me all over with mud . . . a camel spits in my face! Here, a cabbage-seller drives by on his donkey and kicks me in the stomach. There, a porter hooks the feathers in my hat on his basket. And now this guttersnipe attacks me with his smelly sheep!

SHEPHERD : But, lady! . . .

JOEY :

MARIA : } Baaaa! . . . Baaaa! . . .

LADY : Don't talk to me. Let me pass! Wretched slumchild! Take those sheep out of my way instantly!

SHEPHERD : But, lady! . . .

LADY : "Lady?" I'll give you "lady!" Take them away! Don't drive them nearer, do you hear?

JOEY :

MARIA : } Baa! . . . Baa! . . . Baa! . . .

LADY : Oh! The noise! . . . And the stench! Their wool isn't even clean. You should bathe them more often.—Oh! Look! Look! There is one in front! Another one behind me! . . . They are surrounding me! . . . Help! I am a prisoner! Marooned in a flock of sheep!

JOEY :
MARIA : } Baa! . . . Baa! . . . Baa! . . . Baa! . . .

SHEPHERD : I can't help it, ma'am. There is such a crowd! . . .

LADY : You have no right to bring sheep into a crowd.

JOEY :
MARIA : } Baa! . . . Baa! . . . Baa! . . .

LADY : Keep them quiet, for Heaven's sake! (*Raising her umbrella.*) I shall strike!

SHEPHERD : It's no good. We are stuck.

LADY : I shall complain to the police. Rome will hear of this, young man. I have a brother in the State Department. And if the Secretary! . . . I mean, Cæsar Augustus . . .

JOEY :
MARIA : } Baa! . . . Baaa! . . . Baa! . . . Baa! . . .

LADY : It is intolerable! Intolerable!

SHEPHERD : There is no way out, ma'am. We shall have to wait.

LADY : Police! Police!

SHEPHERD : It is a complete traffic jam.

LADY : I shall not forget Bethlehem! What a hole! . . . Disgusting roads! . . . It took me the entire morning to find a decent room in a hotel! And that has no bathroom. There is only one—reserved for Civil Servants, of course.—How shall I get rid of this smell? It is all over me. I am soaked in it! I shall smell of sheep for the rest of my life!

SHEPHERD : Ha! Ha! Ha! Ha!

LADY : Are you laughing at me, brat?

SHEPHERD : Well, I'm not crying! You should think yourself lucky to get a room.

LADY : Lucky! Lucky! I should think myself lucky! Have you any idea whom you are speaking to?

SHEPHERD : No, I haven't: but I should like to know.

JOEY :
           } Baa! . . . Baa! . . . Baa! . . . Baa! . . .
MARIA :

LADY : There they go again! Stampeding about! (*Suddenly.*) Oh! There's a ram under my skirt!

SHEPHERD : No . . . it's only a lamb! Hi! Come out! Come out! Don't worry—I have got him.

LADY : Aaahh! This census! What a business! I wanted to send my maid to represent me, but they would not allow it. The days of government are past. This—is anarchy!

SHEPHERD : Don't worry, lady. The road opens out a bit farther down.

LADY : That does not help me. It is packed here—just where my hotel is. I shall miss dinner—and I know I have caught a cold on my chest!

VII

(*At this moment, Joseph, who has advanced slowly from the right, supporting Mary, stops near the young Shepherd.*)

JOSEPH : Excuse me, sonny.

SHEPHERD : Yes, sir?

JOSEPH : Do you happen to know an inn—a small inn—where we could stay the night?

SHEPHERD : There is this lady's hotel, but that is a big place, I think. Still—if she put in a word for you . . .

LADY : It is full, my boy, but even if it were entirely empty, it would not take them. My hotel does not cater for workmen.

JOSEPH : Yes, I am a workman. A carpenter, ma'am. I do fairly well at it. But journeys are expensive, and I have to watch the pennies.

LADY : My hotel is excessively dear.

JOSEPH : Then it is no good talking about it. But this is a special case. He that shall come . . .

LADY : He that shall come? . . . Oh! I see. Your wife is expecting.

JOSEPH : Yes, ma'am, any time now. She doesn't feel well. But if we are lucky enough . . .

LADY : Lucky? Well, that may be one point of view. I have no children. I should not want one, not for an empire . . .

JOSEPH : Maybe you are wrong. It is well worth one child—for the empire of the world.

LADY : What *are* you talking about?

JOSEPH : Yes . . . He that shall come. . . . You would not understand.

LADY : Too stupid, I suppose?

JOSEPH : I didn't say that. But God works in a mysterious way . . .

LADY : God? . . . Oh, I don't believe in God! . . . Anyway, which God do you mean? You are Jews, are you not?

JOSEPH : Yes, we are Jews.

LADY : I can't bear Jews.

JOSEPH : Lots of people feel like that. They have their faults, I know. . . . Yet God chose them.

LADY : Really! What rubbish!—The prophets were all killed off. I shouldn't advise you to take to prophesying, or they may kill you . . . and this child you are expecting, if He resembles you.

JOSEPH : Heaven protect Him, sweet child! Shepherd, you live in these parts. Do you know any little inns? The Child must be born somewhere, and His poor mother must find a bed . . .

SHEPHERD : There are no beds to be had. They have put up notices saying all the inns are full. One of the townsfolk might squeeze you in, but most of them have friends or relatives staying.

MARY : Joseph! I cannot stand!

JOSEPH : Lean on me! Lean on me, Mary! Where can we go? Lord, where can we go?

SHEPHERD : Come along with me, and we will look together. It is all right now. The traffic is moving again.

LADY : About time, too! Drive on your flock, and let me go.

SHEPHERD : Good-bye, lady. The road is empty now. It only needed a bit of patience.

LADY : Patience! I have no patience! A lady of my rank does not need patience!

JOSEPH :
MARY : } Good night, madam.

LADY : Good night.

SHEPHERD : (*coming back*) Wouldn't you let her have your bed, if they cannot find anything? You could make yourself comfortable in an armchair for one night.

LADY : My bed! . . . My bed! . . . Oh! I shall remember Bethlehem! (*She goes out.*)

SHEPHERD : (*followed by Joseph and Mary*) Sheep! . . . Sheep! . . . Sheep! . . .

(*They go out.*)

MELCHIOR : The whole world will remember Bethlehem! She spoke truer than she knew.—Isn't it so? The world remembers it still. (*Reading.*) "But the little shepherd found no lodging for them, nor for himself,—not even in his sheepfold, which had been taken by a nomad tribe, who stayed there for lack of other shelter. They ate, drank, swore and told stories: and Joseph and Mary went on their way, while the young shepherd, leaving them regretfully, lay down in a field with his flock." (*Again we hear* "Baaa! . . . Baaa! . . ." *off stage, and the young Shepherd comes on again with his flock.*)

VIII

SHEPHERD : Come on, lie down! Here. Don't be afraid of huddling up to me. You will keep me warm. (*Half lying down.*) What an awful situation! Perhaps they have found a stable—or a cave in the rocks. The country people here have hearts like flint. (*A pause.*) If only the baby is not born to-night, they will be able to find something in the morning. It is easier by daylight. (*Looking up at the sky.*) What a wonderful sky! It will freeze hard to-night . . . (*To his sheep.*) Huddle together! Keep close! They are worse off than we are, poor folk. . . . (*He stretches out, begins falling off to sleep, and drowsily murmurs the mysterious words of Joseph.*) He that shall come! . . . He that shall come! . . .

MELCHIOR : (*rising*) He that shall come, little shepherd, shall be poor and strong, reviled and glorified. He shall bear our burdens and give joy. Holy! Holy! Holy! His hour is come. His kingdom is at hand. He is freeing His hands and feet. Rejoice, and be exceeding glad! Midnight strikes! The Child is born!

THE OTHERS : (*off*) The Child is born!

MELCHIOR : Glory to God in the highest, And on earth, peace, goodwill toward men!

THE OTHERS : (*off*) Peace, goodwill toward men!

MELCHIOR : "At the last stroke of midnight, the angel of the Lord came upon the shepherds, abiding in the field, keeping watch over their flocks by night: and these shepherds had never failed in their hope of His coming." (*He advances majestically towards the sleeping Shepherd.*) "And he cried, 'Awake!' "

THE OTHERS : (*off*) Awake!

(*The Shepherd gets up and looks about him.*)

MELCHIOR : "Fear not, for behold, I bring you good tidings of great joy, which shall be to all people. For unto you is born this day, in the city of David a Saviour."

THE OTHERS : (*off*) A Saviour!

MELCHIOR : "Which is Christ the Lord."

SHEPHERD : The Messiah is born?

THE OTHERS : (*off*) The Messiah is born!

MELCHIOR : "And this shall be a sign unto you: you shall find
the babe wrapped in swaddling clothes, lying in a manger."

SHEPHERD : And that will be Him?

THE OTHERS : (*off*) The Lord Jesus!

MELCHIOR : And suddenly there was with the angel a multitude
of the Heavenly host praising God, and saying,

> "Glory to God in the highest,
> And on earth, peace, goodwill toward men."

SHEPHERD : Peace, goodwill toward men . . . !

(*He rises, stretches out his arms, then prostrates himself. Melchior goes back to his place. A pause. The Shepherd stands again.*)

I did not dream it? They have gone . . . (*To the sheep.*)
Sleep! . . . Sleep! The Angel will watch over you. I must go! I
must run! He that shall come, He that shall be born—it is He!
It is He!!

(*Then, after he has run off, the others sing:*)

CAROL:

> Sweet baby, sleep! What ails my dear?
>   What ails my darling thus to cry?
> Be still, my child, and lend thine ear
>   To hear me sing thy lullaby.
> My pretty lamb, forbear to weep.
> Be still, my dear: sweet baby, sleep.

(*A musical setting can be found in The Oxford Book of Carols.*)

IX

MELCHIOR : Is the stable ready?—Can we go on?

VOICES : No!—No! Wait a moment! . . . I'm not ready!—Yes! —No! (*Confused noise.*)

MELCHIOR : What is the matter?

MARIA : Horatio doesn't want to be Jesus.

MELCHIOR : Then take Edward.

MARIA : He has been playing with the tin of boot-polish, and it's all over his face!

MELCHIOR : We will have the baby, then . . .

MARIA : He is asleep.

MELCHIOR : All the better . . .

MARIA : He is sure to cry if he wakes up.

MELCHIOR : Never mind. Don't you think Jesus ever cried as a baby? It will be more realistic.— (*To the public.*) Excuse me, ladies and gentlemen. You can't always do what you like with children. (*To the others.*) Ready now?

BRUNO : No, not yet! The donkey is holding us up—

MELCHIOR : Give him some hay.

COLOMBA : We have run out of hay.

MELCHIOR : Well, let him be. We'll make do without a donkey. We haven't got an ox, anyway. (*To the public.*) Excuse us, ladies and gentlemen—

DONKEY : Hi—han! Hi—han!

MELCHIOR : You will have to be satisfied with his voice.

DONKEY : Hi—han! Hi—han!!!

MELCHIOR : Don't overdo it! That's enough for now. (*The Donkey stops.*) I am beginning!

THE OTHERS : All right, Grandpa. Off you go! (*Bell.*)

MELCHIOR : "Now the young shepherd, having met with the others, soon found himself near a cave in which he saw a candle burning."

X

(The young Shepherd comes on, beckoning to the others—we do not see them—to follow him quietly.)

SHEPHERD : They may be in here. Don't make a noise. Prepare to see a sight that has never been seen before!

DONKEY : Hi—han! Hi—han!

SHEPHERD : That's a donkey: this is it. Why? I don't know. Because he is a friendly beast—obstinate, but friendly—and not at all proud. Quite different from that lady! Oh! if you could have seen her!—I haven't time to tell you about it now. Anyway—right or wrong, I see the Child Jesus with a donkey. It will look well in pictures.

DONKEY : Hi—han!

SHEPHERD : I am sure this is it.

(He goes near, and raises the curtain hiding the platform.)

JOSEPH : (*putting his head out*) Who is that?

SHEPHERD : (*not daring to look at him*) Excuse us, sir. We are three shepherds.

JOSEPH : Why have you come?

SHEPHERD : To worship the Child.

JOSEPH : To worship the Child!

SHEPHERD : (*recognizing him*) Why, it is you! The man who couldn't find a room. Fancy meeting you again!

JOSEPH : (*opening the curtain*) Enter and worship. He is here.

(He retires and takes his place kneeling beside the manger, in which the Child is lying: at the other side Mary kneels too.)

SHEPHERD : Oh!—Oh!—Lord! Lord! (*He kneels.*) I have never seen such a fine baby—and I have had four baby brothers. They don't always look nice when they are newborn,—but He! (*To the other shepherds.*) Look! Come nearer. How gentle He looks. He is our King.

MARY : He is your brother.

SHEPHERD : Are you the Mother of our little King?

MARY : Your Mother, too.

SHEPHERD : You are almost as lovely as He.—No one would believe you had just borne him. You look like a virgin—a dove—a lily.

JOSEPH : She is called Mary.

SHEPHERD : Mary? (*To the others.*) Do you hear? Mary!—Mary! It is a name created specially.

JOSEPH : Of course. Our Heavenly Father looked after every detail.

SHEPHERD : (*rising*) Wait!—We must bring gifts to the Child. I will go and get some figs, butter and cheese. He won't eat them, of course, but they will be a gift, and His father and mother will eat them. And He can play with my flute, if I can find it.—Here it is!

MARY : Play Him a tune.

SHEPHERD : If only my mistress were here! She has hoped for so long, she would dance for joy!

MARY : There is nothing against it. Go and fetch your mistress.

SHEPHERD : I will! You others wait for me here. I will play my flute, and she will dance. (*He goes off singing, and his voice dies away.*)

XI

MELCHIOR : Now, at this time, Melchior the Magus—my great-great-great-great-grandfather, ladies and gentlemen—was visiting his two colleagues, Balthasar and Gaspar, for a congress in astronomy. One evening, resting on the terrace, chatting together, they perceived a star many times larger than the others, but which was not marked anywhere on their maps of the sky. It seemed as if the star beckoned them.

(*He leaves his place, and walks up and down, looking at the sky.*)

It is not possible!—Quite impossible! You are on the wrong track, Melchior, old man.—It is there.—Of course, it is there! As clear as a cluster of diamonds.—Compared with that, the others look like paste.—Then my colleagues are on the wrong track, too. Three wise men all raving at once—and in complete agreement as they rave! A unique case! Entirely unique! (*Reading.*) "Then, as the star moved, they decided to follow, and soon they found that it was leading them to Bethlehem in Judah, where, in fulfilment of the prophets, the King of the Jews was born. And they sought Him with naked feet, their crowns on their heads, bearing precious gifts. And to their little King, they offered the gifts of gold and frankincense and myrrh." (*To himself.*) Come along, old Melchior, you must start! Don't spare your old legs! You must go to worship the Child. You have found a King greater than yourself.

(*He walks slowly, discovers the cave, and prostrates himself.*)

In the name of my ancestor, and in his remembrance, I, Melchior, Ancient of Ancients among the Gypsy folk, give you all I have—although it is little enough. Gold of my faith, frankincense of my hope, and myrrh of my charity. Will You have them, precious babe? (*More softly.*) You will forgive Joey, won't You, dear Jesus?

MARY : Get up, Grandpa, or you will get a cramp in your back.

MELCHIOR : Oooooh!—He will heal me. He came to heal.

XII

(*At this moment, the young Shepherd reappears, dragging his mistress, Colomba, by the hand.*)

SHEPHERD : (*putting down his presents*) Here you are! Figs, butter and a little cheese. I brought a cabbage for the donkey, too. He likes cabbage. (*To Colomba.*) Look, mistress! Do you see Him?

COLOMBA : (*as a Farmer's wife*) Sweet Jesus! In flesh and blood! (*She kneels and mumbles.*) Saint Colomba, our patron saint

SHEPHERD : You said you would dance the day He was born. Dance now! You, too! (*To the public.*) And all of you! It will warm you up.

MELCHIOR : (*lyrically*) Come, dance, dance! In honour of Jesus! The stars dance! The hills dance! King David, harp in hand, sends his golden crown spinning round the ark of alliance! Noah dances on the flood! Moses dances on the Nile! And Gypsy folk seize tambourines, and slap the taut skin!

(*He takes a tambourine.*)

DONKEY : Hi—han! Hi—han!

SHEPHERD : The donkey approves, old man!

MELCHIOR : She's Balaam's Ass! She will dance, too!

SHEPHERD :⎱
COLOMBA :⎰ Come on! Dance! Dance!

MELCHIOR : There is just one person who won't dance—who won't have the least desire to dance—for all that he is so active!

COLOMBA : Beelzebub!—Don't talk of him, Grandpa! (*Crosses herself.*)

MELCHIOR : In honour of the Child Jesus!

MARY : (*sitting*) They are looking at You. See—He has opened His eyes. (*She takes the child on her knees.*)

(*A gypsy dance. Melchior claps his hands: the young Shepherd moves about playing his flute. Colomba dances opposite him, with feet twirling, curtsies, and finger-snappings. And all scan the dance with one cry, which is echoed by the spectators:*)

EVERYBODY : Noel! Noel! Noel!

(*CURTAIN.*)

PART THREE

THE PRESENTATION AND THE RECOVERY

I

(*Bell.*)

JOEY : (*to the public*) Sssh! Sssh! Sssh! We're starting. Silence in court! . . . Go ahead, Melchior!

(*On the platform, Melchior stands praying, representing Simeon. Colomba crouches, old and shrunken, as the prophetess Anna.*)

Half a moment. They won't understand. (*To the public.*) This old man is Simeon. And here is the prophetess Anna. We are in the temple of Jerusalem, one of the seven wonders of the world. What do you think of those columns? Solid marble . . . with gold cornices. They don't build like that nowadays. Look at those lamps! And the ceiling!—Following the Jewish custom, the parents of Jesus will present their child and dedicate Him to the Lord. They will offer a pair of doves as the sacrifice. Go on, Melchior!

SIMEON : (*interrupting his prayer*) Well?

ANNA : Well?

SIMEON : I am listening.

ANNA : I have nothing to say.

SIMEON : You will not prophesy to-day?

ANNA : I am worn-out. See how thin I am getting. I shall soon be eighty-five.

SIMEON : A great age. I am not far behind. In the days of the Patriarchs, this was the springtime of life. They would marry again at a hundred and fifty. (*A pause.*) You fast too much.

ANNA : I wish I could fast more. Fasting preserves the body.— I shall die before you.

SIMEON : Perhaps. I am not ready for death. I have lived my life, but I shall not die until I have seen the Lord's Christ.

ANNA : I would see Him too, but I shall not have such fortune.

SIMEON : God promised it.

ANNA : Not to me. God has revealed many things to me, but not that.

SIMEON : Hope!

ANNA : I do hope, Simeon.

SIMEON : They mock us for our life of hope. I grieve for those who have no hope, but go on living. Why do they live? For what?

ANNA : Hear them laughing, down there.

SIMEON : They think they are fine fellows. He laughs best who laughs last, my lads! Christ could shake hands with them, and they wouldn't believe it. Because they do not hope.

ANNA : Because they do not expect Him. (*She begins getting up.*) I shall stretch my legs a little. Always on my knees . . .

SIMEON : Enjoy the fresh air. It will do you good. I shall wait here. You see, Anna, I am always afraid that He may come just when I have left the temple.

ANNA : You will warn me if He comes?

SIMEON : You will hear my cry of joy.

ANNA : Warn me, all the same.

SIMEON : I will.

(*Anna goes out slowly.*)

II

SIMEON : (*alone*) God of Abraham, of Jacob, of my ancestor Melchior, grant me patience. I am impatient for myself, for my earthly life is done. Each one of my joints creaks like a rusty old machine. I doze during my prayers. Nothing but

death can give me sufficient rest . . . until the resurrection o
my carcass. Above all, I am impatient for *them*. They are
not worth much, I agree, and they have their deserts. If the
wish to run round in circles, let them. You'd think they were
going through life on a roundabout. As soon as they stop, the
are bored—they have time to think . . . and they are so scared
of thinking of You! If You could catch them suddenly by
thought—like Habakkuk by one hair! Oh, they suffer . .
they suffer, I assure you. They suffer from their whirling
their everlasting whirling round in circles. What will they d
when they see You? They will have to stop, to face You, t
pray to You. Life goes by and they make nothing of it.—Go
of Abraham! God of Jacob! Pity them, and pity Simeon!

(*He lowers his head and meditates.*)

III

(*Mary and Joseph come forward. She holds the Child in he
arms: He carries a little cage.*)

MARY : Joseph—dear Joseph! How good it is in our Father'
house!

JOSEPH : Yes.

MARY : You do not agree?

JOSEPH : There are too many stalls and shopkeepers.

MARY : The shopkeepers are needed to sell candles.

JOSEPH : Oh! They sell everything.

MARY : I did not notice. Since Christmas Eve, when the shep
herds danced before us, when, for the first time in the world
men paid homage to the Son of God delivered from my womb
I have felt nothing but joy. I do not have even those natura
fears that mothers feel for their children. Such a fragile crea
ture! Yes, but Son of God. Any other child would have perishe
in that icy cave. He is kept. He is guarded. The Angels are
about Him and surround Him with their wings. God has sen

His salvation to man. The Holy Child can bring us nothing but joy.

JOSEPH : Yes, you are right, Mary. But if you only knew men. They are hard, evil-minded, thoughtless. I know them. You are too pure to see their evil.

MARY : Yet I must purify myself to-day.

JOSEPH : The law commands it, and we must obey the law. But you do not need it.

MARY : Let us be full of joy, Joseph.

JOSEPH : Believe me, Mary, I am. (*They stop.*)

MARY : (*raising her child in her arms*) Lord, on the threshold of Thy temple, I present this small child, who is my son, and Thy Son, and my Saviour. Keep me pure, as He is, and joyful, that He may know nothing but joy—the joy that He brings to this world, and which must return to Him.

(*While she says this, Simeon raises his head, sees the Child and comes forward, as if dazzled. He holds out his arms. Mary gives him the Child.*)

SIMEON : (*overcome*) "Lord, now lettest thou thy servant depart in peace,
According to thy word:
For mine eyes have seen thy salvation,
Which thou hast prepared before the face of all people;
A light to lighten the Gentiles,
And the glory of thy people Israel."

MARY : (*wondering*) Your name, good man?

SIMEON : I am Simeon. (*Blessing the Child.*) I bless Him who has already blessed me by His touch and His presence. (*A pause. Serious.*) "Behold, Mary, blessed mother of the living God, this child is set for the fall and rising again of many in Israel: and for a sign which shall be spoken against——"

MARY : But God will protect Him?

SIMEON : "Yea, Mary, a sword shall pierce through thy own sou
also———"

MARY : Joseph! (*She leans on him.*)

SIMEON : "That the thoughts of many hearts may be revealed."
(*He gives back the Child to His mother, and turns aside
saying:*) I have seen Thy Salvation, Lord, and I must wee
for Him.

IV

(*Anna arrives at this moment.*)

ANNA : Simeon, Simeon, you are weeping?

SIMEON : I weep for joy.

ANNA : (*kneeling at Mary's feet*) My Lord! . . . (*She rises an
cries.*)—

> "Lo, this is our God:
> We have waited for him,
> And he will save us:
> This is the Lord;
> We have waited for him,
> We will be glad and rejoice in his salvation."

(*Softly.*) Saint Colomba, our patron saint . . . (*The rest i
lost.*)

MARY : (*straightening herself*) Come, Joseph. We still have t
offer our two doves. One shall be for joy, and the other fo
grief. (*As she goes out with Joseph.*) Sweet child . . . swee
child . . .

(*Anna follows them. Melchior stays on the stage in the sam
place.*)

V

MELCHIOR : And already the sword is drawn. At the mere nam
of Jesus, the sword issues forth.

Herod, King Herod, Herod the Wicked, had made the three Kings promise to bring word of where the Child was born, that he might go to worship Him also.

But they, being warned of God in a dream that they should not return to Herod, departed into their country another way. And the sword was drawn!

(*Entering into the character of Herod.*)

I am Herod, King of the Jews. The *only* King of the Jews.

Do you think a King will let himself be supplanted by a child at the breast?

Oh, treacherous Melchior! Treacherous Gaspar! Treacherous Balthasar!

I order you to reply!

Where have they gone? Follow them!

Saddle my camels! Harness the zebras!

To horse! To horse! They bear with them my secret of death.

—He is to be born in Bethlehem of Judah?—Search Bethlehem!

Scour the houses from attic to cellar.

Bring out the children: the new-born babies, and all those up to two years old.

I will soon discover the "king."

—There! That one! He has a sign on his forehead. I can read these signs!

—No, this boy, with his head carried high, like an Assyrian god.

—That one laughing at me!

—This one whose eyes sparkle fire!

—That child who looks like David!

—That brat wringing his hands like a soul in torment!

Which is the regicide? Come here! Stand before me, women!

Look in my eyes. Which of you is mother to a King?

—You there, shielding your child! It is he! Yes! . . .

—Or can it be yours . . . ! (*A pause.*)

Will none of you speak?—Will none reveal the enemy of my throne and my peace? . . .

Then kill them all! Spare none! Massacre them!

And let a torrent of innocent blood wash away the blood of the
usurper!

(*Changing his manner.*)

> "In Rama was there a voice heard,
> Lamentation, and weeping, and great mourning,
> Rachel weeping for her children,
> And would not be comforted,
> Because they were not."

And the blood of the first martyrs flowed from under each door,
And a multitude of innocent souls fled, like a flight of swallows,
to the subterranean haunts of the dead.
But Joseph, warned in a dream, was already fleeing with the
Child,
Whom Mary clasped to her breast, like the sacrificial lamb.
And the Child Jesus prayed for His brothers, and secretly
promised that He would deliver them one day,
When He himself should have fallen under the burden of crime
and hatred.
And they dwelt in Egypt until their enemy the king was dead.

(*Melchior comes down to his previous place. Then he reads, in
a calmer voice:*)

"And the Child grew, and waxed strong in spirit, filled with
wisdom: and the grace of God was upon him."

VI

(*Joseph enters, carrying a plank on his shoulder, which the
apprentice Jesus supports behind. [Jesus is Bruno.] Mary
enters from the other side with a workbasket: she seats herself
on a stool.*)

JOSEPH : Down here, son. (*Jesus helps him to lower the plank to
a corner of the platform.*) Where is the set-square? (*Jesus gives
him the square, and he marks the line to saw on.*) Have you got
the saw?

JESUS : Here it is, father.

JOSEPH : Hold the plank firm. (*Jesus obeys. Joseph saws until the end drops.*) Good. That's it.

MARY : (*to Jesus*) I haven't a fine enough needle. There is one in the little green box on the table. Do you mind, Joseph? (*Joseph nods.*)

JESUS : Yes, Mother.

MARY : He must fetch the milk from the farm soon, or they will have sold out.

JESUS : Yes, Mother.

JOSEPH : He may as well go straight away, Mary. We aren't busy. He can plane this off at any time.

JESUS : Yes, Father. I shall not be long.

(*He goes out.*)

JOSEPH : As for me . . . I must tidy myself up. I have to see the pilgrims, to arrange about our journey.

MARY : Shall we be leaving early to-morrow?

JOSEPH : Before dawn, to avoid the heat.

(*Jesus comes back and gives His mother the little green box.*)

JESUS : I have brought them all. I was afraid I would bring the wrong one, Mother. I don't know anything about needles.

JOSEPH : Oh, that's not a boy's job.

MARY : Thank you, Jesus.

JESUS : I am going for the milk.

MARY : Yes, dear. Don't get too hot on the way. Take your time.

JESUS : I have my prayer-book here. I shall read that.

MARY : Yes, do.

JESUS : Good-bye, Mother. Good-bye, Father.

MARY : } Good-bye, dear. (*A pause. They watch Him walking*
JOSEPH : }   *away.*)

VII

MARY :   How big our son has grown!

JOSEPH :   You can hardly recognize Him.

MARY :   He is the same underneath. To think they wanted to kill Him! You remember, Joseph . . . when we had to fly to Egypt?

JOSEPH :   He did some travelling on that donkey . . . He saw some country. That's a long while ago. Don't let us think of it, Mary.

MARY :   I shall never forget my fear then.

JOSEPH :   Well, well, there is no reason to fear for Him now. Our life has settled down. We work, without interference. We have a splendid son—obedient, thoughtful, affectionate—a boy just like any other.

MARY :   Without others' faults.

JOSEPH :   Certainly. He has none. But I meant by that, that He has come back to being a carpenter's son—He doesn't have visits from shepherds, or kings, or angels any more, neither do people send Him gifts as if He were a sultan. He is back where He belongs. Except for your cousin Elisabeth, nobody seems to suspect the marvellous secret of His birth. Does He even know it Himself?

MARY :   We never talk about it. (*A pause.*) He hasn't the slightest touch of pride in Him, that boy. He might boast of being more virtuous, more intelligent, than others—of knowing more than His parents do,—yet He thinks only through us. He listens carefully to our lessons and advice, as if we were really teaching Him something.

JOSEPH :   Knowledge wasn't born *in* Him.

MARY :   No, but He surprises us, at times.

JOSEPH :   I don't know what the Lord wants to make of Him. Alas! I may not live long enough to know. But it often worries me.

MARY : Let us not try to see into the future. We will simply take what God gives us:—three hearts, knowing each other in love, blessed with peace and work, and united as if they were a single heart.—May God keep Him as He is! Let Him be a journeyman carpenter, setting up later on His own account, and closing our eyes in this house!

JOSEPH : We cannot ask for more. (*He makes to go out, then thinks better of it.*) I will just plane off this plank. We are going on a long journey, and He mustn't get too tired. (*He does as he has said, humming.*) There, that's it. I am going to wash.

(*He goes out. Mary examines the linen that she has been mending, collects her things, rises, and looks around her.*)

MARY : The peace of it! The calm! Perhaps *this* is earthly salvation.

(*She goes out, too.*)

VIII

MELCHIOR : (*reading*) "The pilgrims from Nazareth set off to Jerusalem for the feast of the Passover. The weather was magnificent, and flowers covered the land. With the permission of his parents, Jesus went in front among the boys of his own age, and with them he admired the rebirth of creation.

"After the days had been fulfilled, they made their way home again. Suddenly, Joseph and Mary noticed that Jesus was not with them."

(*Mary and Joseph enter from the right, accompanied by an old neighbour [Colomba], all with their pilgrims' belongings: basket, cloak, staff, etc.*)

MARY : (*distracted: to invisible pilgrims*) Have you seen our child? Have you seen our boy?—No? No? Where is He? Where is He, Joseph?

JOSEPH : We must not despair, Mary.

MARY : God will protect Him, I know.

NEIGHBOUR : Of course! Look at you, all of a flutter, as if He was never coming back again! He will catch us up, with His young legs. He is just playing about somewhere.

MARY : Playing about? Jesus?

NEIGHBOUR : Why not Him, more than any other boy? Don't talk to me about boys! As soon as you let them off your apron strings—they want to see everything and know everything. Well, what can you expect? In a town, there's the shops with their windows—the traffic, soldiers marching by, everything a boy could want! I bet you He has gone to the pictures. He couldn't resist it. He's only a boy.

MARY : Oh, I am sure . . .

NEIGHBOUR : Yes, yes, yes, yes! Because He stays quietly at home, runs errands, and works with His dad—— Well, what of it? You never know with kids. They say what they know you want them to say. And they keep the rest to themselves!

MARY : He has never given us cause to worry.

NEIGHBOUR : He will, I can tell you.

JOSEPH : He would have to change a lot, then.

NEIGHBOUR : He will change, as they all do. The voice begins to break, and it's then the demon comes out. The little chap begins to feel His strength. He feels His body waking up. It is the awkward age, and you will have to put up with it, like everyone else. One fine day, before you know it, you'll realize that your plaster saint is nothing but a young rascal.

MARY : They are not all like that. I am speaking of my boy.

NEIGHBOUR : Oh! Mothers are all the same. All positive they have given birth to a phœnix!

MARY : But you don't know—This boy! . . .

NEIGHBOUR : This boy?—He isn't a special kind, is He? He is a Jew and a man. God didn't make a new pattern just for Him. Go on with you! I've had some experience in my time. You will live to know that I am right.

JOSEPH : Let her talk, Mary.

MARY : Well . . . it is enough that I love Him—and He is my child. Where is He? Where is He?

JOSEPH : We will go back to Jerusalem, but we mustn't lose hope.

MARY : Could He have been run over?

NEIGHBOUR : He might have been. He's very vague. He crosses the roads in a dream. Oh, so long as He's only broken an arm or a leg, that will teach Him to be careful in future.

JOSEPH : You are a great comfort!

MARY : (*going out*) Have you seen Jesus? Have you seen Jesus? A tall boy, with fair curly hair. No? No? (*In the distance.*) Oh God, give me back my boy!

(*They have all gone off.*)

IX

MELCHIOR : Now the Doctors were debating in the Temple. And since they could not agree, many stayed there listening to them. They were dealing with such complicated matters that it is difficult to tell you what they said. There were two in particular, who contradicted each other with incredible obstinacy, because they were the wisest—or thought they were.

(*He mounts the platform.*)

The elder—that's me—marched up and down scratching his head and tugging at his beard, as if he could shake a new argument out of it each time he was stumped. (*He does as he says. To the others.*) My mortar-board, please. (*A hand passes him the mortar-board, and he puts it on.*) The younger one kept jumping up from his stall, taking a step forward, and throwing himself down again—as if the itch of proving his point was hurting him somewhere.

(*At these words, Joey, rigged out in a beard and cap, has climbed onto the platform with his stool under his arm. He sits down, gets up again, and sits with increasing agitation.*)

JOEY : You must agree that the prophecy is not clear, Zadoch. (*To the others, who are invisible.*) What do you think, Nathan? And you, Jehu? . . .

MELCHIOR : My dear Baruch, the whole point of a prophecy is that it can be interpreted in more than one way. But you are deliberately confusing the issue.

JOEY : I appeal to my colleagues. Isaiah writes: "People of Zion, a Saviour shall come to save the People."

MELCHIOR : *Ad salvandum gentes. Gentes* is the key-word. I translate that as Gentiles. Or alternatively, pagans. (*To the others.*) Isn't that so?

JOEY : Blasphemy! That interpretation is sheer blasphemy, Zadoch. There is only one chosen people—ours: and consequently, only one people can be saved. (*To the others.*) Do you agree?

MELCHIOR : *Gentes* is plural.

JOEY : Of course. The people in question number more than one man. So, according to you, the Jewish people cannot expect salvation?

MELCHIOR : I do not say that. The Jewish people—certainly: *and* the others, too. It is them that Isaiah is speaking of.

JOEY : I will not admit that God will save the others!

(*At this moment, Jesus appears, comes forward, and makes a gesture.*)

X

JESUS : Allow me, sirs.

JOEY : What do You want, my boy? The sacristy is along there.

JESUS : I do not want the sacristy. I wanted to say, that in My opinion——

JOEY : In His opinion! . . .

JESUS : All people are equal before God.

JOEY : Oh, no!

MELCHIOR : No! . . . I agree with you on that point, Baruch. I stick quite firmly to the chosen people. They will be served first. If the others can pick up a few crumbs, so much the better for them. And that proves . . .

JESUS : A few crumbs? You cannot believe that. As I see it, there is . . .

JOEY : As He sees it!—As *He* sees it!——

JESUS : There is enough grain in the granaries of the Lord to feed all peoples.

MELCHIOR : What is He interfering for?

JOEY : Go away, my lad. Go back to Your school-bench, and study the A B C of Mosaic Law. Doctors sitting in the Temple are here to give lessons, not to receive them.

JESUS : I have every respect for the Doctors, sir, but when they are wrong, they are wrong. Man is fallible . . .

JOEY : Fallible—fallible—fallible! He uses words He doesn't understand.

JESUS : I mean: subject to error. The primeval sin wounded him, even in his mind.

MELCHIOR : True! True!

JESUS : For that was a sin of pride against the spirit.

JOEY : Where does He get all this from?

JESUS : And pride blinds the spirit of man.

MELCHIOR : Very good, my boy.

JOEY : Well, if you're going to encourage Him . . . (*Rising.*) Let Him seat himself! Let Him take my chair! I give Him my place.

MELCHIOR : Calm yourself, Baruch, calm yourself. There have been child prodigies. Remember David.

JOEY : He is no David.

MELCHIOR : (*giving Him a stool*) Sit down, my boy. Please. And tell us all You know.

JESUS : I should be ashamed, sirs. I am only a child.

MELCHIOR : No, no! (*Softly, to Joey.*) We shall see. (*Aloud.*) First of all, who are You?

JESUS : A carpenter's son. I work with My father.

JOEY : A carpenter's son!

JESUS : No craft is foolish, they say.

MELCHIOR : Where do You live?

JESUS : At Nazareth. I came to Jerusalem with My mother and father for Passover.

JOEY : Nazareth, eh? I expect You know what they say about Nazareth—that no good comes out of it?

JESUS : They say that, sir.

JOEY : How old are You?

JESUS : Twelve.

MELCHIOR : And who taught You?

JESUS : My Father.

JOEY : The carpenter? (*He laughs. Jesus does not reply.*)

MELCHIOR : Well, we have been talking of the Messiah—He that should come. What is Your opinion of that?

JESUS : I have no opinion of My own. I have nothing of My own. It is sufficient to read the Books.

JOEY : Have You read them? And understood them?

JESUS : I try My hardest.

JOEY : What do they say of Him?

JESUS : He shall be great among men, and men shall receive Him ill.

JOEY : But He *will* save them?

JESUS : Certainly. If they received Him well, perhaps He could not save them. At least, the Prophets tell us that He does not intend to save them so. He must be despised, rejected, wounded, —worse, perhaps. He must suffer——

JOEY : The Prophets did not say that.

MELCHIOR : Yes. Something of the kind—but He is exaggerating.

JESUS : Consult David, Isaiah,—Job, who is an image of Christ. And Jonah, too. But it would take too long to tell them all.

JOEY : There you are!—There you are! He's talking all over the place—mixing them all up.

MELCHIOR : Hum! Hum! It is strange. Who can have stuffed all that into His head?

JOEY : Why, His father!

JESUS : My Father.

JOEY : Good night! (*He gets up.*) I'm not listening to any more. A twelve-year-old kid, who knows more than the Doctors——! (*To the other, imaginary ones.*) Well! Well! You haven't a word to say! All sitting there tongue-tied! You can stay! I'm going home.

(*He goes out.*)

XI

MELCHIOR : In your opinion, what is the greatest sin?

JESUS : Denial, arising from pride. (*A long pause.*)

(*Melchior walks up and down. Then, mysteriously—*)

MELCHIOR : Tell me this, my child. Do the Prophets say *when* He shall come?

JESUS : Who?

MELCHIOR : The Messiah.

JESUS : They do not say when. But they counsel vigilance. He must be watched for at each hour of the day and night, as if He might knock at the door. A fire should be kept in among the ashes, to light the lamp at His coming.

MELCHIOR : What is the meaning of that flame under the ashes?

JESUS : The love of God, and of one's neighbour.

MELCHIOR : And who is one's neighbour, do You think?

JESUS : Every man. (*More childishly.*) You see that My knowledge is not of a very high order.

MELCHIOR : Perhaps not! But never mind—if it is the truth! We have never taught that. Yet it should be taught. Hum! (*Going towards Him.*) I thank you, and I embrace you, dear child.

(*During the end of the dialogue, Joseph and Mary have come in quietly. They have seen, listened, and are moved. When Jesus comes down from His seat to embrace Melchior, they hurry forward.*)

MARY : My son! . . . My son!

JESUS : Mother! (*He kisses Mary and Joseph.*)

MELCHIOR : Is He your son? He is advanced for His years. How long has He been at school?

MARY : Two years.

JOSEPH : He works at home, though—serving His apprenticeship as a carpenter. Did He come here alone?

MELCHIOR : Quite alone. He joined in our discussion, a thing no child has ever done before. He interested us, and we kept Him. Were you worried?

JOSEPH : Yes, sir. A mother—and father. He is our only child.

MELCHIOR : Take care of Him, then. He is worth many others. My colleagues will tell you—He astonished us, and perhaps taught us something. Would you allow Him to stay in Jerusalem? He could continue His studies here, and——

JESUS : Oh no, sir. You are very kind, but I am too young——

MELCHIOR : Then, good-bye. We may meet again. Who knows?

(*He bows and goes to one side, but listens to what is said.*)

MARY : I told you we were setting off, you naughty boy! Why cause us all this worry? Your father and I have been looking everywhere, with our hearts in our mouths.

JESUS : Why should you seek Me?

MARY : (*stupefied*) Why?

JESUS : Did you not know that I must be about My Father's business?

MELCHIOR : (*coming back*) What does He mean?

MARY : Nothing—nothing, sir. You cannot understand. We—we can hardly understand. You have to know Him——

(*Melchior makes a vague sign, and goes away.*)

MELCHIOR : Good night. (*He goes to his place as the Reader.*)

JESUS : I will go with you now, Mother.

MARY : You promise You will not leave us again? (*Jesus does not answer.*)

(*Mary and Joseph go out. Jesus follows them. Mary leans against Joseph, sobbing.*)

MELCHIOR : (*reading*) "Then Mary knew that her child had a duty higher than to her. And that he must leave her again."

THE OTHERS : (*in Chorus*) "And that he must leave her again."

COLOMBA : (*arriving and changing the mood*) Come on, Mary. Joseph.—Maria, Joey! Sing! (*She brings them back onto the stage.*) Your little Jesus, your little Bruno, is still here. You have found Him, and He will stay with you. It will be time to weep for Him later. Sing! Dance! (*To the public.*) You must all be off to church now.

(*Bells are heard.*)

MELCHIOR : (*rising gravely*) The bells are ringing! At the last stroke of midnight, the Child will be born . . . eternally!

THE OTHERS : Eternally!

MELCHIOR : This is just a simple story we strung together one evening to amuse our gypsy friends. If it has filled in your time until that moment when you all share the living reality of our Lord's nativity, it has served its purpose.—Thank us, good people! And show us that you have enjoyed our play by joining in a carol—"God Rest You Merry, Gentlemen!"

(All sing the carol, and the Curtain falls to end the play.)

by
Nathaniel Banks

THE CURATE'S PLAY

THE CHARACTERS

THE CURATE
THE NARRATOR
THE DOCTOR
THE LADY WITH FUR COAT
THE DISGRUNTLED WOMAN
FIRST ANGEL
SECOND ANGEL

CHILDREN OF THE TABLEAUX

MARY
GABRIEL
JOSEPH
THE INNKEEPER
CASPAR
MELCHIOR
BALTHAZAR
THREE SHEPHERDS

THE CHOIR

PRODUCTION NOTES: If the names "curate" and "vicar" are inapplicable to the specific church where a performance is planned, substitutions can easily be made. For example, in a Methodist church, it might be called "The Pastor's Play" and the Vicar might become the District Superintendent or the Bishop.

It is suggested that as many avenues of entry and exit as possible be utilized for maximum effectiveness in the staging. However, the only essential "off-stage" area is the room described in the play as the "vestry." This might be the choir's changing room, or the minister's study, or any room or passage near the chancel area.

Sources for music used in the play, both the short chanted passages and hymns, are found in the acting version of the text, distributed by Dramatists Play Service, Inc.

Whenever possible, the play should be presented without preamble or introductory remarks of any kind, since much of its effectiveness depends on the element of surprise.

There is a platform in the center of the chancel with a simple wooden frame for the proscenium (perhaps trimmed with holly or other winter greens) across which a curtain is drawn. The Choir enters singing "Adeste Fideles." During the Processional the Curate enters with the Narrator. The Curate is an intense young man; the Narrator is younger still—preferably an adolescent who looks as though he may have recently outgrown a role in the pageant. The Curate accompanies the Narrator to the pulpit and then starts toward the vestry with the book containing the narration. Realizing his blunder he returns quickly and gives it to the Narrator. He exits into the vestry, which opens off the chancel, and reenters with the twelve Children, ranging in age from about nine to twelve, who appear in the tableaux. He places the First Angel at one side of the platform to operate the curtain, and he leads the Second Angel, who will perform various other chores, to the opposite side.

CURATE : Are you ready, children? Take your places now . . . (*When the Choir is seated he helps the little girl who plays Mary, wearing a blue, hooded robe trimmed with gold, to ascend the platform.*) Shh! The pageant's about to begin! (*He signals the Narrator, and the lights come up on the chancel. When the Narrator begins speaking the Curate hurries Off into the vestry.*)

NARRATOR : "The book of the generation of Jesus Christ, the son of David, the son of Abraham. Abraham begat Isaac; and Isaac begat Jacob; and Jacob begat Judas and his brethren . . ." and so on for sixteen verses. As you see, Matthew starts with genealogy—that is, the genealogy of Joseph, who one might say is the terrestrial father of Jesus. But the most extensive genealogy can never account for divinity. Hear how St. John proclaims the mystic origin of our Lord.

MALE VOICE FROM CHOIR : (*Chanting No. 1.*) "In the beginning was the Word, and the Word was with God, and the Word was

305

God . . . And the Word was made flesh, and dwelt among us, (and we beheld his glory, the glory as of the only begotten of the Father), full of grace and truth."

NARRATOR : It is to Luke we turn for the more homely events attending Jesus' birth. He tells of a virgin espoused to a man named Joseph . . . (*The First Angel draws the curtain, and we see Mary sitting on a stool, her hands clasped in prayer.*)

FEMALE VOICE FROM CHOIR : (*Chanting No. 2.*) "And the virgin's name was Mary."

CHOIR : (*Singing.*)

> I sing of a maiden
> That is makeless
> King of all kings
> To her son she ches . . .

(*At the end of the first verse the Curate rushes On from the vestry showing signs of great perturbation.*)

CURATE : Stop, please! Stop! (*Turning to the stage.*) Children, I'm sorry. (*To the congregation.*) I apologize for this interruption. It's really too bad, for we've been rehearsing for weeks on end, and I think we're finally letter-perfect. This is the sort of thing that's always happening to me. If I prepare a sermon on divine providence I'm sure to trip and fall on my way to the pulpit. I often wonder why the Lord tolerates a servant as clumsy as I am.

FIRST ANGEL : What's happened, sir?

CURATE : I feel somehow that it's my fault!

SECOND ANGEL : *What*, sir?

CURATE : I was watching the performance from the vestry. The door to the street was unlocked, and suddenly it flew open and a woman stumbled in. In broken English she asked if she could stay a few minutes to take shelter from the cold. I'm afraid she's ill. Is there a doctor in the congregation? (*A Doctor in one of the front pews rises and makes his way to the chancel.*)

DOCTOR : I'll take a look at her.

CURATE : How do you do, Doctor? We haven't seen you here for a long time—not since Christmas a year ago.

DOCTOR : Now, now, you're exaggerating. I attended the Easter service.

CURATE : (*As he ushers the Doctor into the vestry.*) Doctor, I think—I think she's going to have a baby! (*Turning back toward the platform.*) Children, you may as well continue. (*The Curate follows the Doctor Off, and Mary resumes her prayerful pose.*)

CHOIR : (*Singing.*)

> Mother and maiden
> Was never none but she
> Well may such a lady
> Godes mother be.

(*The Curate reenters as the First Angel closes the curtain.*)

CURATE : Oh, the poor woman! She's moaning, and though it's quite warm in there she's shivering like a sparrow in the snow.

LADY WITH FUR COAT : (*Rising from her pew.*) I beg your pardon —but may I offer her my coat?

CURATE : How kind of you! I'm sure she'll be grateful. (*The Curate and the Lady With Fur Coat exit into the vestry. During the Narrator's speech the Second Angel changes the position of the stool, and an older boy dressed in a flowing white robe, representing Gabriel, mounts the platform.*)

NARRATOR : Have you noticed that in medieval paintings of the Annunciation Mary is often depicted shrinking from the Angel and his awesome message? Luke says, "When she saw him she was troubled . . ." (*The First Angel opens the curtain, and we see Mary sitting on the stool on one side of the stage and Gabriel kneeling opposite her. Gabriel is holding a large white lily, and Mary's hand is raised as if in protest, her face half-averted.*)

MALE VOICE FROM CHOIR : (*Chanting No. 3.*) "Fear not, Mary: for thou hast found favour with God. And, behold, thou shalt conceive in thy womb, and bring forth a son, and shalt call his name Jesus. He shall be great, and shall be called the Son of the Highest."

NARRATOR : "And Mary said, Behold the handmaid of the Lord; be it unto me according to thy word." (*The Lady With Fur Coat enters from the vestry.*)

LADY : (*Addressing the congregation.*) Why, it's the most extraordinary coincidence. (*Nodding toward the vestry.*) I know her! She's a cleaning woman; she's often worked for me by the day when I've needed some extra help. She was brisk and efficient, and as pretty as could be—but she rarely ever smiled. I learned that her husband was a shiftless fellow who bullied her and spent all their money on drink. One day when I asked if she was going to have a baby she denied it so violently—and then burst into tears—that I never dared to mention it again. I must confess, as I watched her going about her work with a look of stubborn resentment, I was often filled with envy. You see, my husband and I have never had children—and here was this unhappy girl despising the condition which seemed to me more desirable than anything in the world. Watching her quicken with life I felt as barren as a rock! Yes, I confess, I was guilty of covetousness. But seeing her just now I no longer felt bitter at what I had considered God's mismanagement. She seemed changed somehow. Until my dying day I'll remember the look in her eyes, as deep and still as the black pools in a cypress swamp. When she recognized me she smiled and said, "Que contenta estoy. I am content."

FEMALE VOICE FROM CHOIR : (*Chanting No. 4.*) "Behold the handmaid of the Lord; be it unto me according to thy word."

(*As the First Angel closes the curtain, the Curate enters from the vestry.*)

CURATE : She's in dreadful pain! I feel so helpless!

LADY : I'll wait here, shall I?—in case the doctor needs me.

CURATE : It suddenly occurred to me in there that Mary for all her holiness was a real woman who suffered the anguish of childbirth, as this woman is suffering now. I wonder if she too clenched her fists and moaned and bit her lip until it trickled blood? (*Cocking his head toward the vestry.*) I hear her crying out! Oh, I wish—I *wish* there were something I could do! (*The Curate exits into the vestry, and the Lady moves to one side of the chancel.*)

NARRATOR : "And it came to pass," according to St. Luke, "that there went out a decree from Caesar Augustus that all the world should be taxed. And all went to be taxed, every one into his own city. And Joseph also went up from Galilee, out of the city of Nazareth, into Judea, unto the city of David, which is called Bethlehem, to be taxed with Mary his espoused wife, being great with child."

CHOIR : (*Singing.*)
    Din, din, din, Came the awaited day,
    Din, din, din, When they set on their way.
    Mary, blessed Virgin, Beautiful was She.
    With Her, gentle Joseph; Kind and good was he . . .

(*The bell sound from the organ continues softly under the Narrator's speech. The Second Angel sets a prop donkey on the stage.*)

NARRATOR : From what we know of life in Palestine in the days of the Roman empire, we can picture the town of Bethlehem when Joseph and Mary came from Nazareth to be among those who were counted and taxed. It was a mean, provincial town bristling with soldiers and crammed with strangers impelled there against their wills . . .

CHOIR : (*Singing.*)
    Din, din, din, To Bethlehem they came, Din, din, din . . .

NARRATOR : The crowded streets, the dust and the noise must have oppressed and frightened Mary, for it was near her time to deliver . . .

CHOIR : (*Singing.*)
    Shelter they must find them as the night did fall.
    No place was too humble, No place was too small . . .

NARRATOR : Joseph sought lodging for her, but he sought in vain. Unfortunately, there was no room for them in the inn. (*The First Angel opens the curtain, revealing Mary sitting on the donkey and Joseph standing beside her; they are confronted by the Innkeeper with arm thrust forward, palm outward, refusing them entry.*)

CHOIR : (*Singing.*)
> Crowded was the city, Fruitless seemed their quest,
> As the humble Joseph Begged for place to rest.
> One there was who helped them,
> Scorned the heat and cold;
> 'Twas the faithful donkey Which the Virgin rode.

(*The Curate reenters from the vestry.*)

CURATE : (*To Lady.*) The doctor asks if you'll please come and help him?

LADY : Of course! Perhaps now at least I'll have a godchild! (*As the Lady exits hurriedly into the vestry a Disgruntled Woman in the congregation springs to her feet.*)

DISGRUNTLED WOMAN : I'm not going to put up with this another minute!

CURATE : I beg your pardon?

DISGRUNTLED WOMAN : The interruptions, the confusion—it's just too much. (*She goes to the chancel and confronts the Curate.*) I came to this church today as I've come Christmas after Christmas, to sit quietly in the dimness, to be soothed by the conventional scriptures, enthralled by the traditional music. Suddenly I'm jolted out of my reverie and like Humpty Dumpty plunged headlong into chaos . . .

CURATE : But madam, I—

DISGRUNTLED WOMAN : This beautiful service with these adorable children has been utterly spoiled—and for what?

CURATE : Why—er—

DISGRUNTLED WOMAN : I'm telling you, sir! For a situation that should never have been allowed to develop in the first place.

CURATE : But madam, we—

DISGRUNTLED WOMAN : The instant that woman appeared off the street you should have called the police. Getting her to a hospital is *their* responsibility. What do you think we pay taxes for?

CURATE : Well—er—

DISGRUNTLED WOMAN : I tell you this is a civil affair—it's nothing whatever to do with the church. Why, the woman's a foreigner, probably not even one of our faith . . .

CURATE : (*Quickly.*) We're all God's children, madam.

DISGRUNTLED WOMAN : I wouldn't be so sure about that!

CURATE : As a minister it's my duty to serve whoever needs me; I can't discriminate. I'm terribly sorry you've been upset. We try our best to please everyone here.

DISGRUNTLED WOMAN : You try to please altogether too many— that's one of your troubles! (*The Doctor enters from the vestry without his jacket and with his shirt sleeves rolled up.*) I insist that you get that woman out of the church and into a hospital and not waste any more time doing it!

CURATE : Madam, I've been trying to explain—

DOCTOR : Excuse me, Curate, there's a simpler answer. (*To the Disgruntled Woman.*) The baby won't wait! My patient is already in labor—she may deliver at any moment. Now will you please sit down?

DISGRUNTLED WOMAN : (*Making her way to the aisle.*) Indeed I will not sit down. I'm going home! At least in the seclusion of my own small apartment I can entertain God without vulgar intrusion. (*The Disgruntled Woman exits up the aisle.*)

NARRATOR : There was no room for them in the inn in Bethlehem. It was not the last time that a door has been closed and an opportunity lost. (*The First Angel draws the curtain across the stage. The Doctor turns back toward the vestry.*)

CURATE : (*Excitedly.*) Just think, Doctor—a baby is going to be born right here in this church! (*The Doctor pauses.*) You

know, I've heard it said that every time the clock ticks, somewhere in the world a child is born. What on earth's more
commonplace than birth?—yet to me it always seems an occasion of wonder and joy.

DOCTOR : I scarcely think in this case there is cause for jubilation.
One more infant delivered kicking and screaming into a life of
ignorance and poverty.

CURATE : But the circumstances, Doctor! The woman might have
perished outside in the cold. Her stumbling in here for shelter
almost seems like—well, like a miracle. But then, there's an
element of the miraculous in every birth, don't you think so?

DOCTOR : Not really. Shall I tell you what I really think? To me a
birth merely represents a statistic in the population explosion—
another increment in a deadly multiplication that will probably
one day swamp the earth!

CURATE : Doctor, what a terrible thing to say!

DOCTOR : Oh, naturally you and I see things from contrary points
of view. By the nature of your profession you're committed to
the celebration of birth—specifically, the birth of a Messiah in
a Palestinian village two thousand years ago. But what you
overlook, Curate, is that there is scarcely any relevance between that civilization and the one we're damned to live in
today. Christ was born into an agrarian society in which men
were sustained by tribal loyalties and mythic beliefs—why, for
generations the Hebrew prophets had been foretelling a Messiah's birth. In this ancient civilization the individual had
stature! . . .

CURATE : Surely, Doctor, in every era there have been individuals
of great character—men of foresight and influence?

DOCTOR : Today? What about our mechanized, our overpopulated
and atomized society today? Our prophets are purblind; the
influence of our messiahs is measured solely by applause meters
and IBM machines. I tell you, in a society in which birth is not
a blessing but a threat, the primary function of the Church
should be to regulate that society—to impose its authority on

civilization that will require increasingly stringent regulation if it's to survive at all. Though it may surprise you, Curate, I'm really a traditionalist at heart. I believe in a sort of unofficial coalition of church and state, of lawyers and teachers, politicians and business men—of all the elements that make for an orderly society—all working together for the welfare—no, let's just say, the *survival* of man. If I attend services here at Easter and Christmastime, it's because I still believe in the efficacy of the Church as a member of the coalition. (*Mischievously.*) Besides, I like the music.

CURATE : The *music!* Why, it's like saying you go to the theatre for the orange drink! I assure you, Doctor, the Church is—why, it's—that is, it isn't—! (*The Lady With Fur Coat appears in the vestry door.*)

LADY : Doctor! Doctor, I think you'd better come!

DOCTOR : (*Going quickly toward the vestry.*) Excuse me, Curate, I'll hear your rebuttal another time. I have to go and deliver a statistic! (*As the Doctor exits the First Angel, impelled by curiosity, starts to follow him.*)

CURATE : Johnny! Come back here! The pageant's still going on.

(*The First Angel resumes his position. During the Narrator's speech the Second Angel places a stepladder on the platform.*)

NARRATOR : The gospels of Matthew and Luke tell how the heavens proclaimed the birth of Jesus. From Matthew we learn of the wise men from the east who followed an extraordinary star . . .

MALE VOICE FROM CHOIR : (*Chanting No. 5.*) "When they saw the star, they rejoiced with exceeding great joy." (*The Curate fusses about the ladder as the Second Angel, holding a pole, climbs to the top.*)

CURATE : Be careful! Remember what happened to Tommy at rehearsal last week. (*The First Angel draws the curtain to reveal Caspar, Melchior and Balthazar, richly caparisoned in Oriental finery, standing transfixed by a star dangling from the pole held by the Second Angel atop the ladder.*)

CHOIR : (*Singing.*)

What star is this, with beam so bright,
More beauteous than the noonday light?
It leads them on with power benign
To seek the Giver of the sign . . .

(*During the hymn the Vicar comes down the aisle from th*
rear of the church.)

CURATE : (*Going forward to meet the Vicar.*) Oh, Vicar, than
goodness you're here! I've been having an awful time!

VICAR : Now, now, I've been watching from the back of th
church, and I think you've managed everything splendidly. It'
too bad we don't have a Curate's Medal for heroism above an
beyond the call of duty.

CURATE : Never in my life have I felt so inadequate! First th
disgruntled woman who seems to regard religion as a kind c
tranquilizer storming out of the church—and then the Docto
speaking in such a cynical way about birth and survival. Thei
sentiments were as chilling as a killing frost! I should have ha
the answers for them on the tip of my tongue, and all I coul
do was stammer and blush.

VICAR : Ah, my boy, when you've been at this game as long as
have you'll realize there aren't any easy answers. (*Indicatin*
the stage.) Like the wise men from the east—like you and m
for that matter—the socially oriented Doctor and the unsoci
woman are seeking religious truth. Well, the truth is immens
it shouldn't distress you that they've only found a small pa
of it.

CURATE : But it *is* distressing! They come here to worship—an
they've scarcely a clue to what they're worshipping or why
There may be others here in the same predicament. I want s
to help them but I don't know how! (*During the Curate*
speech the First Angel draws the curtain.)

VICAR : Well, we'll have to do something about that. Suppose w
pretend for a moment that you're the Doctor and that I'm you
—and we'll see if we can find some of the answers. Now fix m

with a sceptical gaze. (*The Curate looks embarrassed but finally manages to strike a pose.*) That's the idea. (*Clearing his throat.*) Well, Doctor, I must say you talk very persuasively indeed, but I'm afraid you're overlooking some fundamental truths. May I remind you that as Christians we believe every man is created with a spiritual as well as a physical being? Do you realize the tremendous implications? In all ages, in every society, every man through the exercise of his will possesses an infinite capacity for good.

CURATE : What about man's infinite capacity for evil! (*Diffidently.*) Er—you understand, sir, I'm speaking for the Doctor?

VICAR : Yes, yes, go on.

CURATE : Well, I mean—I think the Doctor would say that today man's evil impulses have to be restrained more forcefully than ever, since he now has the means at his disposal to blow himself to smithereens.

VICAR : As a practicing churchman I'm naturally in favor of restraining evil impulses—though as a Christian humanist I'm equally committed to safeguarding man's freedom to choose for himself between evil and good. The trick is to impose decent social restraints without denying this essential freedom. You see, Doctor, I believe that survival in itself is meaningless unless we continually assert the worth and dignity of each one of God's creatures. However grave the dangers of overpopulation or massive destruction, the great task for the Church today is to affirm and reaffirm a simple, eternal truth—that the crucial battles are still fought where the final victory lies—in the solitude of the human spirit.

CURATE : Yes, that's what I want to say! Thank you, sir! . . .

(*The Narrator coughs significantly.*)

VICAR : (*To the Curate.*) Sh! (*Nodding toward the platform.*) Let's listen.

NARRATOR : Matthew tells the story of the wise men. Luke tells about the shepherds . . .

MALE VOICE FROM CHOIR : (*Chanting No. 6.*) "And there were in the same country shepherds abiding in the field, keeping watch over their flock by night . . ." (*Gabriel takes the place of the Second Angel on the ladder and raises a trumpet to his lips. The First Angel opens the curtain to reveal three Shepherds hearkening to the angel's song.*) "And, lo, the angel of the Lord came upon them, and the glory of the Lord shone round about them: and they were sore afraid. And the angel said unto them . . ."

FEMALE VOICE FROM CHOIR : (*Singing.*) "Fear not: for, behold I bring you good tidings of great joy, which shall be to all people. For unto you is born this day in the city of David a Saviour, which is Christ the Lord." (*The First and Second Angels join Gabriel on the ladder.*)

MALE VOICE FROM CHOIR : (*Chanting.*) "And suddenly there was with the angel a multitude of the heavenly host praising God, and saying . . ."

CHOIR : (*Singing.*)
"Glory to God in the highest, and on earth peace, good will toward men."

(*The Curate closes the curtain.*)

VICAR : Do you understand the angels' message? A Saviour is born, which is God made flesh—the deity's profoundest engagement in the lives of men.

CURATE : Then how can the Church stay aloof from earthly matters, when the crux of our faith is God's commitment? There's the answer for the disgruntled woman!

VICAR : Ah, my boy, there's the answer for the whole blessed world.

NARRATOR : The shepherds hearkened to the angels; the wise men followed the star. Shepherds and wise men travelled to Bethlehem and there found Mary and Joseph and the babe, lying in manger. (*The Curate opens the curtain. Mary is hovering over the crib with Joseph standing beside her. The Wise Men are*

the Shepherds are kneeling in adoration while the Angels look down from above.)

CURATE : (*Whispering.*) Be careful, boys—don't shake the ladder!

CHOIR : (*Singing.*)

> O come, little children, O come one and all.
> To Bethlehem come to the crib in the stall.
> O see, little children, who lies in the stall.
> In clean swaddling clothes is a dear Baby small . . .

CURATE : (*Whispering to Mary.*) Cathy, you're supposed to lift the baby Jesus from the crib . . . (*Whispering frantically.*) Has someone misplaced the doll? Johnny, have you been playing tricks again? Oh, why do these things always happen to me?

(*At this moment there is an infant's cry from the vestry.*)

SECOND ANGEL : What's that?

FIRST ANGEL : Let's go see! (*The Children break the tableau, jump down from the stage and crowd around the vestry door.*)

JOSEPH : Is the lady sick?

INNKEEPER : I'm scared! (*The Lady With Fur Coat appears at the entrance to the vestry.*)

LADY : Hush, children. Something wonderful has just happened . . .

MARY : Oh, look! It's a baby!

CURATE : (*Kneeling.*) Thank you, oh God, for a love so profound, for an involvement so passionate, for a gift so marvellous, that this child born here today in misery and pain—even this child contains a seed of spirituality which may burgeon in glory at last! (*The Choir sings "Gloria in Excelsis Deo."*)

NARRATOR : (*Speaking above the music.*) "For God so loved the world, that he gave his only begotten Son, that whosoever believeth in him should not perish, but have everlasting life." (*As the music swells again the Curate shepherds the Children Off, and the Narrator closes his book. The Choir exits singing the Gloria.*)

by
James Forsyth

EMMANUEL

CHARACTERS

MARY	*The Women in the Play*
THE INNKEEPER'S WIFE	
1ST WOMAN OF BETHLEHEM	
2ND WOMAN OF BETHLEHEM	
JOSEPH	*The Men in the Play*
HEROD	
A SHEPHERD	
THOMAS	The Innkeeper
JUSTINIUS	Roman Procurator
THE THREE WISE MEN	1. Of Astronomy
	2. Of Medicine
	3. Of Chemistry
OLD SIMON	
A YOUNG MAN OF BETHLEHEM	
NICOLUS	Servant of Herod

Other people of Bethlehem, as crowd—if required. NICOLUS and THE YOUNG MAN can be played by young women if necessary.

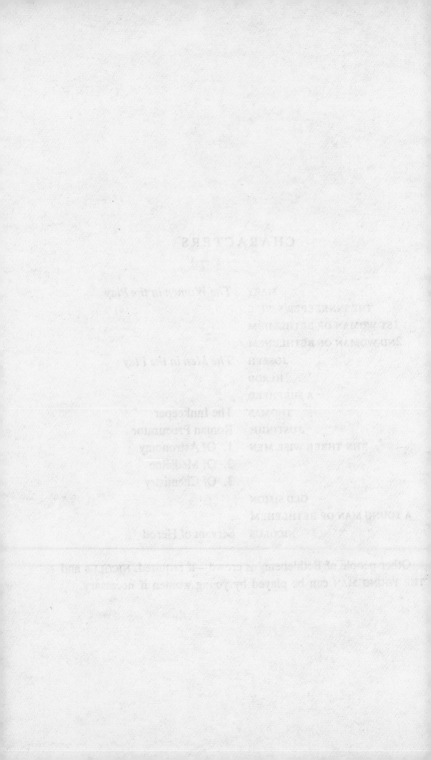

CHARACTERS

MARY	The Women in the Play
THE ANGEL GABRIEL	
1ST WOMAN OF BETHLEHEM	
2ND WOMAN OF BETHLEHEM	
JOSEPH	The Men in the Play
HEROD	
A SHEPHERD	
THOMAS	The Innkeeper
JONATHAN	Roman Procurator
THE THREE WISE MEN	1. Of Astronomy
	2. Of Medicine
	3. Of Chemistry
OLD SIMON	
A YOUNG MAN OF BETHLEHEM	
NICHOLAS	Servant at Herod

Other people of Bethlehem, as required: SHEPHERDS, NICHOLAS, and THE YOUNG MAN can be played by young women if necessary.

ACT I

Scene I
On the Hills Around Bethlehem, Sunset—Warm

Sound of little sheep-bell ringing, and approaching. A Shepherd comes in, carrying a lamb wrapped up in his cloak. The bell hangs from his staff or crook. Laying the lamb down, he raises his eyes to heaven:

SHEPHERD : Lord God of High Heaven, in this coming night
spread your starlight around these hills,
and drive away all darkly ills
from me and my white flock of sheep—
not forgetting this little black lamb. (*Looking down on it.*)
For though he's now lying there sweet and calm
and lost to the world in a lambikin sleep,
he's just all but bleated him out of his mind
for a mother who is, for the moment, mislaid
and a father even I cannot find—
least not without some heavenly aid.
And, Dear Jehovah, don't let him start crying again
when I lift him up into my two arms—
at a certain cost in muscular pain (*smiling*)
to me and my back. Mnah!! (*as he stoops and picks up lamb.*)

(*Joseph is heard calling from offstage left.*)

JOSEPH : (*off*) Shepherd! Shepherd!

SHEPHERD : (*turning*) Who is this now? (*peering off*)
—with a limping ass.
and with a woman upon the poor animal—
rocking gently along this way
in the last royal redness of the sun.

323

JOSEPH : (*off and nearer*) Shepherd!

(*Joseph comes in.*)

Shepherd . . .

SHEPHERD : Yes, traveller?

JOSEPH : Can that really be Bethlehem
spread on the dark hillside below?

SHEPHERD : (*looking to where Joseph points*)

Bethlehem? Aye. It can't be aught else—
unless, since I stooped to pick up this lamb,
God has been very busy indeed
behind my back. Why, brother?

JOSEPH : She . . . (*indicating off*) and myself
must be in Bethlehem before sundown.

SHEPHERD : (*looking off*) You and your wife?

JOSEPH : Yes. And our ass is lame.

SHEPHERD :   So I see.

(*Turning curiously to Joseph.*)

But your voice is from the North.

JOSEPH : From Galilee. Why? (*Unaccountably sharp.*) *Why?*

SHEPHERD : Sh! You must keep your voice low,
or you may waken my youngest.

JOSEPH : (*quietly*) Your youngest? A child? Up here?

SHEPHERD : No, brother, a lamb—and a black one too.

JOSEPH : (*turning off to where Mary is*) It is a little lamb,
Mary.

SHEPHERD : Perhaps the lady would like to hold . . .

(*As though going off to show it to Mary.*)

JOSEPH : (*shortly, interrupting*) . . . No.
And my voice may be from the North,

but its first bleat was in Bethlehem.
I must rise there early tomorrow to pay
the Roman Tax. (*Turning to go.*)

SHEPHERD :   The Roman Tax!
Aye, there's a wearisome burden on us all.
And your sweet wife dragging all that way too!
Tcha! From Galilee, did you say?

JOSEPH : From Nazareth in Galilee. (*Shortly.*) Good-night!

SHEPHERD : Nazareth! Wait! (*Stopping Joseph.*)
                              Why, only today,
another, a potter, came this way
from Nazareth in Galilee,
and he had a strange tale to tell.
Perhaps you can . . . (*stopping as he sees Joseph's
    face.*)
What's the matter, brother?

JOSEPH : (*wearily*)   Nothing.
But idle talk discovers no truth.
And it may waken your little lamb.
We both bid you good-night.

SHEPHERD : Well . . . I hope you know somewhere down there
        to lodge;
for your wife seems in no condition to . . .

JOSEPH : (*exasperated in his desire to get away*)
We shall sleep tonight at the new Inn.

SHEPHERD : Well . . . you can try. But I doubt it.
And with your wife in her condition it . . .

JOSEPH : Let my poor wife be! (*With surprising anger.*)
In Jehovah's name, is she never to have any peace
    again?
Are all minds so anxious to harry the nest where the
    dove has come!

MARY : (*off, calling, tenderly but reprovingly*) Joseph! Jo-
        seph!

SHEPHERD : Tcha! (*As lamb bleats.*)* And now we have wakened
my little lamb.
It's all right, Emmanuel. (*Speaking to lamb.*)

JOSEPH : Emmanuel?

MARY : (*off*) It is the name, Joseph. It is the name! Come!

JOSEPH : Yes, Mary!

SHEPHERD : Mary? (*Looking off curiously.*)
What was that she said?
Did she ask something of me?

JOSEPH : (*wearily*) All we ask, Shepherd, of you is the way.
On which side of Bethlehem does this new Inn lie?

SHEPHERD : (*turning to him and watching Joseph's face as he
speaks*)
See that clump of olives on the slope below?
Go on and down to the right of them.
And as you begin to climb again
you'll see it—on the rocky breast of the hill.
Lamps will be buzzing round it now,
like Samson's little foxes. So
you'll not miss it, Master. (*With a new deference.*)

JOSEPH : Thank you, Shepherd.
And forgive me my anger. (*Turning.*) I am very
tired. (*Going.*)
God rest you, and your little lamb!
(*As Joseph goes.*)
Mary! This is the way! (*Off.*) We begin to go down.
Mary, come!

SHEPHERD : Mary! (*To himself.*) That was the name.
(*Calling after them.*)
God rest you both!—and your "little lamb"!
(*To lamb.*) Emmanuel! (*Urgently.*) Emmanuel!
Just cast your sheepy eyes that way.

* By judicious use of his cloak throughout, the Shepherd may bleat for
his lamb.

For the loveliest creature I did ever see
is riding the lowliest one away—
limping against the cooling sky.
And, if I am not wrong, in the warmth of her
she carries a "little lamb" too.
But she's gone. We must move our flock on. (*Turning.*)
And there's no need for all this trembling in you.
Aye, but—born out of season in a bad time,
you'll need the horns now coming through
that soft, curly, innocent brow.
A bad time, Aye! (*Looking off and down.*)
For these little red lamps down below
are flickering about on that far brow
because Bethlehem is chockful now
of lost sheep—with two legs apiece.
Cæsar Augustus is fleecing his sheep.
Emmanuel! (*Softly.*) He's asleep.
Well . . . (*rocking him as for a lullaby*)
dream your dreams of the great milky ewe,
for the world will turn you all too soon
into a hard-horned, grey old ram.
And yet, my Emmanuel, if you grew
and kept that curly beauty too
you'd be so special a sort of thing,
that they'd covet you up in Jerusalem.
And you'd end in the temple of Herod the King
in some new blood-sacrifice.
So, sleep you! Sleep you! (*Looking up.*)
For the little stars are coming through,
like a crop of crowfoot growing through
a dark lake. The sun has gone. (*Looking off.*)
Aye, but high in the palace in Jerusalem,
in a room whose gold walls still hold the red sun,
Herod, hunched, glowers down—
like a Roman eagle ready to swoop
on any lamb that raises the hope

of a new sort of majesty.
Come, my sheep! Come!

(*He rings the little bell to lead flock.*)

Aye . . . (*Sighing.*)

(*As the figure of Herod sitting on his throne is disclosed.*)

Emmanuel (*as a parting thought*) there's another thing!
You're better born Lamb than king.
For to be killed and devoured is one thing—
but to devour yourself . . . well (*as he goes*)
ask the King. Aye, ask the King.

(*The Shepherd moves off, ringing his little bell.*)

ACT I

Scene II

The Palace in Jerusalem—The Throne—Afterglow of Sunset—Cool

As Herod sits like a brooding eagle in his throne . . . Justinius comes in. He is the typical colonial officer of a foreign and "occupying power."

Justinius : (*approaching*) Do I interrupt the evening meditations of the King?

Herod : (*looking at him, unmoved*) It remains a Roman right, Justinius, to interrupt anything I may do—as King.

(*Herod, who is a person of no small scale, has a cleverness whetted by obsessive suspicion. Under his superficial and oriental suavity he watches like a hawk.*)

Yet, peace attend you, Justinius! This was not meditation. Having fed my doves, I was watching them circle round and round in the air, snatching insects. And meanwhile the sun turned the great eagle on the Temple dome from green-gold into red. (*Rousing himself from reflection.*) Are there "incidents" already? Or why have you come to the palace at this hour?

JUSTINIUS : Do you anticipate some special "incident"?

HEROD : (*laconically*) It is a way to keep peace, Procurator—to anticipate. And my peace is never fostered by your Cæsar's taxation. But, in all honesty, why have you come?

JUSTINIUS : (*blandly*) To render thanks before sleep. For in my message to Rome I shall be able to say—with all honesty—"in the kingdom of Herod in Judah my task has been made the lighter by the iron rule with which he sways all his people." Yet (*trying to provoke information*) I did come also to say—before tomorrow's tax-gatherings overwhelm me—that in the event of whatever "incident" you "anticipate," you may anticipate that all Imperial guards now standing within my command are at your disposal.

HEROD : What I, Justinius, anticipate need never come to anything which will either make demands upon you or crease the pale imperious brow of your Augustus.

JUSTINIUS : Yet, together, we have done much to keep that pale brow smooth. And any service I may still do—even for private, not public, peace—is yours to command. Such peace be yours! (*About to go.*)

HEROD : Justinius! (*Justinius turns back.*) When your registers of the tax-payers are complete, it would be of service to me to have copies for my private scrutiny. For it is some little comfort to know what strangers I entertain tonight within my little kingdom.

JUSTINIUS : (*provoking the matter further*) Might it be some further aid to private peace, if I were to have the symbol of David's star inscribed opposite to all those who are named . . . "Emmanuel"?

HEROD : (*angrily breaking his false calm*) I do try at least to keep my mind beyond Roman supervision! (*Shouting.*) Is my mind too, to be under Roman mandate!

(*Herod rises from his throne and would go.*)

JUSTINIUS : (*placatingly*) My King . . . This anticipation of the coming of your Messiah must occupy my mind too. Is it not my duty?—even to you. For it is something always in the ebb and flow of popular unrest. Our unfortunate overcrowding of the towns and villages now must raise such a high tide of unrest. And though I cannot share your view that the danger of a Messiah is a reality, yet I am fully aware that at such a time, though in fact no real Messiah will come, it is the highest of probabilities that some sect or faction will invent one. Such "inventions" must be crushed at their birth. For a new King of the Jews must certainly be as grave a concern to Rome as to you. That is, simply, why I must say that if anything should happen then . . .

HEROD : (*cutting him short*) Nothing will! Not beyond mere invention. Your registers would help me if you choose to help.

JUSTINIUS : By nightfall of tomorrow they will be in your hands; your sensitive and powerful hands. Peace be with you! (*Turning at the exit.*) And I would have you know how much I understand, that it is easier for me to find peace in all this than you. For you must believe, must you not, that some time the true Messiah will come?

HEROD : I believe that when He does come, neither you nor I shall have any doubts. (*Coldly.*) While I do have doubts I shall— as you—assume that a false Messiah has come; and leave my actions to the correctives of God. For should my actions be wrong . . . (*gesture*) it will be Jehovah's Son. The Lord's dominion is greater than mine. He will protect him. (*Turning.*) Peace attend you this night! For me there can be no peace— nor for many Jews—for many nights. Send the registers . . . unmarked.

(*Herod sweeps out past Justinius who follows out.*)

ACT I

Scene III

Outside the Stable—Bethlehem—The Same Evening—
Twilight—Mild

*Sound of Thomas singing off. The Innkeeper's Wife bustles in with
a lantern in her hand, calling:*

Wife : Thomas! (*And to self.*) Why do they all want to come and
sleep at our Inn?—and not sleep when they do come! Oh,
where will they all sleep? Where will they all sleep? (*Going,
calling.*) Thomas! Thomas! (*She bustles out. Off, and going.*)
Thom-as!

(*A light streams out of the stable door. Thomas comes to the
door, sweeping out the stable with a broom, and singing, happily, a song as he sweeps.*)

Thomas : "Adam was the father of Cain,
but who was the father of Adam?
        The rain?
                No.
        The sun?
                No.
        The West Wind?
                East Wind?
                South Wind?
                        No!
        Then who was? Do you know?
                The Lord Jeh—ho—. . . . (*stopping*)
        What? (*Listening and stopping sweeping.*)

(*His wife can be heard approaching calling.*)

Wife : (*off and approaching*) Thomas! Tho-mas! Tho——

(*Wife comes in. Thomas is younger than his wife, who is serious even when he pokes fun at her.*)

Oh, there you are! Where have you been?

THOMAS : (*lightly*) I've been sweeping out the stable, wife-for-ever-adored.

WIFE : But why do that now? You should be finding people places to sleep.

THOMAS : I am. (*Continuing sweeping and singing.*)
"Adam was the father of . . ."

WIFE : You can't mean in there, Thomas!

THOMAS : I can mean in there, wife.

WIFE : In the stable? (*Incredulously.*)

THOMAS : It's fit for a king now, incredible wife.
"Adam was the . . ."

WIFE : But, Thomas! (*Stopping him.*) They're all dancing up in the wine-room above, and teasing me about you. And they won't let me have their names for the Roman registers.

THOMAS : "Adam was . . ." Won't they now, my turtle dove?
"But who was the father of Adam? The rain?
No! . . ."

WIFE : Oh. (*Exasperated.*) And what have you got to sing about, I'd like to know?

THOMAS : Everything. (*Stopping sweeping and sweeping her into his arms.*) A new wife like you—a new Inn like this—up to the knees in new straw—and so up to the ears in custom now, that they'll have to sleep in that stable! Kiss me!

WIFE : Oh, why did I marry a man who behaves like a boy!

THOMAS : (*wickedly*) There may be an answer to that! Take care!
"Adam was the father of . . ."

WIFE : And is this place really fit for sleeping in?

THOMAS : Positively purified, precious spouse!

WIFE : (*seriously*) And have you put the asses in next door with the other beasts?

THOMAS : Yes, delectable wife! Put the asses with the oxen, put the goats with the swine, and all the birds under one roof. I feel like Noah putting to sea with a shortage of partitioning. Lord knows what we are letting ourselves in for in the way of animal offspring! But . . .

WIFE : (*sharply*) Hold your silly tongue! You've been drinking!

THOMAS : (*wickedly*) Incontestable, inexhaustible wife!

WIFE : And is that fresh straw in there?

THOMAS : The freshest of fresh golden straw, superb wife! (*Going in to get lantern out.*) "West Wind? East Wind? South Wind? No!! . . ." (*Coming out again.*) Even in the mangers too. For if there are young children coming . . . And that reminds me. Talking of cradles . . . I heard a story today. . . . (*Confidentially, as he leans on his broom.*)

WIFE : (*shortly*) I've no time now for your stories! (*But as he turns away.*) What was the story?

THOMAS : (*eagerly, laying down lantern*) It was a fisherman from the Sea of Galilee told it to me. He had it from a sail-maker, who had it from a potter, who had it from a publican, who had it . . .

WIFE : (*exasperated*) What was the story!

THOMAS : A carpenter in the village of Nazareth took a virgin woman to wife, and she told him that she was going to have a child, and that the child would not be his. And he didn't have her put away from him.

WIFE : Oh. (*Serious.*) Why?

THOMAS : Because she said that the Lord God had conceived in her, before she was his. And the carpenter, so they say, saw in a vision that this was true. And they say he's a wise sort of man.

WIFE : (*simply*) But can it be true?

THOMAS : Well, you know what the prophets say—"A virgin with child—house of David—stem of Jesse." And this carpenter is of the house of David. So! (*As if she should draw her own conclusion.*)

WIFE : The Messiah! Oh, Thomas! But then it's not true about Him going to be born in Bethlehem?

THOMAS : Ah! (*Knowingly.*) But don't you see! If he is of the House of David, then he will have to come back to Bethlehem here in order to pay Cæsar's tax. In fact, he will be in Bethlehem now—unless he's determined to break the law—as well as the conventions! (*Taking up the lantern.*) And if he doesn't keep her close by his side after all this, it will be a wonder, won't it? Eh?

WIFE : What did you say her name was?

THOMAS : I didn't. For I don't know. But his name—the father . . . well, I mean the husband—is Joseph, son of Jacob, of Nazareth, a carpenter. And now that I've finished my purifications of this place, I'll bolt the door and come up to help you with the registers. Oho! (*Looking off.*) Here's a lantern coming our way, with a man attached.

WIFE : And a white ass. (*Looking off.*)

THOMAS : A white ass attached to him. And a woman, to whom he seems rather attached. Is she ill—or just weary? Jehovah proceed you! (*Calling.*) Leave the ass there!

(*Joseph comes in with Mary, who leans on his arm. One should not see her face or figure clearly.*)

WIFE : (*uneasily, as Joseph says nothing, but just looks at them*) What is it that you want?

JOSEPH : They said up in the Inn that we might find you here. Are you not the Innkeeper's wife?

THOMAS : Yes, and I'm what keeps her. (*Pleasantly.*) What can we do for you?

JOSEPH : It was said that you might have some other place for us to sleep in.

THOMAS : And I have. But is your wife ill? (*Raising lantern.*)

JOSEPH : (*standing between the lantern and Mary*) She is exhausted. We have travelled a long way. Where is the place?

WIFE : (*troubled*) I am afraid there is nothing better to offer you than the stable.

THOMAS : Nothing better! It's fit for a King! I've seen to that. Look! (*Turning to unbolt door.*)

WIFE : (*as Thomas is getting door unbolted*) Master, before I get lost again among my guests up there, perhaps you would tell me your name and where you have come from—and your occupation too. It is for the Roman registers. They must have the lists by the morning.

(*Mary moves towards the door.*)

JOSEPH : Yes, I see. (*Wearily.*) Joseph . . . son of Jacob . . . carpenter . . . and this is Mary, my wife, who has . . . (*Stopping, as he sees that the woman is looking at Mary and not listening to what he says.*) What is it, woman?

WIFE : Oh. (*Speechless.*) Oh!! . . . (*crying out involuntarily.*)

(*Thomas turns to see his Wife run away.*)

THOMAS : Wife! Come back! T! t! I'm sorry, Master. (*He too stares at Mary.*)

MARY : Oh, why did the woman run away? (*Distressed.*)

THOMAS : Oh, dear lady, it's not her fault. But there are a lot of people in our Inn, and some from Galilee, Master Joseph, and people talk, and, and . . . (*stopping in distress.*)

JOSEPH : The woman had no right to distress her.

THOMAS : Oh, I am sure that she didn't mean to do that. She's really very gentle. I'll fetch her back and perhaps we can offer you our own room in the house.

MARY : No. Joseph (*gently and wearily*), if the stable is clean and warm I would rather be there. It will be away from the stir in the house and the voices of people.

THOMAS : (*eagerly*) Oh, yes, it is clean, and comfortable too. But it is only a sort of a cave of a place for animals. And you . . . well . . . you . . . (*lost for words.*)

JOSEPH : Open the door.

THOMAS : Well, of course, it must be up to you, Master. (*Fumbling with door.*) And it will be quietest and farthest away from the dancing and the drinking up there. Though perhaps the animals that I crowded in next door will make a bit of noise in the night. We have an ox that snores and . . . (*throwing door open.*) Will I help you in, Master Joseph?

JOSEPH : No. But our animal needs a place to rest. So . . .

THOMAS : (*eagerly*) Leave that to me. And take my lamp in too. It is dark for her in there. You look so tired, Master. And so does she. In the morning I'll leave a pan of milk by this door. My name's Thomas. And anything I can do for you. . . . Well. . . . Good-night! . . . May the Lord God bless. . . . But of course! . . . (*stopping in confusion*) . . . of course . . . (*Thomas goes.*)

MARY : (*calling after him, compassionately*) God rest you, Thomas!

JOSEPH : Now, let us go in.

(*As they stand before the open door.*)

MARY : It is like a cave—cut into the rock.

JOSEPH : (*holding up lantern and looking in*) It is empty. It is warm. And it is clean. (*Turning to her.*) Lean on my arm. For this is the end of the long journey.

MARY : No. Please, go you first in. I shall follow.

(*Submissively Joseph goes in with the light. Music—softly—plaintively. Mary drops her dark hood as she looks up and we see her face.*

For a moment Mary looks around, as one looking at the earth and the sky for the last time, then, bowing her head, goes in through the low stable door.

Music to grow and continue over scene change.)

ACT I

Scene IV

Inside the Stable

*A Manger (which is a simple, shallow wicker basket from which
cattle would eat) with straw in it, and some trusses of straw. Night.
Joseph guides Mary in and helps her to rest on the straw beyond
the manger. Music gently—ends.*

MARY : (*looking up and around*)
I feel strangely at peace in this place.

(*As Joseph puts his own cloak around her and lays out
some of their belongings.*)

Joseph, no others will come into this stable now.
May we bring in the poor lame ass—
who has carried me so devotedly—
so that I may bathe and attend to his leg,
without stirring out. May we?

JOSEPH : (*resignedly*)
It must be as you say in this place.
It must all be, Mary, as you say.
I will first unpack the animal where he is.
Lie you back against the sweet straw.

MARY : (*closing her eyes in relief*)
It smells of the Summer still.
And this manger is like the flat boat we saw
ferrying harvest to Magdala. (*Touching it.*)
Joseph, why was the woman afraid of me?

JOSEPH : Because, beloved, are you not chosen to be above all
others?

MARY : (*simply, thoughtfully*) No, not *above*—favoured—
and for my time.

JOSEPH : For all Time! (*With tender pride.*)

MARY : (*with almost worried simplicity*)
        No, Joseph—now.
    And not above. God does not sow
    the seed of His Spirit in the proud.

JOSEPH : (*in great pride of her*)
    Nor lets that priceless pearl grow
    but in elect and flawless flesh.

MARY : The proud Queen of Sheba might envy me
    the flaws of my humble flesh, had she
    this . . . visiting glory. (*Almost trancelike.*)
    It came from above—
    the Spirit was about me,
    is in and is of me now.
    Yet it is not I—it is He,
    He who will ascend—
    but only through me.
    There is my glory.

JOSEPH : (*with adoration*) Oh, Mary! Mary!

MARY : In the eyes of the world I make it hard for you,
    but the truth is in . . .

JOSEPH : (*fervently*) The Truth is in you!
    And the revelation of it is to come.
    And the Lord would not seek an easy way
    to accomplish the impossibly good!
    Rest. It has been a long journey—
    for us both. (*Turning to go.*)
    I shall leave both lamps in here.
    Outside they will not be necessary,
    for it is a great night of stars.

    (*Music—softly.*)

    I shall bolt the door on the outside
    so that no one will disturb you.

MARY : Yes, bolt the door, and I shall pray
    for my submission, to what must be.

JOSEPH : Pray also, beloved (*in self-despair*) for me.

> (*Joseph goes. Slowly Mary kneels before the empty manger, with the lamp at either side. Music to end.*)

MARY : (*raising her hand in simple supplication*)
As Ruth, in this same Bethlehem,
laid down her body at Boaz' feet,
I lay my body in this sweet straw
—at Your feet.

> Teach me, Lord, how
—in this small cave in this dark earth—
this weak body may bring to birth
the seed You have sown, to make the sea
of stars above turn silently
away from chaos.

> For how dare I
mother God out of the uttermost sky?
How, hinged upon Heaven, dare I be
the door of the cave from which You go
walking forth upon the earth?
(*With final resignation.*)
Yet, Lord, if You will it, let there be
no mortal will remaining in me.
But comfort Joseph, and let me be true,
like the old Shepherd up on the hill,
whose lamb was just a lamb, and who
loved the little animal so,
for no other reason than that he too
loved a young life.

> Let all be . . . true,
and simple, and lovely; and Love drive away
my mortal fears.

> (*In complete peace and relaxation Mary lies down to sleep in the straw. Music to a conclusion.*)

CURTAIN.

ACT II

SCENE I

OUTSIDE THE STABLE—A BRIGHT MORNING—EARLY—COOL

Before rise of curtain there is knocking.
The curtain rises and Thomas is by the door knocking. He has a pot of milk and some barley bread. Thomas knocks and calls timidly.

THOMAS : Master Joseph! It's me! It's Thomas, the Innkeeper!

(*Joseph slips out through the door and closes it behind him.*)

The morning's brightest blessings to you!
It's me—and the morning sun—and the goat's milk—and some barley bread, from my shamefaced wife.

JOSEPH : Bless you, my good friend!

THOMAS : And I hope the beasts didn't disturb you in the night.

JOSEPH : She slept deeply—and she sleeps still. But (*leading Thomas away from the door*) I had a dream of the child and of Herod the King. And it troubles me—deeply, Thomas.

(*Sound of some voices off from the people of Bethlehem.*)

(*Alarmed.*) What are these voices? (*Looking off.*) Who are these?

THOMAS : (*apologetically*) There's some people gathered outside already. Oh, I'm not letting them come near, Master.

JOSEPH : But you must send them away. Their voices will worry her. And they might draw attention to us. They might draw the attention of Herod's men. You must send them away!

THOMAS : Of course, I'll try, Master Joseph. But you see (*whispering*) now that they know who you are . . .

JOSEPH : (*loudly*) Thomas, I am in the world's eyes simply a poor carpenter, who is anxious in the extreme about his beloved wife. For it may be that her time draws near. And . . .

THOMAS : (*awed*) . . . Oh, Master.

JOSEPH : (*nervously*) And I am at a loss who to ask here about our fears. For this is my . . . this is the first child.

THOMAS : (*quickly*) I'll get my wife straight away. She's really a good woman, Master, and good about these things. She's older than me—and wiser. Take the milk, and the bread.

(*Joseph accepts the gifts of food.*)

JOSEPH : Yes, but go at once and fetch her. And (*as Thomas is going*) try to send these people away!

THOMAS : Well, I'll get them to keep silent for her sake. But they'll not go. For it's such an event. I mean, it's not just as if they were curious. It does concern everybody, doesn't it? Watch, Master! You're letting the milk spill! (*Going.*) I'll fetch my wife.

(*Thomas hurries off.*)

(*Off.*) Stand farther off! (*To crowd.*) And keep silent!

JOSEPH : "It does concern everybody." (*To himself.*) Oh, Lord, protect her! Protect her!

(*Joseph goes in.*)

ACT II

SCENE II

INSIDE THE STABLE—IMMEDIATELY AFTER

Mary sits, rocking ever so gently, and quite unconsciously.

MARY : Joseph . . .

(*Joseph brings the milk and bread.*)

JOSEPH : Yes, Mary? (*Gently.*) A woman is coming. Thomas has brought this milk and some barley bread. Drink the milk, beloved. (*As she makes no move to take it and ceaselessly rocks.*) What is wrong?

MARY : I am afraid. (*Simply, softly and innocently*.) I find that I am afraid. Is it faithless of me to be afraid?

JOSEPH : (*gently*)
Surely it is through fear that faith must go
to find its own constancy?
And God has chosen to be like us,
not to exalt us out of our fears
but to give them great meaning.
Break the bread and eat.

MARY : But Joseph . . .

JOSEPH :   Yes?

(*As she is silent.*)

                             Yes, Mary?

MARY : The lamb of that shepherd on the hill
must have been born out of season. And he . . .
had lost his mother in gaining life.
If it were required that I . . .

JOSEPH : (*fearfully*) No!
Oh, no, my beloved, that cannot be.
Oh, is it sinful that I cannot see
beyond you to the child? (*Taking her hands in his.*)
That I cannot love what I cannot touch
—when what I love and touch is you?
that all my prayers are for you,
and not for the child? Is this wrong?

MARY : How can I believe so? For, in longing for Him,
it is your love and care that I need now.
Oh, pray that the child will need me so.
For what a glory will that be—
to be essential to Him.

JOSEPH : (*quietly, sadly*) Yes, Mary. (*Letting her hands fall away.*)

(*Slowly the rocking motion reasserts itself in her.*)

MARY : (*simply, unanxiously*) I wish that the woman might come now.

(*Thomas is seen going through the door.*)

JOSEPH : This will be Thomas with her. (*Rising.*) Thomas!

(*As Thomas comes in alone.*)

THOMAS : (*shamefacedly*) Oh, Master!

JOSEPH : But the woman?—your wife?—where is she?

THOMAS : Oh, it's very difficult. (*Perplexed.*) She's sitting up in the kitchen now—crying, Master Joseph, like to break her heart.

MARY : Crying? The woman crying?

JOSEPH : But why? Why?

THOMAS : Oh, you'll not be angry with her, will you?

JOSEPH : Of course not. (*Impatiently.*) But why?

THOMAS : Because (*haltingly*) she just can't make her weak legs carry her down here. Oh, it's not her fault entirely, Master. You see, she says, as she weeps, how can she with her sinful hands dare to . . . well . . . Master . . . The Messiah! . . . The Christ Child . . . ?

JOSEPH : (*in anger*) It is not for her to choose. It is not for any of us to choose! (*His fears finding voice.*) Do you think I choose to be in this hard responsibility?

MARY : Joseph! Joseph! (*Gently, reprovingly.*) It is the woman's humility that keeps her away—as it is your love which makes you angry. Tell her, Thomas, that I feel more unworthy than she, in face of my greater responsibility. Tell her simply that I need and want her near.

THOMAS : I will. Oh, I will. (*Perplexed.*) But will she have the courage to come? You see, if something did go wrong . . .

MARY : But it will not, Thomas.

THOMAS : Oh, I'm ashamed, my lady, I am. But how am I to give her the faith to come?

JOSEPH : (*distractedly*) Is there no one else?

THOMAS : There's only one of all the women who is not afraid. And she's not afraid at all. For she's just as you'd suspect—so full of herself and falseness, Master, that nobody should trust her. You mustn't have her!

JOSEPH : Then, in God's name! (*Thundering in his distraction.*) Tell your wife that she has been chosen of all for this time and this place! And that all of us, to our poor capacities, must play false or true to the event! But for those who simply turn away, fires of torment will follow! For, if love of God will not bring her here, then let fear of God do so!!

MARY : (*softly*) Thomas . . . let love of life bring her to me. Tell her that whether she comes or not, the child will come. Tell her that I am lonely for a woman's hand.

THOMAS : I'll tell her just that. (*In tears.*) And I'll tell her the glory I see in your face—my lady! Oh, my lady! (*Turning to go.*) I'm sorry, Master Joseph, but it's as if something was so precious to you that you just didn't dare touch it at all. But I'll hurry. She'll come. I know she'll come now.

(*Thomas goes. Mary, in weariness, bows her head.*)

JOSEPH : Oh, Mary, will it always be so?
    and everything be so critical?
    and you, who are so calm, so gentle, so shy,
    never again taste simple joy?

MARY : (*as she raises her head, with great serenity*)
    I am in pain—and I am filled with joy.

(*Music—gently, behind. Joseph sinks on his knees before her.*)

JOSEPH : Mary, it is you—(*in adoration*) you—
    it is the quality of what you are—
    it is your utter trust makes all things true
    conform around you. I adore you.

MARY : No, Joseph (*distressed*) you must not kneel to me. It is not to me that you must pray.

JOSEPH : That, beloved, you may not say.
             (*With intense passion.*)
             For I must! I must!

      (*Music—rising to conclude. The curtain excluding the stable
      falls as he prays before her.*)

ACT II

SCENE III

BEFORE THE PALACE IN JERUSALEM—NOON—HOT

Before rise of curtain a cry of anguish.
*The Three Wise Men come in anxiously. The Three should differ
in size and shape—remembering that Air is the element of the
first: Water of the second, and Fire of the third. Their professional
intensity and wit provide comic effect, but they are not burlesque
characters. They carry serious meaning.*

1ST W.M. : I heard a cry of pain. (*Looking up.*) What was that
cry of pain?

2ND W.M. : And from where did it come? (*Turning to First
Wise Man.*) Did it not come from your sphere of Wisdom,
my learned friend?—from the skies?

1ST W.M. : From the skies? Did it?

3RD W.M. : (*dryly*) It came from an upper room of this high
palace of the King, my dear astronomer. It appears that this
King Herod is questioning a man—an astronomer. (*Meaningfully.*)

1ST W.M. : Oh. (*Apprehensively.*) Come. Let us shake from our
weary feet the sands of the courtyards of this king. Oh! (*Stopping and looking off.*) Our camels! Our camels!

3RD W.M. : (*pointing*) They are dragging our three camels away!

2ND W.M. : (*calmly*) There I must differ with you, Persia. They are simply leading the thirsty animals through to the outer court. I propose, however, that we keep calm, and do not run from Herod—or he will simply follow and cut us down. For if he will torture his own astronomer about a star, what more might he do to us who are necessarily at variance with him, not only in Astronomy, but in Medicine and Chemistry. (*Indicating their respective departments.*)

1ST W.M. : I suppose we must wait and face what transpires (*Looking up.*) The sun's at its zenith. The Roman officer has been a long time in coming back down from the King.

2ND W.M. : (*placidly*) Well . . . (*looking around*)
It is a palace of great height and many stairways.

1ST W.M. : (*seriously*) But, my brothers in Wisdom, when we do come
before the throne of this cruel King,
is it agreed between us three
that we must be guarded in what we say?—
about the star.

2ND W.M. : Very guarded. His humours are violent.

3RD W.M. : Let us not lose our heads—(*dryly*)
or we shall.

1ST W.M. :   So . . . (*taking them aside in conference*)
within our three spheres of wisdom shall we
pursue one desperate policy of polite evasion?
You agree?—Media, for Medicine?

2ND W.M. : I do, my soul of Astronomy.
And when one finds himself in difficulty,
let him pass the question to another, and he
pass to the third, and so on—till we
confound the question.

3RD W.M. : (*dryly*)   And the King too.

1ST W.M. : Avoid seriousness, for seriousness might grow into universal catastrophe.

2ND W.M. : Smile; fear God; and let The Evil One be his own
destruction.

1ST W.M. :   I agree.
And you, my analyser of substance?

3RD W.M. : Yes, I agree—(*dryly*) in substance.
And we must keep his mind off one substance—gold
or he may retain me forcibly
to transmute all his metals. For don't you agree
that gold would appear to be (*looking round*)
this ruler's ruling passion?
Consider that great golden door. (*Pointing off.*)

2ND W.M. : Yes. But consider who comes through it now.

1ST W.M. : The Imperial Roman!
Can I take it that we all agree
that he constitutes no threat at all
to the Empire of Ideas?
          (*As they all nod assent.*) Sh!

(*Justinius comes in.*)

JUSTINIUS : (*imperiously*) March this way! All three.
I said, march this way!

3RD W.M. : (*dryly*) We march. (*Following him, muttering.*)
A man of some metal! . . . But which?

JUSTINIUS : (*turning, nettled*) What did you say?

ST W.M. : My friend said: "We march"—to the best of our
ability, according to the suitability of our ridiculous clothes.
(*Falling in line.*) We follow, Imperial Procurator. It has become our custom to follow in the wake of brilliance. The star,
you see . . .

ND AND 3RD : Sh! (*Cautioning him.*) We follow.
(*Justinius goes.*)

ST W.M. : Oh! (*Realising his gaff.*) I follow you, I follow.

(*The Three Wise Men go out after Justinius.*)

ACT II
Scene IV
Herod's Palace—Immediately After Sunset

Herod sits on his throne. Nicolus, a personal servant, comes in.

Nicolus : My Lord (*with the smiling deference of a pampered servant*), my King, you called for me? Is the "examination" over?

Herod : Yes, Nicolus. (*Stroking his head.*) And it is to be published, through all the streets of Jerusalem that this last fool, whom I have been "questioning," has seen no new star and there is no such thing in our heavens now.

Nicolus : No new star. No star?

Herod : No. I shall let the people know that the man is mad. For if he is not so now (*meaningfully*) he soon will be. Have the Roman Procurator now bring in his Three Wise Men.

Nicolus : Yes, my King. I shall send them to you.

(*Nicolus goes out.*)

Herod : (*to himself*) The prophecies . . . "And also a star . . ." (*Troubled.*) "Also a star . . ."

(*Justinius peremptorily ushers in the Three Wise Men, who bow before the King and remain bowed.*)

Peace rest upon your heads! Raise your wise heads, my learned friends! I would see your distinguished faces.

1st W.M. : (*raising his head*) For my breathless self, and on behalf of these my brilliant brothers on this pilgrimage, I do salute you, great King of Judah! May the sun and may the moon never gild your golden roofs and not find peace thereunder.

Herod : (*coolly*)
And may the stars not be unpacific either.
For are you not astronomers?

1st W.M. : (*with airy pleasantry*)
I, myself, do attempt the stars.

My two friends devote themselves, severally,
to the Forms and to the Substances of Life.
They are as Water and Fire to my vapourings.
For it is vocational to me
to utter airy nothings—mathematically. (*Smiling.*)

HEROD : (*liking the intellectual pleasantry but not diverted
from his deadly serious intention*)
And, being of the company of the Magi,
I do take it that you are—all three—
devoted to . . . Truth?

1ST W.M. : (*with a glance at the others*) That is true.

HEROD : And this friend of my household, Justinius—
who is procurator of The Empire of the West—
tells me that you have travelled far
before presenting yourselves here.

1ST W.M. : That too is true.

HEROD : And what can lead you to travel so far,
and cause you so suddenly to appear?—
so abruptly—so unannounced?

1ST W.M. :   Ah . . . (*in trouble*)
(*The Second Wise Man makes a sign to him to pass
the question on.*)
Ah! the *cause* of our sudden arrival, O King,
being much less a matter of astronomy
than of . . . anatomy and formality,
I defer to our Medical scholar of Man—
Media?

2ND W.M. : (*calmly, coming forward*) The cause, O King,
of our sudden arrival thus breathlessly,
when viewed with any immediacy (*turning*) . . .
is this swift-marching officer of the Empire of the
West.

JUSTINIUS : Fool!

(*Herod is secretly amused.*)

You show disrespect before a King!

HEROD :   I notice no disrespect to *me*. But
           viewed with less "immediacy" (*playing their game*
           what led you out of the Realms of the East?

2ND W.M. : (*smoothly*)
           That . . . er . . . being a matter which might b
           best
           astro-geographically assessed,
           I defer to my friend from The Ultimate East.

           (*Bowing himself "out of play."*)

1ST W.M. : As, O Wise King (*a little unprepared for thi
           move*)
           is in the case of . . . all our wanderings,
           the *cause* of our present journeying . . .
           is the Pursuit of Truth!

HEROD :   (*relentlessly playing his moves in their polite game*
           Yet I had understood it thus—
           again from my friend Justinius—
           that what you pursued was in fact . . .
           (*watching them*) . . . *a star.*

1ST W.M. : Ah! "In fact" our Pursuit of Truth, it is true,
           has seemed to simplify itself into
           the pursuit of a . . . (*coughing*)

2ND W.M. : . . . a form in the sky (*coming to his assistance*

1ST W.M. : which (*recovering*)—being biased towards Astroi
           omy
           and governed by the verbal necessity
           of making myself ridiculously clear,
           for the sake of our Roman conductor here—
           I had *"in fact"* called *a star.*

JUSTINIUS : (*superciliously*)
           And if it is not *in fact* a star,
           what in Heaven's name is it?

1ST W.M. : In Heaven's name?—(*blandly*) nothing.

3RD W.M. : (*quickly*)
Having no substance, by any name,
and having no essence but what we imply.

1ST W.M. : (*quickly*)
From a trace drawn by The Heavenly Hand
across the insubstantial sky.

2ND W.M. : (*quickly*)
And which according to the human eye
is caused by a light which yet may be
a complete illusion!

JUSTINIUS : (*bursting out*)
This is outrageous evasion!
And if you persist I . . .

HEROD : (*curtly*) Peace, Justinius! This is not Rome.
(*Turning to the three.*) My wise friends,
though it is beyond my poor wisdom to advise you
upon what it is that you pursue,
yet it does seem—beyond what you say—
that you anticipate something more;
and that something seems to be *a star*.
Nor does your anticipation stop there.
(*Presenting his case with relish and authority.*)
For you anticipate that this star—
which you refuse to award so far
any more substance than that of a sign—
is the sign of something which is quite new.
Further, that knowing—as you surely do—
the signs in which our prophecies abound,
you do now anticipate and pursue
the fulfillment of a prophecy;—
that under that star there should be found
a child, of an equal glory to
the formless brilliance of that star.
That (*watching its effect*) is what my dull mind in-
    forms me;
and what I have the audacity
to present to you.

JUSTINIUS : (*challengingly, as he is caught up in the tense intellectual "cat-and-mouse" despite himself*)
What do you say to that?

1ST W.M. : Well . . . my Imperial Procurator (*thinking furiously*)
and, O wise . . . O most wise King!
There is so much "anticipation" in what you say
and anticipation is such a human thing,
that again I must defer to my more humane friend
(*And, giving 2nd W.M. time to prepare argument.*)
Though—as to star, as star—
I do admit to a professional desire
towards finding that this celestial fire
should fall within my special sphere
of Pure Astronomy.
But that is a human weakness which I am sure
my medical colleague may yet cure.
Media?

2ND W.M. : Hm. (*Clearing his throat.*)
Let us agree, O King, that we know
of a certain local prophecy,
by which—through no active desire of your own—
you must affect "anticipation."
I mean of your Messiah's coming.
And of course this is correct for you.
But for *us*—in so far as we do pursue
a *universal* devotion to Truth—
it may not be that we should so
anticipate local conclusion to
this . . . moving sign.
We pursue it—we hope—in pure hope.
True, it did lead us to your kingdom, *and*
—so far as the mathematics of my friend
can with accuracy ascertain—
it now leads us on through Jerusalem.
But who knows!

In some years' time we may pass through Rome,
and greet this lord Justinius,
with the same equivocal degree
of quite essential uncertainty—
and then find ourselves re-approaching you
from the opposite direction!
For beyond what we know we must not presume,
and behind what we know there will always be
our abysmal ignorance. (*Bowing.*)

1ST AND 3RD : (*involuntarily applauding*) Beautiful!

JUSTINIUS : This is intolerable!

HEROD : (*tensely*) But not to me,
not so intolerable as it would be
if the world should lose, too suddenly,
such triple brilliance (*standing and calling.*)
Nicolus!

(*The Three Wise Men exchange uncertain glances.*)

My dear companions in the pursuit of Truth,
I have bathed in the brillance of your minds;
yet let none here forget how Truth may be
dependent on behaviour; and wisdom may come
through crude—Nay, indeed I fear—
through brutal action. (*Sighing. Nicolus comes in
and waits.*)
But do me this honour; to accept of me
my full hospitality for this day.
For I presume—if presumption is allowed me—
that to follow a . . .
light in the sky, at the height of the day,
is unwise behaviour.

1ST W.M. : As you in your great wisdom do know,
all must bow to such *forceful* wisdom as yours.
(*Not quite sure if they are now prisoners.*)
And may we sometime be free to return to you
this overpowering generosity?

HEROD : The return—which I do desire—
need in no way affect your freedom now.
I would simply ask this of you:
(*Coming down from throne, and they retreating.*)
that if this sign which you pursue
should ever blossom forth as a star—
and if beneath it you should find
what my dull mind has long looked for—
that, immediately, you should send to me.
Then I too may touch and see
the wonder of this child!
(*With a strange passion.*)
For there burns no greater desire in me
than that a true Messiah should come.
For, only through *His* Majesty (*voice rising*)
can the realms of the restless world become
One Kingdom of God Upon Earth!—
and Peace reign among men!
Peace is my passion!
(*Exhausted.*) Go in peace! (*Turning back towards
the throne.*)
This servant of my household, Nicolus,
will conduct you down to cool rooms
and splendid raiments. Go in peace!

(*Herod subsides wearily on his throne as the Three
Wise Men, awed to silence by this frightening show
of passion, are led off by Nicolus. Justinius hesitates
to go.*)

Well, Justinius . . . ?

JUSTINIUS : Well . . . King of Judah! (*Solemnly.*) In my des-
patch to Rome what dare I say that this Herod of Judah now
believes—and *hopes* from his belief?

HEROD : He *believes* nothing, Justinius. But what he *hopes* to
know is what *is,* and what is about to be—for the sake of
anticipating strife, and keeping the King's—*and* the Emperor's
—Peace.

JUSTINIUS : I think I shall devote myself to the receipts of taxes. Your meanings are too subtle for me. (*Turning to go.*)

HEROD : Justinius! (*He turns.*) If it rescues you from Eastern subtlety, you may know that when the three leave my palace— and perhaps until the day they die—*they will be followed.*

(*Nicolus approaching and calling.*)

NICOLUS : (*off*) My Lord Herod! My Lord!

(*Nicolus comes in, excitedly carrying the three gifts of the Wise Men in his arms.*)

Look, my Lord Herod!

HEROD : What is it, Nicolus? What are these?

(*As Nicolus offers them up to Herod and Justinius examines them.*)

NICOLUS : (*excitedly*) They are three gifts which were found in the camel panniers of the Three Wise Men. The Roman guards of lord Justinius have just brought them up the Great Stair.

JUSTINIUS : A casket of alabaster.

NICOLUS : (*handing it up to Herod*) Containing frankincense.

HEROD : (*taking it slowly in his hands*) And in the shape of a crown.

JUSTINIUS : A casket of silver.

NICOLUS : Containing myrrh.

HEROD : (*taking it*) In the shape of a scroll.

JUSTINIUS : And what is this?

NICOLUS : A talisman of gold.

HEROD : (*taking it*) In the shape of a . . . cross.

JUSTINIUS : Presents fit for a King.

NICOLUS : What shall be done with them?

HEROD : (*handing them back, his mind lost in thought*) Put them back where they were found—on the camels. They must continue to their destination—which obviously is not here. Leave me, both. (*Suddenly hysterically, as Justinius is about to question him.*) Leave me!

JUSTINIUS : (*withdrawing*) Peace be . . .

HEROD : (*interrupting*) Peace! . . . (*Sitting and looking bitterly ahead of him.*) Peace . . .

(*Justinius and Nicolus without another word, go.*)

CURTAIN.

ACT III

SCENE I

THE HILLS AROUND BETHLEHEM—STARLIGHT—CHILL

The Shepherd is lying back snoring with his lamb tucked up and hidden under his cloak. His little bell tinkles as his staff falls to the ground. There is a bright light shining down upon him, as he wakes up.

SHEPHERD : I . . . I dreamt of . . . (*looking up*) . . . of angels . . . "Peace on earth" . . . ? (*Lamb bleats.*) What? (*Sleepily.*) What is it, my lamb? Oh, yes. I may have been snoring. But time and custom have made it so that I can snore with an eye open. Eh? (*Lamb bleats.*) (*Sitting up.*) What is it now, Emmanuel? You would think that I hadn't provided you with the best bed on these bare hills— next to your mother's woolly bosom. You what? Think my bosom's too bony? Eh? (*Arranging cloak.*) Well, so do I. But my cloak is soft, and warm too, if you'd only stop wagging your wicked little tail

at this ridiculous hour of the night.
Why, what *is* it that's troubling you?
(*Looking round.*) Where? Oh . . . I see! I see.
Camels amove on our dark horizon!
(*Peering off.*)
Three camels!—Aye, and a fourth one too.
Well!! Here's a night of novelties!—
A strange star in the sky,
and camels up here!
(*Getting up.*)   They've lost their way.
And we'd better stop them coming on, Emmanuel,
or they'll scatter our sleeping flock. Hey!
Stop there! (*Picking up and ringing his little bell.
    Calling to them off.*)
Masters, don't come further this way
—least, not with your camels!
My flock is down that way!
Have you lost your path in the dark?

(*First Wise Man comes in on foot.*)

I said, have you lost your path?

1st W.M. : Lost our path, Shepherd? No. We have no path,
but the path traced upon this earth
by that star slowly traversing the sky.

Shepherd : Traversing? (*Looking up.*) That star?

(*Second and Third Wise Men come in.*)

So you know something about that bright star?

3rd W.M. : We should.

1st W.M. : Having followed it half-way across the world.

Shepherd : Half-way across the world! (*Incredulously.*)
What, all four of you?

1st, 2nd, 3rd : We have, Shepherd.

1st W.M. : What? (*Thinking twice.*) Did you say four?—
four of us?

Shepherd : Yes, four . . . I think. (*Puzzled.*)

1ST W.M. : And how do you make us four?

2ND W.M. : If by force of habit he reckons in animals, it would make us six, not four.

3RD W.M. : (*dryly*) If he's truly disposed to zoology he can reckon us up to infinity, by counting the fleas. (*Scratching*.)

SHEPHERD : (*smiling*) Ah, but, now you are closer, I can see that you are only three. (*Looking off*.) And a camel apiece. It was while you were further off you seemed four.

2ND W.M. : This confirms my suspicion. Ever since leaving Herod's palace we have been followed.

3RD W.M. : Suspicion supported, Media.

1ST W.M. : My eyes have so constantly been on the star, that perhaps I would have been quite unaware had all of Jerusalem followed in the rear.

SHEPHERD : Well, if there's somebody following you leave him to me. I've had long experiences of wolves—human and animal. I'll keep my eyes open as you pass on. But what are you all following this star for anyway?

(*The Third Wise Man is keeping his eyes fixed intently on the star.*)

1ST W.M. : Because where that star shall come to rest, there shall be born upon the earth below a Child of Heaven.

SHEPHERD : On the earth below?—where it comes to rest? (*Interested*.) Is that so? Do you hear that, Emmanuel?

3RD W.M. : (*with suppressed excitement*) My friend! Quickly! Persia! Fetch our colleague's astral calculator from off his camel. Quickly! (*As he is about to ask why. Second Wise Man hurries off*.)

SHEPHERD : His what calculator? (*Looking off*.)

3RD W.M. : (*to 1st*) While you have talked it has seemed to me— and I hesitate to say it with certainty—that *the star has ceased to move on!*

(Second Wise Man hurries in with what looks like some sort of sextant.)

2ND W.M. : What?—not moved on! Here is the instrument!

3RD W.M. : Then perhaps our astronomical friend will calculate and confirm the observation of my naked eye.

1ST W.M. : But immediately! *(Seizing instrument and raising it.)*

(As First Wise Man does business with "astral calculator.")

SHEPHERD : *My* naked eye, sirs, is used enough to telling the movement of stars without . . .

2ND AND 3RD : Hush! Be quiet, Shepherd! Be still!

2ND W.M. : *(whispering)* While he calculates he must not be distracted.

3RD W.M. : *(teasing Shepherd)* Or what should have been added will be subtracted! What's the conclusion?

1ST W.M. : *(turning to them in excitement)*
The star is at rest!
It stands steadfast above the earth now.
Shepherd! Shepherd *(pointing)* what lies there below? I see some lights.

SHEPHERD : Why, Bethlehem, of course. Bethle . . . Oh! *(Suddenly recollecting.)* Glory to God! If this is true . . . *(Slowly.)*

1ST W.M. : Why, what is it, Shepherd?

SHEPHERD : I think that my little lamb and I did see the mother of this Child of Heaven pass by. *(Urgently.)* I'll be your guide to Bethlehem. I'll guide you to her and him. I know where this babe is to be born, I do.

2ND W.M. : Then blessed are you!

SHEPHERD : Aye *(excitedly)* blessed, am I? *(Turning to go.)* Come. Oh! . . . *(Again recollecting and stopping as he sees something off.)* I think I saw that wolf of Herod's up among the rocks. You make for the corner of that olive grove down there. (*Whispering.*) Wait among its black shapes, and I will join you—aye—(*slyly*) and on a camel too—a fourth camel . . .

1ST W.M. : But how will you manage to . . .

SHEPHERD : Now don't ask me how. (*Impatiently bundling them off.*) There will be a deal of wisdom in it, I dare say. But it's of little concern to you and the Wisdom of the East. Go on! But, master, perhaps under your gorgeous coat you'll carry my little black lamb, till I join you.

(*Shepherd hands "lamb" to the embarrassed Third Wise Man who holds it the wrong end up.*)

It's all right, Emmanuel! He's a wise sort of man—even though he may not know which end wags. (*Righting the lamb.*) Now, off with you to your camels! And if I don't come soon, make for the new Inn! (*After them.*)

1ST W.M. : The new Inn! (*Going.*)

(*As the Three Wise Men go off, the Shepherd goes stealthily about his business.*)

ACT III

SCENE II

BEFORE THE STABLE—LATER THE SAME NIGHT

Throaty lowing of oxen, chained and restless in background. One or two people including 1st Woman of Bethlehem, 2nd Woman of Bethlehem, and Old Simon, "a local worthy," edge in cautiously.

1ST WOMAN : (*almost whispered*) Just think what a wonderful thing it would be, to be the one to hear this child's first cry.

(*Thomas comes in from behind them.*)

THOMAS : Have I not told you to stand away? Have you no respect at all? Get back!

(*He shepherds them back.*)

(*Looking to door.*) Has nobody come out yet?

2ND WOMAN : No.

(*Thomas goes anxiously, and gradually they all edge back in again.*)

OLD SIMON : (*in his high pipe*) Is Thomas's wife in the stable there?

1ST WOMAN : What did Old Simon say? Eh?

OLD SIMON : Are you all as deaf as I am? (*Querulously.*) I said, is Thomas's wife in there still?

1ST WOMAN : Yes! (*Loudly into his ear.*) Fancy a stable to be the chosen place! (*To 2nd Woman.*) These animals in the next place are restless, eh?

(*A Young Man strolls in. Old Simon views him with suspicion.*)

2ND WOMAN : Do you think that animals know?

OLD SIMON : Animals know what?

2ND WOMAN : Don't you think that animals sense what's in the air?

OLD SIMON : What's in the air? (*Seeing Young Man. Looking up.*)

1ST WOMAN : Well, I couldn't say.

2ND WOMAN : Well, look how just a moment ago they were all lowing and bellowing as if they knew.

YOUNG MAN : (*overhearing*) It's nothing to the noise that you would make if half the folk of Bethlehem were gathering out-side your door and arguing the whole night through what you did or did not know. (*Turning to go.*)

2ND WOMAN : (*angrily following him up*) Young man—nobody asked you your opinion! Who are you, anyway?

YOUNG MAN : A man, I hope. Why (*insolently*), who are you, come to that?

2ND WOMAN : (*bitingly*) A woman—and it's more than hope! Keep your Jerusalem tongue to yourself and let me talk to my neighbours in peace. Why, I've got sons as big as you and many smaller—and wiser!

YOUNG MAN : All right, Mother of Millions! (*Trying to avoid her.*)

1ST WOMAN : Mother of Millions, indeed! (*Flaring up.*)

YOUNG MAN : (*blandly*) Why, mother, have *you* more?

1ST WOMAN : I have one dear child, young man, and I hope to God that he will never grow up as disrespectful as you!

(*Old Simon, who has been watching and wondering, taps the Young Man on the back. The Young Man jumps nervously.*)

OLD SIMON : Young fellow, what do you say to that star?

(*Old Simon points up with his stick.*)

YOUNG MAN : What star, grandfather?

OLD SIMON : That bright fellow straight above us now. Eh? What do you think?

YOUNG MAN : I think it's bright! (*Shouting into his ear.*)

OLD SIMON : I'm deaf, young man—not unconscious. But what do you say to its brightness? Eh? What do you say to it?

YOUNG MAN : That it has a lot of light to give—and it's giving it freely. I say: "Thanks, star!" Why?

OLD SIMON : They are saying that it is The Messiah's star. And that it moved up out of the East—growing brighter as it came. And I haven't seen it before. Have you? Eh?

YOUNG MAN : No, I've not seen it before. And that applies to half the stars in the night sky. I work hard in the day and sleep at night. (*Turning away.*)

1ST WOMAN : (*confronting him*) Young man, don't you *want* The Messiah to come?

YOUNG MAN : Mother-of-One (*grimly*) I think I want The Messiah to come as much as you will want him to be gone when he does come. For he'll come with a sword and sacrifice! (*Fanatically.*) God, how I long for a just King for Israel!— for one who is a true Jew! Not a Roman puppet of Idumean blood with Greek ideals and an Egyptian Guard who will murder to order!

OLD SIMON : Young cockerel, you'll do well to be more careful how you crow. Herod has spies all around.

YOUNG MAN : Then the more fools you!—to be hanging around this stable now, attracting their attention. (*Angrily.*) Has no one told you that Herod killed his own wife and murdered his sons? That when my friends had the courage to go and tear that Roman eagle down from the top of our Temple dome, he butchered them? And what do you think he'll do to our Messiah?

OLD SIMON : Young fellow, for all the many years I have been here, every birth in Bethlehem with any signs of hope at all has drawn Herod's attention. He won't do a thing until all the signs are fulfilled. And then perhaps . . .

YOUNG MAN : (*interrupting*) . . . Signs! Signs! You old gossips, with your waiting for signs, have been the ruin of Judah!

2ND WOMAN : Gossips are we? (*As it boils up into a quarrel.*)

YOUNG MAN : Oh, why don't you go home to your millions, mother?

2ND WOMAN : And why don't you go home to *your* mother!

YOUNG MAN : Because I have none! (*Turning on her savagely.*) And ask Herod about that too!!!

OLD SIMON : Not so loud, young fellow.

YOUNG MAN : Yes (*shouting*) and the gossips who gave her away!!

OLD SIMON : Quiet!

(*At this quarrel and the raised voices Joseph comes out through the door.*)

JOSEPH : Stop! (*As they turn.*) In Jehovah's name, think shame on yourselves for raising your voices in anger here. Your voices have troubled her. Please, go away from this door, or keep silence for her sake.

(*As they are all retiring, ashamed, Thomas leads through them the Shepherd with his lamb on his arm.*)

OLD SIMON : That's old Antony—Antony the shepherd!

SHEPHERD : Simon, my old friend! But where is . . . (*seeing Joseph.*) Master Joseph! (*Going to him.*)

THOMAS : He says that he met you up on the hills, Master.

JOSEPH : Yes, I remember. (*Wearily.*) But I am sorely distressed now, and would rather not talk with anyone.

SHEPHERD : But, Master Joseph, you'll not turn me away when you know that I have had the honour of guiding to you these three greatly wise men.

(*The others fall back in silence as the Three Wise Men come in and bow before Joseph.*)

They have travelled half across the earth to bring presents to your wonderful son.

JOSEPH : I have no son. (*Turning away in despair.*) And why need there be all this light shed around?

1ST W.M. : Can it be that he has not seen His star?

JOSEPH : (*turning to him*) What star?

SHEPHERD : Look up, Master Joseph. In your despair, look up!

(*As Joseph for the first time turns his eyes to the heavens.*)

JOSEPH : Oh . . . (*slowly, in wonder.*) Mary . . . the star! His star! Oh . . . (*turning to door.*) Mary! . . .

(*Quickly Joseph goes into the stable and the door is closed.*)

YOUNG MAN : (*incredulously*) The star! (*Looking up.*) It seems to grow. As I look at it, it seems to grow!

THOMAS : Yes, it seems to grow.

SHEPHERD : Masters (*to the Three*) the star is growing in the sky!

(*As all look up.*)

1ST W.M. : Oh, my brothers, we were wrong! For the star has not ceased to move at all. It has changed direction. It has turned towards us! The star is approaching the earth! And so— (*excitedly and awed*)—it seems to grow!!

YOUNG MAN : Look at it now!

THOMAS : Soon it's going to be too bright to look at!

(*As the Men look up the Women draw apart and Old Simon sits with his eye on the door.*)

2ND WOMAN : Aye, it's like the men to look up to the sky.

1ST WOMAN : It's the nature of men, to scan the sky
or, looking to the sea, and far away,
to plan all their hopes to infinity.
But it rests with us—it rests with her,
the Mother of The Son of Man—
to bear the burden of their plan.

2ND WOMAN : Aye, the star grows brighter up in the sky
and captures every up-turned eye
now out-of-doors in Bethlehem,
but she's with God in there in the rock.
And in behind that wooden door
is a truth of which no man will talk
much hereafter.

(*Old Simon mutters something.*)

What did you say, Old Simon? Eh?

OLD SIMON : I said, I was there when they put up that door—
and turned the cellar of rock into
a stable for an ass. I knew
the gnarled hands of the man who blew
the bellows in the forge below—
as they hammered those bolt heads that show
like dark studs on the weathered wood.

1ST WOMAN : He's off again! (*Smiling tolerantly*.)

OLD SIMON : (*lost in reverie*)
Aye, and it's a strange thing too;
though boards have rotted and worn away
top and bottom, and in its day
it's had many a bolt, and many a shoe
has rusted above it; and many a colt
grown out of its white coat into its grey;
aye, and many children now men bored holes
to peer through at the animals;
still—do you know what I'm telling you—
there's one thing not altered one bit since the day
they hung it on its hinges. Eh? (*Catching 2nd Woman's eye.*)
But it's true!

2ND WOMAN : Yes, but what *is* the thing, Old Simon?

OLD SIMON : What thing? Oh . . . (*scratching his head*)
Didn't I tell you? The creak of that door. Oh!

(*He rises as the door creaks and Joseph comes out through the doorway. He carries a lamp. He looks up at the star.*)

THOMAS : (*going to him*) Master Joseph, has he come?

JOSEPH : He? (*Shaking his head.*) No.
(*Turning to Wise Men.*)
Oh, if you are accounted so wise, sirs,
then in your wisdom comfort me.
You are familiar with this great star.
But its approach fills me with fear.

(*During all this the light should grow from a faint to an intense white light. Where dimmers are not available let the addition of light step-by-step take place when the focus of attention is not on the sky but on a character or on the door.*)

1ST W.M. : (*coming forward*)
But, Master Joseph, why should you despair?

For this star has not come to destroy,
but to create!—to impregnate the very air
with The Creator's universal joy.

JOSEPH :   But in its growing brilliance may it not be
too great a brilliance for us of this earth?
(*Feverishly.*)
For our flesh is too weak for divinity,
and the finite, taxed with infinity
in such a universal event,
may be split asunder! and infinite gain
be God's and our loss and the world's pain.
(*In crescendo.*)
For I know the woods with which I work,
and I know that no wood will stand more strain
than, in the structure of its grain,
it has the natural strength to withstand.
But in His desire to create may not God—may
not He—
overtax the nature of flesh and *she* . . .
(*burying his face in his hands*)
. . . Oh, Mary! (*Softly.*) Mary! . . .

2ND W.M. :   (*compassionately and calmly*) Master Joseph,
the star is by nature of the Heavens.
It may rush towards Earth, but it cannot come here
—not in the form of a star.
Though, indeed, it may come so near
as to alter some natural forms as they are.
The tides may even change in the sea.

JOSEPH :   (*raising his head*)
But in its nearness all life may be
devoured by fire. Oh, Mary! Mary!
(*Inconsolable.*)

3RD W.M. :   (*coming forward*) Master Joseph.
Master Joseph, I have often seen,
within my white-hot crucibles,
the red devoured become green,

and the metal apparently destroyed by fire
deliver the metal of my desire
out of seeming destruction.
For near-chaos has often been
but the prelude to re-creation.

JOSEPH :   Yes! (*Unconsoled.*)
But has there not always been—
at the seething heart of what you have seen—
something destroyed, something cast away?
And in this event if it should be she
who . . . (*turning to the Shepherd*)
Oh, Shepherd! Shepherd, can *you* comfort me?

(*The Shepherd comes forward.*)

SHEPHERD :   (*simply and gently*)
I have not the power, Master Joseph, in me
to comfort such a great despair—
nor the great wisdom of these three—
but this I *do* know to be true:—
that every glassy-eyed, great ewe
disburthening herself of her lamb
is, to herself at that time,
the whole Universal in upheaval.
                              And we
must stand outside, and must not try
to intrude in that Universe, until we see
the lamb do so. (*With quiet assurance.*)
                              For, you see,
though that star may become too bright for my eye
I believe that your lady in labour in there
is a brighter being than even you know—
and can stand God's brilliance better than we.

JOSEPH :   (*humbled and infinitely grateful*)
Blessed are you, Shepherd, who have taught me
      to see
my own belief in my despair.
For I *do* believe that behind that door

she equals the glory of His star—
and I will kneel now, in trust, and in prayer.

(*As Joseph kneels, so also do the Wise Men and others. Only the Young Man and Old Simon do not kneel. 1st Woman goes across to Old Simon to tell him to kneel.*)

OLD SIMON : (*loudly to 1st Woman*)
Yes, and soon that same old door
will be treated like the gate of Heaven! Eh?

1ST WOMAN : Shush, Old Si! Simon, Joseph is kneeling to pray.
What did you say? (*Whispering.*)

OLD SIMON : (*loudly*) What did I say?
I was talking about the door. Do you know.

1ST WOMAN : Yes, but Simon, kneel! Simon!

OLD SIMON : I said, do you know . . .

(*She gives up, and kneels herself as Simon turns to the Young Man for audience.*)

I remember how one night, that door
was rent from its hinges by the storm—
a thunderstorm—this was years ago—

(*The Young Man is still fascinated by what he sees in the sky, and lets Simon ramble on, while there is a murmur and mutter of prayer from the kneeling figures.*)

and as the thunder muttered away
there came a great dark swishing wind.
And that wind swirled around this hill
for just a few minutes, but in those few
it blew with all the ferocity
of years of tempest! (*Getting excited.*)
                                    It tore away
the new wooden bolts and the rain swept
        through—
it crashed like a wave on the old pine door;

it swung it wide: the ox ran amok!—
The mule in stark terror uprooted his rope
and thrashed at the wind with flashing
    hooves . . .
and split the loose door from lintel to lock!

2ND WOMAN : Simon! Si! Sh!

OLD SIMON : Yes, the animal's hooves split the door.
And people were afraid to go out after.
It was so suddenly calm after the stir—
so still and calm. And all you could hear
—above the thunder far beyond—
was the wreck of the desolate old door—
in the gentle after-wind—
creaking, just as it creaked before. Eh? What?
Oh! (*Turning and seeing them all at prayer.*)

(*Simon goes slowly onto his knees. Only the Young Man now stands, looking up and shielding his eyes from the bright light. The murmur of prayer goes on.*)

YOUNG MAN : Stop that noise! (*Harshly.*) Stop your praying! For God's sake, stop!

(*There is quiet as the Young Man listens attentively.*)

1ST W.M. : What is it, young man?

YOUNG MAN : There is a *sound* that comes from the star.

(*No sound effect should be used at this point.*)

1ST W.M. : Yes. (*Listening.*) There is a strange sound in the air.
(*Quickly.*) But do not look up at the star!

2ND W.M. : The star is too bright for the human eye!

1ST W.M. : (*warningly to those who raise their heads*)
Keep your heads bowed! Bow your head, young man!

YOUNG MAN : Listen! (*Impatiently.*) Listen!

    (*All in quick, hushed succession.*)

1ST WOMAN : Is it the angels?

2ND WOMAN :   Is it the choirs of Heaven?

3RD W.M. : It comes from the fires that burn in the star!

1ST W.M. : It is the music-making of the spheres!

2ND W.M. : It is simply something created in our ears by the great agitation in the air!

    (*A faint sound just audible, as of a taut string plucked and dying away, or a single voice at a great remove. If this is more than just heard it will make anticlimax.*)

YOUNG MAN : (*triumphantly*)
It is the coming of the King through the clouds!
The King is coming in the star! (*Staring up.*)
The King from above!—from another
  world! . . .

1ST W.M. : Young man! (*Shouting to him.*)
Not with your naked eyes or . . .

YOUNG MAN : I can see! (*Crying out in pain.*) Ah! . . .

    (*He turns his head in agony from the light and gropes around.*)

It's gone! It's dark!

    (*The light is brighter than ever.*)

1ST W.M. : (*awed*)
Let no one else look up! For now
it is brighter than ever! And he was blinded.

YOUNG MAN : Blind? I am blind. (*Appalled.*) I *am* blind!
  Guide me.

    (*As he stumbles over the other prostrate figures.*)

I am blind! (*Going.*) I am blind!! . . .

2ND W.M. : Let no man look with the naked eye upon the star!
(*Solemnly.*)
But you, my friend, take up your dark glass
and with that try to see for us
what is taking place in the star.

1ST W.M. : I shall try. I shall try.

(*The 1st Wise Man, taking a dark circle of glass
from his satchel holds it up before his eyes and
looks up.*)

SHEPHERD : Master, what can you see up there?

2ND WOMAN : Is it the bright winged angels themselves?

3RD W.M. : What is there at its nucleus?

1ST W.M. : (*still looking*) Only an intensity of light.

2ND W.M. : But is there no shape, no form, to the light.

1ST W.M. : Only a sort of flame—no form.
(*Suddenly, excitedly.*)
But a tongue of flame forks out and down!

(*Faintly, sound of one sustained and quivering
note.*)

And now all the light is tinged with red!

2ND WOMAN : Red! It's a falling ball of fire!

1ST WOMAN : We'll all perish! (*Terror-stricken, going to rise.*)

THOMAS :   Stay where you are!
Keep calm!   (*Holding her.*)

1ST W.M. :   It is like a red flower,
It blossoms forth! It's white at the heart!

3RD W.M. : It is the regenerating part
of the heavens' ever-renewing fire!

2ND W.M. : What more do you see at the heart of the star?

1st W.M. : Something erupts from the heart of the star!
Ah!! (*Crying out in wonder.*)
It sheds hundreds of tiny tongues of flame!

(*His voice rising in crescendo against decrescendo of sound.*)

And a thousand now plunge from each of them!
And from each thousand millions, till
the curving canopy of the night
is streaked with minute tracks of light!!—
falling down (*decrescendo and covering*)
        and down,
                and down . . .! . . . down . . .

(*The sound and all the light have gone.*)

(*Raising his head slowly.*)
Raise up your heads! For the star is spent.
And the fiery atoms of all its light
are engulfed in the cold sea of night.
Raise up your heads!

(*As, murmuring, they raise their heads.*)

JOSEPH : (*in a voice hoarse with exhaustion*)
How dark it is. How utterly dark!
Was there ever such utter darkness on Earth?
(*Then, fearfully recollecting her.*) Mary . . .
Oh, my beloved . . .

OLD SIMON : There *is* a light, you know.

(*As the stable door is unbolted and a ray of light falls on the people as it creaks open.*)

Since the day of the storm, that
door has never fitted as . . .

1st WOMAN : (*on verge of tears*) . . . Be quiet, Simon!
The door is opening.

(*In the light from the door the exhausted Wife of the Innkeeper stands.*)

WIFE : (*quietly, triumphantly*) Master Joseph.
Master Joseph . . . He is come.

(*Music gently, behind.*)

JOSEPH : (*rising, in slow amazement, from his knees*)
He? . . . (*incredulously.*) He . . .?

WIFE : He is come. (*Gently.*) Come you in—alone.

(*Joseph goes, almost fearfully in his joy, in past
her into the light of the stable. She closes the door
and leans wearily upon it. As Thomas runs forward to embrace her the people break their
silence.*)

1ST WOMAN : (*crying out*) He is come!
Run and tell them in the streets that the child is
born.

SHEPHERD : Woman, take care! (*Calling out in alarm.*) Hush!
We must not tell the wolf of the lamb;
Let all go in joy! But keep the joy in your
hearts as yet!—For His sake! Come. (*Shepherding
them off.*)

(*As all rise and go.*)

2ND WOMAN : (*almost whispered*) The Messiah! (*Going.*)

1ST W.M. : The Son of Heaven! (*Going.*)

2ND W.M. : The Son of Man! (*Going.*)

3RD W.M. : The substance of God Incarnate! (*Going.*)

(*As Thomas takes his wife off, he stops and, in
pride and tenderness, kisses her. Music to conclude
as they go. As silence again falls, the curtain rises
on the manger.*)

ACT III

SCENE III

IN THE STABLE—LATER—THE EARLY HOURS

Mary lies beyond the manger, leaning against the trusses of straw.
The child is in the crook of her arm, and hidden by the fall of her
cloak.
A lamp burns on the ground by the manger.
Joseph kneels with his head bowed.

MARY : Joseph! (*In the tenderness of exhaustion.*)
Joseph, you must not weep.

JOSEPH : (*tearful with joy and relief*) Oh, Mary! These are
a new sort of tears to me. For He *is*. He has come
into *being*. He . . . (*speechless.*)

MARY : He cried as He came. But He is here.
(*Smiling down at the babe.*)

JOSEPH : And he is thirsting for life—so it seems.
For . . . (*almost laughing through his tears with in-*
expressible happiness) he is . . . a baby!
. . . a perfect baby!

MARY : He is perfection—and of us.

JOSEPH : Oh, the Heavens cried out in praise of you!

MARY : I think that the Earth cried out in me!
(*Closing her eyes in exhaustion and peace.*)
But now it seems as though God's wings
were around and supporting me;—
or as though I were afloat in that world of cloud
which you and I would sometimes see
—when watching the thunderstorms die—
sailing away out of the sky
in the evenings, beyond Galilee.
There, now. (*Whispering.*) He sleeps. He sleeps.

JOSEPH : Yes. (*Rising and looking down at them with great*
tenderness.)

For he has tasted the world;
and, as all his world is yet you,
he has found it sweet. (*Gathering his cloak around
      them.*)

MARY : Emmanuel—(*softly*)—God with us.

JOSEPH : Such a trust to be lodged in us—
that in that vulnerable form,
breathing within your pulsing arm,
the hope of God in Man should sleep.
Sleep, my love—(*touching the child's head*)
and O, my love—(*touching Mary's head*)
sleep!

(*Music—softly. Lifting the lamp, Joseph goes, quietly.*)

CURTAIN

ACT IV

SCENE I

THE PALACE—THE NEXT DAY—EARLY MORNING

Justinius is waiting, nervously.

HEROD : (*off, and calling*) Justinius! Where is the Roman Procurator!

(*Herod comes in.*)

JUSTINIUS : I am here, my Lord Herod, and more than curious.

HEROD : That fool, Nicolus, told me that you were still below.
(*In some agitation.*) Justinius, in the night the child was born
—in Bethlehem—in a stable—of an inn. I must ask your
assistance immediately.

JUSTINIUS : It has always been yours to ask.

HEROD : I dare not send my own guards to Bethlehem now. The
people would simply hide the child. And I must see the child

JUSTINIUS : With what end in view?

HEROD : (*pacing restlessly*) It is necessary for me to see the child —and for you, Justinius, to trust me.

JUSTINIUS : But if you merely seek its destruction, then I . . .

HEROD : (*violently*) . . . *I must see the child!*

JUSTINIUS : (*coldly*) Can it be that you really fear—or hope—to find your *true* Messiah?

HEROD : I did not create this star! (*Pacing.*) I could not prevent the star's approach. I could not prevent the child being born! But now I . . . (*shouting hysterically*) . . . I *will* see the child!!! And if in this you refuse to help me then . . . ! (*about to go.*)

JUSTINIUS : (*standing in his path*) But I did not say so. (*Quickly and calmly.*) In fact, I myself will go to Bethlehem, to hold the child in custody till you come. Peace (*scornfully*) remain with you!

(*Justinius turns abruptly and goes.*)

HEROD : (*calling after him*) When the place is fully guarded I will come! Already the people in Bethlehem may be in open defiance!

(*Following after Justinius.*)

And (*calling*) let the Great Gate be closed behind the Roman Procurator! (*Going, calling.*) Nicolus! Nicolus!

ACT IV

SCENE II

IN THE STABLE—THE SAME DAY—TOWARDS EVENING

Mary sits, gently rocking the manger, in which the child lies, unseen. Joseph comes in.

JOSEPH : Mary! (*Gently.*) The day is far spent. And the Wise Men must depart. But they will not depart without seeing him. The Shepherd is with them. May they come in? They have presents.

MARY : Yes, Joseph, let them come in.

JOSEPH : (*turning to go*) If I could, I would let the world come in, to adore him. How could I have foreseen this . . . adoration?

(*Joseph goes to door and ushers in the Three Wise Men and the Shepherd. Joseph stands by Mary and the manger as the Three hesitate and the Shepherd hangs back.*)

MARY : (*simply*) His eyes search towards the brilliance of your garments. Come forward.

(*As they kneel before her.*)

1ST W.M. : Glory be to the Creator of All things!

2ND W.M. : And to you among all women!

3RD W.M. : And to Him, Whose substantial glory I see!

2ND W.M. : Whose form is the beauty of purity.

1ST W.M. : And in whose eyes I seem to see the star still shine.

SHEPHERD : And in whose fleecy head I see a power of tenderness.

1ST W.M. : In the presence of true splendour we kneel and offer these our trivial gifts:

(*As each offers his and lays it by the manger.*)

I bring you Frankincense from Arabia,
In this alabaster box—
which is in the shape of a *crown*.

2ND W.M. : I bring you a silver casket of Myrrh—
which is in the shape of a *scroll*.

3RD W.M. : I bring you a talisman of Gold—
which is in the shape of a *cross*.

SHEPHERD : I bring you, my lady, this little lamb—
which is in the shape God made him;
for he is what I most love.

MARY :   In the name of my child I accept these gifts.
          The presents from The East are precious to me.
          And yet, of all, I must love best the living lamb.

*(Thomas calling: "Master Joseph!" As they all turn, alarmed,
he comes in.)*

THOMAS : Master Joseph!

JOSEPH : Thomas! What is wrong?

THOMAS : *(breathlessly)* The Roman Governor, Justinius has
ridden into Bethlehem. And he is mustering a special guard.
And I think they are coming on this way. I sent all the crowd
off into the streets to hinder them coming on—so far as they
can without open strife. But you must get the dear child away.

JOSEPH : But where could we go that we would not be easily
followed?

SHEPHERD : *(thinking hard)* They'd better lie hidden till nightfall, Thomas. Then I can guide them up into the hills. And you
three gentlemen *(turning to Wise Men)* had best not be seen.
I have some sheepskins in my hut at the back. You could throw
them over your fine robes. And I dare say—if the bargain ap-
peals to you—that I could change your three camels for mules.

1ST W.M. : *(anxiously)* Yes, but where will you hide the mother
and the child?

SHEPHERD : *(wasting no time)* We'll think of somewhere. And
Master Joseph, put your belongings out on the ass now and
I'll lead him up to my hut right away.

*(As Joseph gathers things together and assists Mary to take the
child in her arms.)*

Now, Thomas, this place next door—*(to Wise Men.)* I won't
be a moment!—is it full of beasts?

THOMAS : Yes, but if there's time I could turn them all out.

SHEPHERD : *(quickly but unruffled)* No, don't do that. For what I
was thinking now, is that a place full of livestock is one that
they'll not look into very closely. See?

THOMAS : Yes. *(Worried.)*

SHEPHERD : There will be space at the back for them to hide. No animal is going to hurt them. And if the child did happen to cry, while they were searching about in here, it would be a simple matter for Master Joseph to rouse the beasts—and so drown his cry. For that's a danger—his crying.

THOMAS : Yes. I see. I suppose it is as good as we can do. And the Lord is with us.

SHEPHERD : If you three have made your farewells . . . (*Impatiently*.)

1ST W.M. : Our quest is completed. (*Preparing to go*.) And tomorrow, as the new rays of the rising sun touch all the temple towers in turn, crossing our countries—so we shall go calling to the sentinel towers of The East: "A creature is come within the world, in whom God must manifest the full nature of Heaven!" And as we journey on, so the silver trumpets one by one striding from tower to tower will begin to outpace this news we bring, in pure silver notes of joy!

(*Hurried by the Shepherd, the Three Wise Men go.*)

JOSEPH : (*anxiously*) And may joy attend you all the way? Mary we must go.
(*As he helps her to her feet.*)

SHEPHERD : Yes, Master Joseph! (*Urgently*.) Thomas will see you hidden safely next door. I'll carry the lamb, my lady, till later. For when it is dark I shall come back. Outside the other door I shall say aloud, as though to my little lamb, "Emmanuel prepare yourself! We must part for a time!" Then rise you up and come forth unafraid. Coming, my Wise ones! And Thomas lose no time!

(*The Shepherd's little bell tinkling as he goes after the Wise Men.*)

(*Curtain as Thomas, Mary with the child, and Joseph go in the opposite direction.*)

ACT IV

SCENE III

BEFORE THE STABLE—EVENING

Thomas's Wife comes in weeping. The 1st Woman follows and takes up on her.

1ST WOMAN : What did they do to him?

(*2nd Woman comes in with Old Simon. Sound of Shepherd's bell.*)

2ND WOMAN : Here's Antony the Shepherd coming back now. Antony! (*Calling him cautiously.*)

(*The Shepherd comes in and they lead him aside to where Thomas's Wife stands weeping.*)

SHEPHERD : What is she weeping for? What is the matter, my dear?

OLD SIMON : It's Thomas, isn't it? Eh?

WIFE : They've taken my man away. (*Sobbing.*)

SHEPHERD : Taken Thomas away? Who, the Romans?

WIFE : And they'll hurt him—for he'll not tell them anything.

SHEPHERD : Why, what happened? What happened, Simon?

OLD SIMON : Oh, they threw open the old door as if they expected to be struck down—and they searched—and they found nothing.

2ND WOMAN : They didn't look beyond the animals in the second place.

SHEPHERD : And have they gone away?

1ST WOMAN : No, that's the trouble. There are two standing guarding the way in here. They'd see anybody going into the other place—or coming out.

OLD SIMON : See? But not in the dark—not when it is dark.

SHEPHERD : Not so loud, Old Si—or they'll hear us.

WIFE : And when it's dark they have asked to have a lantern from me.

SHEPHERD : (*scratching head*) Well—it's a problem. And I have their ass packed, and all ready, and tethered up among the olives. (*Suddenly.*) Listen. Have you given the Romans that lantern yet?

WIFE : No, not yet.

SHEPHERD : Well, listen (*gathering them close*) when it's getting dark, you keep delaying the bringing of that lantern down. Then, when it is really dark, I will bring it down to them. I'll say that my little lamb is sick and has to go into the other place. Then I . . .

1ST WOMAN : (*stopping him*) Quiet! (*Whispering.*) There's some one coming.

(*Thomas comes in.*)

OLD SIMON : It's Thomas.

WIFE : (*running to him*) Thomas! Thomas!

THOMAS : Aye, it's me, my dear delectable wife. (*Smiling and holding her to him.*) Now, don't cry. I'm all right.

2ND WOMAN : And have they simply set you free?

OLD SIMON : You're hurt, Thomas, my son? Eh? (*As he winces as Simon touches his shoulder.*)

THOMAS : Not much. That Justinius tried to force something out of me. But he gave it all up when Herod's decree got to his ears. He hates Herod. (*Trying to avoid saying more.*) Let's go into the house. I'm thirsty.

SHEPHERD : Herod's decree? (*Thomas is silent.*)

OLD SIMON : What decree, Thomas? A new one? Eh?

THOMAS : (*grimly*) It's trumpeting now, into the deserted market-place. Ah, let's go into the house.

ST WOMAN : Deserted? Wait, Thomas. What is the decree?

THOMAS : (*slowly, bitterly*) That if the child is not delivered up to the King, every child under the age of two, in and around Bethlehem . . . (*forcing himself to say it*) . . . will be put to the sword.

ND WOMAN : (*crying out*) No!

OTHERS : No! (*Appalled.*) Oh, no!

SHEPHERD : There's a legion of devils deep down in that King.

ND WOMAN : But my Rachel is not two. . . . Oh . . .

ST WOMAN : (*urgently*) But, Thomas, did he say what he'd do with the child—if it *was* delivered up to him?

THOMAS : Kill it (*sighing*), I suppose.

ST WOMAN : Yes, but do you *know!* Did the decree *say* so?

SHEPHERD : Ah, woman (*sadly*) a wolf might even suckle a lamb, but, when it knew the nature of that lamb, do you suppose it could tolerate it long? No, don't blind yourself. He'd destroy that dear child.

ND WOMAN : (*in the anger of despair*) But you don't know for certain!

ST WOMAN : No, all you do know is that if this child is let slip away, our own children are certain to lose their lives!

OLD SIMON : (*in querulous sadness*) Woman, are you so soon prepared to betray the Saviour of Mankind?

WIFE : I saw his body come to life. I cannot bear to think of that life taken away.

ND WOMAN : (*fiercely*) And can I bear to see my last-born die? If he is God's Son then let God protect him! For how can we at such a price?

THOMAS : And must we have it hereafter set in The Book that the faithless people of Bethlehem sacrificed God's Son to save their own children?

1ST WOMAN : (*passionately*) You have none of your own! And would it not be a more terrible thing to face a future in which you had found that you had sacrificed your own child for an unfulfilled hope!

OLD SIMON : Unfulfilled hope? (*Shocked.*) I'm afraid, woman that you have just got to make up your mind whether you believe in this great event or not. For among the prophecies there is one that we are all too ready to forget. Was there not to be great lamentations? Eh?

2ND WOMAN : You are old. (*Bitterly.*) You have forgotten what it is to love your children. What right have you to speak?

OLD SIMON : (*quietly*) Perhaps I can speak *for* the children. For it is said I am "become as a child again." And I find that I do not really care for the things I whimper and fuss over. But for what I do care——What can destroy or give being to me—and maybe to the child—is that which is sown in the corner of my eye, or seeds in the mystery of my mind, about utter right and utter wrong. And it seems now utterly wrong to me that The Lamp of the World should be cast away, to keep a little lantern alight in any one house.

1ST WOMAN : (*in despair*) It is not *right* that we should have to choose!

WIFE : (*appalled at the thought*) It is a terrible thing that we might decide the fate of the world.
(*She looks at them all in turn in silence.*)

OLD SIMON : Shepherd, my old friend, I've not heard you say anything. What would you say? Eh?

SHEPHERD : Well (*shaking his head*), I don't know. If a wolf was about to destroy my best lamb, I don't suppose I would stand and argue. And if he was just too powerful for me to kill, and if in rescuing my little lamb I must let him play havoc among the flock . . . Well . . . (*sighing*) . . . I think I'd not think at all, but seize up my lamb in my arms and run. And there might be the knowledge prompting me that I held the best of all breed in my arms. The grass grows green on many a hill

And many a fine flock of sheep are still in the Mind of God. (*Turning to 2nd Woman.*) But, woman, if you are not strong enough for this, I don't see why you shouldn't take your own little one up into your arms and go—warning as many as you may, before you slip out into the dark. It's not sacrifice that God would commend, but fidelity—to the end—however bitter. So all I would say is help me to get the little Lord away; then do whatever your heart prompts you. But . . . if you don't choose to put him first, perhaps your heart will stop prompting at all. That's all I'd say. (*To Thomas's Wife.*) Now, will you show me where that lantern is.

WIFE : Yes.

(*The Shepherd goes off with Thomas and his Wife. Old Simon goes shaking his head sadly. 1st and 2nd Women look at each other and unable to meet each other's eyes go off in different directions.*)

ACT IV

SCENE IV

THE PALACE—NIGHT

Herod and Justinius, voices raised, come in quarrelling.

JUSTINIUS : . . . But it is dark, beyond your golden walls! It is now pitch dark! Utterly dark! And I tell you that in less than a day it was utterly impossible for me to search every house thoroughly! How could it be?

HEROD : I do not seek the reasons, Justinius. (*Bitingly.*) All that concerns me—and may concern your Cæsar too—is that *you have not found the child!*

JUSTINIUS : (*turning on him, livid*) Nor, my King of Judah, has your infamous decree done more than make it impossible for me!—with half of Bethlehem creeping away in stark terror!

And may it not therefore be thought by my Cæsar too—as well as by me—that *you have wanted this child to escape!*

(*Herod turns on the step of the throne.*)

HEROD : No! (*Crying out.*) You fool! No! For he cannot escape That cannot be. He cannot want to fly from me! Am I not King? Was not I too called Christ in Judah! (*Hysterically.*) And can he be other than Prince of Peace too! There is no gulf For Majesty is indivisible! I am in Him and He in me! Thus the child is mine! Mine!!! . . . (*sitting on throne.*)

JUSTINIUS : (*appalled*) He is mad! Nicolus! (*Calling.*) Nicolus Ah! (*In surprise as . . .*)

(*Nicolus runs in carrying something.*)

NICOLUS : (*recovering his breath*) Herod! . . . my King . . . have come from the guard by the Great Gate. (*Hesitantly.*) Word has come . . . from Bethlehem.

HEROD : Word? (*Dangerously calm.*) And what word, my Nicolus?

NICOLUS : The child (*fearful to say it*) has escaped to the hills

HEROD : (*in calm, shocked voice*) Escaped?
(*Slowly he sinks back into his throne.*)

HEROD : (*softly*) Fools!

JUSTINIUS : But how can you be sure of this?

HEROD : (*softly*) Fools!

(*The "fools" is almost like the toll of a bell.*)

NICOLUS : (*looking nervously to Herod, who sits in a sort of stupor*) In the place next to the stable cell there was found— in the manger—a little black lamb.

HEROD : (*almost sobbing*) Fools!

NICOLUS : (*fearfully hurrying on*) And beside this lamb there lay in the straw, these three gifts which we knew to have come from the camels of The Three. (*Producing the gifts.*)

HEROD : (*sobbing*) Fools!

NICOLUS : (*tumbling it out with his eyes on Herod*) A woman, taken fleeing with her own child, confessed that the lamb had belonged to a Shepherd. He was in the plot too. And she said that the gifts and the lamb must have been abandoned in their flight into the hills. She said this because she feared for her child. And she . . .

HEROD : Fools!!!!! (*Screaming it out.*)
(*Herod rises, trembling.*)
Fools, to steal the child from me! (*Suddenly quiet.*) Then let it all be as decreed. And let all who can—suffer, for me. (*Almost sadly.*) Nicolus, my child, go below and have them sound . . . the Night Trumpets.

NICOLUS : My lord . . . (*aghast*) the Night Trumpets? The signal to begin . . . (*turning to Justinius*) the massacre of the . . . of the children?

JUSTINIUS : (*in flaming anger*) What possible purpose can such slaughter serve now? Stop! (*Seizing Nicolus as he makes to go.*)

HEROD : It can serve me, Justinius! (*Viciously.*) It can serve me!! Sound the Night Trumpets!

(*Herod comes down from his throne and thrusting Nicolus and Justinius aside goes out shrieking.*)

(*Off.*) Sound the Night Trumpets! Sound the Night Trumpets! . . . Sound the Night Trumpets!

(*Nicolus wrenches himself from Justinius's grasp and runs out in fear. Justinius, wearily, confused, sits in the throne, his head in his hand. Distant trumpets or Herod's voice very distant "Sound the Night Trumpets."*)

ACT IV

Scene V

The Hills Around Bethlehem—Just Before Dawn

The Shepherd comes in, leading Joseph and Mary.

SHEPHERD : Master Joseph, this way! (*Breathlessly.*) Master
        Joseph,
        I think we have climbed up high enough.
        It is hard to tell in the darkness, but now
        I think it is safe for us to talk.
        For we have put the olive groves between us here
        and those down in the village below.
        The ass is tied along there (*pointing off*)
        by the last and the highest tree.

JOSEPH : Without you, Shepherd, we should have been lost.

SHEPHERD : And how is it with your lady and the babe?

JOSEPH : (*softly*) Mary?

MARY :   All is well with us, Shepherd.
        But until we are many many nights away
        and the walls of our home are around me
        I shall not feel that he is safe.

SHEPHERD : (*troubled*) Home—did you say?

JOSEPH : Mary, (*sadly and gently*) we cannot go home.

MARY : Not home? (*Perplexed.*)

SHEPHERD : My lady, if you did go where you were known Herod
        or the Romans would come for him—to take him
        away.

MARY : Then . . . we may not ever . . . take him home?

JOSEPH : When Herod is dead, it may be.

MARY : Perhaps many years?

JOSEPH : Yes, many years.

MARY : (*in desolation*)
In the place I most love I had seen him grow.
(*Her voice drained of all emotion.*)
Where shall we go?

JOSEPH : Towards Egypt.
What is it, Shepherd?
(*As the Shepherd pulls him aside.*)

SHEPHERD : Don't delay.
I see many torches marching below.

JOSEPH : But she still knows nothing of the decree.

SHEPHERD : Aye, but the sinful slaughter has begun.
Dreadful sounds drift up in the wind.
She must not hear. Hurry her on.
My lady (*turning to Mary*), I must leave you now.
And I have no words for what I feel.
But may I once touch his tender head
with lips that remember another brow—
for I think that little Emmanuel has sped
on the best of errands down below.
(*Fervently and conquering his tears.*)
Now, God speed you!

MARY : And the Love of God rest with you!

JOSEPH : God will reward you, Shepherd!

SHEPHERD : Oh, but He has! (*Going.*) He has!

(*The Shepherd goes.*)

JOSEPH : Come, the night wind and the ordinary star
are now our guides. Mary—come. (*As she hesitates.*)

MARY : (*listening*) Joseph!
A noise drifted up from Bethlehem!
What was that noise from the dark below?

JOSEPH : (*quickly, quietly*)
A sheep bleating on the slopes. Come.

MARY : (*with simple persistence*)
But there was a sound beyond that—below.
Where those little torches now come and go.

JOSEPH : A dog howling from Bethlehem. Come! (*Pleading.*)

MARY : Listen. The sound comes again. (*Troubled.*)
It is women's voices wailing, in pain?

JOSEPH : (*quickly, desperately*)
The night wind moans through the olive groves.
Speak softly or the child may wake. Come!

MARY : (*with sudden and dreadful conviction*)
O Joseph!
It is the voices of mothers who cry—
for their lost children! O, my child, why?
(*Agonisedly.*) Why?

JOSEPH : Mary, for you and for me, there is no choice.
We must go on.

MARY : (*full of dread*) Oh, my child!

JOSEPH : For there is no joy, and there is no pain,
that will not, through His body be
forever and ever reconciled.
Set your dark eyes to the hills again.
For this night was in us and was foreseen;
but in him is the unforeseeable dawn—undefiled!
Come.

(*Music—softly behind. As Mary goes passively with
Joseph.*)

MARY : Oh, my child! My child! (*Off.*) O, my child . . . !

*   *   *

(AUTHOR'S NOTE: The action of the play ends here and many
directors will prefer to bring down the curtain at this point. There
follows a form of conclusion which can provide a meaningful
tableau and colorful ending—in place of a curtain or as a special

ceremonial conclusion where appropriate. This ending can be considered optional.)

> (*Below on either side come in the Men and the Women of Bethlehem, the Three Wise Men, the Shepherd. Music concludes.*)

1st Woman : (*softly, in sorrow*)
Woe unto us that the world's gain
is our loss and our pain!

1st W.M. : (*loudly, in joy*)
Sound!—silver trumpets! The Seed of Truth has
found fertility on earth!

Shepherd : The white lamb of God has come
from the cave of night out into the sun!

> (*Final music behind.*)

1st and 2nd Woman : (*softly in sorrow*)
One lamb from all this fold!

3rd W.M. : (*jubilantly*)
Sound the trumpets of red gold!

2nd W.M. : For out of our joy—

1st Woman : and out of our pain—

1st W.M. : There shines beyond all loss and all gain—

2nd W.M. : The Word made Flesh!

3rd W.M. : God in Man!

All : Emmanuel! . . .

> (*Music to conclusion.*)

FINAL CURTAIN.

THE END.

by
Laurence Housman

ABRAHAM AND ISAAC

CHARACTERS
IN ORDER OF APPEARANCE:

SARAH
ABRAHAM
ISAAC

SCENE 1

For the right setting of this play there is no need that scenery or costume should be correct either as to date or locality; indeed, better not; for although eastern in origin, it retells a story so deeply human in its appeal that wherever it has become known, it has taken a native coloring in the minds of its readers. So, in the form in which it is here presented, there has been no attempt to preserve the archaic and biblical character of the original, but only to express in simple everyday language the painful heart-searchings of a rather primitive mind seeking to discover the Will of God in the terms of a command coming from without; and, in agonized obedience to that supposed Will, finding at last that the Will of God is truly within the heart of of man, and in no other place.

In a plain tent-like interior sits Abraham, sunk in deep dejection. He is now an old man, but his mood makes him look much older than he is; strength seems to have gone out of him. He wears the dress of one who lives on the land—an owner of flocks and herds, but also a worker.

Sarah, his wife, enters from the inner tent, carrying a pail and a milking-stool. On her way out she stops, looks at him, puts down pail and milking-stool, and goes toward him.

SARAH : Abram, what's the matter?

ABRAHAM : Matter? Nothing.

SARAH : What's worrying you?

ABRAHAM : *You.*

SARAH : It's you that's worrying me, Abram. You've got something on your mind. It's as if ye'd done a crime.

ABRAHAM : I've done no crime! God keep me from it; that's all I ask.

SARAH : Well, sure He will. What's tempting ye to it?

397

ABRAHAM : Maybe 'tis God. Quit asking!

SARAH : Abram, I can't let it be. This last week, how much have ye slept o' nights? I've heard ye get up from your bed, and kneel down and pray; and I could hear the sound of it, but not the words. And after all your praying, you groaned as though it had brought you no comfort, and you've come back to bed, and there ye have lain, sighing your heart out; and never a wink of sleep have ye had, nor I either—thinking, but not daring to speak to you, for *you* not speaking to *me*. What is it, Abram?

ABRAHAM : Nothing I can tell you, Woman; it's a trouble that's come to me from the Lord—if 'tis the Lord that's tempting me. Maybe He'll let me know in His own good time. But He's told me nothing yet. Quit asking!

SARAH : (*with a sigh, giving it up*) Well, it's no use my going on about it, if you won't tell me anything.

ABRAHAM : No use at all. We'll just leave it at that.

SARAH : While I make some better use of myself. (*She picks up pail and stool, then turns to him again, and inquires cheerfully*) How have things gone in the field today?

ABRAHAM : Well,—all well.

SARAH : Isaac's getting to be a real help to you now, isn't he?

ABRAHAM : Yes; he is that.

SARAH : He's getting a big lad.

ABRAHAM : Yes; so he is.

SARAH : Growing so fast, he'll soon be a man.

ABRAHAM : So you think he'll soon be a man?

SARAH : Why yes; he almost looks it now; so tall as he is for his age, and so strong.

ABRAHAM : Aye; tall and strong—a fine lad; and we so late in the making of him.

SARAH : Yes; God was good to us, Abram, when He gave us such a son to our old age. If he goes on like he is, he'll soon be able to take things over for you. Why don't you let him now for a bit—just as a trial? For you're older now for your age than you used to be.

ABRAHAM : Yes; older for my age now.

SARAH : And you're tired.

ABRAHAM : Aye; tired I am.

SARAH : And it's because you won't give yourself enough rest. That's what's the matter; that's what has made you so out of heart these last days.

ABRAHAM : Out of heart, you say? I've too much heart in me: that's what's the matter with me. I wish I'd no heart at all. 'Twould be easier then.

SARAH : What would?

ABRAHAM : Nothing . . . everything!

SARAH : You are talking daft, Abram.

ABRAHAM : Yes, Woman; I'm talking daft. I don't want to talk.

SARAH : Then I'll go and milk the goats for better company.

(*She goes out; Abraham remains seated; he bows his head into his hands, and groans. Presently he raises himself and lifts his hands in supplication.*)

ABRAHAM : O Lord, what is the truth of this thing ye're telling me to do? Let me know, let me see Thy Face; and if I know that it *is* Thy telling, I will do it, though it be to the death. But if Thou show *not* Thy Face, how am I to know that it is Thy telling? All in darkness now; no light. Lord, show me Thy light!

(*He pauses, but seems to get no answer; with a hopeless gesture he rises and turns toward the door. Isaac enters. Abraham stands and looks at him: something in his look causes the lad to hesitate, a little shy in his greeting.*)

ISAAC : Hullo, Father. Here I am back.

ABRAHAM : Isaac, have you done your work? Have you brought in and penned all those sheep I told you?

ISAAC : Yes, Father.

ABRAHAM : Where had you been gone that I lost sight of you?

ISAAC : Only up on the hill, Father.

ABRAHAM : What did you go there for?

ISAAC : Just to look out—and see.

ABRAHAM : See what?

ISAAC : Whatever was to see—further away where the world begins. I'd like to see the world, Father. Here at home one sees so little; never any change—all days the same.

ABRAHAM : D'you want change, Isaac?

ISAAC : Yes, sometimes. And from top of the hill one sees more of the world than down here. That's why I go there.

ABRAHAM : And what did you see—this time?

ISAAC : I saw a great company of travellers, going south; all their beasts with loads on them. Who were they? . . . Where were they going, Father?

ABRAHAM : Merchants, my son, from foreign parts, maybe; going from city to city to find sale for their merchandise.

ISAAC : What are cities like, Father?

ABRAHAM : Like nothing you've ever seen; streets and streets of houses all shut up in walls . . . full of people, thousands of 'em, rich and poor, with their kings to rule over them, and their temples set up to false gods.

ISAAC : What is a false god, Father?

ABRAHAM : One that deceives his worshippers, telling them lies, making them do wicked things.

ISAAC : Are there many of them?

ABRAHAM : Aye; the world is full of them—more than a man can count. And all going strong.

ISAAC : Why strong, Father?

ABRAHAM : Because the hearts of men are evil—and what their false gods tell them to do, they wish to do. Aye, they like doing it well. But when it's the true God that speaks, He tells you to do hard things:—hard, hard.

ISAAC : How many true Gods are there?

ABRAHAM : There's only one true God, my son.

ISAAC : Your God, Father?

ABRAHAM : Aye; my God and your God.

ISAAC : But *I* don't know Him, Father. What's He like? Have you ever seen Him?

ABRAHAM : No man can see God, Isaac.

ISAAC : Then how do you know He's there at all—anywhere?

ABRAHAM : You hear His voice speaking.

ISAAC : But how do you know that it's *His* voice, if you've never seen Him?

ABRAHAM : If you heard my voice from far off, calling to you, my son, you'd know 'twas me.

ISAAC : Yes, Father; because I've heard your voice other times, when I've seen you.

ABRAHAM : If you'd been born blind, my son, you would still know my voice. Man has been born blind to the ways of Heaven; but he knows the Voice of God speaking in his heart.

ISAAC : But has God ever spoken in mine, Father?

ABRAHAM : I don't know, my son. Maybe you're so young that He hasn't spoken to you yet. But when a hard thing comes for you to do that you know you've got to do, then it'll be God speaking.

ISAAC : Why must it be a *hard* thing, Father?

ABRAHAM : Because God is much greater than man—and wiser. And God's ways not being man's ways, man finds it hard . . .

(*This talk is too hard for Isaac to follow. He moves toward the door, and stands looking out. His Father watches him.*)

ABRAHAM : So you like change, you say? And you like going up a hill . . . Then I've a bit of news for you . . . Tomorrow you'll be going with me to a place where God tells me He wants us to go . . . to a hill much higher than yon; aye, more than a hill, a mountain—Mount Moriah, they call it. We are going right up to the top of it, you and I. You'll have a large look from there on the world lying down beneath you, and the world out away beyond, farther than ever you or I'll have feet to go. You'll see a lot from up there—that you'll never see again . . . And you'll like to go there—won't you?

ISAAC : Yes, Father. I'll like to go up there. I shan't want ever to come down again . . . But why are we going, Father? What shall we have to do when we get there?

ABRAHAM : We shall do what God wants us to do. Leave that to Him. Ask me no more.

ISAAC : How far is it?

ABRAHAM : A three days' journey, my son.

ISAAC : That's further than I've ever been.

ABRAHAM : Yes; much further it'll be.

ISAAC : Oh, I wish tomorrow were come! . . . Why couldn't we start today, Father?

ABRAHAM : There's no need to hurry. Tomorrow will be time enough. The day'll keep.

(*He goes to the door, stands looking out, and speaks only to himself.*)

Down goes the sun . . . This day's over . . . I have made the Lord's will to be mine.

(*He goes out. Isaac stands puzzled.*)

ISAAC : Why is he so sad? He says God has told him; but he doesn't want to go. How funny!

(*Enter Sarah carrying her pail of milk.*)

Mother! Have you heard? Did you know? Has Father told you?

SARAH : Told me what, child?

ISAAC : We are going away, Mother: he's taking me with him— a three days' journey to somewhere I've never been: to a great high mountain, Mother; we are going right up to the top where one can look out and see all the world. Just think of that!

SARAH : (*setting down her pail*) I think your Father is out of his senses, Isaac. What for does he want to go climbing mountains at his age? There's no sense in it.

ISAAC : Oh, yes, there is, Mother. He says it's a hard thing to do, but that God told him. And that's why.

SARAH : God told him?

ISAAC : Yes, Mother; he says that if anything is hard to do, you must do it; because doing hard things is God's will.

SARAH : Well, if it's only a hard thing God wants him to do, he could just as well have done it at home: he might have stood on his head—or something a bit harder maybe, if that didn't satisfy him. You know, Isaac, God is not making your Father happy; he's not treating him right. Night after night he can't sleep: he gets up out of his bed, goes off and prays, and comes back more miserable than he went. It's not reasonable praying to a God who does that to you. He'd better try a change, I think. There's plenty of other gods to choose from.

ISAAC : But you can't change from the true God to a false god, Mother.

SARAH : How does he know he's got the true God? You've only his word for it. Men all think they've got the true God, whichever it is: but whether they have or no, that's not left for a woman to say. When I married your Father, his God became my God; and had I married some one else 'twould have been a different one; so there's where I leave it . . . Ah, but you're not listening to a word I say—just like your Father—always dreaming.

ISAAC : No; I was only thinking, Mother.

SARAH : Thinking what?

ISAAC : Of the world.

SARAH : Eh? What of it?

ISAAC : I want to see it.

SARAH : Well, you've only to look round.

ISAAC : More of it. What I see here's nothing.

SARAH : No, only what's going to be your life and what's made it: the sheep and the goats, and the cattle and the serving men; and your father and mother. We're nothing—or we'll not be much longer.

ISAAC : (*protesting*) Oh, Mother!

SARAH : And because your father's taking you on a journey, where you'll see new things, you're happier than I've ever been able to make you, for all the care I've had of ye. Well, it's natural, I suppose, that you should want to see the world, and what it's like, and all that's in it—the good and the bad. What are you most wanting to see?

ISAAC : I don't know, Mother. Things . . . places . . . people.

SARAH : People—ah, ye mean women . . . Young maidens, with eyes looking at you, eh? Now, isn't that true, Isaac?

ISAAC : How did you know, Mother?

SARAH : Mothers don't have to know, when their sons begin to be men . . . Well, who is she?

ISAAC : I don't know, Mother: I shall never know . . . 'Twas a month ago, when those travellers came by, and stopped, and asked for their water-skins to be filled. There was one with them; she wore a veil; and when she put it aside, I saw one of her eyes—only one, Mother. And I've been seeing that eye of hers ever since—sleeping and waking.

SARAH : Aye; it's begun for you! And now, till you've seen the other eye and all the rest—of her, or of another—you're never going to have peace.

ISAAC : I don't want peace, Mother; I want life. Peace isn't life.

SARAH : No? Maybe you're right. Anyway peace isn't your Father's life; though it's peace he should be having now he's so old. You know, Isaac, I shouldn't wonder if it isn't to please you that he's doing this, taking you to the top of a mountain just for you to see what you call the world. For he was always a yielding man; and you could make him do wrong things if you went on at him long enough . . . Ah, I did that once. And I remember (after he'd done it), he made himself think 'twas the Lord's will and not mine as had made him. Seems he liked better to think 'twas the Lord had made him do what was wrong, than that his wife should have made him. Ah, that's like a man. For so being 'twas the Lord's will—made it right . . . But it wasn't.

ISAAC : What was it, Mother?

SARAH : I'll tell you. I was sorry for it, after; but 'twas too late then. There was a woman named Hagar. Your Father had had a son by her; thirteen years before you were born that was. I'd wished for it to be, having no son of my own. But when you came I was jealous; for Ishmael was a fine lad, and your Father was fond of him. And because I feared he'd be fonder of him than ever he'd be of you, and would put him first, maybe, I made him send both of 'em away. He didn't want to, but I would have it. And when he'd done it, then he said 'twas the Lord's will. That's your Father's way; when he's done something he didn't want to do he thinks 'twas God made him do it. So now he tells you 'tis God sending him off to this mountain he's got to climb when he's no longer the strength for it; but

I think it's for you he's doing it, because it pleases you. And you do want to go?

ISAAC : Yes, Mother.

(*While she has been speaking Abraham enters, and stands listening.*)

SARAH : To go away and leave your poor old mother alone.

ISAAC : But I'm coming back, Mother.

SARAH : Oh yes, you're coming back; but you'll come back with your head so full of all the things you've seen that there'll be no keeping you. Aye; it's what a mother has to learn, and to bear—having given all her care and all the love of her heart to the son she's borne, she has to give him up—and let him go to another. Aye, she may keep her old man, till both be grey; but a woman is ever widowed of her sons. And I'll forgive the woman that takes you from me that you may have joy of her, and children of your own. But if God took you from me, Him I would never forgive.

ABRAHAM : Woman, you are speaking wickedly.

SARAH : Yes, Abram, I'm speaking wickedly, but I'm speaking truth. For if God dealt so with me, He'd be no God of mine; nay, though He were your God, He should not be mine!

ABRAHAM : You don't know what you're saying, Woman: you don't know what you're saying! And this is my word to you, and my command—that you speak not another word, lest God strike you dead. Get in!

(*Sarah, frightened, runs in to the inner tent.*)

ISAAC : What did Mother mean, Father?

ABRAHAM : Nothing . . . Woman's words . . . Man has no right, Isaac, to make God do man's will. If he did, man would be his own God. We live to do *His*, not ours. (*He goes to the door, and stands looking out.*) Come here to me, Isaac . . . See yonder sun setting; see it go. Some day you'll see it set for the last time.

ISAAC : I shall see it rise again tomorrow, Father.

ABRAHAM : Aye, tomorrow, maybe, you'll see it rise; and the next day and the next. But a day will come after, when you'll not. Our lives are in God's hands, Isaac—yours *and* mine. If God would take my life this day, surely I would be thankful—for a great mercy it would be! (*It begins to get dark.*) Go in, my son, to your mother, and be kind to her; be very kind. To-morrow, we start early; when the sun rises we start on our way.

(*Isaac goes in. Abraham stands motionless. It gets darker and darker.*)

Oh, the black sunrise it'll be! Shall I ever see sunrise again? No light to the darkness of my days will ever come to me now . . . Only the darkness of the grave!

SCENE 2

On the top of Mount Moriah is a low hillock; on it a stone roughly shaped like an altar. Dawn has hardly begun; it is still twilight. Abraham enters, followed by Isaac, bearing a load of wood. He halts and looks round. Isaac stands looking at him for some time, in silence, then speaks.

ISAAC : Are we there, Father?

ABRAHAM : Aye; we're there. We've no further to go now. This is the very place. 'Twas here He told me we were to come.

ISAAC : What are we here for?

ABRAHAM : For a meeting.

ISAAC : Who with?

ABRAHAM : With God.

ISAAC : With God? Am I going to see God, Father?

ABRAHAM : I don't know, my son. But if, after this day, there's any life in you, you'll be seeing God better than I, maybe.

ISAAC : You talk strange, Father.

ABRAHAM : Aye, for a strange thought has come to me. I would to God now that you were not my son.

ISAAC : What are you looking like that for, Father? Are you angry with me? Have I done anything wrong?

ABRAHAM : Only by being born, my son.

ISAAC : Why was I wrong to be born, Father?

ABRAHAM : There's some born that better hadn't been born. I was one; now you're another.

ISAAC : What do you mean, Father?

(*Abraham seats himself, and draws Isaac toward him. Isaac sits at his knee.*)

ABRAHAM : Listen, my son. You know that all your life I've cared for you, and loved you, and done all for you that a father could do. Do you remember one day when I saved your young life, when you'd fallen down into a pit; and three days you were lost to us? And I came and found you and drew you out again?

ISAAC : Yes, I remember, Father.

ABRAHAM : If now I asked your life of you, would you give it me?

ISAAC : My life, Father?

ABRAHAM : If I asked you to give me the life I saved, would you give it me?

ISAAC : If it was to save your life, Father.

ABRAHAM : I said not to save *my* life. I said, if I asked it, would you give it me?

ISAAC : I would wish to give it you, Father, if I had the courage for it.

ABRAHAM : Have courage, my son; for the day may come soon . . . Listen again, son. If there was one that had cared for me all my life, as I have cared for you—that had saved my life as I saved yours, but more times than one; if He came and asked of me my life, should I not give it Him?

ISAAC : Yes, Father.

ABRAHAM : And if He came, and asked—not *my* life, but yours, should I not give it Him?

ISAAC : Why should he ask mine, Father?

ABRAHAM : I do not know why. But if He *did* ask it—

ISAAC : He? Who is it you mean, Father?

ABRAHAM : I mean God. There's none other that could ask it—only God.

ISAAC : How would He ask? Would you hear Him speak?

ABRAHAM : Aye; as I have heard Him speak often—before. Day in, day out, I could not get away from Him; could not get Him out of my mind, out of my heart—always there—speaking. Ever asking me—did I love Him? Was I ready to do anything He told me to do—*was* I? So—the better to satisfy Him, and my own mind—I began to think of all the things I *would* do for Him. 'Yes,' I said, 'Yes, and yes; Lord, I would do that, and I would do that, and I would do that—aye, willingly—if it were Thy will I should do it' . . . But that wasn't enough for Him. (*His face becomes terrible.*)

ISAAC : Father!

ABRAHAM : For one day the thought came to me, all of a sudden, of one thing I would *not* do for Him. And then I knew that was the very thing He would have me do.

ISAAC : How did you know it?

ABRAHAM : My heart told me. For there, in my heart, was the wickedness—that I hadn't the will to serve Him in that thing, in that one thing . . . And because I hadn't the will for it, sure and certain I knew then that it was His Will.

ISAAC : What was it, Father?

ABRAHAM : A sacrifice, my son.

ISAAC : What sort of a sacrifice?

ABRAHAM : Blood; the blood of a lamb.

ISAAC : That's no great thing, is it, Father?

ABRAHAM : In God's eyes maybe not . . . maybe not. As God sees we cannot see—poor mortals as we be. So, here we come to the place, and this the appointed time for the lamb to be slain . . . We've no further to go now.

ISAAC : But, Father, though we have the wood and the fire for kindling, where is the lamb?

ABRAHAM : God has provided the lamb, my son.

ISAAC : Then it's not yours, Father?

ABRAHAM : No, not what I can call mine—everything that is mine being His . . . Unbind the wood, my son. Aye; and give me the rope. Now lay the wood. There's a stone that you can lay it on. For a stone has no heart, so the heart of it won't break, as mine'll break when the fire's lighted, and the sacrifice, with its life gone out, laid on it.

ISAAC : (*stopping*) Father, you frighten me.

ABRAHAM : Aye; and if 'twere not the Lord's will, I'd tell you now to run for your life—for your dear life; for 'twas not to *you* that the bidding came—only to me. And because when word of it came, piercing my heart, so that my heart breaks and bleeds—so, surely, I know that 'tis only God can have laid this bidding on me—to do His will . . . Stand up, my son, stand up, and let me bind you. And for pity of your Father's heart that's breaking, stand still and do not strive. (*He starts binding him.*)

ISAAC : But why are you binding *me*, Father?

ABRAHAM : Because 'tis the Lord's will.

ISAAC : But are you going to kill *me*, Father? Am I the lamb?

ABRAHAM : Aye: you are the lamb, my son.

ISAAC : And killing me, do you do God's will, Father?

ABRAHAM : Killing you—I do—His will.

ISAAC : Willingly, Father?

ABRAHAM : Aye—God helping me—willingly.

ISAAC : Then He knows, Father!

ABRAHAM : Knows what?

ISAAC : That your will is to do His Will . . . If He knows *that*—
what more does He want, Father? . . . What more does He
want?

(*Abraham raises himself, and stands rapt in the revelation that
has come to him. Slowly the light of dawn grows brighter.
Isaac kneels at his feet.*)

Oh, do not hold me bound! I too am willing, Father!

ABRAHAM : (*lifting his hands*) O God, God, hast Thou heard?
'Twas the lamb that spoke, not I: but surely he spoke truth.
If with my whole heart I have been willing to serve Thee—
to the death, and have not withheld my son, my only son, from
Thee, then is my truth known unto Thee, and my condemna-
tion is over, and Thy reproof has gone from me. O Searcher of
hearts, what more dost Thou need? Is not life dearer to Thee
than death? Is not *my* son Thy son? Aye, plainly now, in light,
not in darkness, Thou speakest to me again. I have heard Thee
with the hearing of my ear, but now mine eye seeth Thee.

ISAAC : You see God, Father?

ABRAHAM : I see God.

ISAAC : Where?

ABRAHAM : In the land of the living, in the heart of man whom
He hath made. We are His children and He careth for us. In
Him we live . . . In Him there is no death. Thou wast my
Father, when I was ignorant of Thee. I wake in Thy likeness,
and am satisfied. For Thou art the God not of the dead but
of the living. And from Thee comes no darkness but light!

(*The sun rises, and shines fully upon him. He stoops, looses Isaac from his bonds, raises him, and stands holding him embraced. And presently they will hear the bleating of a ram caught in a thicket; and an alternative sacrifice will present itself, and be thankfully accepted as a sign that the controversy between Abraham and his God is over.*)

SCENE 3

In the tent Sarah stands waiting and looking out. It is near the end of the day; the sun is setting. Abraham comes slowly in, rather weary upon his feet; he carries his traveling-pack in his hand.

SARAH : (*a little hard of tone*) Well, Abram: so you are back, are you?

ABRAHAM : I am—back.

SARAH : I'd been hoping, maybe, you'd give up, and come back sooner.

ABRAHAM : You shouldn't have done, Woman.

SARAH : No: I suppose I shouldn't have given it a thought, as 'twas no affair of *mine*. Well; you've had your outing; and I hope it's done you good.

ABRAHAM : It has done that. Here, Woman—take this!

(*He hands over his bundle.*)

SARAH : Ah! but it's tired you out; I can see that.

ABRAHAM : Aye . . . But it's good to be tired after doing what's been so well worth doing.

SARAH : (*drily*) Well, if you like to think so! (*Then relenting*) But there! I'm sorry I spoke sharp to you. Sit down, Abram, and rest yourself.

ABRAHAM : No, I'll go in, I'll go right in; and lie down for a while. (*He moves to the inner door.*)

SARAH : Where's Isaac? What's *he* doing?

ABRAHAM : He's out there with the ass, stabling her for the night. He'll be with you in a minute.

(*He moves to the door. Meanwhile Sarah has undone the bundle.*)

SARAH : Why, Abram! Whatever made you take your holy robes with you? You didn't need *them* on top of the mountain, did you?

ABRAHAM : I did, Woman.

SARAH : What for?

ABRAHAM : That's no concern of yours, Woman. I'd reason for it, you needn't doubt. Have you never heard of a holy mountain —aye, holy to God? (*He goes in.*)

SARAH : Holy? Oh, it's that God of his that's always leading him astray. I wish he'd get another!

(*Enter Isaac.*)

ISAAC : Well, Mother, here I am back!

SARAH : Aye, back at last; and time too. Aren't you going to give your mother a kiss? (*He kisses her.*) D'you think I haven't missed you, all the long days you've been away?

ISAAC : Only six, Mother.

SARAH : Seemed more like a month to me, left here all alone, with all the pens to see to, and the milking to do; and every night lying awake, thinking of your old father, and him not fit to go anywhere—the state he was in—so low and out of spirit as he was.

ISAAC : He's all right now, Mother.

SARAH : Say what you like; but he was looking well nigh worn out when he came in just now. And he's gone in to lie down: which he wouldn't, if he was feeling as 'all right' as you say he is.

ISAAC : It's been a hot day and a long journey. But when we were going he seemed never to sleep at all. Now—these last three days, he's slept well. The first night, coming back, he was off before ever I was. I lay and watched him for hours.

SARAH : What kept you awake?

ISAAC : (*evasively*) Oh, just thinking; and wondering what it would be like to be old and wise and good like him. In his sleep, he put his hand over me, and I lay in his breast.

SARAH : Aye; he loves you well, Isaac.

ISAAC : He does, Mother.

SARAH : Well, tell me, now, all that you've been doing. Your Father's so shut up he won't tell me anything. Where is it you've been?

ISAAC : (*avoiding her eye*) To the top of a mountain.

SARAH : Ah! 'twas there he said he was going when he first talked of going away. And I said—at his age, whatever for? 'To do something hard,' he says. And when I said—why couldn't he do that at home? he'd no answer except some foolishness about the ways of God not being the ways of man . . . And what did you do when you got there?

ISAAC : (*who is finding this difficult*) Oh . . . we sat down, and rested.

SARAH : Well—and then?

ISAAC : And then we talked—and looked at the view. (*This gives him something to talk about.*) 'Twas a fine view, Mother, right up over the world; you could see for miles and miles. Down below us, in the valleys, 'twas all dark, for 'twas early; the sun hadn't risen.

SARAH : (*astonished*) You went up before the sun was risen?

ISAAC : Yes, Mother.

SARAH : Why?

ISAAC : Because we wanted to get to the top, and see the view.

SARAH : Before sunrise?

ISAAC : Yes; it's the best time for it, just when the sun rises, it makes everything so clear.

SARAH : Well—and then?

ISAAC : Then we came down again.

(*But this is not going to satisfy Sarah; the more she thinks of it, the less does she find in it.*)

SARAH : D'you mean to tell me you only went up to see the view?

ISAAC : (*reluctantly*) No, Mother, of course it wasn't only to see the view. 'Twas to make a burnt-offering for a sacrifice.

SARAH : What had you to sacrifice?

ISAAC : A ram.

SARAH : You didn't take a ram *with* you?

ISAAC : No, we found it. 'Twas there caught in a thicket.

SARAH : (*puzzled*) Well, but did you know you were going to find it?

ISAAC : No, Mother; it just so happened 'twas there.

SARAH : Well, it's being only a woman, I suppose, and having no understanding, as your father is always saying; but this beats *me*. I can see no sense in it! You went up to make a sacrifice, and you didn't take the sacrifice with you? Then how did you mean to make it? What of?

ISAAC : That's what *I* said, Mother. I asked him. And Father said that God would provide the lamb.

SARAH : The lamb? Just now you said 'twas a ram.

ISAAC : 'Twas a young ram, Mother. Anyway, it wasn't any older than I am now.

SARAH : 'Twould need no *young* ram to be that.

ISAAC : (*trying to satisfy her*) Well, this *was* a young ram, Mother.

SARAH : And so, you made a sacrifice of it?

ISAAC : Yes, Mother—Father did.

SARAH : (*taking up the robe from the opened bundle*) Oh, so that's why! I was wondering how ever there came to be blood on it! If you hadn't told me, I might have thought your Father had done a murder, and was afraid to tell me of it. For when he went in just now, it seemed like as he didn't want to talk to me about it. Ah, well! men's ways aren't women's ways, and never will be. We shall never understand them, not if we were to stand on our heads to do it . . . And now, I'll go and be getting you something to eat, for you must be hungry.

ISAAC : Yes, Mother; I'm very hungry.

(*Sarah goes off to get the meal. Presently through the curtain over the inner door, Abraham looks out cautiously to see if the coast is clear. Isaac gives him a gesture of reassurance. Abraham comes in.*)

ABRAHAM : Has your Mother been asking you things, Isaac?

ISAAC : Yes, Father.

ABRAHAM : (*apprehensively*) What have you told her?

ISAAC : Only so much as she could understand, Father.

ABRAHAM : How much was that?

ISAAC : About the ram, Father; and the sacrifice. I saw her looking at those blood marks; so I told her what was the cause of them.

ABRAHAM : Aye, you've a wise heart, and an understanding mind, Isaac. There's things a woman hasn't the mind for; so being it's better to leave them not said . . . And your old father —what have you in your mind about him, Isaac?

ISAAC : Understanding, Father.

ABRAHAM : God bless you for that, Isaac. Surely 'twas one father that went up the mountain, 'twas another that came down. But *that* your mother would never understand; she's always have it against me. It's a great doubt I have, Isaac, that she'd never look at me the same, did she know what had been in my heart to do, before God made His meaning clear to me. She's a good woman, is your mother, and a good wife to me has she been. But she loves you better than she loves me.

ISAAC : Why do you think that, Father?

ABRAHAM : 'Tis natural, my son. A woman's child is of her own flesh and blood; the bearing is hers, and all the travail, and the pain, and the joy that comes after. And that being the way of it, she'd find it hard—maybe—if she knew—not to think ill of me.

ISAAC : She shall never know from me, Father. There's no need.

ABRAHAM : (*much relieved*) You're a good son to me, Isaac. God's blessing be on you.

(*Sarah comes in, and begins laying the table with the meal.*)

SARAH : Ah! so you're up again, Abram. Are you rested?

ABRAHAM : I've had all the rest I need for now. And please God, this night I shall have more—and, in my dreams, peace.

SARAH : Then now, maybe, you'll be ready for a meal.

ABRAHAM : I *am* ready, Woman.

SARAH : (*as she lays the table*) There's not much that I've got for you; not knowing when you'd be coming back.

ABRAHAM : It's enough, Woman.

SARAH : I'd have had more for you yesterday, had you come then —soon enough. 'Twas near noon when four travellers came to the door wanting food and drink; so I killed the kid for them, and what they could not eat, I gave them to take away.

ABRAHAM : Had they come with so little food of their own?

SARAH : Ah. So it would seem; for they'd come off in haste, flee-ing for their lives.

ABRAHAM : Where did they come from?

SARAH : Zoar, the hill-city, so they told me. 'Twas a man with his wife and his two children.

ABRAHAM : And fleeing for their lives, you say?

SARAH : Yes, from the gods of that city, and their own people, where they'd been born and bred. 'Twas a strange tale, and hard to believe; but it sounded true. They've a god there called Moloch.

ABRAHAM : Aye, Moloch, one of their false gods.

SARAH : And when they make a feast for him, they cast lots for those that shall give their children for a burnt sacrifice—'to pass through the fire to Moloch' is their word for it. Well, this time 'twas on one of their sons the lot had fallen, a fine lad— the same age as Isaac, he was. So, in the very dead of night, before the feast day, they got up, secretly, and came safe away. And they'll never be able to go back, they say. They'd be all put cruelly to death, because they would not give their god what he required of them . . . Is your God like that, Abraham?

ABRAHAM : No; He is not like that, Woman.

SARAH : Well, that's a good thing to know—that He'd never wish you to do a thing like that.

ABRAHAM : Aye; it's a good thing to *know,* Woman. But maybe, a man, for lack of understanding, might think that He *did* wish it.

SARAH : If He did, He'd be no God o' mine. I'd find me another.

ABRAHAM : You cannot choose God to your own liking, Woman. There's only one true God and true He is, but hard to find, man being so slow of understanding. But when you *have* found Him, you know that He is the one true God, and that there is none like Him in all the world.

SARAH : And you've found Him?

ABRAHAM : Aye: I've found Him—or He's found *me;* and dark and difficult was the way. Mighty and merciful is He: slow to anger, and of great goodness.

(*Sarah goes out to fetch the last dish for the meal. Father and son sit silent, looking at each other. Sarah returns and sets the dish down.*)

SARAH : There! that's the best I can do for you. (*She starts helping them.*)

ABRAHAM : Wait, Woman, wait! Would you have us eat without first asking a blessing?

(*Sarah sits down. Abraham rises.*)

God be merciful to us, and bless us, and shew us the light of His countenance, and be merciful unto us. That His way may be known upon earth, and His saving health among all nations.

Let the people praise thee, O Lord: yea, let all the people praise thee.

Then shall the Nations rejoice and be glad, and the far Nations shall run unto Thee. Then shall the earth bring forth her increase; and God even our own God shall give us His blessing. God shall bless us: and all the ends of the world shall fear Him. Thus shall the man be blessed that feareth the Lord. Yea, he shall see his children's children: and peace upon Israel.

(*Having ended the blessing Abraham sits down.*)

ISAAC : Who is Israel, Father?

ABRAHAM : I know not, my son. The word just came to me. And though I see not the end thereof, now I see the beginning of his day, and I am rejoiced because of it: and in Him my heart is glad.

(*In the first part of the blessing Sarah and Isaac have joined. While it is being said the light of day dies slowly; it becomes almost dark. At the end of the blessing Sarah goes out, and brings in a lamp just before the scene closes.*)

by
Philip J. Lamb

GO DOWN MOSES

Published in 1947 for the Religious Drama Society of Great Britain by
the Society for Promoting Christian Knowledge. Acting copies may be
obtained from the Walter H. Baker Company, 100 Summer Street,
Boston 10, Mass. Permission for an amateur stage performance may be
obtained from Baker's at a rate of $15.00 for each performance.

NOTES

Stage

No scenery is needed for the performance of this play and a front curtain is not indispensable. It is convenient to use one or more daises to give enriched opportunities for grouping the Chorus and to provide a place where Michael and Satan may take their stations when they are not actively interposing in the drama.

Costume

Costume is partly stylised, partly naturalistic. Michael and Satan are represented as warriors at the beginning of the play. Their costume had better be identical except in colour. If the torso is left bare, that will facilitate Satan's quick change into a different skirt and head-dress to appear as Pharaoh. As the Golden Calf he wears a mask. Moses appears as an Egyptian, a shepherd and a bedouin leader. There is no need to represent his extreme old age in the last scene. The Chorus on its last appearance must be recognisable as representing the Christian Church.

PART ONE

Scene I

Michael and Satan in position, clad as warriors.

MICHAEL : Michael, the Archangel, Prince and Captain of the Host of Heaven,

Of Abraham's seed, the Chosen People, champion; such am I;

And guardian in particular of Moses. Moses.

The mouth of the Omnipotent has named that name,

Inexorable Mercy chosen the man for a certain function.

God has assigned the part which he must play,

And he must play it.

Who can forbid the high decree of God?

SATAN : Not exactly forbid, but you must modify must.

MICHAEL : May the Creator not compel His creature?

SATAN : No doubt.

God is omnipotent and can compel;

But will not.

Between that can and will not, I step into the picture,

I, Satan, the accuser of the brethren,

I, the chance of sin in the will's freedom,

I, the tempter from the intended good.

Moses, mark you, is no automaton

But a human being with free will.

He may do as he pleases.

And shall do as he pleases. I, Satan, say it.

I defy you, Michael.

If you want Moses, you will have to fight for him.

MICHAEL : And am made for fighting.

Equivocal existence for a time is yours, Satan.

God suffers you, abroad among the sons of men,

> To fight down with pride the holy aspiration,
> And when you win, to ruin. So be it.
> We fight each other for the soul of Moses
> And what depends upon the soul of Moses.
> Let the fight begin.

SATAN : Let it begin.

They address themselves to the audience.

MICHAEL : Abraham begat Isaac, and Isaac begat Jacob, and Jacob,
> Whose name is Israel, begat the twelve Patriarchs,
> Judah, Reuben, Gad, Asher, Naphtali, Dan,
> Simeon, Levi, Issachar, Zebulun, Joseph and
> Benjamin.
> These men went down into Egypt with their families.

SATAN : And in the land of Egypt they found
> Fear, for they were many,
> Hatred, for they were feared,
> Persecution, for Egypt was more mighty.
> Israel was enslaved in Egypt's brick-kilns,
> And their sons slaughtered.

MICHAEL : One child escaped the slaughter,
> Moses, son of Amram, of the tribe of Levi.
> His parents hid him in the bulrushes,
> Where Pharaoh's daughter found him,
> The Princess of Egypt.
> Moses was brought up in Pharaoh's house,
> Nurtured as a prince,
> Learned in the lore and wisdom of Egypt.

SATAN : Meanwhile his kith and kin laboured in degradation,
> Toiled and sweated, gave up hope, gave up self-esteem,
> Cowering under the whip, yet still spawned and multiplied,
> Brought forth more sons in the stink of slavery.
> Moses, grown to be a man, went to visit his people,

And learnt the limitless degradation of man.
He spied an Egyptian smiting a Hebrew, one of his
    brethren,
And he looked this way and that way,
And when he saw that there was no witness,
He slew this Egyptian, and hid him in the sand.
And when he went the second day . . .
On guard, Michael.

MICHAEL : Ready.

The Chorus enters.

CHORUS : Abraham, Isaac, Israel,
And the twelve sons of Israel,
Were blessed by the mighty God.
And we, that are their children,
Are in bondage, bondage, bondage.

Israel went down into Egypt,
And Jacob was a stranger
In the cursed land of Ham.
And we, that are his children,
Are broken, broken, broken.

MAN 1 : And there is only lechery left,
Dirtiness in secret, rubbing the itch, scratching the
    sore,
Breaking out in coward anger
And futile cruelty.
Cruelty.
Where is that scab that sold me to the officer?
Ah, there you are!
This is a quiet spot, suitable for the purpose.
Come here, Pharaoh's spy.
Something is going to happen to you.

WOMAN 1 : What is it? What's the matter?

MAN 2 : Matter. There's going to be a bloody execution.
We're going to take it out of a traitor to the people.

MAN 3 :   I'm not a traitor. I'm not. I'm not really.

MAN 1 :   Be quiet, you. Save your breath for squealing with.
You'll need it.

WOMAN 1 :   There's going to be an execution.
A man's been caught spying.

WOMAN 2 :   What fun. Who caught him?

MAN 1 :   Now you, you shall have your trial.
I'm the judge and the plaintiff, and I'm the chief
witness.
And soon I'm going to be the executioner.
You told the officer on duty, didn't you?
That I wasn't baking his blasted mud into bricks,
Didn't you?

MAN 3 :   I . . .

MAN 1 :   Shut up. But was taking a quiet hour off in the straw
loft
With a lady friend. Didn't you?

MAN 3 :   With my wife, damn you.

WOMAN 3 :   And if it was with your wife,
You might feel honoured.
At least he's a man, not a half-dried cod-fish.
Much fun I've had with you in five years, husband.

MAN 3 :   Oh, he's a mighty fine fellow, he is.
Mighty fine he looked when the rods came down on
his back,
One-two. One-two.
His squeals were music.

MAN 1 :   And now it's your turn to do the squealing.
Hold him still.

MAN 3 :   Mercy. Mercy.

WOMAN 2 :   Look out. There's someone coming.

MAN 3 :   Help. Help. Murder. Help.

MAN 1 :   Quick. Stop his mouth.

Moses enters.

MOSES :   Let that man go. Let that man go, I say.
          What, must I use the whip? That's better.
          Like curs you snarl and fight, but one crack of the
              whip
          And like curs you cringe.
          And now stand up. Stand up.
          For pity's sake stand up, man. Use your backbone.

CHORUS :   We meant no harm. Let my lord forgive us.
          A private quarrel, settled behind a wall.
          It is time for us to go back to work.
          Let my lord not have heard. Let him take no notice.

MOSES :   Stand still. Let me see you. You are Hebrews!
          If I were an Egyptian, I would use you as they do.
          Your backs invite the whip.
          Sodden in slavery, your souls give off
          A nasty exhalation of slave vices.
          You have no pride. Behind your eyes
          There is no spark of fire.

CHORUS :   It is true. We have no pride. My lord speaks truth.
          We may go back to the bricks now, may we?

MOSES :   And you are Hebrews! You are Abraham's seed;
          Of the lineage of blessed Isaac.
          Crafty Jacob founded your families.
          What has befallen you, O my people?

CHORUS :   Why does he use those names,
          The Egyptian stranger?
          Abraham, Isaac, Jacob,
          The great men, the ancestors.
          Who are you, Egyptian,
          That speak so boldly names were best forgotten?

MOSES :   I am no Egyptian, though my nurture
          Was Egyptian. I am your flesh and blood.
          I am a Hebrew, one of Abraham's seed,

Son of Amram of the tribe of Levi,
My mother, Jochabed. My name is Moses.

CHORUS : Moses!

MOSES : I am weary of the palace by the Nile,
And the dark gods of Egypt's temples
Oppress my soul. I, who grew up a stranger
In the house of my people's enemy,
Am hungry for kith and kin, for a brother's greeting.
I have came back to my own people.
Friends, will you welcome me? Will you say friend?

They mutter together uncertainly.

You do not know what it is to be lonely.
Your quarrels are brothers' quarrels.
I have had no brothers. I have been the stranger,
The changeling Hebrew. I have come back where I
belong.
Why do you look so strangely on me?

WOMAN 3 : So this is Moses!
What a brave, fine man it's grown to be,
The little baby in the bulrush cradle.
Pharaoh's daughter gives him goodly perfumes.
What strong hands he has.

MAN 2 : Strong enough to strangle an Egyptian.

MOSES : What did you say?

MAN 2 : Strong enough to strangle an Egyptian.
I said your hands could strangle an Egyptian.

MOSES : Your meaning?

MAN 2 : The body of an Egyptian officer
Has been found hidden in the sand,
Done to death by violent strangulation.
A Hebrew captured near the site of the crime
Has confessed under torture to have been an eye-
witness
And has named the murderer, one Moses.

CHORUS :　We have heard the name delated in the camp,
　　　　　The violent man who turned on Egypt
　　　　　And raised his hand against the granite sphinx.

MOSES :　The thing is known then?

CHORUS :　The thing is known. And through the camp
　　　　　Pharaoh's officers are seeking one Moses,
　　　　　Whose death Pharaoh intends.

WOMAN 3 :　O lovely Moses, you are going to die.
　　　　　I do not think you will die easily.

MOSES :　Brothers, let me hide myself among you.
　　　　　Let the anonymous, drab horde engulf
　　　　　Him who was Moses. No longer a prince
　　　　　I'll share the hard lot of my father's children.
　　　　　My strength shall be your succour.
　　　　　Israel shall rebel. One man died yesterday.
　　　　　He shall not die alone;
　　　　　We'll give them many bodies to embalm.
　　　　　I'll teach you not to kiss the hand that whips you,
　　　　　But grin beneath the whip, till when chance comes
　　　　　The quick blow pays the debt; you strike the striker.
　　　　　Open your ranks, comrades. Let me come in.

CHORUS :　(*severally*) No. No. No. No. No.
　　　　　Why should we hide you, who come so proud among
　　　　　　　us?
　　　　　We are offended by your pride.
　　　　　Your contempt makes us uneasy.
　　　　　You are dangerous. We do not want you.
　　　　　A man like you makes trouble round him.
　　　　　We want no trouble, but only to keep quiet,
　　　　　Making the best of things.

MAN 3 :　Stand up, he says, stand up, man. Use your backbone.
　　　　　Lording it like a very prince of Egypt.
　　　　　And he nothing better than ourselves, a mere Hebrew,
　　　　　A man with a price on his head.

CHORUS : Egypt at least has nothing against us.
We do our work and escape notice.
He is a marked man. He is a doomed man.

MOSES : Against your enemy my hand was lifted,
I could not stand the sight of Jacob's wrong.
As a Hebrew I have killed an Egyptian,
You will not betray me?

CHORUS : We will not betray you. It might be dangerous.
It might not pay.
We will go back to our work where we are safe.
We will take no further steps in the matter.
We will efface ourselves among the bricks.

The Chorus goes out. Moses sits dejected.

SATAN : A bad start, Michael.

MICHAEL : The human race made a bad start.
It is what follows that matters.

SATAN : Meanwhile it is still my turn, I think.

MICHAEL : It is still your turn, Satan.

Satan stands behind Moses.

SATAN : Moses. Moses.

MOSES : Who is it speaking?

SATAN : Look and see.

MOSES : You!

*He is looking straight ahead and does not actually
look at Satan.*

SATAN : Have we met before?

MOSES : I have seen you before, but never before so clearly.
You have been there and not there,
Present to the abstracted attention, but gone when
one looked.
What have you been saying to me all these years?

SATAN : Nothing but what you have said to yourself.

MOSES : What am I saying to myself now?

SATAN : Your mind says nothing. It is your belly that speaks,
Heaving with an intolerable nausea.
You are a Hebrew. These are Hebrews.
The same blood runs in all of you.
Horrible, isn't it? And your pride.
You will never forget what they did to that.
Personally I found the spectacle a trifle comic—
From my point of view, of course.
"Brothers, let me hide myself among you."
"We do not want you, Moses."
The scene will not fade quickly from your memory.
And now you are saying to yourself you were a fool
to come here,
Greater fool to murder the Egyptian,
Greatest fool of all to give anything of yourself away
to the Hebrews.
Am I right?

MOSES : Yes.

SATAN : One chapter has ended. A new one must begin.

MOSES : Yes.

SATAN : Out of Egypt.

MOSES : Out of Egypt.

SATAN : Out of reach of the unpleasant Hebrew smell.
Also out of Pharaoh's reach. Pharaoh will have no
mercy
On a Hebrew agitator. There are many ways to die,
And few of them pleasant. Get out of the country
quick.

MOSES : Out of Egypt. It is a pleasant thought. Whither?

SATAN : Consult your own inclination.

MOSES : A quiet land where a man can be alone,
And think or not think as he pleases.

Decent work to do; the mind concerned only
With technical problems; a country landscape;
A woman, or women; peace in the heart.
Is there such a land?

SATAN : Over the desert to the foothills of Sinai.

MOSES : Where there are sheep farms.

SATAN : And strong arms are welcome.

MOSES : There will be quiet in the fields,
Where the shepherd at evening tells his flock,
And fountains murmur through the palm-trees.

SATAN : You will forget the sons of Jacob.

MOSES : In my single self find my integrity.

SATAN : Quickly then, for Pharaoh is active.

Moses goes out.

SATAN : Let not your steps turn back towards the People.
It is my mission to keep you apart.
This is defeat. I see the tiny figure
In flight over the desert, fugitive, in fear;
In fear of man, in fear of his own conscience,
From the first stirrings of divine vocation headlong
away.
Moses, who fancied himself a hero,
Has chosen the country life, married and settled down
Where—

MICHAEL : Where by the natural scene refreshed, his eyes
Will see again the Way, his ears more clearly
Discern the insistent, more and more articulate
Formulation of the divine decree . . .
On guard, Satan.

SATAN : Ready.

Scene II

Michael and Satan in position. Four Women enter dancing. As they dance they say:

WOMEN   Sifting sands between the porphyry crags,
1, 2, 3, 4 :   Sifting sands and dryness in the desert;
           But in the foothills of the mountains,
           The fall of water, the palm-tree waving its branches.
           This is the grass land, the land of delight;
           Here cattle and sheep can find good pasture.
           In the cool arms of the Shepherd's daughter
           There is oblivion.

WOMAN 1 : There was oblivion, and should be still, but . . .

WOMEN   This is the land of all sweet sounds; harp, pipe and
2, 3, 4 :   flute
           Mingle with music of falling water,
           The singing of songs, and rhythm of bare feet dancing,
           When shepherds are jolly round the fire at nightfall.

WOMAN 1 : My shepherd is not jolly any longer,
           For a month past has not joined in the singing,
           Will not dance, stands cold and aloof;
           His brittle happiness is breaking.
           The old pain returns. There is something he cannot
               forget.
           Even in sleep the pain hurts him.

WOMEN   Do not grieve so for your husband, Zipporah.
2, 3, 4 :   He is a great man, he has been a prince.
           Ambition dies hard, but with lapse of summers
           Use brings comfort; the heart will grow accustomed
           To littleness, as the hands do to labour.

WOMAN 1 : Summers have come and gone, but Moses does not
               dwindle.
           The biting sand wears not that rock away
           Nor dripping water.

He will never be content like other shepherds.
I have seen a look in his eyes that makes me afraid.

MICHAEL : What you say is true.
Shepherd's daughter, you have married no shepherd,
But a prince among men, one whose way
Will lead him back from quiet to turmoil,
From water to sand, from pasture to desert.
Today you will see enacted
The breaking of bondage, that another bondage may
    be broken,
The end of retreat, that a journey may begin.
You will see the living God commandeer a soul
That cannot resist, appropriate it for purposes
Unintelligible to this little oasis.
Moses, come forth and meet your destiny.

Moses enters.

MOSES : I was with the sheep. Who called?
There is nothing unusual here, and yet I am certain
That out of the very quietness of the atmosphere
My name sounded. I am drawn here
By a compulsion that is not my own desire or will.
Who called?

WOMEN   Was it our voice you heard?
2, 3, 4 : Prince among shepherds, foremost in work,
Strongest in fight, lightest of foot at the dance,
We are always ready to bid you welcome.

MOSES : I know you are, and thank you.
I have found integrity here among country folk
Not known in palaces.
The bird on the rock, the sheep by the pool,
Laughter of falling water and friendly women,
I know these voices. They welcomed me out of the
    desert
And are round me at all times.
But this was different. Who called?

WOMAN 1 : I called you, husband.

MOSES : It was not your voice either.

WOMAN 1 : But I called you, Moses. Why will you not hear?
When you came among us bitter and angry,
Your pride bruised by some grief we did not under-
stand,
Who was it taught you to smile again,
Coaxed you to be human,
Kissed away the hurt and made you whole?
Let no voice sound above mine in your ears.
I have a right to call you.

MOSES : You are my wife, and your right a right not to be
gainsaid.
But this voice was not yours. Who called?

WOMEN
1, 2, 3, 4 : There are no voices here but our voices,
Bird on the rock, sheep by the pool,
Falling water and friendly women;
The sun's brightness out of the air
Falls on green water and bright petal,
The common bush afire with beauty . . .

MOSES : Stop! The bush. The voice began at the bush.
Around me were the sheep, my back against a
boulder,
And before me the bush, blossom, branches, stem,
Roots running into the earth;
Fire running up from the good earth
Broke into flame in the yellow blossom.
I marvelled the wood could bear such brightness and
not be consumed.
Oh, I was happy!

WOMAN 1 : Hold that happiness, Moses. Do not seek beyond it.
Here where the bush flames and waters fall from the
rocks,
Here among us is peace.

WOMEN
2, 3, 4 : Year by year the blossoms kindle in Spring,
Dwindle in Autumn, kindle again in Spring,
As the fire mounts up in the youth of a man

And sinks in age, till his body is laid low,
Earth into earth. You have caught our rhythm at last.
You will be happy among us, Moses.

MOSES : You do not understand.
I was watching the bush, warming my heart by its fire,
When a voice called.
The bush was not the voice.
The voice was something beyond, far more important.
Look, I have taken off my sandals;
I am in dread; the voice has abashed my spirit.
I do not know who called, but I am afraid before him.
Let me know who called.

WOMAN 1 : What is it that has happened?
Such exaltation is not friendly to the simple quiet
That has filled our love for each other.
Yet let the crisis come, if come it must.
Let the precise word be spoken, the way made plain.

MICHAEL : Amen.

MOSES : Amen.
Let the moment of vision precipitate the clear decision.
Let the precise word be spoken, the way made plain.

MICHAEL : Ask, and it shall be answered you.

MOSES : Whose is the voice?

MICHAEL : The Lord, the God of your fathers,
Abraham, Isaac and Jacob,
Speaks by his messenger.

MOSES : The Lord, the God of my fathers,
Abraham, Isaac and Jacob,
Half obliterated names that once had power over the
imagination;
It seems strange to me now that the names of my
fathers,
The voice of their God,
Should mingle in the substance of this revelation.

The awe weighs more heavily upon me.
What is the message?

MICHAEL : It is a command.

MOSES : Concerning?

MICHAEL : Concerning the People.

MOSES : Ah!

MICHAEL : Concerning the People in Egypt,
Whom the Lord will have delivered from their
bondage.

MOSES : The People in Egypt.
I have seen the People in Egypt.
I have also seen rats in the sewers of Memphis,
And preferred them to my brethren,
The spawn of Abraham.

MICHAEL : In spite of which the ancient purpose of the Lord
stands firm.
Moses, son of Amram of the Tribe of Levi,
Will return to Egypt,
Perform there certain portents upon Pharaoh,
Rally the degraded tribes, and lead their host,
Their bondage broken, to such a land
As shall be indicated to him in due season.

WOMEN   It is impossible, unthinkable;
2, 3, 4 : Over the burning sands is no returning.
Let the voice be lost,
Let the past sink into oblivion;
Drink of the musical waters,
Let the leaves wrap you round;
Let the shepherd's daughter
Stand between you and the voice,
Annihilate the voice.

MOSES : Fire in the bush has become lightning
And shrivelled to black ash the pretty camouflage
Wherewith I hid myself from my own eyes.

I challenged the voice to define its meaning,
The moment of vision to speak plain.
Earth, air, water and fire, all I have ever known of
    good,
With something wholly other, awful, eluding the
    mind's grasp,
All these become articulate in answer;
Repent, the voice says, change your mind. Change
    your ways.
Go back over the desert. Face Pharaoh. Face your
    brothers
(The rotting souls, repulsive in decomposition),
Break the dream and take up the burden.
Go back over the desert to the slums where you
    belong.
Oh, I am afraid to face it. I am afraid.
The thought hurts me. I am afraid.

WOMAN 1 :   I knew there was fear at the heart of his peace;
As he lay in my arms his dreams have infected mine.

WOMEN   He shall yet discover peace among the palm-trees.
2, 3, 4 :   Easy, quiet, calmly meandering days
Shall soothe the riot of dreams, shall dissipate the
    burden
That grieves; here, among leaves, balm shall drip
    from the branch
And staunch the interior hurt, heal the ancient
Wound in the heart. Smoothly, softly, the soul shall
    grow accustomed
To ways . . .

WOMAN 1 :   Be quiet, sisters.
The voice is in his ears; he cannot hear
Such music as we make.
Our flowers are shrivelling in this strange fire.
Do not expect Moses to be again
Moses as we have known him;
He has come face to face with his own fear,

And now must fight or yield himself a craven.
You do not want a bogus hero,
A sham gallant to cheer you,
A man that goes in terror of his own thoughts.
Let him be.
Let his destiny lead him where he has to go.

MOSES :   Who is it that is doing this to me?

MICHAEL :   It is the Lord, the God of your fathers.

MOSES :   That is only a name,
The Tabu of my petty tribe.
There are gods in Egypt;
I have known their priests,
Isis, Osiris, Thoth, Anubis,
Powerful gods, with impressive magic.
This voice is different,
Overriding the human will remorselessly,
Exercising a compulsion not known in the temples.
I have heard an authentic imperative.
In the name of that for which I have no name.
Tell me its derivation.

MICHAEL :   There is no God but God, and the Lord is God.
The Lord who spoke to your father Abraham,
He is the God of Heaven and Earth
And of all things that move therein.
Thus saith the Lord, the one true God;
Before Abraham was, I am.
Before Pharaoh was, and Egypt, I am.
Before man stood upright, before the beasts were
    made,
I am.
Before the heaving rocks lay quiet, and molten lava
Crumpled in rain and shine to fruitful soil,
Before the earth, before the sun,
Before the myriad stars first hurtled on their courses,
Before Time was,

                    I am.
                    Dust that I have made and made into man,
                    I am, and I am the Lord.

MOSES :   O Lord, the God,
                    God of my fathers and of everything that is,
                    I acknowledge myself to be your creature,
                    I acknowledge you to be my Lord.
                    And there is nothing within me, in mind, heart or will
                    That can offer you any resistance.
                    Take me and use me
                    In whatever way, in whatever place
                    You choose.

MICHAEL :   Amen.

MOSES :   Amen.

WOMAN 1 :   Is it Egypt, Moses?

MOSES :   It is Egypt and the People,
                    And the Lord's purpose for His People.
                    Come.

Moses and Woman 1 go out.

WOMEN   Sifting sands between the porphyry crags,
2, 3, 4 :   Sifting sands and dryness in the desert,
                    With his back to the delightful land,
                    The dreaming land of palm-trees, the land of waters.

They go out, dancing.

Scene III

Michael and Satan in position.

SATAN :   To be brought up as a poor waif in the palace of
                    princes
                    Has a dreadful effect on the subconscious reactions.

Voices, compulsions, inability to settle down and live
  a profitable life as a farm labourer,

The masochistic return to a painful experience,

These are signs of a deep psychological maladjustment.

Moonstruck Moses goes back to the place he hates
  and the people he despises

And becomes a political agitator. Quite unnecessarily.

The people are well fed, and housed according to their
  social station,

The standard of life approximating to that of the rest
  of the working class in Egypt.

The hours of labour are not too vexatious;

Conditions have improved considerably in the last
  generation.

The people are contented and happy; at least they
  believe themselves to be so.

It is only under the restless influence of Moses

That they find it necessary to get excited about their
  rights.

Moses will now appear and give one of his perorations.

(*To Michael*) In the action which follows I am to
  play the congenial part of Pharaoh.

MICHAEL : Wherever the contingent claims to be the absolute,
  The limited infinite, the part to be the whole,
  The dot on the circumference to be the centre,
  There Satan is in his element.
  Play Pharaoh.

Moses and the Chorus enter. Satan goes out.

MOSES : When you have heard this word by my mouth spoken,
  And your chains fall broken from you;
  When your will, afire with desire for God,
  Makes possible the divine visitation,
  You shall become the nation.
  Your dingy days, sour with slavery, shall blaze with
    purpose,
  Power irradiate your shrunken spirits.

Time for ignominy is past; the sun at last
Hurls the dark headlong; dawn greets your eyes.
Israel, hearken. Hearken, O people of God,
And arise.

CHORUS :   Our hearts are dull harp-strings, slack to the finger,
Why will he be for ever plucking music from us?
It is hard to shake off the insensible sleep,
To feel life eddy along the quickened nerve,
Blood stir again in the stagnant artery.

MOSES :   God, whose voice by the bush was vibrant eternity
Speaking in stillness, speak to your people;
Let your breath set the chill cinders aflame.
It is a task beyond my rhetoric.

CHORUS :   It would be good to change the mud of Egypt
For fields and vineyards in a land of our own,
To grow up bright and new like a white lily.
It would be good to have a look at hope again.
We shall be a people, minding our own business.
Our fathers' God is a great God,
We shall be an exalted people,
Prosperous, imperial, significant.
There will be no end to the glories of Israel.
Israel is God's people, chosen from all peoples.
Let the secret go round; man to man whisper it
In the chain gang, woman to woman grinding the
        meal.
Resent the whip; resist the oppression.
Let the mind be free and the will be free
That the body may win freedom.
Great things are about to happen.
The Lord and Moses will deliver us.

During this speech Satan enters, dressed as Pharaoh.

SATAN :   It appears to me that among my slaves
The Hebrews are distinguishable for loquacity and
        idleness.

Where the tongue wags, output is diminished
And unrest increased.
Let heavier burdens be laid upon them.
Since they have time for talking, let them go seeking
    straw.
Let no straw be given to the Hebrews for their brick-
    making,
But let not the tale of bricks be lessened.

CHORUS : Ah! This is what happens to hope.
We look up at the sun, and the sun is the sneer of our
    master.
On our faces uplifted the lash of the whip descends.
Pharaoh is strong.

SATAN : Pharaoh is strong, stronger than you, and armed with
    the whip.
To your burdens, Hebrews.

CHORUS : How can we be a people
Under the whip?
At our work he is always there, the man with the
    whip.
From the hearthside, through the open doorway
We can see him, watchful, malevolent,
Walking about with the whip.
If we speak together of better conditions
His eye is upon us,
His hand on the whip.
In our dreams he stands astride our bodies,
And the noise which freezes our blood and wakes us
Is the crack of his whip.
Fear of fear had hidden our fear; we battened it down;
But now it stalks in the open,
Intolerable, not to be endured.
It is better to die than continue in this bondage,
In fear of the whip.
Pharaoh, our master, let us breathe, give us respite.

Give us leave to go on a journey
Out of the reach of the whip.

SATAN : If you worked harder you would have less vivid
imaginations.
Get back to your burdens.

CHORUS : From the edge of hope and despair,   Moses
You who have been where   Moses
Faith was vivid and bright,   Moses
You have seen   Moses
Assurance beyond our sight,   Moses
Moses, Moses.
Stand up for us,
Call on your God to save us,
Deliver us.

MOSES : Thus saith the Lord to Pharaoh of Egypt:
My people have too long endured bondage.
It is my will that they leave your land
And serve me in the wilderness.
Let my people go.

SATAN : A hundred generations have my fathers ruled in this
place,
Not without acquiring some skill in the art of govern-
ment.
I command here by a concentration of power
That has not yet found its equal.
In the name of a god who has hitherto escaped my
attention
You are bold to utter an imperative.
Enforce it if you are able;
Thirty centuries of Egyptian civilisation
Stand up and deny your request:
I do not let the people go.

MOSES : I am grieved for the grief that shall be unloosed.
I am moved for Pharaoh, the little man,
Armed in conceit of his own might and power,
Who would try conclusions with his Maker.

Pharaoh of Egypt, be merciful to yourself and to your
subjects,
Let my people go.

SATAN : I am weary of words.
Let us see with what sanctions
You back your impertinence.
Show us the Lord's arm unbared.
Let him act.

MOSES : You cannot retract the word that you have spoken.
It was necessary an example should be made
For this and future generations.
For this end God made you Pharaoh.
Men of Israel, look up and behold
The arm of the Lord unbared.

CHORUS : Look at the river, look at the pools,
The fountains in the palace garden,
The cooking pot on the kitchen hearth.
Blood.
All the water in your land is turned into blood,
Pharaoh,
And the stink of it rises to Heaven.

MOSES : Pharaoh of Egypt, let my people go
That they may serve me in the wilderness.

SATAN : This is strong magic and unpleasant,
But I shall not be convinced by tricks like these.
My own experts can do as much.
I do not let the people go.

CHORUS : What are the bodies that flop beside you,
Cold as the tomb, clammy and horrible?
Frogs from the river.
Lice in the air, in the hair, in the mouth,
Lice like dust over polluted Egypt.
The land is carrion crawling with flies;
You cannot open your eyes for them, Pharaoh,
Black, soft bodies in a maze 'twixt you and the sun.

MOSES : Pharaoh of Egypt, let my people go.

SATAN : Natural calamities fall on the earth at certain seasons,
But involve no reversal of determined policy.
Bad times will modulate to good times,
The will come through unbroken.
I do not let the people go.

CHORUS : Your cattle are sick. A murrain is on the beasts.
How loathsome are the fair bodies of your people;
Boils and blanes, on the face, in the armpits,
Foul excrescences on the white flesh of your singing
girls.
An odour of pus is in all men's nostrils.
The harvest is ruined; hailstones mingled with fire
Ravage the flax, fling havoc among the barley.
Do you see the cloud in the East, Pharaoh?
Do you feel the wind blowing up from the East?
It brings locusts, locusts, locusts.
On every green thing they alight;
There is no green thing left,
Only the stalk, close bitten.

SATAN : Stop. Money speaks. You are wasting money.
Ruined fields mean barren harvests,
Empty granaries, empty purses;
Let us come to an accommodation, a compromise.

MOSES : There can be no compromise with bondage.
Without conditions, men, women and children,
With cattle and gear, and all else belonging,
Let my people go.

SATAN : No.

MOSES : Then come the penultimate plague,
Almost the most terrible.

SATAN : What is the horror of great darkness that is fallen
upon me,
Darkness that may be felt?

For three days there has been no light.
Where has the light hidden itself?

CHORUS : But upon the Children of Israel
The sun shines all day long.

SATAN : No light. No light. Where is the light?

MOSES : Let my people go.

SATAN : Give me light and I will do your bidding. (*Moses drops his hand.*)
No. Now that the light is returned,
Shall my imperial will bend before God or man?
I do not let the people go.

MOSES : Yet one more plague shall break upon impotent Pharaoh,
That Israel may know, and all the world may know,
There is no power but of God,
And that by the will of God
Israel must be a people.
Prepare for a journey, people of God.
Gird your loins, bind your shoes, take staff in hand,
Eat while yet there is time
Lamb's flesh roasted, bread without leaven,
A handful of herbs from the garden.
Sprinkle your lintel with blood
That he may discern you and spare you,
The Angel of Death.
For the Angel of Death passes over the land of Egypt
And the first-born in every house
This night must die.

SATAN : I have felt the blow
And know not whence it has come.
From regions my science cannot command
A power has broken loose to destroy me.
The clamour of my people bereaved fills my ears.
Get you gone.
Your wives and your children. All. All.

Everything you have.
Void the land. Let no trace of you remain.
Get you gone out of Egypt.

Satan goes out.

CHORUS : Not our own strength wrought it: we had no strength.
We were drained quite dry, shrivelled. We were dead.
Oh, glory be to God, we have come alive again.
Look up, you men, the sun is bright in Heaven.
Breathe deep, you women, for the air is free.
By a straight, wide road to a glorious future
We can walk out of Egypt; we can be
God's own imagination of us. Alleluia.
Set this day apart from all other days,
The Lord's Passover to all generations
Of your children's children. God has performed
Even as he promised. Alleluia.
Alleluia, Alleluia, Alleluia, Amen, Alleluia.
Forward to our destiny.

MOSES : Forward to our destiny.

*Moses and the Chorus go out. Satan enters, having
put off the guise of Pharaoh.*

MICHAEL : Go forth, People of God, to the determined future.
Go to the place that the Lord has named,
With the pillar of cloud by day to guide you,
The finger of fire by night to point the way.
Triumph over Pharaoh, whose chariots pursuing
In the Red Sea shall perish.

SATAN : You shall not triumph so easily
Over yourselves.
Yes, I am here, Michael. You have won that bout,
But the battle is still joined. I am still here.

MICHAEL : Did you imagine I thought otherwise?
Moses is human, and God deals delicately
With human wills. Moses by his own choice

Shall hold the place God's plan appoints for him.
By his own choice, Satan. There lies your chance.
Use it.
When time and place cohere we meet again.

SATAN : I shall be at your service.

Michael and Satan go out different ways.

PART TWO

Scene I

Michael and Satan in position.

MICHAEL : From the ponderous, slow-wheeling nebula to the
mere atom,
From the worm in the dust to the choir of seraphim,
Upwards and downwards through the scale of being
All that is is God's. He made and rules it.

SATAN : All that is is God's, but man is less than God's,
Being his own master if he wills to be.
I spy a flaw in the roundness of creation,
Detect dissonance in the heavenly music.
We have to deal not with obedient angels, animals or
atoms,
But with proud man, with one man, even Moses.

MICHAEL : Moses, whose will swings in the rhythm of God's will,
Obedient Moses. You have seen his spirit
Ride up to its place in the orbit of mercy,
God's fire strike unhampered through him. You have
seen
Israel delivered. Even now their feet
Tread the straight way to the mountain of God,
Where covenant shall be made, and will with will,
God's will and his People's ring a chime in concord.

SATAN : So be it. The People come to the mountain,
The desolate mountain, eerie, crepuscular
With dark clouds, with the glow of dark fire
Unillumined, the harsh block of stone
That rises sheer from the inhospitable desert.
Let the People come to the mountain.

MICHAEL : There shall Moses receive the Law,
And Israel make his covenant with God.
To be His people and serve Him.

SATAN : There shall other happenings befall
That have no place in the purpose, no part in the plan.
Moses goes seeking wisdom in the mountain. So be it.
The saint's abstraction is Satan's opportunity.

They go out different ways. The Chorus enters.

MAN 1 : Forty days since Moses left us.

MAN 2 : Forty days since he climbed the mountain,
Left us here in the lonely desert.

MAN 3 : Forty days in a barren desert
Is a long time.

MAN 1 : Too long.

MAN 2 : Too long.

WOMEN : Well, what are you going to do about it?

MAN 3 : What I say is, How do we know he will ever come back?
There are dangers up there in the mountain.

MAN 2 : There are dangers down here at the foot of the mountain:
The food and water are giving out.

WOMEN : Well, what are you going to do about it?

MAN 3 : I didn't know there was shortage of water.

MAN 2 : It isn't a question of food and water,
But of something deeper, more fundamentally wrong.

CHORUS :   What do you mean, what do you mean, what do you
              mean?

MAN 2 :   I mean this, though you won't admit it:
              We're not together like we used to be;
              We've lost something.

CHORUS :   What have we lost?

MAN 2 :   I don't know . . .
              But I tell you this,
              When we stood in triumph by the Red Sea Shore,
              I was myself and something more.
              Now I'm only myself again,
              And I'm afraid of the desert.

WOMEN :   Look at the desert.

MAN 3 :   It's come closer.

MAN 2 :   It's creeping closer all the time.
              Now can you see what I mean?
              I feel as if I were alone in the desert.

CHORUS :   The stony desert with basilisk eye,
              Bones in the desert are white and dry,
              The sun stares at you all the day,
              Bare and bright is the sand; the way
              You lost in the night will never be found;
              You will go in circles round and round
              Till the fear creeps out upon you,
              The beast leaps out upon you.

MAN 1 :   Stop, stop, stop.
              We mustn't get into a panic; we mustn't give way to
                 panic.
              Find something quick and hold on hard,
              Something that will keep us together.

WOMAN 3 : Look!

              Satan appears as Golden Calf. Slow kettle-drum.

CHORUS :   What is it?

MAN 1 :   Do you recognise it?

WOMAN 3 :   I think I do. I think I *do*.
            It's one of the dear old gods of Egypt!
            Years ago we were well acquainted.

MAN 3 :   Is it a god?

WOMAN 3 :   I should say it's a god,
            A god you can see, a friendly god,
            Come to help us just in time.
            Golden Calf, permit me to introduce you.
            The Golden Calf, the Hebrew People.

MAN 3 :   Do I understand you to say
            That this animal, this god, excuse me,
            Is really made of gold?

MAN 1 :   I wonder how you can ask such a question.
            The Golden Calf is made of gold.

MAN 3 :   Quite remarkable.
            This god sounds like a first-class financial proposition.
            Depend upon it, there's money in this religion.

MAN 1 :   The Golden Calf is made of gold,
            But money can wait till we've all grown old.
            There's other things to attend to now
            (You can see by his eye he's thinking of cow).
            Life's kind of freer when the Calf's around,
            There's something you've lost, but there something
                you've found.
            Come on now, get together.

MEN 2, 3   We're not quite used to this kind of thing.
    and   We're a little nervous; we tend to cling
WOMEN 1   To out-of-date conventions and rules,
    2   :   Instructions received in our Sunday Schools,
            However, the new god seems to approve;
            We'll follow your lead, we'll make a move.

CHORUS :   Down in the dark place under the hill
            (No one's watching except the Calf),

Take off your clothes of mind and will,
Strip yourself naked of thoughts until
Control is gone and the body must
Obey the urge of animal lust.
Scrap your old convictions,
Break the old restrictions.
Let pride loose. Avarice.
Sloth. Gluttony.
Drunkenness. Envy. Hate. Let them loose.
Down in the dark place nothing is told
(No one's watching except the Calf)
Of the claims of the poor, the sick and the old.
Break them, grind them, forget them. Gold
From the Calf at your feet is hurled,
Gold is the demon that rules the world.
Scramble your way to it,
Trample your way to it.
Get money. Get more money. More money.
Money. Money. Money.
Down in the dark where the shadows glower
(Watch the gleam in the eyes of the Calf)
The strongest hand will seize the power.
This is the year and the night and the hour
When the Golden Calf demands its price,
Demands our blood in sacrifice.
Bring out the knife. Let the hand not falter.
Extend the throat. Spurt blood on the altar
Not of sheep or goat,
But man's blood, woman's blood, child's blood,
Blood, blood, blood.

*Cymbals. Satan slips out. Moses enters, with Michael
glorious behind him.*

MOSES :   For forty days and nights I have not eaten nor drunk.
I have been wrapped in contemplation of the will of
God,
Displayed before me in ordinance on ordinance.

I have had a vision of mankind living in peace and
    harmony together,
And of the way in which it could be managed.
I have been entrusted with the Law,
Ponderous, with the finger of God engraven,
Perfect to the last jot and tittle,
The paradigm of the good society.

CHORUS : Moses, Moses,
    How his face is shining!

MOSES : It was all there. I held it in my hands,
    The way men should live together,
    Lovely laws, clearly formulated,
    Covering all life.
    And you have smashed the Law to atoms.
    When your lustful noises invaded the holy mountain
    There was no holding the stone tables.
    As though they were made only of imagination,
    They slipped from my fingers,
    Hurtled down the steep places,
    Shattered, dissipated, annihilated.
    Do you think you will not have to pay for what you
        have done?

CHORUS : We understand that there will be a price to pay.
    We have been used to the whip and know when to
        expect it.

MOSES : I have seen you cringe before Pharaoh's bondsman,
    Terrified of the whip in a slave's hand.
    You, who have seen Pharaoh himself put down,
    A bubble on the cataract of the wrath of God,
    Before God who did it have not cringed,
    But stood with upright backbone and mouth wide in
        defiance,
    Bawling blasphemies beyond the sun.
    What has happened to you, my children, that you
        have grown so bold?

What has made you such reckless heroes
That you have no fear of God?

CHORUS : Body's agony is sharp, but soon forgotten.
The lash descends, the blade bites,
The flesh quivers and is still again.
We have already passed the portal of that pain.
We are afraid now with a more terrible fear,
For the eye of God rises in the desert,
Red and wrathful. Night phantasms have fled.
In the clear light of dawn we stand exposed
To the chastisement of self-knowledge. Below the
bone,
Deeper than the beating heart, a sickness invades us,
Disgust, disillusion, disintegration,
And fear. We have no place to shelter from God.
O Moses, pray for us.
Moses, pray for us. Pray for us.

MOSES : I have already prayed.
My hands above your heads have held back the
lightning.
You are still God's people, and the promise stands.
You may put away your fear, for see, the sun is be-
nign,
The day is warm and friendly now,
And you have work at your fingers' ends.

MAN 2 : Under the mercy of God a new day is breaking,
And Moses has come back to us again
With words of forgiveness.
Thanks be to God.

CHORUS : Thanks be to God.

MOSES : The perfect law that I perceived in solitude
Is dust in the wind, is a dream vanished,
Not to be known again, I think, this side the grave.

CHORUS : But we cannot live without the Law.

MOSES : I tell you sin has shattered the Law.

MAN 2 :   Give us a law, Moses.

Maybe not the perfect Law, seen by you in vision,

But a law suited to our littleness.

Hedge us about with thus thou shalt and thus shalt thou not.

We are children in need of comfort.

We are frightened of life and frightened of ourselves.

Space is too big for us, too empty.

Hedge us about with a law we can understand.

MOSES :   I will give you a law.

Come near and listen as children to your father,

And in the tablets of your hearts imprint these admonitions.

This is what God says to you.

Hear, O Israel,

I am the Lord thy God, who brought thee out of the land of Egypt,

Out of the House of Bondage.

Thou shalt have none other Gods but Me.

The Chorus may repeat each command after Moses.

Thou shalt not make to thyself any graven image.

Thou shalt not take the name of the Lord thy God in vain.

Remember the Sabbath day, to keep it holy.

Honour thy father and thy mother.

Thou shalt do no murder.

Thou shalt not commit adultery.

Thou shalt not steal.

Thou shalt not bear false witness.

Thou shalt not covet thy neighbour's house, thou shalt not covet thy neighbour's wife, nor his servant, nor his maid, nor his ox, nor his ass, nor anything that is his.

And now stand up.

This is the contract God offers you.

Keep this Law and He will bless you.

Obey His voice and He will bring you to peace.
He will make you a People above all peoples.
In your seed shall all nations of the earth be blessed.
What is your answer?

CHORUS : All that is written in this Law of the Lord
We will do.

MOSES : Think well. It is no easy calling.

CHORUS : We will be the Lord's People, come what may.
All that is written in this Law of the Lord
We will do.

MOSES : Lord, have mercy upon us
And write all these Thy laws in our hearts,

CHORUS : We beseech Thee.

MOSES : Come. We have a journey to make.

Moses and the Chorus go out.

Scene II

Michael and Satan in position.

SATAN : More uncouth than a calf are some of my disguises,
But underneath abides always the same Satan,
The chance of ill in the will's freedom,
In the straight path the crooked fork that leads to
Hell.
They have gone forth into the desert, Michael.

MICHAEL : Their destiny accepted, the Covenant made sure,
The will committed to the strict service,
A royal people, a holy nation,
A nation of kings and priests.
From them in the fulness of time shall spring
The Day-star to the zenith. Christ shall come.

SATAN :   The fulness of time shall come in time's fulness;
             Meanwhile the present.

MICHAEL :   The People go forth from Sinai
             To seek their own place, the lovely land
             Their God has appointed.

SATAN :   Still slaves at heart
             For all their Covenant, they are disappointing.
             Oh, the heavy grief in the soul of Moses,
             Day by day to keep such company.
             Hunger, thirst, rebellion, the faint heart sighing always
             For the fleshpots of Egypt, the tired hope
             Rejecting the Promised Land.

MICHAEL :   Ah, but faith always steadfastly shining,
             Power day by day renewed in the chosen leader.
             Moses works miracles, for God works through him.
             In the desert there is bread; water never fails;
             Meat is not lacking. Moses shoulders aside
             The very course of Nature that the plan may go
                 forward.

SATAN :   But Moses grows old. Forty years are past.
             Time has marched on to another man's station.
             The day draws near of a shrewder trial, the last of life.
             It is for his end I fight you, Michael,
             The dying moment that pays for all the rest.
             Concede the miracles, concede the journey ended,
             Moses has brought Israel to the Promised Land,
             And the next move is Death's.

MICHAEL :   The common end of mortals.

SATAN :   Guard yourself well, Michael. This is no easy stroke.
             The common end of common men is death.
             Moses is not common; neither is his death.
             His eyes are not dim, nor his natural force abated.
             He will not be glad to be thrust aside
             And die before the triumph,
             Punished like a child for a peccadillo. Listen.

For forty years he wrestled with the People,
With their stubborn will, their endless gainsaying,
Their fertility in low forms of annoyance,
Till once his patience snapped.
Water, they said.

CHORUS : (*off*) Water, give us water.
Have you brought us all this way to die of thirst?
Give us water.

SATAN : And he, taking his staff, with anger in his heart
That spoke louder than patience or the voice of
God . . .

MOSES : (*off*) Hear now, ye rebels, must we draw water for
you from this rock?

SATAN : And smote the rock. What happened then, Michael?

MICHAEL : Water gushed out of the stony rock for the People's
need.

SATAN : True. But what else happened?

MICHAEL : God, who is wise and meets men's need with knowl-
edge,
Pronounced of Moses that he must die,
And never set foot in the Promised Land.

SATAN : That is my moment.
Forty years in the wilderness with the hope always
before him.
Now he must die, and the hope unfulfilled,
Disappointed at last, and never set foot in the Prom-
ised Land.
He may see the Land only, but never enter.
That is where we take up the combat.
Let Moses appear on the heights of Pisgah
To see the Promised Land and die.

MICHAEL : As you will. Let Moses enter, see the Promised Land
and die.

Moses enters.

MOSES :   So that is the Land, and my life ends here.
          Grey, quiet hills, and beyond them lies the sea.
          The tribes of Israel approach their resting place,
          But as for me, I must look only
          And then lie down; on this mountain top
          Finish the journey that a long time ago
          Began, and has reached now a conclusion,
          Inconclusive, uninspired, unexpected, unsatisfactory.
          God has decreed I should not tread those hills,
          And when the glory, long expected, long desired,
          Breaks at last dazzling on the People's sight,
          Sightless and still below this turf,
          I shall not know the issue.
          O Lord, protect this People.
          What I heard by the Bush, let them hear;
          Sunlight and singing, the water from the rock
          Drop dropping, peace and a quiet heart
          Attuned to the Voice that speaks out of silence,
          Pronouncing your holy will.
          What power I wielded in Egypt endue them with.
          What I saw in the Mount let them in life's em-
              bodiment
          Fashion, giving the command a content
          In joyful communion, every man with his neighbour.
          O Lord, bless them and keep them,
          O Lord, make your face to shine upon them and be
              gracious to them.
          O Lord, lift up your countenance on them and give
              them peace
          Unto the ages of ages. Amen.

SATAN :   There kneels Moses, a man disappointed and un-
              fulfilled,
          Wrestling with a doubt that will not down.

MICHAEL : There kneels Moses, the man of God,
          Subduing as often before, so now in his last and
              bitterest hour,
          The natural will to the divine.

SATAN :   Hating the divine will,
          Resenting frustration, resenting death
          That comes before the purpose is made plain.

MICHAEL : Beating down rebellion with knowledge of the truth.

SATAN :   Desperately fighting anger against God with lies.
          Moses is lying to himself about the future,
          In imagination peopling the Land with peace that shall
              not be;
          If resigned, resigned only to a fiction,
          A sequel fashioned in thought to his own fancy.
          Dare Moses face the truth?
          Could he guess what shall follow, would faith stand?
          Dare he know the fate of this People?

MICHAEL : He is in your hand.
          God gives clearness of vision. Moses may see
          Not only the physical contours
          But that which shall be,
          The point of the Promise, the meaning and fate of the
              land.

SATAN :   (*taunting Moses as he kneels in prayer*)
          After such promise no fulfilment,
          Gone down to the grave with no fulfilment,
          Long expected, long desired,
          Unsatisfactory, the end is unsatisfactory.
          To die within sight of the land
          And never to be quite certain,
          Never to be quite certain.
          If only the People were dependable.
          How should the purpose be served by such as these,
          After forty years still unbroken to the purpose?
          Gazing west across the river, libidinous,
          Lust of blood, lust to possess,
          Tightens the lips, tenses the finger on the javelin.
          Dregs of the desert, avid for the spoil,
          Was it for them the story was woven, the tale told?

MOSES :   What meaning else should the story hold?

SATAN : Suppose the story held no meaning?

MOSES : Out of the past a voice speaks.
Out of the shadows of memory
The contradiction of hope and purpose
Through layers of long years and the effort of prayer
Worms its way to consciousness.
Come forth, Satan, and make your meaning plain.

SATAN : Plain meaning and plain dealing are not for me.
My name at the moment is doubt.
I am your own doubt. Have you not suspected
That after all the story is pointless, there is no
meaning?

MOSES : Come into the light where I can see you.

SATAN : Doubt comes out from the obscure corner
To stand his trial. The question at issue,
Was the meaning a mirage, the promise deceitful,
The purpose empty, the journey vain?

MOSES : It is unthinkable.

SATAN : No, for you have thought it.

MOSES : I see you now. You are the enemy
And would have me die in despair.
I have to admit I am a little afraid of you.
And yet you might as wisely deny the solid firmament
As deny the Voice.
Will you tell me that there was no voice
When I stood by the Bush?
Will you affirm I did not see the Truth
When forty days and nights I fasted on Mount Sinai?

SATAN : There is no doubt that you have had the most impressive
Revelations.

MOSES : And what of the Exodus from Egypt?
Was that a dream?
Will you impute to mere imagination

The dreadful sequence of Plagues
And Pharaoh's overthrow in the reedy sea,
Or tell me that Manna was a mirage?
Whence came water from the dry rock?
How came this people so far afield,
Raggle-taggle slaves turned into steady cohorts
Disciplined for battle?
In all these marvels will you deny the manifest pur-
    pose of Almighty God?

SATAN : The mind that is critically aware
Requires for every statement evidence,
Choosing at last as its hypothesis
The theory that accounts for the greatest number of
    facts.
As for purpose, I neither affirm nor deny it.
I merely reiterate your own question:
Granted that you yourself must be denied access
To the Land you have travelled so far to reach,
Granted that now and in this place you die,
What is to happen after your decease
To the People whom you have led so far?
What will follow when your cohorts cross the border?

MOSES : I die, but the People march.
Through open gates they shall throng to a land of
    laughter.
After the journey, rest; and peace shall smile upon
    them.
They shall not hurt nor destroy any more.
They shall not be slaves to men or to their own lusts.
Milk shall flow, the bees store honey in the clefts.
The Burning Bush shall flame, lambent and lovely.
They shall obey the Voice and live the Law.
In widening circles from this the centre
To the world's margin joy shall ripple.
Here shall God consummate desire that moved Him
When He made the world.

SATAN : Do you believe all that, Moses?

MOSES :   I believe that God keeps faith;
          I believe I have not done His will in vain.

SATAN :   I tell you, Moses, you mock yourself with fancy.

MOSES :   I tell you I speak truth, if there is truth.

SATAN :   If there is truth! Your lips have said it.
          Listen, Moses, I will give you facts, facts.
          Open your eyes again over the land and see.
          See plunder and rapine, the dirty tricks of war,
          Power cankering to cruelty, self, self, self,
          Always self, the slimy passions always predominant;
          The diseased will suppurates, secretes the pus
          That issues in poisonous action.
          See judges and kings, venial, tyrannical,
          Oppressed peoples in misery turning to idols,
          Animal idols, narcotic rites, the jig and crazy rhythm
          Of evil, inhuman abominations;
          For the real world holds too much pain.
          See the fate of the prophets, alternately mocked and
               neglected,
          Persecuted to the death from generation to generation.
          See Moses, look carefully.
          Not tomorrow only, Moses:
          Not a dream that troubles the night and is gone at
               cock-crow,
          But year in, year out, as far as the eye can see.
          See Moses. Fifty generations hence, fifty generations,
          What is afoot among the Chosen People?

          He beckons the Chorus onto the stage.

SATAN :   See, the men and women of Israel assemble.
          Before them stands a prophet, whom they have
               accused at law,
          One who has spoken to them as no man spoke,
          (Not even you, Moses) the word of God. His name is
               Jesus.
          A prophet beyond all prophets;
          Never was such holiness seen in Israel

Nor such mighty works;
Yet he stands bound before their ruler.

He addresses the Chorus.

Men of Israel, you have brought this man before me,
And I, having examined him, find no fault in him.
I advise you to withdraw the charge and let the man
   go free.

CHORUS : Let him not go free. We want him out of the way.

SATAN : Why, what evil has he done?

CHORUS : Words, words. He speaks words that hurt us.
Where he is there is no peace and quiet.
He forces on us the effort of thought;
Tricks our pride; disturbs our self-esteem.
He calls us to a journey we do not care to take.
We are afraid of him. Away with him. We will have
   none of him.
Put him out of the way. Stop his mouth with earth.
Crucify him. Crucify him.

SATAN : Shall I crucify your King?

CHORUS : Ah, a fine King that!
At least he has a crown, a crown of thorns!
Listen, Pilate, we want no king but the State,
Hard and inhuman, to rule us on our own terms.
You're not doing your job to speak for such as this.
Crucify him.

MOSES : But this man is just and righteous.
Will you bring innocent blood upon your heads?

SATAN : Go down, Moses. You have been dead fifteen hundred
   years.

CHORUS : Crucify him. Crucify him.

SATAN : Well, you eager men must have your way.
Take him and crucify him, but remember,
I am innocent of the blood of this just man.

CHORUS : His blood be on us and on our children.

MOSES : No, no, no, no! Unsay the curse!
Or ever they reach the ears of God,
Children of my children's children,
Call those words back.

The Chorus mimes the erection of the Cross.

SATAN : Go down, Moses, you have had your day.

CHORUS : (*looking up at the Cross*) His blood be on us and on
our children.

MOSES : There is a film of blood over my eyes.
The Promised Land is red with blood,
As though red rain had fallen. A shadow is thrown,
Stark black on red, across the mountains,
And the shadow is a cross.
What is this sigh that breathes among the mountains,
Twists in the valleys and mounts and grows
To an intolerable clamour in the mountains,
To an iron reverberation of appalling pain:
My God, my God, why hast Thou forsaken me?
My God, shall it come to this?
Did I bring them all this way for this?
Long expected, long desired, I have seen the Land
polluted,
The plan in fifteen centuries warped, ruined, twisted,
Horribly distorted to a deed of blood.
And I can see no further.

SATAN : Yet look further, Moses, hopeful Moses.
Your hope is done for, the proud purpose
Sinks bloodied into the dust; yet see the sequel.
There are more facts yet to look on.
Shall I show you the Chosen People cast out again
from the Promised Land?
Reuben and Gad, Asher and Naphtali,
Simeon, Levi, Issachar, Dan, Zebulun and Joseph
All gone down into oblivion,

And only Judah left. And as for Judah—
Go out, Judah, onto the ways of the world and tread
 them,
With any man's boot to help you on your way.
Be the stranger on the foreigner's doorstep,
The Wandering Jew, everlastingly not at home.
Wear the yellow badge; be segregated in the ghetto;
Be from generation to generation the universal scape-
 goat,
All the world's whipping boy.
Go, get you gone.

The Chorus goes out.
Ah, Moses, you have set a crown on the head of your
 People,
Imagined a nation of kings and priests.
I tell you that on earth no race shall be so poor
Its abjects dare not spit on Israel's beard.

MOSES : Gone, gone, gone, gone! I have seen them go.
       From the Land still unattained I have seen them slink
        away
       To a desolate future, no bright light from the finger of
        fire
       In their eyes shining, but blood-shot misery,
       And my heart quails to imagine what they shall suffer.
       O my God . . .
       O Lord, God of my fathers, why must you do this
        thing to them?

SATAN : Curse God and die.

MOSES : Is there no answer but the mocking of despair?

SATAN : The laughter of God's unconscionable sense of
        humour,
       Who has played this prank upon you,
       To bring you all this way and show you
       The end of hope. Curse him and die.
       Well, what will you do?

MICHAEL :   What will you do, Moses?

MOSES :   I shall pray. I shall give glory to God.
I gave Him my allegiance once and do not swerve
  now at the last.
Though all this shall be, even so as I have seen,
Though His ways are as unsearchable as the grave,
I know Him in whom I have hoped.
Under the unconceived and inconceivable failure
Some purpose stands.
O God, God, God, God of my fathers,
God of the Burning Bush and of the Mountain,
Before my eyes that look into the dark be darkened
  for ever,
Before the earth press heavy on my eyelids,
Make your meaning plain.

He bows himself in prayer.

MICHAEL :   Satan, have you anything more to say?

SATAN :   It would not be worth while.

MICHAEL :   Satan, have you lost or won?

SATAN :   What has befallen is what had to befall,
And Moses is reckoned with the saints.
I have lost.

MICHAEL :   Do you think you had better go now,
Quietly, while Moses is praying?

SATAN :   As you will; I can watch from the wings. (*He goes
out.*)

MICHAEL :   In the name of the Father and of the Son and of the
Holy Ghost. Amen.
Glory be to God on High and in earth peace,
Good will towards men.
O all ye angels of God, rejoice.
Rejoice, ye multitudes of the heavenly squadrons.
Rejoice, Nature, in your intricate devices,

Beasts, birds and things that grow.

Sing your bright way, bright stars, across the firmament.

For fallen man, our brother, in the filthy pit of sin is stirring;

Sinful man gropes upwards to the universal light.

Rejoice for this man, Moses.

Moses has gathered Abraham's seed, and led

To the appointed place the appointed People.

The story of salvation is well begun.

Angels in timeless apprehension holding

Past, present and future, rejoice that in time this moment

Holds its place in the appointed pattern of progress.

Rejoice for what is purposed for this People.

Rejoice for co-operation

And Incarnation.

Now is the time I must lay down my charge.

Now is this man come to the border of a Land more holy

Than the Holy Land.

Come forth, you smiling citizens of Heaven,

And greet him here. While mortal sight

Still clothes his apprehension, let light break about him.

O angel guards, show him the way wide open.

A company of Angels enter and group themselves about Moses.

ANGELS : We are the watchers on the frontier,
Angel obediences. The way is open.
He need not tarry.

MOSES : Glory be to God,
My prayer is suddenly lifted. There are wings beneath me,
And I ride with ten thousand companions on beating pinions,
Confident and strong.

MICHAEL :   For the hour of deliverance is at hand.
             Now does God vindicate His servant,
             And, as death approaches, makes plain to the traveller
             According to His promise the journey's purpose.
             Come forth, O Church of God,
             Transcended all barriers of time and place,
             New Israel from Old Israel descended,
             Let him see of the travail of his soul and be satisfied.
             Let him see his true children.

The Chorus enter as the Church.

CHORUS :   We are the New Israel, children of the New Covenant.
             Israel is dead in Christ and with Christ is risen.
             And we are Israel.
             From all nations, kindreds and peoples and tongues
             By the mercy of God gathered,
             We are the Church.

MICHAEL :   Israel from all nations, that are not Moses' People,
             And yet are his People,
             Tell him the ground of your joy,
             That in your company he may rejoice.

CHORUS :   How shall we tell him, how make him understand?
             Shall we say, Israel was there when the time came;
             When God Himself would stoop to the low portal,
             Enter the world by parturition, Mary was waiting,
             With will made perfect and with words of wel-
                 come . . .
             Behold the handmaid of the Lord . . . Shall we say
                 this?
             Shall we speak of the Church in the world,
             Smiting the heathen with the hammer of love,
             On the anvil of history welding the nations of Chris-
                 tendom?
             Shall we speak of saints and martyrs, prophets and
                 statesmen,
             The Communion of Saints in the heavenly places?
             We must show him the Christ.

How can we make him see and believe,
How can he know and bow down and adore
And rejoice, if he see not the Christ?
Christ is the ground of our hope.
We must show him the Christ.

MOSES : There are many beautiful words that voices are saying
Around me, in the darkness.

MICHAEL : It is in the dark the light shall shine,
The light of Christ.

CHORUS : We must show him the Christ.
The light shineth in darkness,
And the darkness comprehendeth it not nor over-
cometh.
The light that lighteth every man coming into the
world.
The light of the knowledge of the glory of God
In the face of the Christ.

MICHAEL : Once more open his eyes, O God,
That he may see and believe.

CHORUS : And show him the Christ.

MOSES : What light is this that blooms in the darkness
And moves towards me, bright like the Bush,
But whiter and more lovely?
There is one walking to me on this hilltop,
And through the glory round him I discern

CHORUS : The face of the Christ.

MOSES : The face of my race.

CHORUS : The face of your race,
For Christ is of your race,
Israel made perfect.

MOSES : Oh, incandescence of beauty,
Oh, splendour incomparable.
This face that looks down upon me
Is the face of God.

CHORUS : God of God, Light of Light,
Very God of very God,
For us men and for our salvation
Come down from Heaven,
Made flesh in Israel.

MOSES : God, made flesh in Israel.
Yes, Lord. I understand.
Here am I.
I come.

The lights begin to ebb away, leaving a tableau of Michael, Angels and Chorus grouped round the body of Moses.

MICHAEL : And the Lord buried him in the land of Moab by the hand of angels,
And no man knoweth of his sepulchre unto this day.